PREFACE.

THIS small work treats of that portion of the law which has solely reference to the trade of Banking. The author has endeavoured to deal fully with his subject within the limits he prescribed to himself, and hopes the pains he has bestowed may make his work of service to the profession.

J. DOUGLAS WALKER.

6, CROWN OFFICE ROW, TEMPLE,
May, 1877.

ISBN 978-1-331-21877-7
PIBN 10159903

FB &c Ltd, Dalton House, 60 Windsor Avenue, London, SW19 2RR.
Company number 08720141. Registered in England and Wales.

For support please visit www.forgottenbooks.com

A TREATISE

ON

BANKING LAW.

BY

J. DOUGLAS WALKER, Esq.,

OF LINCOLN'S INN, BARRISTER-AT-LAW.

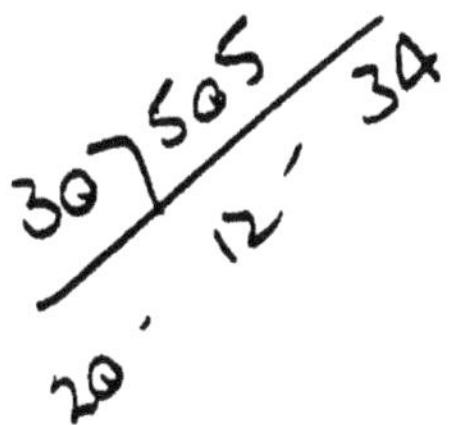

LONDON:
STEVENS AND SONS, 119, CHANCERY LANE,
Law Publishers and Booksellers.

1877.

LONDON:

STEVENS AND RICHARDSON, PRINTERS, 5, GREAT QUEEN STREET,

LINCOLN'S INN FIELDS, W.C.

CONTENTS.

APPENDIX.

LIST OF STATUTES.

LIST OF STATUTES.

TABLE OF CASES CITED.

ERRATA.

Page 3, line 1, *should run*, "or copartnership exceeding six persons in number other than the Bank of England."

" 58, " 10, from bottom, *insert Gatty* v. *Fry*, 2 Ex. D. 265.

" 67, " 3, from bottom, *for* "drawer," *read* "drawee."

" 100, " 8, from top, *for* "1875," *read* "1876."

A TREATISE

ON

BANKING LAW.

CHAPTER I.

BANKS OF ISSUE.

THE scope of this treatise is a statement of those points of the law which are involved in the present practice of banking. It is, therefore, out of place here to trace in detail the progress of legislation from the year 1694, the commencement of legislative interference with the trade of banking, to the present day. At the same time it is difficult without some knowledge of the history of banking to understand the reason and object of the successive Acts of Parliament, and an attempt will be made in the following pages to state enough for the comprehension of the present state of the law.

BANKS OF ISSUE.

Banking, as practised in the United Kingdom, has two distinct branches—the one, that of issuing on the credit of the bank promissory notes payable to bearer; the other, that of receiving the deposits of customers with an obligation to repay them either at the place of deposit or elsewhere, and either on demand or at some longer period.

It is true that all banks of issue happen to be also banks of deposit, but the existence of the one branch is not by law dependent on the co-existence of the other;

BANKS OF ISSUE. and the note issue of banks in England has been the subject of a series of Acts of Parliament from 1694 to 1844, the year of the passing of the Bank Charter Act. It will be convenient to discuss this series of Acts at once and so dispose of the law involved in the note-issue; and to turn afterwards to the various possible constitutions of banks with their respective liabilities under the law as it at present stands.

Previously to the year 1694, banking, in both its branches, had been carried on by individuals and copartnerships, but the system of receiving deposits, which now forms the chief business of the banks of this country, formed but a small part of the business of that day, and indeed was hardly known as banking at all. The circulation and issue of notes or bills payable to bearer on demand was then thought the chief function of a bank, as it was, in fact, the source of the chief profit; and the term bank meant a bank of circulation and issue, and had no reference to what is now known as a bank of deposit. See *Bank of England* v. *Anderson*, 3 Bing. N. C. 589.

5 & 6 W. & M. c. 20. In the year 1694, the 5 & 6 W. & M. c. 20, empowered their Majesties to incorporate the subscribers to a loan by the name of the Governor and Company of the Bank of England. A privilege was conferred on the bank (sec. 28) of making their bills obligatory and of credit under the seal of the corporation transferable by endorsement under the hand of the holder, and allowing the assignee to sue thereon in his own name. The charter of incorporation was shortly issued, and was followed by a 8 & 9 Will. 3, c. 20. statute passed two years afterwards (8 & 9 Will. 3, c. 20), which enacted (as was explained by 15 Geo. 2, c. 15, s. 5), that no other bank should be erected, established, or allowed by Parliament. This was followed by the statute 6 Anne, c. 22. of Anne which enacted (6 Anne, c. 22, s. 9) that no body

other than the Bank of England, or co-partnership *exceeding six persons* in number, should "borrowe, owe or take up any sums of money on their bills or notes payable on demand, or at any less time than six months from the borrowing thereof," thus preventing competition with the Bank of England by laying a check on the issue of negotiable bills or notes having the security of a large number of co-partners, and made payable on demand, but not interfering with the issue of notes by a co-partnership not exceeding six in number, nor with the trade of a bank whose business was confined to receiving deposits.

The prohibition in the statute of Anne, against the issue of notes payable on demand, by co-partnerships of more than six persons, was repeated in succeeding Acts with little variation of form, and less of meaning, up to the year 1826. In this year the 7 Geo. 4, c. 46, was passed for (amongst other things) better regulating co-partnerships of certain bankers in England. The object of this Act was to allow the issue of notes payable on demand by co-partnerships of more than six persons, outside a radius of sixty-five miles from London, on the security of all the persons composing the co-partnership.

7 Geo. 4, c. 46.

Under this Act many banks were formed outside the sixty-five mile radius. Their note issue, begun under this Act, is now entirely regulated as to its amount by 7 & 8 Vic. c. 32, but the right to issue is still conditional on their carrying on business wholly outside the sixty-five mile radius, so that banking co-partnerships of issue formed under this Act must surrender their right to issue notes if they set up a house of business or an establishment in London. See 27 & 28 Vic. c. 32, s. 1.

By a subsequent Act of 9 Geo. 4, c. 23, any persons carrying on the business of a banker or bankers in England (except within the city of London, or within three miles

9 Geo. 4, c. 23.

BANKS OF ISSUE.

thereof), were empowered to issue notes payable on demand, if they obtained a licence and gave security.

3 & 4 Will. 4, c. 98.

In the year 1833 the legislature passed a restrictive Act (3 & 4 Will. 4, c. 98, s. 2), whereby co-partnerships of more than six persons were expressly prohibited from issuing notes payable on demand, in London or within sixty-five miles thereof, but were allowed to carry on the business of banking within those limits provided they confined their issue to bills at not less than six months date (sec. 3).

Still no restrictions were imposed on the issue of notes by co-partnerships not exceeding six persons in number; but the effect of this legislation was to enable the Bank of England to monopolise the whole issue of notes payable on demand in the metropolis.

7 & 8 Vic. c. 32.

In the year 1844 a new departure was made by an Act, which still regulates the whole note issue of England. It is entitled "an Act to regulate the issue of bank notes, and for giving the Governor and Company of the Bank of England certain privileges for a limited period," and is commonly known as the Bank Charter Act (7 & 8 Vic. c. 32).

This Act separates the banking and issue department of the Bank of England, and authorises the issue department to issue to the banking department notes payable on demand to the amount of fourteen million pounds, on the credit of securities of equivalent value; the amount of notes may be increased and exchanged for gold coin or gold or silver bullion, and power is given under certain circumstances to increase the issue of notes.

The issue by other banks in England and Wales of bank notes for the payment of money to bearer on demand, is thus dealt with by the 7 & 8 Vic. c. 32, viz.:—

No new bank of issue.

By sec. 10, after the 19th of July, 1844, no person, other than a banker, who, on the 6th of May, 1844, was lawfully issuing his own bank notes, shall make or issue bank notes in any part of the United Kingdom.

BANKS OF ISSUE.

Restriction against issue of notes.

And by sec. 11, after the 19th of July, 1844, it shall not be lawful for any banker to draw, accept, make or issue, in England and Wales, any bill of exchange or promissory note, or engagement for the payment of money payable to bearer on demand, or to borrow, owe or take up in England and Wales, any sum or sums of money on the bills or notes of such banker, payable to bearer on demand, save and except that it shall be lawful for any banker who was on the 6th of May, 1844, carrying on the business of a banker in England or Wales, and was then lawfully issuing in England or Wales his own bank notes under the authority of a license to that effect, to continue to issue such notes to the extent and under the conditions hereinafter mentioned, but not further or otherwise; and the right of any company or partnership to continue to issue such notes shall not be in any manner prejudiced or affected by any change which may hereafter take place in the personal composition of such company or partnership, either by the transfer of any shares or share therein, or by the admission of any new partner or member thereto, or by the retirement of any present partner or member therefrom; provided always, that it shall not be lawful for any company or partnership, now consisting of only six or less than six persons, to issue bank notes at any time after the number of partners therein shall exceed six in the whole.

The result of these sections is that within the city of London and three miles round, the Bank of England can alone issue notes payable on demand to bearer. Beyond that limit and within sixty-five miles, such notes may be issued by banking partnerships of less than six members, who were lawfully issuing their notes under a license on May 6, 1844, and by the Bank of England;

BANKS OF ISSUE.

and beyond the sixty-five miles limit by the Bank of England and by partnerships of six or more or less partners who were lawfully issuing their notes under a license on May 6, 1844.

Banker's license.

The license referred to is a license charged with a duty of thirty pounds, enabling (under 55 Geo. 3, c. 184, s. 24) bankers, or banking co-partnerships not exceeding six persons in number, to issue stamped promissory notes payable to bearer on demand for sums not exceeding one hundred pounds, or enabling (under 9 Geo. 4, c. 23, s. 1) all bankers carrying on business, except within the city of London or within three miles thereof, to issue, on unstamped paper, promissory notes for five pounds and upwards payable to bearer on demand, or bills of exchange payable to order on demand, if drawn as therein prescribed. This license is to be issued by the Commissioners of Stamps (9 Geo. 4, c. 23, s. 2), and (7 & 8 Vic. c. 32, s. 22) each banker is to take out a separate license for each town where he issues notes requiring such a license, but is not to be required to take out more than four licenses.

The license has (55 Geo. 3, c. 184, s. 24; 9 Geo. 4, c. 23, s. 4) to specify the proper names and places of abode of the persons, or the proper name and description of any body corporate to whom the same shall be granted, and the name of the town or place where, and the name of the bank, as well as the partnership name, style, or firm, under which such notes are to be issued, and where granted to persons in partnership, shall set forth the names and places of abode of all persons concerned in the partnership, but where (24 & 25 Vic. c. 91, s. 35) the partnership consists of more than six persons, it is sufficient to specify the names and places of abode of any six or more of such persons.

The number of the bankers entitled to issue notes being thus fixed by 7 & 8 Vic. c. 32, a method is provided for ascertaining at once the existing average issue of each banker, which, when ascertained, is to be the limit of issue for the future (sec. 13), and the penalty enacted on a bank issuing in excess is a sum equal to the amount by which any future average monthly circulation shall have exceeded the amount which such bank is authorised to issue (sec. 17).

BANKS OF ISSUE.

Already, bankers issuing notes were bound (3 & 4 Will. 4, c. 83, s. 1; 4 & 5 Vic. c. 50) to make returns every four weeks of the amount of their notes in circulation, and by 7 & 8 Vic. c. 32, s. 18, a return of the amount of bank notes in circulation on every day during the week ending on the next preceding Saturday, and an account of the average amount of the bank notes of such banker in circulation during the same week, verified by the signature of the banker or chief cashier, are to be made weekly, on some date to be fixed by the commissioners in the form prescribed by the Act.

Banker's returns of issue.

Bank notes payable to bearer on demand for less than five pounds were prohibited to be issued or re-issued by the Bank of England, or any banker in England, after the 5th of April, 1829 (7 Geo. 4, c. 6, s. 3).

No bank notes of less than £5.

Any society or company, or any persons in partnership, carrying on the business of banking, may draw, accept, or endorse bills of exchange not being payable to bearer on demand (7 & 8 Vic. c. 32, s. 26).

Banks may accept, &c., bills not payable on demand.

Bank notes for the purposes of the Stamp Acts are at present defined by two Acts of Parliament, the 17 & 18 Vic. c. 98, and the 33 & 34 Vic. c. 97, but the duty is fixed by the latter Act.

Definition of bank note.

The 17 & 18 Vic. c. 98, s. 11, defines a bank note in the following terms:—

That all bills, drafts, or notes (other than notes of the Bank of England), which shall be issued by any banker, or the agent of any banker for the payment of money to

BANKS OF ISSUE. the bearer on demand, and all bills, drafts, or notes so issued, which shall entitle or be intended to entitle the bearer or holder thereof without endorsement, or without any further or other endorsement than may be thereon at the time of the issuing thereof, to the payment of any sum of money on demand, whether the same shall be so expressed or not, in whatever form, and by whomsoever such bills, drafts, or notes shall be drawn or made, shall be deemed to be bank notes of the banker by whom or by whose agent the same shall be issued.

Definition of "banker;" The 33 & 34 Vic. c. 97 (The Stamp Act, 1870), enacts: Sec. 45. The term "banker" means and includes any corporation, society, partnership and persons, and every individual person carrying on the business of banking in the United Kingdom. of "bank note." The term "bank note" means and includes (1) any bill of exchange or promissory note issued by any banker other than the Governor and Company of the Bank of England, for the payment of money not exceeding one hundred pounds, to the bearer on demand; (2) any bill of exchange or promissory note so issued which enables, or is intended to enable, the bearer or holder thereof, without endorsement, or without any further or other endorsement than may be thereon at the time of issuing thereof, to the payment of money not exceeding one hundred pounds on demand, whether the same be so expressed or not and in whatever form such bill or note is drawn or made.

Re-issue of notes. Sec. 46. A bank note issued, duly stamped or issued unstamped, by a banker, duly licensed or otherwise authorised to issue unstamped bank notes, may be from time to time, re-issued without being liable to any stamp duty by reason of such re-issuing.

Penalties. Sec. 47. (1) If any banker, not being duly licensed or otherwise authorised to issue unstamped bank notes, issues or causes or permits to be issued any bank note not being duly stamped, he shall forfeit the sum of fifty pounds; (2) if any person receives or takes any such bank note in payment or as a security, knowing the same to have been issued unstamped contrary to law, he shall forfeit the sum of twenty pounds.

Duty on bank notes

By the schedule the duty imposed on bank notes is as follows:—

BANK NOTE.

For money not exceeding £1		£0	0	5
Exceeeding £1 and not exceeding £2 . .		0	0	10
.. £2 ..	£5 . .	0	1	3
£5	£10 . .	0	1	9
£10	£20 . .	0	2	0
£20	£30 . .	0	3	0
£30	£50 . .	0	5	0
£50	£100 . .	0	8	6

may be compounded for.

The duties payable on bank notes may be compounded for under 9 Geo. 4, c. 23, s. 7, at the rate of three shillings and sixpence for every £100, and for the fractional part of £100, of the average amount or value of the notes in circulation during each half year; and before a licence is granted to issue notes on unstamped paper, security must be given for the payment of the composition.

No bank issuing notes is entitled, on registering under Part VII. of 25 & 26 Vic. c. 89, to acquire limited liability in respect of such issue (s. 182).

CHAPTER II.

BANKS OF DEPOSIT.

BANKS OF DEPOSIT. THE constitutions of banks of deposit may best be considered in groups arranged in chronological order.

I. *B*anks formed under 7 Geo. 4, c. 46, and still carrying on business under that Act, subject to a few modifications in its details introduced by later Acts.

II. *B*anks formed under 7 Geo. 4, c. 46, and reconstituted under 7 & 8 Vic. c. 113.

III. Banks formed under 7 Geo. 4, c. 46, and registered under 20 & 21 Vic. c. 49.

IV. *B*anks formed under 7 Geo. 4, c. 46, and registered under 25 & 26 Vic. c. 89.

V. Banks formed under 3 & 4 Will. 4, c. 98.

VI. *B*anks formed under 1 & 2 Vic. c. 73.

VII. Banks formed under 7 & 8 Vic. c. 113, and registered under 20 & 21 Vic. c. 49, or under 21 & 22 Vic. c. 91.

VIII. Banks formed and registered under 20 & 21 Vic. c. 49, and 21 & 22 Vic. c. 91.

IX. Banks formed under the Companies Act, 1862 (25 & 26 Vic. c. 89).

X. Private Banks, *i.e.*, banks composed of any number of persons not exceeding ten.

Banks under 7 Geo. 4, c. 46.

I. Banks formed under 7 Geo. 4, c. 46.

These are co-partnerships of more than six persons, carrying on business prior to May 6, 1844, beyond a radius of sixty-five miles from London. For convenience sake, under this head, will be considered banks formed under 3 & 4 Will. 4, c. 98, for carrying on business within a radius of sixty-five miles from London, since the privileges of banks, formed under the last-mentioned Act, are, as will be seen, dependent on their making returns similar to those of banks under 7 Geo. 4, c. 46.

BANKS OF DEPOSIT.

As we have seen, no restrictions were imposed up to 1826 on the trade of receiving deposits, either as to the number of partners or the locality of the business; but the attention of the legislature was directed to prohibiting the issue of notes by co-partnerships of more than six persons within the radius of sixty-five miles of London, and controlling the issue by like co-partnerships beyond that radius. But, under the Act 7 Geo. 4, c. 46, already mentioned, co-partnerships were formed outside the sixty-five miles combining the functions of issuing notes and receiving deposits; and carried on their business with considerable success. It had been long thought that within sixty-five miles of London the Bank of England was the only Joint Stock Company which could receive deposits, as well as the only company that could issue notes: but it began to be doubted whether the privileges of the Bank of England did extend beyond forbidding the issue of negotiable instruments. These doubts were set at rest by 3 & 4 Will. 4, c. 98, which enacted (sec. 3), That any body politic, or corporate, or society, or company, or partnership, although consisting of more than six persons, may carry on the trade or business of banking in London, or within sixty-five miles thereof, provided such body, &c., do not borrow, owe, or take up in England, any sum or sums of money on their bills or notes payable on demand, or at any less time than six months from the borrowing thereof during the continuance of the privileges granted by this Act to the Governor and

Banks formed under 3 & 4 W. 4, c. 98.

BANKS OF DEPOSIT.

Are to make returns, 7 & 8 Vic. c. 113, s. 47.

Company of the Bank of England. And (by 7 & 8 Vic. c. 113, s. 47) all such companies can sue and be sued in the name of a public officer, and may have judgments, decrees, and orders enforced against them, in the same manner as is provided for companies under 7 Geo. 4, c. 46, provided they make out and deliver similar accounts and returns.

27 & 28 Vic. c. 32.

By 27 & 28 Vic. c. 32 s. 1, banks discontinuing their issue of notes and commencing to carry on their business in London, preserve their privilege of suing and being sued in the name of a public officer and their privileges as to the enforcement of judgments, decrees, and orders.

The 7 Geo. 4, c. 46, therefore, still governs the constitution and liability of all banking co-partnerships exceeding six persons in number and carrying on business on the 6th of May, 1844, who have not obtained letters patent under the 7 & 8 Vic. c. 113, or registered themselves under the Joint Stock Banking Companies' Act, of 1857, or under the Companies' Act of 1862, and it becomes necessary to examine the 7 Geo. 4, c. 46, in detail.

Responsibility of members of co-partnership under 7 Geo. 4, c. 46.

By section 1, the members of such co-partnerships are to be responsible for the payment of all bills and notes issued and all sums of money borrowed or taken up or owed by the co-partnership; and this liability attaches to every person who is a member at the date of the bills or notes, or becomes or is a member before or at the time of the bills becoming payable, or a member at the time of the borrowing of the money, or while any money remains due or at the time of its becoming due.

Public officers of co-partnership.

Returns to be made of members.

Secs. 4 to 8. The copartnership having nominated two public officers, who are to be members of the co-partnership, and having made a return of its original constitution and places of business, is to make yearly returns between February 28 and March 25 of each year, in forms provided by the Act, of the name of any new or additional public officer, of the name of any person who shall have ceased to be a member, and the name of any person who shall have become a member, either in addition to or instead of any former member. These returns are to be delivered to the Commissioners of Stamps and filed by them. A copy of such return certified under the hand of one of the commissioners is, upon proof of the handwriting of the commissioner, to be evidence of the facts therein alleged. A certified copy of the return is evidence of the facts pertinently stated in it; it is not necessary to prove that the affidavit verifying it was made by the public registered officer (*Bosanquet* v. *Woodford*, 5 Q. B. 310).

The fact of the return having been made, is not a condition precedent to the public officer's right to sue on behalf of the company (*Bonar* v. *Mitchell*, 5 Ex. 415).

Copartnership to sue and be sued in the name of public officer.

By sec. 9, all actions, suits, petitions in bankruptcy, and all proceedings at law or in equity, by or against the co-partnership, and whether against or by members of the co-partnership, are to be commenced and instituted in the name of or against any one of the public officers (25 & 26 Vic. c. 89, s. 205, 3rd schedule, part 2). No more than one action or suit is to be brought for the recovery of one and the same demand, in case the merits have been tried in such suit (7 Geo. 4, c. 46, s. 10; 1 & 2 Vic. c. 96, s. 2; 25 & 26 Vic. c. 89, s. 205).

Members may sue and be sued.

The co-partnership may sue and be sued by any person who has been or is a member of the co-partnership (1 & 2 Vic. c. 96, s. 1; 25 & 26 Vic. c. 89, s. 205).

A member's share in the capital of the co-partnership is not to be set off against any demand which such co-partnership may have against him (1 & 2 Vic. c. 96, s. 4).

Decrees and judgments made or obtained against the public officer are to take effect against the co-partnership (7 Geo. 4, c. 46, s. 10).

Banks of Deposit.

Execution upon judgment may issue against members.

The 13th sec. (7 Geo. 4, c. 46) provides that on a judgment obtained against any public officer, execution may issue first against any member, for the time being, of the partnership (*i.e.*, at the time of issuing the *sci. fa.*, *Bradley* v. *Eyre*, 11 M. & W. 432), and secondarily against any person who had ceased for not more than three years to be a member, but who was a member when the contract recovered on was entered into; but the 25 & 26 Vic. c. 89, affords a means of escaping this personal liability for the whole amount of the judgment which will probably be adopted by members in such cases; it enacts (25 & 26 Vic. c. 89, s. 199c), that whenever execution or other process issued on a judgment, decree, or order against a person authorised to be sued as a nominal defendant on behalf of the company is returned unsatisfied, the company may be wound up; any person (sec. 200) liable to pay or contribute to the debts of the company is deemed a contributory, on whose petition the company may be wound up, and after the order for winding up is made, no suit, action, or other legal proceeding can be commenced or proceeded with against a contributory without leave of the court (sec. 202).

25 & 26 Vic. c. 89.

Powers to wind up co-partnership if judgment unsatisfied.

The distinctive features of a co-partnership under this Act were thus summed up by Quain, J.:—

"The company is not a corporation, and has therefore no common seal. It is a co-partnership created by deed or articles of co-partnership for a particular purpose, with certain statutable privileges. It can sue and be sued only in the name of one of its public officers, and in all litigious business the company is represented by one of its public officers, who must be a member of the company, and individual members cannot be sued in respect of transactions with the company till a judgment or decree has been first obtained against the company, through one of its public officers. In *Powles* v. *Page*, 3 C. B. 16, a company established under this Act was considered a quasi corporate body, so as not to be affected by what may have been known to any individual member. The Act contains no provision as to the manner in which the company shall make or sign deeds, contracts, or documents of any description. It confers no authority on the public officer to bind the company, but makes him the representative of the bank only for litigious purposes, and although he must be a member of the company, he may have nothing to do with the management of its affairs. It seems obvious, therefore, from the nature of its constitution, as a fluctuating and numerous body, that the company cannot affix its signature to documents otherwise than by the hand of some individual or individuals who, by the articles of co-partnership, are appointed to represent the general body in such matters" (*Swift* v. *Winterbotham*, L. R. 8 Q. *B.* 244, 250).

BANKS OF DEPOSIT.

Returns to be made under 7 & 8 Vic. c. 32, s. 21, of members of co-partnership.

This kind of bank is bound to make returns, under 7 & 8 Vic. c. 32, s. 21, which enacts that—Every banker in England and Wales who is carrying on, or shall hereafter carry on business as such, shall on the first of January in each year, or within fifteen days thereafter, make a return to the Commissioners of Stamps and Taxes, at their head office in London, of his name, residence, and occupation, or in the case of a company or partnership, of the name, residence, and occupation of every person composing or being a member of such company or partnership, and also the name of the firm under which such banker, company, or partnership, carry on the business of banking, and of every place where such business is carried on.

Penalty for not making returns.

And if any such banker, company, or partnership, shall omit or refuse to make such return within fifteen days after the said 1st of January, or shall wilfully make other than a true return of the persons as herein

Banks of Deposit.

required, every banker, company, or partnership so offending, shall forfeit and pay the sum of fifty pounds; and the Commissioners of Stamps and Taxes shall, on or before the 1st of March in every year, publish in some newspaper circulating with each town or county respectively, a copy of the return so made by every banker, company, or partnership, carrying on the business of bankers within such town or county respectively, as the case may be.

Banks under 7 Geo. 4, c. 46, and 7 & 8 Vic. c. 113.

II. Banks formed under 7 Geo. 4, c. 46, and re-constituted under 7 & 8 Vic. c. 113.

Any company of more than six persons, carrying on the trade or business of bankers in England before May 6, 1844, might, after the passing of 7 & 8 Vic. c. 113, petition the Queen to grant them letters patent under that Act; and (sec. 45) if upon their compliance with the provisions contained in the Act, letters patent were granted, it then became lawful for them to carry on their trade and business of bankers according to 7 & 8 Vic. c. 113, and not otherwise.

A company re-constituted under these conditions was in all respects similar to a company formed under 7 & 8 Vic. c. 113, whose incidents will be found below, p. 21.

Banks under 7 Geo. 4, c. 46, and 20 & 21 Vic. c. 49.

III. Banks formed under 7 Geo. 4, c. 46, and registered under 20 & 21 Vic. c. 49.

Banks formed under 7 Geo. 4, c. 46, might register under 20 & 21 Vic. c. 49, if they consisted of seven or more persons, and had a capital of fixed amount and divided into shares of a fixed amount.

Since 1862, the provisions of the 25 & 26 Vic. c. 89 apply to such companies as if they had been registered, but not formed under the last-mentioned Act, and there seems to be no difference now between the constitution of companies formed under 7 Geo. 4, c. 46, registered under 20 & 21 Vic. c. 49, and those registered under 25 & 26 Vic. c. 89, which are considered in the next section.

IV. *B*anks formed under 7 Geo. 4, c. 46, and registered under 25 & 26 Vic. c. 89.

BANKS OF DEPOSIT.

By sec. 180, a copartnership, formed under 7 Geo. 4, c. 46, existing on November 2, 1862, may register under the 25 & 26 Vic. c. 89, according to the terms of its deed of copartnership, either as a limited company, or a company limited by shares, or a company limited by a guarantee, for the purpose of carrying on business, or with a view to winding up.

Under 7 Geo. 4, c. 46, may register under 25 & 26 Vict. c. 89,

Sec. 181. Such a company, if it have a permanent paid up or nominal capital of a fixed amount divided into shares, also of a fixed amount, or held transferable as stock, may be registered as a company limited by shares on giving thirty days' notice of its intention to register as a limited company to its customers (sec. 188).

on giving notice as a limited company;

But (sec. 182) no banking company claiming to issue notes can limit its liability in respect of such issue.

but not as to note issue.

The effect of registration (sec. 196) is to make the deed of settlement, contract of copartnership, letters patent or other instrument constituting or regulating the company, equivalent to a registered memorandum of association and articles of association under the Act; and all the provisions of the Act are to apply to such company and the members, contributories and creditors thereof, in the same manner as if it had been formed under the Act: except that—

Effect of registration.

1. The regulations for management of a company limited by shares in table A of the schedule shall not apply.
2. That the provisions of the Act relating to the numbering of shares shall not apply to any joint stock company whose shares are not numbered.
3. That no company shall have power to alter any

provision in any Act of Parliament relating to the company.

4. Nor without the leave of the Board of Trade in any letters patent relating to the company.
5. In the event of the company being wound up, persons liable before registration are to continue liable to all debts and liabilities of the company contracted before registration and to the costs of winding up.
6. That a company having power to alter its constitution before registration shall possess such power after registration and not otherwise.

Changes caused by registration.

These appear to be the main changes affected by the registration of a copartnership formed under 7 Geo. 4, c. 46—

1. The liability of a past member to contribute to the assets of the company ceases at the expiration of one year from the time he ceased to be a member (sec. 38).
2. Public officers have not to be appointed, as the company can sue and be sued in its own name, being a body corporate (25 & 26 Vic. c. 89, s. 18).
3. The duty of making the returns prescribed by 7 Geo. 4, c. 46, is removed, but the following returns have to be made under the 25 & 26 Vic. c. 89, to the Registrar of Joint Stock Companies by a company having capital divided into shares (sec. 26), an annual list of members, with names, addresses, and occupations, and the shares held by each; a summary specifying the amount of capital and number of shares into which it is divided; the amount of calls made on each share; the total amount of calls received; the total

amount of calls unpaid; the total amount of shares forfeited; and the names, addresses and occupations of the persons who, since the last list was made, have ceased to be members. Returns have to be made by a company not having a capital divided into shares (sec. 45), of the names and addresses, and occupations, of its directors and managers with a notification of any change that may have taken place since the last return. This return is in addition to the one required of bankers by 7 & 8 Vic. c. 32, s. 21. See *infra*.

BANKS OF DEPOSIT.

4. The late copartnership being after registration a corporation, either the corporation or a member may, in an action by the other of them, claim to set off any debt or cause of action; and by sec. 17, all moneys payable by any member to the company, in pursuance of the conditions or regulations of the company, are to be deemed a debt due from such member to the company.
5. The registered company must (sec. 39) have a registered office, to which all communications and notices may be addressed: it must (sec. 43) keep a register of all mortgages affecting the property of the company: and (sec. 49) hold a general meeting at least once a year.

The company is bound, under 7 & 8 Vic. c. 32, s. 21, to make returns yearly on the 1st of January, or within fifteen days after, to the Commissioners of Stamps and Taxes, at their head office in London, of the names, residences, and occupation of every person composing such company, and of the name of the firm under which, and the place where, the business is carried on.

Yearly returns to be made.

Shares in a copartnership formed under this Act are

BANKS OF DEPOSIT.

chargeable by a judge's order (*McIntyre* v. *Connell*, 20 L. J. Chanc. 284).

V. Banks formed under 3 & 4 Will. 4, c. 98.

These banks are in fact governed by the 7 Geo. 4, c. 46, and are treated under the head of banks formed under that Act. *Ante*, p. 11.

Banks under 1 Vic. c. 73.

VI. Banks formed under 1 Vic. c. 73.

The Crown has power under this Act to grant by letters patent under the great seal any privileges which could be granted by a charter of incorporation to any body of persons associated together for trading and other purposes though not incorporated. The privileges may be (sec. 3) power to sue and be sued in the name of an officer of the company, and (sec. 4) a limitation of the individual liability of the members of such company.

A deed of partnership is to be executed (sec. 5), containing, amongst other things, a division of the undertaking into a number of shares, and an appointment of two or more officers to sue and be sued. Returns (sec. 10) are to be made of the changes in the members of the company, and (secs. 20 and 21) membership begins or ceases from the date of the registration of the return.

Judgments against the company are available against the members individually to the amount unpaid on their shares (sec. 24).

Such a company may register under the 25 & 26 Vic. c. 89, Part VII., as its deed of settlement may allow, and after registration the Act applies to it as to a partnership formed under 7 Geo. 4, c. 46.

These banks are bound to make yearly returns under 7 & 8 Vic. c. 32, s. 21. See *ante*.

Banks under 7 & 8 Vic. c. 113; 20 & 21 Vic. c. 49; 21 & 22 Vic. c. 91.

VII. Banks formed under 7 & 8 Vic. c. 113, and registered under 20 & 21 Vic. c. 49, or under 21 & 22 Vic. c. 91.

This Act was the first Act to regulate joint stock

banks in England. It provided that from the 6th of May, 1844, all banks in future should only carry on business under letters patent to be obtained in the manner pointed out in the Act. The deed of partnership of the company was to be prepared according to a form to be approved of by the Board of Trade, and to contain the specific provisions for the following purposes:— Banks of Deposit.

1. For holding ordinary general meetings every year.
2. For holding extraordinary general meetings on the requisition of at least nine shareholders, holding among them, at least, twenty-one shares.
3. For the management of the affairs of the company and the election and qualification of the directors.
4. For the retirement of a certain proportion of the directors. (This clause has been repealed by 19 & 20 Vic. c. 100, s. 112.)
5. For preventing the company from purchasing any shares or making any advances to any person on the security of a share in the partnership business.
6. For the publication of assets and liabilities once at least in every calendar month.
7. For a yearly audit of the accounts by two auditors chosen at a general meeting.
8. For the yearly communication of the auditors' report and of a balance sheet and profit and loss account to each share-holder.
9. For the appointment of a manager.

It was a condition precedent to the issuing of the letters patent that the amount of each share should not be less than £100 (sec. 2). Companies formed under this Act were compelled to register under the

BANKS OF DEPOSIT.

Joint Stock Banking Companies Act 1857 (20 & 21 Vic. c. 49, s. 4).

This Act was repealed by 25 & 26 Vic. c. 89, with the proviso that this latter Act should (sec. 176) apply to companies registered, but not formed, under 20 & 21 Vic. c. 49, in the same manner as to companies registered, but not formed, under 25 & 26 Vic. c. 89; and that a company registered under 7 & 8 Vic. c. 113, should be deemed to be registered under the Companies Act 1861 from the date of their registration under 7 & 8 Vic. c. 113.

Effect of registration.

The effect of registration (sec. 196) is to make the deed of settlement under 7 & 8 Vic. c. 113, equivalent to the memoranda of association and articles of association under the Companies Act 1862, and to place the company generally under the provisions of the last-mentioned Act, but subject to certain provisions which have been set out above (p. 17).

It was further provided (as the regulations respecting the transmission of shares in 20 & 21 Vic. c. 49, were repealed by 25 & 26 Vic. c. 89, s. 12), that any such company (sec. 178) may cause its shares to be transferred in manner hitherto in use, or in such other manner as the company may direct.

In all other respects a company formed under 7 & 8 Vic. c. 113, is governed by the Companies Act 1862.

Power is given to a bank registered under 20 & 21 Vic. c. 49, to register itself again as a limited company under that Act (21 & 22 Vic. c. 91), and to a company which so registered itself the Act of 1862 applies as if the company had been formed and registered under that Act.

Companies under these Acts are bound to make yearly returns under 7 & 8 Vict. c. 32, s. 21. See *ante*.

Banks under 20 & 21

VIII. Banks formed and registered under 20 & 21 Vic. c. 49, and 21 & 22 Vic. c. 91.

BANKS OF DEPOSIT.

Vic. c. 49; 21 & 22 Vic. c. 91.

The 20 & 21 Vic. c. 49, The Joint Stock Banking Companies Act 1857, incorporating The Joint Stock Companies Acts 1856 and 1857, extended the principle of joint stock companies to banking companies by allowing (sec. 13) seven or more persons associated for the purpose of banking to register themselves under 20 & 21 Vic. c. 49, as a company *other than limited*, but subject to the condition that the shares into which the capital was divided should not be of less amount than £100.

The 21 & 22 Vic. c. 91, was passed in the next year, to enable banking companies to be formed on the principle of limited liability, and repealing the prohibition in 20 & 21 Vic. c. 49, s. 13, allowed companies to register themselves under the last-mentioned Act as of limited liability. The incorporation, constitution, and government of such banks, whether of limited or unlimited liability, were regulated by the Joint Stock Companies Acts 1856 and 1857. These last two Acts, together with the 20 & 21 Vic. c. 49, and the 21 & 22 Vic. c. 91, have been in terms repealed by the 25 & 26 Vic. c. 89, which, by sec. 176, is to apply to all companies formed and registered under the above Acts in the same manner in the case of a limited company, as if such company had been formed and registered under this Act as a company limited by shares; and in the case of a company other than a limited company, as if such company had been formed and registered as an unlimited company.

1. But the date of their registration under the 25 & 26 Vic. c. 89, is to be taken to be that of their registration under the 20 & 21 Vic. c. 49.
2. Such companies have the power of altering by special resolution any provisions contained in the table marked B (being the regulations for management of the company) annexed to the Joint Stock Companies Act 1856.

Banks of Deposit.

3. Such companies, if unlimited, have the power of altering by special resolution any regulations relating to the amount of capital or its distribution into shares, notwithstanding such regulations are contained in the memorandum of association.

In other respects, therefore, these companies are governed like other joint stock companies by the 25 & 26 Vic. c. 89.

Banking companies under these Acts have to make yearly returns in pursuance of 7 & 8 Vic. c. 32, s. 21. See *ante*.

Banks under 25 & 26 Vic. c. 89.

IX. Banks formed under the Companies Act 1862 (25 & 26 Vict. c. 89).

This Act regulates all partnerships exceeding a certain number of persons formed for the acquisition of gain from November 2, 1862; and as it is impossible in the limits of this treatise to give a useful abstract of this and subsequent Acts, those sections alone will be cited which deal exclusively with the business of banking.

Prohibition of banking partnerships exceeding ten persons unless registered as a company.

By sec. 4, no company, association, or partnership consisting of more than ten persons shall be formed after November 2, 1862, for the purpose of carrying on the business of banking, unless it is registered as a company under this Act, or is formed in pursuance of some other Act of Parliament or of letters patent.

Company to publish statement

Sec. 44 provides that every limited banking company under this Act shall, before it commences business, and also on the first Monday in February and the first Monday in August in every year during which it carries on business, publish a statement in the form marked D in the schedule, and a copy of such statement is to be put up in a conspicuous place where the business of the company is carried on, and if default is made a penalty is enacted of £5 for every day during which the default continues.

BANKS OF DEPOS'T.

Sec. 47. A promissory note or bill of exchange shall be deemed to have been made, accepted, or endorsed on behalf of any company under this Act, if made, accepted, or endorsed in the name of the company by any person acting under the authority of the company, or if made, accepted, or endorsed by or on behalf of or on account of the company by any person acting under the authority of the company.

Promissory notes and bills.

Sec. 56 empowers the Board of Trade to appoint one or more competent inspectors to examine into the affairs of a banking company under this Act, and to report thereon, on the application of members holding not less than one third part of the whole shares of the company at the time being issued.

Examination of affairs of company by inspectors.

Sec. 182 provides that no banking company claiming to issue notes in the United Kingdom shall be entitled to limited liability in respect of such issue.

No limitation of liability for note issue.

By sec. 188, a banking company that desires to register itself with limited liability is to give thirty days' notice to each customer.

Notice of registration to be given.

Banking companies under this Act have to make yearly returns in pursuance of 7 & 8 Vic. c. 32, s. 21, in the same way as private banks. See *ante*.

X. Private Banks. It has been lawful, ever since the year 1857, for any number of persons not exceeding ten to carry on the business of banking (20 & 21 Vic. c. 49, s. 12, re-enacted 25 & 26 Vic. c. 89, s. 4, third schedule, part 3) without being registered under the Joint Stock Acts.

Private banks.

Clergymen holding office in the Church are practically excluded from carrying on the business of private banking, either singly or in partnership with less than six others; every contract made by them being

Disability of clergymen.

BANKS OF DEPOSIT.

void under 57 Geo. 3, c. 99, s. 3, which enacts that no spiritual person, having or holding any dignity, prebend, canonry, benefice, stipendiary curacy of lectureship, shall by himself or by any other for him or to his use, engage in or carry on any trade or dealing for gain or profit, and that every bargain or contract so made by him or by any to his use in any such trade or dealing contrary to this Act shall be utterly void and of none effect. This section having been held to apply to the trade of banking (*Hall v. Franklin*, 3 M. & W. 259, 268), carried on by a partnership under 7 Geo. 4, c. 46, in which two of the partners were spiritual persons within the Act, a subsequent statute (4 Vic. c. 14) rendered legal and valid contracts entered into by associations or copartnerships of more than six persons, though such spiritual persons were members of or interested in the copartnership, provided that it should not be lawful for a spiritual person beneficed, or performing ecclesiastical duty, to act as a director, or managing partner, or to carry on the business in person.

Private bankers, as all other bankers, are bound to make yearly returns, under the 7 & 8 Vic. c. 32, s. 21.

Purchase and sale of bank shares (30 Vic. c. 29).

In the year 1867, an Act (30 Vic. c. 29) was passed prescribing certain formalities in the purchase or sale of bank shares.

It enacts (sec. 1) that all contracts, agreements, and tokens of sale and purchase, for the sale or transfer of any shares, stock, or interest in any joint stock banking company, shall be void, unless such contract, &c., set forth in writing the numbers by which such shares, &c., are distinguished on the register of the banking company ; or if there be no register, the contract, &c., is to set forth the person in whose name such shares, &c., shall at the time of making the contract stand as the registered owner on the books of the banking company, the person inserting

Banks of Deposit

a false number or name is to be deemed guilty of a misdemeanour.

By sec. 2, joint stock banking companies are bound to show their list of shareholders to any registered shareholder during business hours, from ten of the clock to four of the clock.

CHAPTER III.

BANKER AND CUSTOMER.

RELATION BETWEEN BANKER AND CUSTOMER.

THE relation between a banker and his customer is that of debtor and creditor, with the obligation superadded that the banker is bound to repay his debt when called for by the draft of the customer (*Foley* v. *Hill*, 2 H. L. C. 28; *Pott* v. *Clegg*, 16 M. & W. 321; *Goodwin* v. *Robarts*, L. R. 10 Ex. p. 351).

The customer, by paying in money, makes a loan to the banker: the money when paid in becomes the money of the banker.

There is nothing of a fiduciary character in the relation of banker and customer with respect to the money paid by the customer to his account; consequently, a bill in equity will not lie to recover the money so paid (*Foley* v. *Hill, supra; Smith* v. *Leveaux*, 2 De G. J. & S. 5). The banker is not responsible to the customer for the use he may make of such money (*Ex parte Waring*, 36 L. J. Chanc. 151).

The relation of debtor and creditor is not altered where the account has been overdrawn, and in fact the banker is the creditor and not the debtor of his customer (*Hardy* v. *Veasey*, L. R. 3 Ex. 107).

Several accounts of one customer.

A customer may and frequently does open several accounts with different headings; all these accounts are, unless in the case of trust accounts, which are discussed below, in reality one account (*In re European Bank, Agra Bank Claim*, L. R. 8 Ch. Ap. 41), and may be so treated by the bank.

Banker may blend several accounts,

Even where the accounts are at different branches the bank may blend them if they are of the same character, and dishonour a cheque drawn against one account, if by combining the accounts a balance in favour of the customer at the branch drawn against is turned into a balance against the customer on the general account (*Garnett* v. *McKewan*, L. R. 8 Ex. 10).

unless otherwise agreed,

But where several accounts are opened by one customer they may be kept separate, either by special agreement or by notice to the bankers of such cogent character that the banker will be inferred to have agreed to keep the accounts separate.

or account is a trust account.

As a banker need not allow his customer to open several accounts unless he pleases, it has been held that sufficient notice has been given him of the character of the account by the terms of the heading under which it was opened if the account is headed in such a way that the banker cannot fail to know it is a trust account. Thus an account opened as "Police Account" was held to be one which the banker could not fail to know was a trust account, and to be kept separate from the customer's private account (*Ex parte Kingston, in re Gross*, L. R. 6 Chan. Ap. 632). Again, though an executor, by transferring his testator's account to his own account as "executor," creates a personal debt between himself and the bank; the effect of the account being opened as an executorship account is to affect the bank with notice of the equities, if any, attaching to that fund (*Bailey* v. *Finch*, L. R. 7 Q. B. 34).

Where the banker has notice that an account is a trust account, the balance standing to the credit of that account will, on the bankruptcy of the person who kept it, belong to the trust, and therefore cannot be set off by the banker against a debt due on the private account of the bankrupt (*Ex parte Kingston, in re Gross, supra*). And

BANKER AND CUSTOMER.

such a trust account is so distinct from the private account, that if a customer having overdrawn his private account asks that he may further overdraw it for the purpose of paying money into the trust account, the banker is entitled to refuse such accommodation (*Ex parte Kingston, in re Gross, supra*).

When banker held liable for breach of trust by his customer.

A banker is not bound, as a general rule, to inquire either the purpose for which a cheque is drawn upon any account (*Ex parte Kingston, in re Gross*, L. R. 6 Ch. Ap. 639), nor the source from which moneys have come that are paid into an account (*Boddenham* v. *Hoskyns*, 21 L. J. Chanc. 867). But where an executor or trustee has, committing thereby a breach of trust, paid a debt due from him to the banker out of money belonging to his testator's or *cestui que* trust estate, with the knowledge of the banker, the banker will be required to make restitution for the benefit of the estate, for being aware of the intended misappropriation or breach of trust he allowed himself to reap the benefit of it (*Boddenham* v. *Hoskyns, supra*).

If it be shown that any personal benefit to the banker himself is designed or stipulated for, that circumstance above all others will most readily establish the fact that the banker is in privity with the breach of trust about to be committed (per Ld. Cairns, C., *Gray* v. *Johnston*, L. R. 3 E&I. 1).

The bare fact that money standing to the credit of the trust account was transferred to and so balanced an overdrawn account, is not a sufficient benefit within this rule (*Gray* v. *Johnston, supra*).

The benefit must be one stipulated for or designed, as in consequence of demands made for payment of an overdrawn account. Thus, where a receiver of rents who had with the bank two accounts—the one a private account which was overdrawn, and the other an account known to the bank to be a trust account and not overdrawn—transferred, in consequence of demands for payment by the bank, a sum from the trust account to balance his private account, the bank were compelled to make good to the trust account the sum so transferred (*Boddenham* v. *Hoskyns*, 21 L. J. Chan. 867; 2 De G. M. & S. 903).

BANKER AND CUSTOMER.

A banker who is aware that such a breach of trust is to be committed by which he will benefit, is justified in refusing to honour a cheque for that purpose (*Gray* v. *Johnston*, *supra*), and equity will restrain an action against him for such refusal (*Hunt* v. *Maniere*, 34 Beav. 157). If trust money is deposited with a banker, and he receives notice that the trustees are about to draw out the money and apply it to their own purposes, and that a bill for an injunction is about to be filed, and thereupon refuses to pay over to the trustees, equity will restrain an action against him to obtain the benefit of a breach of trust (*Hunt* v. *Maniere*, 34 Beav. 157; 11 Jur. N. S. 28).

A banker who permits a sum of money to be lodged at his house to be applied to an illegal purpose may be indicted for a conspiracy along with those who are to apply the money to such purpose (*R.* v. *Pollman*, 2 Camp. 229).

Bankers liable for proceeds of bills collected by them when customer has no title.

It is the practice of bankers to present and procure payment of drafts and bills of exchange from the payees on behalf of their customers, carrying the proceeds when obtained to the customer's account. But if the customer has in fact no title to the draft or bill, the banker is liable to the rightful owner for the proceeds of the draft or bill, though he has already paid them over to his customer. For the customer having no title, the banker, his agent, can have no better title than his principal (*Ogden* v. *Benas*, L. R. 9 C. P. 513; *Arnold* v. *The Cheque Bank*, 1 C. P. D. 578).

But the 39 & 40 Vict. c. 81, sec. 12, enacts that a banker who has in good faith and without negligence received payment for a customer of a cheque crossed generally or specially to himself shall not, in case the title to the cheque proves defective, incur any liability to the true

BANKER AND CUSTOMER.

owner of the cheque by reason only of having received such payment. See chapter on Crossed Cheques.

Banker liable for neglect in collection.

It has been held in America that a bank receiving bills for collection, whether payable at its counter or elsewhere, is liable for any neglect arising in its collection, by which any of the parties are discharged, whether of the officers or other agents or correspondents of the bank or notary employed by the bank (*Ayrault* v. *The Pacific Bank*, 7 The American Reports, following *Allen* v. *The Merchant Bank of New York*, 22 Wend. 215).

Who may sue for money paid to an account with a banker.

As has been said, money paid in to an account opened in a man's own name is *primâ facie* his money, and a loan by him to the banker which the banker is bound to repay to him. But where a person lends money nominally on his own account, but really on account of and as the loan of another, the real lender may sue for the money (*Sims* v. *Bond*, 5 B. & Ad. 393). If, therefore, any person entitled to the money either jointly with the customer, or as the principal of the customer, can show that the loan though nominally that of the customer, was in reality his own, that is, made by him, he can recover the amount from the banker (*Sims* v. *Bond*). It is not sufficient for such person to show that the interest of the customer in the money paid in was in fact joint with others, or that he was an agent acting on behalf of others, for the loan may still have been made by the customer alone (*Sims* v. *Bond*). The fact that the account in the ledger and pass-book stands in the customer's name alone is not conclusive, but throws on the parties suing the obligation of showing they were the real contracting parties (*Cooke* v. *Seely*, 2 Ex. 746).

Who the banker may sue for balance of an overdrawn account.

On the same principle, a banker, to recover the balance of an overdrawn account from persons other than the customer in whose name the account stands, must show the customer had authority to contract a loan on behalf of the others sued, and that the loan was in fact made not to the customer alone, but to the customer either jointly with or on behalf of the others sued (*Alliance Bank* v. *Kearsley*, L. R. 6 C. P. 433). BANKER AND CUSTOMER.

Banker's duty to keep customer's account secret.

It is improper for a banker to disclose the state of his customer's account except on a reasonable occasion; but whether the law implies a contract to this effect by the banker, or whether from the relation between the banker and customer, a duty is implied in the former not to do anything to the damage of his customer, has yet to be decided (see *Tassell* v. *Cooper*, 9 C. B. 509, 515; *Foster* v. *Bank of London*, 3 F. & F. 214; *Hardy* v. *Veasey*, L. R. 3 Ex. 107). The distinction is one of importance, for if there be an obligation by contract the banker is liable for nominal damages on making the disclosure, though no injury whatever has resulted. In the other case special damage must be proved to make a breach of duty actionable (*Hardy* v. *Veasey*, *supra*).

It is for the jury to decide whether the disclosure was made on a reasonable occasion (*Hardy* v. *Veasey*, *supra*).

even when account over-drawn.

A customer is entitled to the reticence of his banker though his account is overdrawn, and he is in fact the debtor of the banker (*Hardy* v. *Veasey*).

When the customer's assets are insufficient to meet a check presented for payment, the banker is not justified in stating the amount of the deficiency; he should not do more than say, "not sufficient assets," or "apply to the drawer" (*Foster* v. *The Bank of England*, 3 F. & F. 214).

Account with a banker may be barred by the Statute of Limitations.

The Statute of Limitations applies to a banking account as to any other debt. Thus if an account remain for six years without any payment of the principal or allowance of interest by the banker, the statute is a bar to the recovery of money due on the account (*Pott* v. *Clegg*, 16 M. & W. 321), but money paid out to the customer pays off the earliest debt due at the time of such payment

BANKER AND CUSTOMER.

(*Tassell* v. *Cooper*, 9 C. B. 526; and see Appropriation of Payments, *infra*).

Words which pass an account with a banker.

The following terms have been held to include and pass the money standing to the testator's account with his banker, "all my ready money" (*Parker* v. *Merchant*, 1 Ph. 356, *Fryer* v. *Ranken*, 11 Sim. 55), "all debts due to me" (*Carr* v. *Carr*, 1 Mer. 541 n), "money in hand" (*Vaisey* v. *Reynolds*, 5 Russ. 12), "all my moneys" (*Manning* v. *Purcell*, 7 De G. M. & G. 55).

Overdraft is not a loan.

A customer does not by overdrawing his account alter the previously existing relations between him and his banker. An overdraft made in the ordinary course of business, and honored by the banker, is not a loan in the proper sense of the word; and therefore a company who have no power to borrow money are liable for the overdrafts of its directors if made in the ordinary course of business, and applied to the purposes of the company (*Waterloo* v. *Sharp*, L. R. 8 Eq. 501; *In re Cefn Cilcen Mining Company*, L. R. 7 Eq. 90; *Beattie* v. *Lord Ebury*, L. R. 7 Ch. Ap. 804, 805).

Banker entitled to commission.

A banker may receive a commission for his trouble in transacting money negotiations, as any other factor for his trouble (*Curtis* v. *Livesey*, 4 M. & S. 197), or for accepting and paying bills of exchange (*Masterman* v. *Courie*, 3 Camp. 488). The reasonableness of the charge is a question for the jury (*Masterman* v. *Courie*).

Accounts between banker and customer.

Where a banker and customer carry on business for a number of years on a certain specified system, it is to be inferred that both parties are agreed the accounts shall be kept upon that system (*Morse* v. *Salt*, 32 L. J. Ch. 761).

Acquiescence in such accounts amounts to an agreement of the system, but not to a settlement of account (*Morse* v. *Salt*, *supra*).

So where bankers have been in the habit of charging interest with annual rests for a number of years, the customer by acquiescence must be taken to have assented to this system of keeping accounts (*Crosskell* v. *Bower*, L. J. 32 Ch. 540). But to charge a person with compound interest a contract or promise must be shown to have been made at or subsequently to the time from which the compound interest began to run; for an antecedent contract or promise to pay compound interest is invalid (*Ex parte Bevan*, 9 Ves. 223; *Ferguson* v. *Fyffe*, 8 Cl. & F. 140). The making of such a contract may be inferred from the course of dealing between the parties or the course of trade in which they are engaged (*Morgan* v. *Mather*, 2 Ves. 20; 2 Camp. 482; *Eaton* v. *Bell*, 5 B. & Ald. 34; *Morse* v. *Salt*, 32 L. J. Ch. 756). An agreement between banker and customer to pay compound interest is terminated by the death of the customer (*Williamson* v. *Williamson*, L. R. 7 Eq. 542); the balance at the date of the customer's death ceases to bear interest and becomes a simple contract debt due from the customer's estate, on which, in the absence of any binding conrtact no interest can be charged (*Crosskell* v. *Bower*, 32 L. J. Ch. 540; but see *contra*, *Williamson* v. *Williamson*, L. R. 7 Eq. 542. The same result appears to follow where the customer becomes bankrupt, or where the banker dies or becomes bankrupt (*Crosskell* v. *Bower*).

BANKER AND CUSTOMER.

Must be special agreement to enable banker to charge compound interest.

Death of customer terminates agreement.

Where bankers take a mortgage security for a fixed sum owing to them from their customer, the relation of banker and customer ceases as to that sum, and it cannot be included in the customer's banking account so as to entitle the bankers to charge compound interest thereupon (*Morse* v. *Salt*, *supra*).

Documents in the possession of the banker are held to be so far in the possession of his customer that the banker need not be served with a subpœna duces tecum, or called as a witness, but notice given to the party himself will suffice (Taylor on Evidence, p. 434).

Banker holds documents as customer's agent.

BANKER AND CUSTOMER.

Banker's knowledge not privileged.

A banker as a witness is bound to answer what the balance of a party to a cause was on a given day, as the knowledge does not come to him in the nature of a privileged or confidential communication (*Lloyd* v. *Freshfield*, 2 Car. & P. 324).

Banker may be compelled to give evidence.

Under sect. 115 of "The Companies Act 1862," by which the court can summon before it any person whom the court may deem capable of giving information concerning the trade dealings, estate, or effects of the company, these decisions have been given. A summons may issue to the secretary of the bank of a person who supplied a shareholder with money calling on the secretary to attend for examination, and produce all books containing entries as to that person's affairs (*In re Smith, Knight and Co.*, L. R. 4 Chan. Ap. 421). The managing clerk of a bank, at which a contributory had an account, was compelled to attend and state the nature of such account (*Re The Financial Assurance Company, Bloxam's case,* 36 L. J. Chan. 687). And a banker with whom a contributory had formerly kept an account was compelled to produce his books, and give all information in his power relating to the property of the contributory and his affairs (*Re Contract Corporation, Forbes' case,* 41 L. J. Chan. 467).

CHAPTER IV.

CUSTOMERS.

Agent.

Cus-TOMERS. Agent.

No agent has *implied* authority as agent to borrow money on behalf of his principal, except the master of a ship or an acceptor for honour of a bill of exchange (*Hawtayne* v. *Bourne*, 7 M. & W. 599), and he has therefore no implied authority as agent to overdraw a banking account belonging to his principal, but the fact that he has overdrawn such an account with the knowledge of his principal is evidence from which a jury may infer that the agent was clothed with authority to pledge his principal's credit by overdrawing (*Pott* v. *Bevan*, 1 Car. & K. 335).

Executors and Administrators.

Executor

An executor has power to pledge a specific asset belonging to the personal estate of his testator. So where he is authorized by the will to realize the real estate he has power to pledge a specific part of such estate (*Farhall* v. *Farhall*, L. R. 7 Ch. Ap. 123). Where the pledge is valid, the person making the advance has a charge to the amount of his advance on the thing pledged, unless he has notice that the executor was committing a breach of trust and applying the money to his own purposes (*Farhall* v. *Farhall*, L. R. 7 Eq. 289). But except in the cases above put, an executor has no power to create debts against his testator's estate by borrowing money. Credit given to him can only be given to him personally, and not in his representative character, and so through

cannot create debt against his testator's estate by borrowing.

CUSTOMERS.

Executor.

him to the estate. It therefore follows that if the asset pledged by the executor turn out insufficient to repay the advance, he, and not the estate, is responsible for the difference. In other words, a person cannot by contract with the executor acquire a right to prove as a creditor against the estate, though the executor has power to give a lien on specific assets (*Farhall* v. *Farhall*, L. R. 7 Ch.Ap. 123).

One executor can bind all by his receipt.

One of several executors is not the agent of the others so as to bind them by his contracts, but he may dispose of the assets so as to bind the others (*Turner* v. *Hardy*, 9 M. & W. 771). Therefore any one of several co-executors may settle an account due from any person to the estate, and such settlement in the absence of fraud is binding on the other co-executors, though dissenting (*Smith* v. *Everitt*, 27 Beav. 454). It follows that where co-executors have an account standing in their joint names at a bank, payment of a check signed by one of them will discharge the banker as to them all.

The banker is not bound for his own safety to do more than see that the executors or administrators have *primâ facie* a good title; and a payment made *bonâ fide* of a debt due to the estate of a deceased person to the executors or administrators is a legal discharge of the debtor, though their letters of probate or administration afterwards turn out void or voidable (20 & 21 Vict. c. 77, ss. 77, 78).

Companies—Railway.

Railway Companies

Joint stock companies constituted for making railways are generally incorporated by a special Act and regulated by 8 Vic. c. 16, which provides (secs. 95, 96) for the appointment of directors who, either by themselves or by committees of directors appointed by themselves, have the management and superintendence of the affairs of the company and exercise all the powers of the company subject to the provisions of that and the special Act; and by sec. 97 that with respect to any contract which, if made between private persons, would be by law required to be in writing signed by the parties to be charged therewith then such committee of directors may make such contract on behalf of the company in writing signed by such committee, or any two of them, or any two of the directors, and in the same manner vary or discharge the same.

Customers.

Railway Companies.

It will be observed that a check drawn under this Act should be signed by all the committee, since the power to draw is vested in them all, or by two of the directors of the company, and further that the check should purport on the face of it to be drawn on behalf of the company (*Halford* v. *Cameron Coalbroke Co.*, 16 Q. B. 442; *Sewell* v. *Derbyshire Railway Co.*, 19 L. J. C. P. 371).

But it would appear that a check purporting to be drawn by persons authorized to draw checks on behalf of the company, and known by the bank as representing the company in the operations upon the account, is a sufficient voucher for the bank as against the company for the payment of money, though the check does not on the face of it indicate that the company is the drawer (*Mahony* v. *The East Holyford Mining Co.*, L. R. 7, E. & I. 869).

Joint Stock Companies.

The 47th sec. of The Companies Act 1862 prescribes that a promissory note or bill of exchange shall be deemed to have been made, accepted, or indorsed on behalf of any company under this Act if made, accepted, or endorsed in the name of the company by any person acting under the authority of the company, or if made, accepted, or endorsed by or on behalf of the company by any person acting under the authority of the company.

Joint Stock Companies.

Customers.

Joint Stock Companies.

How far the duty of banker to satisfy himself as to authority of drawers.

Therefore a banker should satisfy himself as to the authority of the persons pretending to act on behalf of the company. In the case of a registered joint stock company, he is taken to have notice of the general Act of Parliament, and of the special deed which has been registered pursuant to the provisions of the Act, and if there be anything to be done which can only be done by the directors under certain limited powers it lies upon him to see that these limited powers are not exceeded. If (*Royal British Bank* v. *Turquand*, 6 E. & B. 327) the directors have power and authority to bind the company, but certain preliminaries have to be gone through on the part of the company before that power can be duly exercised, the person dealing with the directors is not bound to see that all these preliminaries have been observed. He is entitled to presume that the directors are acting lawfully in what they do (*Fountaine* v. *Carmarthen Railway Company*, L. R. 5 Eq. 316).

The following case (*Mahony* v. *The East Holyford Mining Company*, L. R. 7, E. & I. 869) illustrates the distinction drawn above. Money was paid into the credit of a company with a bank. The articles of association of the company provided that every sum paid on behalf of the company over £10 was to be paid by a check signed and countersigned as might be directed by the board, and that all acts done by the board or a committee of directors, notwithstanding any defect in the appointment of any director or person acting as aforesaid, should be valid, as if every person had been duly appointed and was qualified to be a director. The bank received a letter dated from the registered office of the company and purporting to be signed by the secretary of the company, and to enclose the copy of a resolution passed relative to the banking account of the company. The resolution requested the bank to pay all checks signed by either two of the following three directors, A., B., and C., whose signatures were supplied to the bank. A., B., and the secretary had signed the articles and memorandum of association. The bank, *bonâ fide*, did pay large sums on checks so signed. The three directors turned out to be directors only *de facto*, and not *de jure:* no appointment of directors having in fact been made by the shareholders and no such resolution as was communicated to the bank was passed. It was held by Lord Cairns that there having been *de facto* directors of the company who were permitted by the majority of those who signed the articles of association to occupy the position and act as directors, and the bankers having, in the full belief that these persons were directors, honored the checks drawn by them, the payment of these checks was a good payment as against the company.

And by Lord Penzance, that a bank having a written authority, of a *de facto* secretary, is not bound before it acts upon that authority to ascertain whether he is the properly constituted secretary of the company, and whether any resolution of which he forwards a copy was properly passed by the directors; but is justified in acting upon such a written authority, provided the transaction appears one which might legally have taken place, and have been legally consummated under the articles of association.

The 42nd section of the Companies Act 1862 imposes a penalty on any directors of a limited company, signing or authorizing to be signed on behalf of the company, any bill of exchange, promissory note, endorsement, check, or order for money, wherein the name of the company is mentioned, in manner directed by the Act, *i.e.*, the name of the company, followed by the word "limited," and makes them personally liable to the holder

Customers.

of any such instrument, unless the same is duly paid by the company.

Joint Stock Companies. Form of checks.

This section is not imperative, but simply provides a particular mode of execution (*In re Norwich Yarn Company*, 25 L. J. Chanc. 201); and where those who draw and those who *bonâ fide* honour checks intend them to operate on a certain account, no objection can afterwards be taken that that account is not specifically mentioned on the face of the check; therefore a check which purported to be drawn in accordance with directions from the board of a company by two directors and countersigned by the secretary, and intended to be drawn on the company's account, being *bonâ fide* paid by the bank, was held a good voucher for the payment as against the company (*Mahony* v. *East Holyford Mining Co.*, L. R. 7, E. & I. 869).

Instrument should purport to be made on behalf of the company.

Directors may be personally liable on the instruments they make if describing themselves as directors, or by any similar form of description, they do not state on the face of the document that they are acting on behalf of the company; and if the instrument does not purport on the face of it to be made on behalf of or on account of the company, the affixing thereto of the seal of the company is not equivalent to a declaration in terms on the face of the instrument that it is signed by the persons who put their name to it solely on behalf of the company (*Dutton* v. *Marsh*, L. R. 6 Q. B. 361).

Effect of a direction to honor checks drawn in a certain fashion.

A direction given by persons who are directors of a company to their bankers, when the company had a balance in the hands of the bankers, to honor checks drawn and signed in a particular manner, does not of itself impose on the directors any personal responsibility as to those checks. This direction is in no sense a misrepresentation so as to make personally liable those who gave it to those who acted upon it (*Beattie* v. *Ld. Ebury*, L. R. 7, E & I. 102).

Joint Stock Companies.

Nor, though that direction should continue to be acted on by the bankers after the company's account has been overdrawn, will it entail on the directors who gave it any personal liability. Nor will it entail any such liability on those who, at a subsequent meeting of the board of directors, confirmed the minutes of the board meeting at which it was given, and who drew checks in accordance with it, though the account was overdrawn when these latter checks were issued and honored (*Beattie* v. *Lord Ebury, supra*).

Banker not an officer of the company.

A banker is not an officer of the company within sec. 165 of "The Companies Act 1862" (*In re Imperial Land Company of Marseilles; In re National Bank*, L. R. 10 Eq. 298). And therefore the court cannot when a company is being wound up make an order upon him to repay any money misappropriated by him.

Company liable for overdrafts of directors.

A company who have no power to borrow money are liable for the overdrafts of its directors if made in the ordinary course of business and applied to the purposes of the company; for an overdraft made in the ordinary course of business is not a loan in the proper sense of the word (*Waterloo* v. *Sharp*, L. R. 8 Eq. 501; *In re Cefn Cilcen Mining Co.*, L. R. 7 Eq. 90; *Beattie* v. *Lord Ebury*, L. R. 7 Ch. Ap. 804—805).

A company may, where money belonging to it has been paid to its account in a bank in pursuance of a fraudulent scheme between its directors and the general manager of the bank, avoid the contract and recover such money back from the bank (*British American Telegraph Company* v. *The Albion Bank*, L. R. 7 Ex. 119). But not where the money paid in to the company's account never belonged to the company, and was paid in under circumstances which made such payment merely colourable (*British American Company* v. *Albion Bank, supra; Gray* v. *Lewis*, L. R. 8 Ch. Ap. 1035, 1052, 1055).

Corporations.

Customers. — Corporations.

Corporations at common law can only contract by writing under their common seal, but a distinction exists between municipal and ecclesiastical corporations and trading corporations in this respect, and the settled law now appears to be that (*South of Ireland Colliery Co.* v. *Waddle*, L. R. 3 C. P. 463, 4 C. P. 617, and the cases there cited) the former are allowed to transact affairs of minor importance only, such as hiring a servant, while trading corporations may make *all such contracts as are of ordinary occurrence in their trade* without the formality of a seal, and by the hands and through the instrumentality of their agents and managers.

A corporation established for trading purposes is from its nature capable of drawing a bill of exchange and making the promise implied by law from making a bill, and is liable to be sued in assumpsit on the bill though a body corporate (*Murray* v. *The East India Company*, 5 B. & Ald. 204). And all such bills of exchange have in practice always been made under hand by an agent authorized to draw or accept as the case may be. There is no case in the books where a bill of exchange made under seal has been sued on (*Crouch* v. *Credit Foncier*, L. R. 8 Q. B. 374, 382; *Bank of Australasia* v. *Bank of Australia*, 12 Jur. 188).

It is presumed that as the use of banks is now universal, other corporations have like power, but this point has never yet been decided.

For his perfect discharge therefore a banker when his depositor is a common law corporation, should require a check signed by some officer of the corporation whose signature the banker has been directed to honor by some instrument under the common seal.

Husband and Wife.

CUSTOMERS.

Husband and wife.

Where a drawing account is opened by a husband in the name of his wife, or the husband pays money into an account opened by his wife, the banker's obligation is to honour the check of either husband or wife during their joint lives (*Lloyd* v. *Pugh*, L. R. 8 Ch. App. 88). If an account be opened by the husband in the joint names of himself and his wife, the balance standing to the credit of such account at his death becomes the absolute property of his widow, provided his intention in so opening the account was to make provision for her in that way (*Williams* v. *Davies*, 33 L. J. Prob. Ca. 127); but it does not become the property of the widow if the intention was only to provide a convenient mode of managing affairs (*Marshall* v. *Cruttwell*, L. R. 20 Eq. 328).

Married woman with separate estate

A married woman having a separate estate can charge and bind her estate by bills and promissory notes, and where she is living ostensibly as a *femme sole*, and contracts debts, the intention will be imputed to her that she intends to charge her separate estate (*Johnson* v. *Gallagher*, 3 D. F. & J. 494; *McHenry* v. *Davies*, L. R. 10 Eq. 88); and further she can bind her estate by engagements made with reference to or upon the faith and credit of that estate (see *Johnson* v. *Gallagher*).

can contract with a banker.

A married woman therefore who has a separate property can keep an account and enter into contracts with a banker with reference to that separate estate, and the banker will have a remedy against her separate estate in equity. She can too charge such separate estate as by giving a lien upon it for advances or to secure an overdrawn account (*The London Chartered Bank of Australia* v. *Lemprière*, L. R. 4 P. C. 572). She can exercise this power whether she has an absolute interest or a limited interest as a life estate with a power of appointment by deed or writing, but not it would appear where the power of appointment is by will only (*Johnson* v. *Gallagher*, *supra*; *The London Chartered Bank of Australia* v. *Lemprière*, *supra*). Under "The Married Woman's Property Act 1870," 33 & 34 Vic. c. 93, a married woman has a complete power of disposition over her wages and earnings acquired by her in her separate trade, and may (sec. 11) bring an action in her own name to recover any property declared under the Act to be her separate property. Under this last section a married woman may maintain an action in her own name to recover damages against her bankers for dishonoring checks drawn by her in the course of a trade which she carries on separately from her husband, and for not duly presenting or not giving due notice of dishonor of a bill of exchange acquired by her in such trade (*Summers* v. *City Bank*, L. R. 9 C. P. 581).

Married Woman's Property Act.

Liquidators.

Liquidators.

Where under a voluntary winding up of a company under the Companies Act 1862, several liquidators are appointed, it would seem checks must be signed by at least two of the liquidators (*In re London and Mediterranean Bank; Ex parte Birmingham Banking Co.*, L. R. 3 Ch. App. 651; *Ex parte Agra and Masterman's Bank*, L. R. 6 Ch. 206).

Partners.

Partners.

A partner has implied authority to act for all his co-partners whether known or secret (*Vere* v. *Ashley*, 10 B. & C. 288), in all things necessary for carrying on the business of the co-partnership (*Sandilands* v. *Marsh*, 2 B. & Ald. 672), and they are therefore bound by all his acts within the scope of the partnership. Thus one partner can make the firm liable for money

Customers. — Partners.

borrowed by him for the purposes of the partnership (*Rothwell* v. *Humphreys*, 1 Esp. 406), but not for money which he was to obtain on his individual credit and bring into the partnership (*Greenslader* v. *Dower*, 7 B. & C. 635; *Fisher* v. *Taylor*, 2 Hare 218; *Emly* v. *Lye*, 15 East 7), nor (without proof of authority) for the balance of an overdrawn account opened in his own name (*Alliance Bank* v. *Kearsley*, L. R. 6 C. P. 433). For he has no implied authority to open an account on behalf of the partnership in his own name (*Alliance Bank* v. *Kearsley*). He can as against his co-partners pledge the partnership funds which are standing to the credit of the partnership in the books of a bank (*Brownrigg* v. *Rae*, 5 Ex. 489). He can direct the bankers of the firm not to pay a check drawn by the firm, and no action will lie against the banker by the firm for obeying such direction (see Lindley on Partnership, p. 288).

He can, if the acting partner, assent to the transfer of the partnership account from one bank to another without the express assent of the others (*Beale* v. *Cuddock*, 26 L. J. Ex. 356).

Checks of partners.

He has implied power to bind his firm with checks not post dated (*Forster* v. *Mackreth*, L. R. 2 Ex. 163), drawn on the bankers of the firm in the partnership name (*Laws* v. *Rand*, 3 C. B. N. S. 442). For as no person can be sued upon a bill or note whose name is not on the instrument (*Lloyd* v. *Ashby*, 2 B. & Ad. 23), a check to bind the firm must be drawn in the name of the partnership, by which the partners have agreed each shall bind the others, and which is the only name a partner is entitled to use for the purposes of the partnership (*Kirk* v. *Blurton*, 9 M. & W. 284). If between the style actually signed and the ordinary style of the firm there is any substantial variation which cannot be shown to be authorized by the partners, the firm will not be liable.

Customers.

The question upon which the liability or non-liability of a firm depends is not, has the firm obtained the benefit of contract, but did the firm by one of its partners enter into the contract?

One partner can bind others by his receipt.

Payment of a debt to one of a firm extinguishes the claim of all (Anon. 12 Mod. 446); and each partner has power to give a discharge or receipt for a debt; but if the payment has been made collusively and in fraud of the other partners, a receipt given by the fraudulent partner will not prevent the firm from recovering the money so paid (*Farrer* v. *Hutchinson*, 9 A. & E. 641). After a dissolution, payment to any one of the partners discharges the debtor (*Bristow* v. *Taylor*, 2 Starkie 50; *Porter* v. *Taylor*, 6 M. & S. 156), unless the debtor has notice the debt has been assigned to one of the partners, in which case he can only pay the assignee (*Duff* v. *East India Co.*, 15 Ves. 213). Co-adventurers in a mining concern are not liable for money borrowed by one of their number for the purposes of the mine, unless the borrower is shown to have had authority to pledge the credit of his co-adventurers (*Ricketts* v. *Bennett*, 4 C. B. 686).

Trustees.

Trustees.

Where a body of persons not partners have deposited money with a banker in their joint names, each one of the body ought in the absence of any special agreement between the body and the banker to sign the check on the joint account; and the banker is entitled to refuse to pay on any check not so signed. "For it is a part of the law merchant that bankers shall not pay one of several jointly interested without the consent of the others, except by express agreement" (Per *Maule*, J., *Husband* v. *Davies*, 20 L. J. C. P. 119, 10 C. B. 645).

One trustee cannot bind his co-trustees by his receipt.

The 12 & 13 Vic. c. 74, § 1, entitled an Act for the Relief of Trustees, enacts that the Court of Chancery may upon

Customers.

the application by the majority of trustees where the concurrence of the minority cannot be had, order a banker to pay money vested in the trustees and deposited with the banker to the accountant general, and that such order shall indemnify all persons acting under such order.

CHAPTER V.

DIRECTIONS TO PAY ADDRESSED TO BANKERS.

ORDERS ON BANKERS. THE communications of a customer to his banker, or of a banker to another banker directing the latter to pay money on account of the customer are of various forms. The forms known as checks, letters of credit, and circular notes are discussed hereafter with all their incidents; but it is convenient here to dispose of some preliminary questions by dealing with such communications generally, pointing out what are the stamp duties payable on them; what are the legal consequences of the issuing of such communications to the customer himself, to the banker, and the payee.

Stamp duties. *First* as to the stamp regulations.

The Stamp Act, 1870, 33 & 34 Vict. c. 97, enacts, sect. 48—

1. The term "bill of exchange" for the purposes of this Act includes also draft, order, check and letter of credit, and any document or writing (except a bank note) entitling or purporting to entitle any person, whether named therein or not, to payment by any other person of, or to draw upon any other person for any sum of money therein mentioned.
2. An order for the payment of any sum of money by a bill of exchange or promissory note, or for the delivery of any bill of exchange or promissory note in satisfaction of any sum of money, or for

the payment of any sum of money out of any particular fund, which may or may not be available, or upon any condition or contingency which may or may not be performed or happen, is to be deemed for the purposes of this Act a bill of exchange for the payment of money on demand.

STAMP DUTIES.

3. An order for the payment of any sum of money weekly, monthly, or at any other stated periods, and also any order for the payment by any person at any time after the date thereof of any sum of money, and sent or delivered by the person making the same to the person by whom the payment is to be made, and not to the person to whom the payment is to be made, or to any person on his behalf, is to be deemed for the purposes of this Act a bill of exchange for the payment of money on demand.

Exemptions.

By the Stamp Act, 1870, Schedule, Tit. Bill of Exchange, the following documents are amongst others exempted from duty:—

2. Draft or order drawn by any banker in the United Kingdom upon any other banker in United Kingdom not payable to bearer or to order, and used solely for the purpose of settling or clearing any account between such bankers.

3. Letter written by a banker in the United Kingdom to any other banker in the United Kingdom directing the payment of any sum of money, the same not being payable to bearer or to order, and such letter not being sent or delivered to the person to whom payment is to be made or to any person on his behalf.

STAMP DUTIES.

4. Letter of credit granted in the United Kingdom authorising drafts to be drawn out of the United Kingdom payable in the United Kingdom.

And the Bills of Exchange Act, 1871, 34 & 35 Vict. c. 74, sec. 2, enacts every bill of exchange or promissory note (drawn after the 14th August, 1871), and purporting to be payable at sight or on presentation, shall bear the same stamp, and shall for all purposes whatsoever be deemed a bill of exchange or promissory note payable on demand, any law or custom to the contrary notwithstanding.

Bills of Exchange payable on demand have by the schedule to the Stamp Act, 1870, a duty of one penny imposed on them.

Bills of exchange of any other kind whatever have an ad valorem duty imposed on them, for which, see the chapter on Bills of Exchange, *infra*.

The Liability of a Customer on his Order to the Payee.

A customer who by an order to his banker, not communicated to the payee, directs the banker to pay money to a third person, incurs no liability by such an order to the payee until the order has been communicated to the latter; for a mere mandate from a principal to an agent which is capable of being revoked, gives no right or interest to the subject of it (*Ex parte Heywood*, 2 Rose, 353; *Scott* v. *Porcher*, 2 Mer. 652). But an order, directing a banker to pay money, communicated to the payee, is a good assignment as against the person making the order, and will create a valid effectual equitable charge on the fund in the banker's, provided the following requisites are complied with:—

1. The order must show a clear intention to charge a

fund in the payee's favour (*Hopkinson* v. *Forster*, L. R. 19 Eq. 74), or an unequivocal engagement that the particular fund shall be made liable to the debt (*Watson* v. *The Duke of Wellington*, 1 R. & M. 602).

2. The order must show that the fund is to be paid to the person who claims the benefit of the assignment (*Bell* v. *L. & N. W. Ry.*, 15 Beav. 548).
3. The fund itself need not be of a certain amount if it be sufficiently indicated (*Riccard* v. *Prichard*, 1 K. & J. 277).
4. Nor the amount of the debt to be paid if a limit be fixed to the sum appropriated (*Hutchinson* v. *Heyworth*, 9 A. & E. 375) to meet the debt.

It is not necessary to the validity of an equitable assignment as between assignor and assignee that notice should be given to the person from whom the debt is due (*Rodick* v. *Gandell*, 1 D. M. & G. 780).

A check is not an equitable assignment (*Hopkinson* v. *Forster*, L. R. 19 Eq. 74) of the sum named therein.

It may here be observed that where an order is given by a debtor with the consent of his creditor on a banker who is the banker of both parties, to transfer on a certain day a sum of money from the debtor's to the creditor's account, and before the day arrives and the actual transfer is made (*Pedder* v. *Watts*, 2 Chit. 619; *Calley* v. *Short*, G. Cooper, Ch. 148), or while the order is entered up as short (*Brown* v. *Kewley*, 2 B. & P. 518), the banker fails, the debtor is not discharged. But if after the money has been transferred in the books of the bank from one account to the other, the banker fails, the debtor is discharged (*Eyles* v. *Ellis*, 4 Bing. 112).

The Liability of a Banker to his Customer on such Orders.

BANKER AND CUSTOMER.

Where the customer has given an order to the payee, who has presented it to the banker, and both payee and banker have treated the order as executory, and before any payment or appropriation has been made the customer has revoked the order, the banker pays the order at his own risk, and cannot charge the customer with the payment (*Gibson* v. *Minet*, 2 *B*ing. 7). But where the customer has ordered payment to a third person, and the banker has promised the third person to pay him, the customer is not at liberty to withdraw his order or authority (*Hodgson* v. *Anderson*, 8 *B.* & C. 342, 354).

Nor where the banker has received notice in writing of any absolute assignment by writing under his customer's hand of any portion of his debt to his customer, 36 & 37 Vict. c. 66, s. 25 (6).

A check is not such an assignment (*Hopkinson* v. *Forster*, L. R. 19 Eq. 74).

Where a banker pays on an order the customer may treat the payment as made by himself, so as to recover the money back in certain cases, as where there is a failure of consideration between him and the payee (*Bobbett* v. P*inkett*, 1 Ex. D. 368).

As has been said, a banker as a general rule is bound to honor his customer's order, and he is not entitled, as between himself and his customer, to set up a justification against his customer's order, or to refuse to honor his draft on any other ground than some sufficient one arising from an act of the customer himself (*Gray* v. *Johnston*, L. R. 3 E. & I. 14, per Lord Westbury).

Therefore, though the customer may have improperly obtained the money he has paid in, the banker is bound to repay it to him on his demand (*Tassell* v. *Cooper*, 9 C. B. 509). Nor is the banker as a general rule bound to enquire for what purpose money is drawn out of the account (*Bodenham* v. *Hoskyns*, 21 L. J. Ch. 864; *Ex parte Kingston, In re Gross*, L. R. 6 Chan. Ap. 639). BANKER AND CUSTOMER.

Thus if the banker become incidentally aware that the customer, being in a fiduciary or representative capacity, meditates a breach of trust and draws a check for that purpose, the banker not being interested in the transaction has no right to refuse the payment of the check, for if he did so, he would be making himself a party to an inquiry as between his customer and a third person (Per Lord Westbury, *Gray* v. *Johnston, supra; Ex parte Kingston, In re Gross*, L. R. 6 Chan. Ap. 632, 639, per L. J. James).

The Liability of a Banker to the Payee.

Before the passing of the Supreme Court of Judicature Act, 1873, the rights of an assignee of a debt or chose in action (other than bills of exchange and like instruments), against the person liable in respect of the debt or chose in action, were different at law and in equity. Both at law and in equity the assignee was bound to derive his title from an absolute assignment (*Hopkinson* v. *Forster*, L. R. 19 Eq. 74; see *ante*, p. 53); but at law he could not sue the holder of the fund except he could prove an absolute contract or binding agreement with him, by the holder of the fund to pay. It was not necessary to prove any consideration moving from the holder of the fund to the assignee, but the contract, promise, or agreement to pay must have been unequivocal and absolute. Thus it was not sufficient for the assignee to prove that the banker held a sum of money in which he, with many others, was entitled to share (*Pinto* v. *Santos*, 5

BANKER AND PAYEE

Taunt. 447); nor that the banker had advised him that he would, if remittances came forward to enable him to meet the wishes of his customer, inform the assignee of their arrival (*Malcolm* v. *Scott,* 5 Ex. 601). Nor that the banker had admitted to the assignee the receipt of bills from the proceeds of which the banker had been directed by his customer to pay over the money due to the assignee from the customer (*Williams* v. *Everett,* 14 East, 592).

But in equity the rule was different. It was not necessary to the validity of an equitable assignment as between assignee and assignor that notice should be given to the person from whom the debt was due. But the debtor was bound from the time the order was shown him or notice given him (see Lord Eldon in *Ex parte South,* 3 Swanst. 392). And it was not necessary in equity that the debtor should enter into any contract for the application of the fund in the manner directed (*Burn* v. *Carvalho,* 4 M. & C. 690).

But now sect. 25, subs. 6, of the Supreme Court of Judicature Act, 1873, gives the assignee, under an assignment by writing of a debt, power to perfect his title against the debtor, by giving notice in writing to the debtor of the assignment; no decision has yet been given on this section, but if it is read with the 11th sub-section of the same section, which enacts that in case of any conflict between the rules of equity and common law, the rules of equity shall prevail, the general result appears to be the same with the rules of equity before the Act as stated above.

Where an order is given by a man to his banker to pay over a sum to a third person to whom the order is not communicated, and, before the payment is made, the order is countermanded, the third party cannot insist on the banker paying to him the money (*Morrell* v. *Wooton,* 16 Beav. 197).

CHAPTER VI.

CHECKS.

Checks.

A check resembles in legal effect an inland bill of exchange (*Keene* v. *Beard*, 8 C. B. N. S. 372, 29 L. J. C. P. 287); it has, however, three distinguishing characteristics —that it is always drawn on a banker—it is payable on presentment without the allowance of days of grace, it is never presented for acceptance but only for payment.

No precise form is essential to the validity of a check: most bankers supply their customers with blank forms to be filled up as required; but any instrument is valid as a check which complies with the following conditions:—

I. It must be written.
II. It must be an order to pay.
III. It must be addressed to a banker.
IV. It should be dated.
V. It must contain the sum to be paid.
VI. It must be stamped before payment thereon.
VII. It must be payable on demand.
VIII. It must be payable to some specified person—to bearer or to order.
IX. It must be signed by the party drawing it.

Must be in writing.

I. A check must of necessity be in writing (*Thomas* v. *Bishop*, Ca. Temp. Hardwick, 1); it is usually written on paper, but might legally be written on any substitute for paper and with pencil (*Geary* v. *Physick*, 1 *B.* & C. 234) or ink.

CHECKS.

Order to pay.

II. It must contain an order to pay, *i.e.*, it should purport to be a demand made by a party having a right to call on the other to pay (Per Lord Tenterden in *Little* v. *Slackford*, M. & M. 171).

Drawn on a banker.

III. A check being like a letter of exchange an open letter of request from the drawer to a third person it should be properly addressed to that person by the Christian and surname; or if to a firm, by the full style of that firm (Com. Dig. Merchant F.). It must be addressed to a bank or banker (Story on Prom. Notes, § 487).

Date.

IV. It should be dated, but a date is not essential to the validity of a check; if there is no date on it it will be considered as dated on the day on which it was made (*Hague* v. *French*, 3 B. & P. 173, *Giles* v. *Bourne*, 6 M. & S. 73), and parol evidence is admissible to show from what time an undated instrument is intended to operate (*Davis* v. *Jones*, 25 L. J. C. B. 9, 17 C. B. 625).

It is not illegal to post-date a check, and the post-dating has now no effect on the instrument itself.

It is established that the Stamp Acts only deal with orders for the payment of money as they appear on their face, and that the date expressed on the face of the check can only be looked at without reference to any collateral agreement or condition by which its operation can be effected (*Whistler* v. *Forster*, 14 C. B. N. S. 248, 32 L. J. C. P. 161; *Bull* v. *O'Sullivan*, L. R. 6 Q. *B.* 209), so that in the absence of controlling words in the body of a check it will be taken to be payable on demand from and after the date on the face of it. A check may be dated on a Sunday, though it is not presentable or payable on that day (*Beglie* v. *Levy*, 1 C. & J. 180).

May be drawn for any sum.

V. Formerly a check could not be drawn for any sum under five pounds; but the 26 & 27 Vic. c. 105, legalises drafts for the payment of sums over twenty shillings and less than five pounds, and the 23 & 24 Vic. c. 111, s. 19, enacts that it shall be lawful for any person to draw upon his banker, who shall *bonâ fide* hold money to his use, any draft or order for the payment to the bearer or order on demand of any sum less than twenty shillings. Therefore a check for under twenty shillings is good where the drawer has a balance at his bankers; but if the drawer have no balance, such a draft is void, and the drawer subjects himself to a penalty. CHECKS.

The relation between a banker and his customer being that of a debtor and creditor—the banker is only bound to pay his debt in the mode in which a debtor in England is bound to pay his—in English money only. The sum, therefore, demanded in a check must be expressed in English and not foreign money.

If the sum in the body of the check differs from that in the margin the sum in the body is the sum which the banker ought to pay (*Sanderson* v. *Piper*, 5 Bing. N. C. 425).

A check drawn for "twenty-five, seventeen shillings and three pence" has been held to mean twenty-five pounds, seventeen shillings, and three pence (*Phipps* v. *Tanner*, 5 Car. & P. 488).

Stamp Duty.

VI. A check for the purposes of "The Stamp Act, 1870" is (by sec. 48) included in the definition of a bill of exchange, and (by the schedule) is, being payable on demand, subjected to a penny stamp, which (by sec. 50) may be denoted by an adhesive stamp, to be cancelled by the drawer. If the check be presented for payment unstamped the banker may affix a proper adhesive stamp and cancel the same, charging the drawer with the amount of the stamp (sec. 54, (2)).

Payable on demand.

VII. A check is payable immediately on presentment without any days of grace. It may be drawn in terms "payable on demand," but it is usually made payable generally, *i.e.*, without the addition "on demand."

CHECKS. Such a check is in contemplation of law payable on demand (*Whitlock* v. *Underwood*, 2 B. & C. 157; *Hare* v. *Copland*, 13 Irish Common Law Rep. 426).

In America a check is sometimes dated on one day and made payable on another, for instance, dated on the 1st March, and made payable on the 24th March. The question then arises whether it is payable on that very day, without any allowance of days of grace. The decisions are conflicting, but the custom is said to be to treat such an instrument as a check payable on demand on the day designated for payment (Story on Prom. Notes, 6th ed., § 490).

Forms of check. VIII. A check may be drawn in one of the four following forms:—

Payable to a person by name as to A. B. This check is not negotiable, and can only be sued on by A. B., or in his name (*Cheetham* v. *Butler*, 5 B. & Ad. 837; *Dixon* v. *Chambers*, 1 C. M. & R. 846.)

Or to A. B. or Bearer. This check is negotiable and transferable by delivery. It may be indorsed, thereby enabling the indorsee to sue the indorser thereon (*Keane* v. *Beard*, 8 C. B. N. S. 372).

Or payable to A. B. or order. This is assignable by the endorsement of A. B., and when endorsed is negotiable, and if endorsed in blank is payable to bearer. A banker on whom such a check is drawn may, if the check on presentment purports to be endorsed by the person to whom it was drawn payable, pay the amount of it to the bearer (16 & 17 Vict. c. 59, s. 19). In other words, the banker who is bound to pay bills of exchange drawn by his customer payable to order only to persons deriving their title through genuine endorsements is relieved from this responsibility as regards checks. But this exemption does not extend beyond the banker upon whom the check is drawn (*Ogden* v. *Benas*, L. R. 9 C. P. 513). The drawer of such a check can, if any one endorsement be not genuine, recover the amount so paid by his banker from the person who received it, even where the latter, being an agent has before action brought, paid the money to his principal (*Ogden* v. *Benas*, L. R. 9 C. P. 513). And the bearer to charge the drawer must make title through the first endorsement. An endorsement of the name of the payee "per procuration" or as "agent," purports to be an endorsement within the Act so as to protect the banker (*Charles* v. *Blackwell*, 1 C. P. D. 548).

Or payable to bearer or order on demand, and crossed either specially or generally, and with the words "not negotiable." The manner and effect of crossing will be discussed hereafter, but it is sufficient to say here that by sect. 12 of the 39 & 40 Vic. c. 81, a person taking a crossed check bearing the words "not negotiable," cannot have or give a better title to the check than that of the person from whom he took it. This kind of check, therefore, is not negotiable, though it may be transferable by delivery or endorsement as it is drawn payable to bearer or order.

A check is payable to bearer when the name of the payee does not purport to be the name of any person, as "J. S. or bearer" (*Hinton's case*, 2 Show. 235), or "Ship *Fortune* or bearer" (*Grant* v. *Vaughan*, 3 Burr. 1516), or if a blank be left for the name of the payee (*Cruchley* v. *Clarance*, 2 M. & S. 90), any *bonâ fide*

CHECKS. holder may insert his own name. A check drawn payable to drawer's order is payable to himself (*Smith* v. *McClure*, 5 East. 476).

Signature. IX. A banker contracts with his customers to pay (to the extent of the customer's funds in his possession) all checks drawn by him; and the usual evidence of their being so drawn is that they bear his signature, that is his name in his own handwriting or of some person authorised by him to sign for him. It is, therefore, necessary that a check be signed; and the signature is usually subscribed in the right hand corner, but it may be written in any other part of the check (*Taylor* v. *Dobbin*, 1 Stra. 399; *Saunderson* v. *Jackson*, 2 B. & P. 238), but the name must appear to be the name of the person ordering the payment.

Presentment of Check.

How to be presented. It was held that a check should be presented at the banker's counter by some person ready and authorised to receive the money; but a presentment by post has now been held to be a reasonable mode of presentment, having regard to the commercial business of the country (*Prideaux* v. *Criddle*, L. R. 4 Q. B. 455; *Heywood* v. *Pickering*, L. R. 9 Q. B. 428).

Within what Time after Issue.

A banker is not bound to pay a check before the day on which it bears date or is due, for his duty to his customer is to pay checks on and not before the day of date; and he cannot debit his customer with such a payment if it turn out to have been made to the wrong person (*Da Silva* v. *Fuller*; Chitty on Bills, cited by Parke B. in *Morley* v. *Culverwell*, 7 M. & W. 178).

CHECKS.

A check is said to be issued when it is in the hands of a person entitled to demand cash for it (*Ex parte Bignold*, 1 Deac. 735).

Must be presented within six years from date.

The receipt of a check is in itself no satisfaction of a debt until it is honored, and the holder may present it at any time within six years from its date, and if things have continued the same and no damage has arisen from the delay in presentment, the drawer is liable on the check if it be dishonored (*Robinson* v. *Hawksford*, 9 Q. B. 52).

Drawer discharged by failure of bank.

Or alteration in his position.

But if before the presentment of the check, the banker on whom the check was drawn has failed (*Alexander* v. *Burchfield*, 7 M. & G. 1061; *Serle* v. *Norton*, 2 M. & Rob. 401), or has ceased to allow the drawer to overdraw his account (*Hopkins* v. *Ware*, L. R. 4 Ex. 268), or by reason of the non-presentment of the check the position of the drawer, with respect to the fund on which the check was drawn, is altered for the worse (*Hopkins* v. *Ware*), and the check is consequently dishonored, the drawer is discharged unless the holder can show that he has not been guilty of unreasonable delay; and what is unreasonable delay is a question to be decided on the facts of each case.

Death of drawer a revocation of his check.

It may here be remarked that by delay in presentment, the holder also runs the risk of a revocation of the banker's authority to pay by the death of the drawer (*Tate* v. *Hibbert*, 2 Ves. junr. 118; *Hewett* v. *Kay*, L. R. 6 Eq. 198), or of some delay in the honoring of the check, since bankers make it a rule not to cash stale checks without inquiry (see *Serle* v. *Norton*, 2 M. & Rob. 461 *in notis*). It is said the holder is bound, where a check is refused for staleness, to give the drawer an opportunity of authorising his bankers to pay it (*Ibid.*).

The time within which presentment must be made, varies with the relation of the parties between whom the question is raised.

What is Delay as between the Drawer and the Payee.

CHECKS.

Payee must present within reasonable time.

The payee of a check who wishes to preserve his remedy for the original debt against the drawer is bound to present it within a reasonable time. He is not bound, leaving all other business, to present the check immediately on receiving it. But his right to sue for the original debt is unimpaired, if he present the check before the close of the banking hours of the day after he received it (*Boddington* v. *Schlenker*, 4 B. & Ad. 752, 759; *Alexander* v. *Buckfield*, 7 M. & G. 1061; *Robson* v. *Bennett*, 2 Taunton 388), even though the bankers have become insolvent between the receipt and the presentment of the checks. If he receive it after banking hours, the time allowed him for presentment seems to run from the first day after the actual receipt on which presentment could have been made. Thus if he receive the check after banking hours to-day he has the whole of to-morrow and next day to present it (*Bond* v. *Warden*, 1 Collyer, 583); and if a check be given to an agent to deliver to his principal, the time begins to run against the principal from the day on which the check might reasonably reach the principal (*Frith* v. *Brooks*, 4 L. T. N. S. 467).

What is reasonable where payee and drawee live in the same place.

The payee of a check does not necessarily, as between himself and the drawer, obtain any more time or any less time for presentment by sending the check to his bankers to present for him. If the payee and drawee live in the same place, the banker ought to present the check not later than the day after it was originally issued (*Boddington* v. *Schlenker*, 4 B. & Ad. 752; *Alexander* v. *Burchfield*, 7 M. & G. 1061). For in the words of Crompton, J., the law makes a difference between the same and a different place; a man need not have an agent if he be in the same town (*Frith* v. *Brooks*, 4 L. T. N. S. 467). CHECKS.

But where the payee and drawee do not live in the same place if the payee send the check to his bankers not later than by the next day's post after he received it, and the banker present it or forward it to his agent the day after, and the latter present it the day after he receives it, the presentment seems to have been made in time to charge the drawer (*Heywood* v. *Pickering*, L. R. 9 Q. B. 428; *Rickford* v. *Ridge*, 2 Camp. 537, commented on in *Alexander* v. *Birchfield; Hare* v. *Henty*, 30 L. J. C. P. 302; *Beeching* v. — *Holt*, 315; disputed in *Frith* v. *Brooks*, 4 L. T. N. S. 467; *Bond* v. *Warden*, 1 Collyer, 583).

Where payee and drawee do not live in the same place.

What is Delay as between the Transferee, i.e., *one who has received the Check from the* Payee, *and the Drawer.*

Drawer and transferee.

The transferee of a check stands, it is apprehended, in the same and no better position than the payee as against the drawer; that is to say, the payee cannot enlarge the drawer's liability by transferring the check, and the transferee is bound to present the check within the time originally allowed to the payee, if he wishes to recover from the drawer.

What is Delay as between the Transferee and Payee.

Payee and transferee.

An action will only lie on a check against the payee, or holder subsequent to him, who has endorsed the check; in which case the indorser is in the nature of a new drawer, and stands in that relation to the subsequent holders of the check. But an action will in many cases lie for the money paid by the transferee to the transferor, and as in these the same point arises of the

CHECKS. diligence of the transferee, both classes of cases will be considered together.

Payee and transferee.

Where a banker discounted a check not drawn upon him for the holder, and took the first opportunity in the ordinary course to present the check, which was then dishonored, it was held that the banker could sue the late holder for the money paid by him for the check (*Rickford* v. *Ridge*, 2 Camp. 537). For the defendant by discounting his check in the country was taken to have assented to that being done which was the usual and necessary course to procure payment (per Tindal, C. J., *Alexander* v. *Burchfield*, 7 M. & G. 1066). But where a bank cashed a check not drawn upon them for the holder, and by pursuing then the course customary in that bank, of transmitting all checks cashed at their branch bank to their head office, presented a check a day later than they might have done by transmitting it direct to the drawee, and the check was then dishonored, it was held that no action by the bank would lie against the holder of the check (*Moule* v. *Brown*, 4 Bing. N. C. 266). For as explained by Patteson, J., in *Robinson* v. *Hawksford* (9 Q. B. 57), *Moule* v. *Brown* was not an action against the maker, and no one said that an action would not have lain against him. As between subsequent parties a third person passing the check had a right to expect that the person taking it from him should present it in a reasonable time.

What is Delay as between Banker and Customer.

Banker and customer.

A banker receiving a check becomes the agent for presentment of the man from whom he receives it, even where the presentment has to be made to himself as banker of the drawer (*Bailey* v. *Boddenham*, 33 L. J. C. P. 252). The payee of a check may intrust it to his banker for presentment and collection, and the banker as between himself and his customer has, generally speaking, the day after his receipt of it to present it for payment. But he may under some circumstances be bound to present the check earlier than he would be in order to preserve the rights of his customer against the drawer. CHECKS.

Thus, in *Boddington* v. *Schlenker* (4 B. & Ad. 752), where a debtor, the defendant, paid his creditor, the plaintiff, by a crossed check; the latter on the same day sent it his banker; the banker negligently (as it was alleged by the defendant) omitted to present it at the clearing house in time for that day (when it would have been paid), and on the next day it was dishonored, it seems to have been thought by the judges, though the point was not involved in the decision of the court, that the banker would be liable to his customer for not having so presented it, though the banker presented it in time to preserve his customer's rights against the drawer.

This point was further considered in *Hare* v. *Henty*, 30 L. J. C. P. 302, where it was held that a banker was entitled as against his customer to the full time allowed by law for presentment, "unless circumstances exist from which a contract or duty on the part of the banker to present earlier or to defer presentment to a later period can be inferred."

Banker may employ an agent.

The banker, if he do not live in the same place as the drawee, may, if he choose, employ an agent to present the check, for the holder is not required to part with the possession of the instrument proving the right to be paid and trust it to the party who has the obligation in paying it. (See *Hare* v. *Henty*, *supra*.) He has the day after his receipt of it to post it to his agent, and the agent the day after his receipt of it to present it to the drawer (*Hare* v. *Henty*, 10 C. B. N. S. 65; 30 L. J. C. P. 302; *Prideaux* v. *Criddle*, L. R. 4 Q. B. 455).

CHECKS. Where the practice is established to send checks for payment through a clearing house, the period of time within which presentment should be made is that consumed in the ordinary course through the clearing house (*Hare* v. *Henty, supra*), but it seems immaterial through whose hands the check is sent, provided it arrives in time (*Prideaux* v. *Criddle, supra*).

What will excuse Delay in Presentment.

It is apprehended that even where delay has arisen in presenting a check and the bank has stopped before the presentment, the drawer would still be liable if it could be shown either, that at no time between the earliest period at which the check might have been presented and the stoppage of the bank were there sufficient assets to meet the check (*Boehm* v. *Stirling*, 7 T. R. 429), or that the drawer had in the meantime ordered the bankers not to pay the check (*Robinson* v. *Hawksford*, 9 Q. B. 52).

Presentment, where made.

The presentment should be made at the banking house of the bankers on whom the check is drawn.

Presentment to agents of drawee insufficient.

Presentment of a check to the London bankers of the drawee, though described on the check as agents, is insufficient to charge the drawer, for the obligation to pay a check must in general depend on the drawee's account, which the London agents may not know (*Bailey* v. *Boddenham*, 33 L. J. C. P. 252).

But the London bankers have for their mutual convenience established an institution called the clearing house (*Boddington* v. *Schlencker*, 4 B. & Ad. 752; *Warwick* v. *Rogers*, 5 M. & G. 348; *Robarts* v. *Tucker*, 16 Q. B. 570; *Bellamy* v. *Marjoribanks*, 7 Ex. 389), by the use of which much economy, both of time and of the circulating medium is attained.

CHECKS.

London clearing house.

The manner of presenting and receiving bills, notes, and checks at the clearing house has been proved to be as follows:—A clerk from each banking firm in London connected with the clearing house attends there daily bringing with him the checks, &c., on other banks that have been paid since last clearing until half-past five, when the clearing house is closed. Each banker has there a separate drawer into which all bills and checks then due and payable at such bankers are put by the other bankers' clerks respectively during the day from eleven o'clock up to four o'clock in the afternoon, but not later. At intervals during the day the clearing clerk of each bank takes or sends the contents of the drawer appropriated to his bank to his principals, in order that his principals may examine them and determine as to the payment of such bills and checks; and such bills and checks as are at the time intended to be paid are cancelled, by drawing lines along and across the names of the party for whom such payment is intended to be made. Such of the bills and checks as the bankers determine not to pay are returned by them to, and deposited in, the drawer at the clearing house of the bankers by whom the same were brought that morning to the clearing house. All bills not returned and deposited before three minutes to five are considered by the respective bankers as paid; the claims of the several bankers on each other being settled at five o'clock, and the final balance then struck.

Marked checks.

If a check be paid in too late for presentment at the clearing house, and consequently, too late, according to custom of the London bankers, for payment on that day, it is usually sent to the bankers on whom it is drawn, who, if it is a "good" check, that is, one which they would pay if banking hours were not over, mark it as such by placing their initials on it (*Boddington* v. *Schlencker*, 2 B. & Ad. 752).

CHECKS.

Marked checks are paid on the next day after presentment, and are considered as entitled to a priority of payment on that day.

Presentment through clearing house sufficient.

It has been decided that presentment in the ordinary course through the clearing house is sufficient presentment (*Robson* v. *Bennett,* 2 Taunton 388; *Reynolds* v. *Chettle,* 2 Camp. 596).

Country Clearing House.

Country clearing house.

Country bankers who use the country clearing house have correspondents in London whose name is printed on their checks. A check drawn on a country bank and paid to a second country bank situate at a distance from the first, is sent to the London correspondent of the second bank, who presents it at the country clearing house, to the London correspondent of the first bank.

The London correspondent does not mark the check at once, or give credit for it, but transmits it by the next post to his country banker, who should advise the London correspondent by return of post to debit his account with the same, when the London correspondent gives a draft for the amount to the banker from whom he received the check (*Hare* v. *Henty,* 10 C. B. N. S. 65; 30 L. J. C. P. 302; *Bailey* v. *Boddenham,* 33 L. J. C. P. 252).

Other instances of clearing houses established for local purposes are to be found in the following cases, *Prideaux* v. *Criddle* (L. R. 4 Q. B. 465), *Pollard* v. *The Bank of England* (L. R. 6 Q. B. 623); and in America, *The National Bank of North America* v. *Bangs* (8 Amer. Rep. 349).

Foreign checks, how presented.

By the custom of London bankers, a banker, when a foreign check is paid to him by a customer, if he have an agent at the place where the check is payable, sends the check to the agent to be presented for payment; but if he have no agent at such place, he sends the check direct to the banker on whom it is drawn, and the latter immediately either remits the money or returns the check. Checks drawn on bankers at Jersey are considered to be foreign checks (*Heywood* v. *Pickering*, L. R. 9 Q. B. 429). CHECKS.

When a Check should be presented.

A check should be presented within banking hours (*Whittaker* v. *The Bank of England*, 1 C. M. & R. 744), and what are the banking hours must be proved in each case (*Lefftley* v. *Mills*, 4 Term. R. 171; *Parker* v. *Gordon*, 7 East. 385; *Jamieson* v. *Swinton*, 2 Taunt. 224; *Hare* v. *Henty*, 10 C. B. N. S. 65, and 30 L. J. C. P. 232). Checks drawn by the Treasury on the Bank of England are not payable after three p.m. (4 & 5 Will. 4, c. 15, s. 21).

Dispensation with Presentment.

The bankruptcy or notorious stoppage of a bank on which a check is drawn would seem to excuse a neglect to present for payment (*Howe* v. *Bowes*, 16 East 112; 5 Taunt. 30 S. C.; *Roger* v. *Langford*, 1 C. & M. 637; *Robson* v. *Oliver*, 10 Q. B. 704).

What is an Engagement to Pay.

There is no privity between the banker on whom a check is drawn and the payee or holder of a check; therefore the lawful holder of a check, if the banker refuse to pay it, cannot sue the banker on the check unless the latter have accepted it, a practice not usual but legal (per Parke, B., *Bellamy* v. *Majoribanks*, 7 Ex. 404).

Nor in America can the holder of a check set it off

CHECKS. against his note held by the bank (*Case* v. *Henderson*, 8 Am. Rep. 590).

Engagement to pay.

But where the banker has pledged himself to the payee of the check either to pay him the money or to hold it as the money of the payee, an action will lie against him at the suit of the payee for money had and received by him to the use of the payee (*Malcolm* v. *Scott*, 5 Ex. 601; *Walker* v. *Robson*, 9 M. & W. 414). Where a check is presented across the counter for payment the bank is bound by the answer of the cashier, who has implied authority on behalf of his masters, to decide whether a check shall be paid (*Chambers* v. *Miller*, 32 L. J. C. P. 30). Where a check, too late to pass through the clearing house, is presented and "marked" by the drawee, this check is as we have seen entitled to priority of payment on the next day, and the bankers thereby become bound to each other (per L. C. J. Cockburn, *Goodwin* v. *Robarts*, L. R. 10 Ex. 351); but it is a matter of some doubt to what extent the bankers become so bound. Lord Mansfield laid down that "the effect of that marking was similar to the accepting of a bill of exchange, for the banker admits thereby assets and makes himself liable to pay" (*Robson* v. *Bennett*, 2 Taunt. 388); but at the time of this decision a verbal acceptance might be binding, whereas now by the combined effect (1 & 2 Geo. 4, c. 78, s. 2; and 19 & 20 Vic. c. 97, s. 6) an acceptance to be binding must be written on the bill and signed by the acceptor or some person authorised by him.

Effect of marking check as good.

It is submitted that the marking is still so far similar to the acceptance of a bill of exchange, that it admits the genuineness of the signature of the drawer and the existence of assets, but not that the check is in other respects genuine, as that the amount appearing on the check is the amount for which it was originally drawn; thus giving the bank presenting the check a right of action if injured by reason of the check turning out to be forged or insufficiency of assets, but not if the amount originally named in the check had been fraudulently raised (see the decision between the two banks on the effect of the American custom of certifying checks *Marine National Bank* v. *The National City Bank*, 17 American Rep. 305). Checks.

It is always open to the banker to show that any marking, cancelling, or entering in account was by arrangement between the bankers merely provisional, and subject to revision at a later period. Thus in *Fernandez* v. *Glynn*, 1 Camp. 426, the facts were these: Plaintiff paid unto the house of Vere & Co. a check upon defendant's house. Vere's clerk took it to the clearing house to be paid, and put it into defendant's drawer. Vere's clerk received it back before five o'clock, cancelled with a memorandum written under it, "cancelled by mistake." After five he would not have taken it back. By the custom checks might be returned up to five o'clock. Lord Ellenborough held that, notwithstanding the cancelling, defendant had till five o'clock to return the check, and having so returned it, this amounted to a refusal to pay (see *Pollard* v. *Bank of England*, L. R. 6 Q. B. 623). Provisional cancelling.

Money laid down on the counter by a banker's cashier in payment of a check cannot be recovered back by action, though it were handed over under a misapprehension of the drawer's account; still less can it be taken by force from the party receiving it. As soon as the money is laid down by the banker upon the counter to be taken up by the receiver the payment is complete (*Chambers* v. *Miller*, 32 L. J. C. P. 30). Money paid by drawee cannot be recovered.

The mere receipt of a check by a banker, who is at once the banker of the drawer and the payee, is not sufficient to make him liable to the payee for the amount of the check. There must be either an actual demand for

CHECKS. payment, followed by a promise to pay, or an acknowledgment with or without an actual demand for payment previously made, that the check is held by the banker as the agent of the payee and not of the drawer.

Mere receipt of check by drawee does not amount to a promise to pay.

Thus where the drawer and payee of a check had the same banker, and the check was paid in by the payee without any distinct notice, whether he presented it as a check to be paid or to be merely placed to his account, and the cashier received it without any remark, knowing at the time that the drawer's account was overdrawn, it was held that in the absence of any intimation by the payee of the character in which he wished the banker to receive it, it must be taken that the banker took it as the agent of the payee, and therefore had till the next day to inform him there were no effects, and that the check had not been paid (*Boyd* v. *Emmerson*, 2 Ad. & Ellis 184).

But where the drawer and payee of a check had the same banker, and the payee paid in the check, which was received without any remark on either side, and the banker informed the payee next day that the check was not paid, but he would keep it in the hope of there being money to pay it; and *afterwards* a sufficient sum was paid in, but appropriated by the banker, to pay off debts owing to him by the drawer, it was held that the payee could maintain an action for money had and received against the banker, who, being his agent for the receipt of the money, could not appropriate it to the payment of the debt due to the bank, nor to the payment of checks presented subsequently to that of the payee (*Kilsby* v. *Williams*, 5 B. & Ald. 815; *Pollard* v. *Ogden*, 2 E. & B. 459).

It has been suggested in America by the Supreme Court that if it could be shown that the bank had charged the check in its books against the drawer and settled with him on that basis, the plaintiff could recover on a count for money had and received on the rule *ex æquo et bono* (*Bank of the Republic* v. *Millard*, 10 Wallace's Rep. 152; and see *Oddie* v. *The National City Bank*, 6 Amer. Rep. 161). CHECKS.

Checks presented unstamped.

By 33 & 34 Vict. c. 97, s. 54 (2), if a check be presented for payment unstamped, the banker may affix a proper adhesive stamp and cancel it, then pay the check, and as he thinks fit, charge his customer with the value of the stamp, or deduct it from the sum paid.

Encashment of Checks.

Legal tender

The banker is only bound like any other debtor to pay his debts in what may be legal tender; and this by 33 Vict. c. 10, s. 4, is defined to be a tender of money in coins which have been issued from the mint in accordance with the provisions of that Act, and have not been called in by any proclamation made in pursuance of that Act, and have not become diminished in weight by wear, or otherwise, so as to be of less weight than the current weight (defined in the Act),—

In the case of gold coins for a payment of any amount.

In the case of silver coins for payment of an amount not exceeding 40s., but for no greater amount.

In the case of bronze coins for payment of an amount not exceeding one shilling, but for no greater amount.

And further, nothing in that Act is to prevent any paper currency which, under any Act or otherwise, is a legal tender, from being a legal tender. This last proviso has reference to 3 & 4 Will. 4, c. 98, s. 6, which is as follows:—

A tender of a note or notes of the Bank of England, expressed to be payable to bearer on demand shall be a legal tender to the amount expressed in such note or notes, and shall be taken to be valid as a tender to such

Checks. Legal tender.

amount for all sums above five pounds on all occasions on which any tender of money may be legally made so long as the Bank of England shall continue to pay on demand their notes in legal coin; provided always, that no such note or notes shall be deemed a legal tender of payment by the governor and company of the Bank of England, or any branch bank of the governor and company; but the governor and company are not to become liable or be required to pay and satisfy at any branch bank of the governor and company any note or notes of the governor and company not made specially payable at such branch bank; but the governor and company shall be liable to pay and satisfy at the Bank of England in London all notes of the governor and company, or of any branch bank thereof.

The notes of the Bank of England are not a legal tender in Scotland (8 & 9 Vic. c. 38, s. 15), nor in Ireland (8 & 9 Vic. c. 37; s. 6), though there is no enactment prohibiting their circulation in either country.

The result of these Acts is—

That the Bank of England and its branches must, if required, pay checks drawn on them for sums above 40s. in gold, provided that the amount of the sum required above 40s. is capable of being expressed in the gold coinage.

At any other bank a check for £100 may, if the banker choose, be cashed, and the bearer cannot refuse to accept payment in the following way: 40s. in silver, the next three pounds in gold, and the remaining £95 in Bank of England notes, "expressed to be payable to bearer on demand," but not, it would appear, in Bank of England notes specially payable at a branch of the Bank of England.

Counterfeit Coin.

Where the banker makes in good faith a payment in

base coin, and the coin is accepted without demur, no question, it would appear, as to its goodness can afterwards be raised by the payee, unless the coin can be traced, as where paid in a bag or marked for the purpose of being distinguished, and discovered within a reasonable time to be bad.

Payment in Forged Notes.

Payment in forged notes.

Payment in forged bank notes, whether purporting to be issued by the Bank of England or any other bank, though made in good faith, is no payment in law—that is "the party negotiating them is answerable for the notes being such as they purport to be" (*Jones* v. *Ryde,* 5 Taunt. 484, 494), and, therefore, if they turn out forged, an action will lie to recover the money paid for them (*Woodland* v. *Fear* 26 L. J. Q. B. p. 204).

In Bills of Exchange.

It is open to the drawer to agree with the banker that payment of a check should be made in any circulating medium other than that made legal tender by law. Thus he may by his check direct payment to be made in bills of exchange or promissory notes; such check it may be observed is for the purposes of the Stamp Act a bill of exchange payable on demand and requires no other stamp than an ordinary check (33 & 34 Vic. c. 97, s. 48 (2), *ante,* p. 50).

But the consequences of a payment in bills of exchange or in promissory notes must be considered separately with relation to the parties to whom payment is made.

1. *Drawer and Banker.*—If the drawer of a check payable to himself accept in return for his check a bill drawn or endorsed by the banker the bill by the statute of Anne (3 & 4 Anne, c. 9, s. 7) is a complete payment of his check as between him and the banker, if

CHECKS. he do not take due steps to get the bill accepted paid or protested.

Payment by bill.

2. *Payee and Drawer.*—But where the payee of a check accepts from the banker in return for the check, a bill of exchange endorsed or drawn by the banker (*Strong* v. *Hart,* 6 B. & C. 160 ; *Smith* v. *Ferrand,* 7 B. & C. 19 ; *Baillie* v. *Moore,* 8 Q. B. 489), or bank post bills (*Tilney* v. *Courtier,* 2 C. & J. 16) ; or another check drawn by the banker (*Wilby* v. *Warren,* 2 C. & J. 18 n.) ; or bankers' promissory notes commonly called country notes, though they afterwards turn out worthless, from the failure of the bank (*Vernon* v. *Bouverie,* 2 Show. 296 ; *Lichfield Union* v. *Green,* 26 L. J. Ex. 140 ; 1 H. & N. 884), the original debtor of the payee, *i.e.,* the drawer of the check is discharged, because the payee having the option of taking cash, elected to take something else at his own peril (*Camidge* v. *Allenby,* 6 B. & C. 373), and he cannot sue the drawer for the original debt.

3. *Payee and Banker.*—And if the bill so taken by the payee be not met at maturity the payee can only recover the amount of the bill from the banker in cases where he has taken all due measures to get the bill accepted and paid, or protested (Comyn's Dig. Tit. Merchant, F. 17 ; 3 & 4 Anne, c. 9, s. 7). The law would appear to be the same where a promissory note indorsed by the banker is taken by the payee of a check. And it is obvious that the same rule applies to the relations between successive holders of a check.

But where the payee accepts from the banker in return for the check a banker's note, commonly called a country note, and the note turns out to be worthless from the failure of the maker, though given and accepted in perfect good faith on either side, the payee of the check, if the note be made by the banker himself, must prove against the banker's estate (*Lichfield Guardians* v. *Green*, 26 L. J. Ex. 140). If the note be made by a company, interest at £5 per cent. will be allowed from the date of the demand for payment on the liquidator (*In re East of England Banking Company*, L. R. 4 Ch. Ap. 14).

But if the banker be not the maker the case resembles those where payment is made by country notes at the time of purchase of goods, which are fully discussed in the chapter on bank notes.

Refusal to pay Checks.

What will excuse a refusal by the banker to pay.

A banker's contract is to pay checks drawn upon him by his customer whenever he has funds belonging to the customer to the amount drawn for in his possession. But unless a space of time have elapsed between the receipt of the money and the presentment of the check sufficient to allow the money to be passed to the customer's account, consistently with carrying on the business of the bank (*Whitaker* v. *The Bank of England*, 1 C. M. & R. 744; see Maule, J., *Robarts* v. *Tucker*, 16 Q. B. 560, 578), the banker will not be liable for refusing to pay a check, even though he have in fact money belonging to the customer in his possession. This point was raised in *Marzeth* v. *Williams* (1 B. & Ad. 415), where the facts were these: On a certain day the plaintiff had standing in his name at his banker's, a balance of £69 16*s.* 6*d.* About eleven the same day £40 was paid into his account; a little before three o'clock a check drawn by him for £87 7*s.* 6*d.* was presented for payment. The clerk after referring to a book said there was not sufficient assets, but that the check might go through the clearing house. The check was paid on the following day. The jury found that a sufficient time had elapsed between the paying in of the £40 and the presentment of the check to enable the banker and his clerks to know that the sum

CHECKS. had been paid in, and found a verdict for the plaintiff with nominal damages. A motion was made for a new trial on the ground that the contract between the banker and customer was implied by law and not express, and that the plaintiff could not recover for the breach of such a contract without proving actual damage, of which there was in this case no evidence. The court discharged the rule, and Lord Tenterden in giving judgment, said: "This action is substantially founded on contract, and the plaintiff though he may not have sustained a damage in fact, is entitled to recover nominal damages. At the same time I cannot forbear to observe that it is a discredit to a person, and therefore injurious in fact, to have a draft refused for so small a sum, for it shows that the banker had little confidence in the customer. It is an act particularly calculated to be injurious to a person in trade. My judgment in this case, however, proceeds on the ground that the action is founded on a contract between the plaintiff and the bankers, that the latter whenever they should have money in their hands belonging to the plaintiff or within a reasonable time after they should have received such money, would pay his checks; there having been a breach of such contract the plaintiff is entitled to recover nominal damages" (1 B. & Ad. 415, 424).

Although no evidence is given that the plaintiff has sustained any special damage, the jury ought to give a reasonable compensation for the injury the plaintiff must have sustained by the dishonor of his check (*Rollin* v. *Steward*, 14 C. B. 595; 23 L. J. C. P. 148). Where a banker who had been in the habit of making advances to the plaintiff against consignments, and not debiting them to the plaintiff's current account until the sale of the consignment did, without notice to the plaintiff, debit his current account with an advance before the sale of the consignment in respect of which the advance was made, and having thus exhausted his assets, refused to pay his check, it was held that the banker was bound to give formal notice to the plaintiff of the change in the mode of conducting business before dishonoring the check (*Cumming* v. *Shand*, 29 L. J. Ex. 129; *Garnett* v. *McEwen*, L. R. 8 Ex. 10). And where bankers retained the balance of a customer to answer a future liability which might arise in respect of bills discounted for him by them to a much larger amount than the balance, and the customer brought an action against the banker for having dishonored his checks and for the amount of the balance, the court of equity, upon a bill filed by the bankers against the customer for an account and for an injunction to restrain the action at law, granted the injunction prayed for (*The Agra and Masterman's Bank* v. *Hoffman*, 34 L. J. Ch. 285).

CHECKS.

Refusal to pay.

Banker may retain funds to meet bills to be discounted for customer.

But no action will lie against the banker for dishonoring checks where the drawer's assets have been previously exhausted by the payment of bills accepted by him and made payable at the bankers, and such acceptances are sufficient authority to the banker to pay the amounts due on the bills (*Kymer* v. *Laurie*, 18 L. J. Q. B. 218).

Banker may pay bills made payable at bank.

In some cases the banker is justified in refusing to honor the check of his customer, though there be assets standing in the latter's name. If an executor draw a check as executor on his testator's funds in the banker's possession to discharge some debt due from himself personally to the banker, the banker would be justified in refusing to honor the check. For the discharge of the debt to the banker out of the testator's funds in his possession would be held abundant proof to him of the breach of trust, and he would be held to have participated in it for his own personal benefit, and to be liable therefor (*Gray* v. *Johnston*, L. R. 3 E. & I. 1).

Banker may refuse to pay check drawn in breach of trust.

CHECKS.

Death of drawer.

Again he would appear to be justified in refusing to pay where he has heard of the death of the drawer before the presentment of the check. For the death of the drawer is a revocation of the banker's authority to pay (*Tate* v. *Hibbert*, 2 Ves. Jun. 118; *Hewett* v. *Kay*, L. R. 6 Eq. 198; *Bromley* v. *Brunton*, L. R. 6 Eq. 275). But a payment made by him in ignorance of the death is apparently a good payment.

Notice of Dishonor.

The drawer of a check payable to a third party is entitled to notice of dishonor, and so is each endorser. The consequence of not giving notice is that the party to whom notice should have been given is discharged from all liability, whether on the check or on the consideration for which the check was paid (*Bridges* v. *Berry*, 3 Taunt. 130; *Bickerdike* v. *Bollman*, 2 Sm. L. C. 59); the reason being, that the law presumes the check is drawn on account of the drawee's having effects of the drawer in his hands, and if the latter has notice that the bill be not accepted, or not paid, he may withdraw his funds immediately. But when a check is dishonored for want of assets, and the drawer has either no assets or not sufficient effects in the bank at the time he might reasonably expect the check to be presented for payment, and further, has no reason to expect it will be paid on presentment, the notice of dishonor is excused (*Carew* v. *Duckworth*, L. R. 4 Ex. 313). But if there are sufficient effects in the bank to meet the check, the drawer would be entitled to notice though he knew the bank would not honor the check, for he would be entitled to say the bank was bound to honor it, even though the bank had told him it would not (per Bramwell, B., *ibid*).

When notice of dishonour excused.

Notice by drawee.

Where a check is forwarded by post to the banker on whom it is drawn he is constituted the agent of the holder of the check for purposes of presentment and dishonor (*Bailey* v. *Boddenham*, 33 L. J. C. P. 252), and on the check being dishonored ought to give notice to the drawer with all convenient speed.

Checks.

Banker has a day to give notice.

A banker with whom a check is deposited for collection is for the purpose of notice to be considered as a distinct holder, and has a day to give notice to his customer, and his customer another day to give notice to the anterior parties (*Robson* v. *Bennett*, 2 Taunt. 388; *Langdale* v. *Trimmer*, 15 East, 291; *Bray* v. *Hadwen*, 5 M. & S. 68; *Prideaux* v. *Criddle*, L. R. 4 Q. B. 454). Where a bill passes through several branches of the same establishment, each branch may be considered a distinct holder, entitled to receive and transmit notice as such (*Clode* v. *Bailey*, 12 M. & W. 51), although the bills may have passed without endorsement. The notice must be given within a reasonable time after the dishonor, and generally speaking, a person has a day within which to give notice to the antecedent parties after the day of dishonor (see Byles on Bills,—Notice of Dishonor). Notice of dishonor may be given on behalf of the principal by the banker in his own name (*Woodthorp* v. *Lawes*, 2 M. & W. 109; *Rowe* v. *Tipper*, 22 L. J. C. P. 135).

In *Himmelman* v. *Hotaling* (6 American Rep. 601, see *infra*), it was held that where the drawer and drawee reside in the same city or town, the reasonable time for presumptive dishonor should not be fixed within more restricted limits than the close of business hours of the day succeeding that on which payment might first have been legally demanded.

Stale or Overdue Checks.

A check, in the words of Parke, B. (9 M. & W. 17, 18), is intended to be presented speedily, and though there is

CHECKS. When stale.

no decision laying down precisely at what period after issue a check becomes stale, or suspicious, it was at one time held that a transferee as he took it after it was due, had no better title than his transferor.

Thus, the owner of a check for £50 having lost it, the check was paid five days after its date to a shopkeeper who received the amount at the bank. Held that the shopkeeper was liable to refund the money to the owner of the check, for having taken it overdue, he acquired no better title than the party from whom he took it, and that it lay upon him to show that the assignor had a title (*Down* v. *Halling,* 4 B. & C..330). But, in a later case (*Rothschild* v. *Corney,* 9 B. & C. 388), it was held, that though the taking of a check six days old is a circumstance from which the jury may infer fraud, it is not conclusive evidence so as to prevent the party taking the check from suing on it, or retaining it, or the money received on it.

So it appears, that the holder of a check, stale, but not dishonored, may recover at any time within six years on the check, or retain the money he has obtained on it, unless he have been guilty of fraud. Negligence is a circumstance from which the jury might infer fraud, but, it is not identical with fraud, unless perhaps, when it amounts to a determination to wink at anything (see Lord Denman, *Willis* v. *The Bank of England,* 4 A. & E. 32).

On this point the following American case may be cited :—

The holder of a negotiable bank check, drawn the day previous presented it for payment which was refused. On the same day he transferred it for a valuable consideration to plaintiff, who took it in good faith, and without notice of previous dishonor, and immediately on the same day, presented it to the drawee, when payment was again refused. Held, that plaintiff could recover of the drawer, a sufficient time after the check was drawn not having elapsed when plaintiff took it, to raise the presumption of dishonor, though the drawer and drawee were residents in the same city (*Himmelman* v. *Hotaling*, 6 American Rep. 601, citing *O'Keefe* v. *Dunn*, 6 Taunt. 305; *Goodman* v. *Harvey*, 4 A. & E. 870.) Checks.

Dishonored Checks.

An endorsee for value of a check after dishonor has a right to recover on the check unless there be an equity attached to the check itself amounting to a discharge, and such equities may be between the indorser and a third party, and not only between the holder and drawer (*Ex parte Swan*, L. R. 9 Eq. 344; *In re European Bank, Ex parte Oriental Com. Bank*, L. R. 5 Ch. Ap. 358).

Forged Checks.

Where the Drawer's Signature is Forged.

It is the banker's duty to know his customer's signature, and if he pay a check to which the drawer's signature has been forged, he pays it in his own wrong, and cannot charge his customer with such a payment. Not even if the customer lost his check book, and so contributed to the success of the forgery (per Parke, B., *The Bank of Ireland* v. *Evan's Charities*, 5 H. L. C. 389.) Banker and customer.

The banker may in some cases recover the money he has paid, from the presenter, even where he was a *bonâ fide* holder for value. Possibly, where the banker discovered the forgery on the day on which he paid the Banker and presenter of check.

CHECKS. check and at once gave notice to the presenter before any alteration in the situation of the prior parties (*Wilkinson* v. *Johnson,* 3 B. & C. 428). Notice given on the day following would appear to be too late (*Cocks* v. *Masterman,* 9 B. & C. 902), and *à fortiori* after a longer interval (*Price* v. *Neale,* 3 Burr. 1354; *Smith* v. *Mercer,* 6 Taunt. 76). But he will not be estopped by payment from recovering from one whose conduct, or whose agent's conduct, has been such as to mislead or to induce him to pay the check, without the usual scrutiny or other precautions against fraud (*Wilkinson* v. *Johnson,* 3 *B.* & C. 428), at least if the mistake is discovered before any alteration in the situation of the other parties, that is, whilst their remedies are left entire, and no one is discharged by laches.

Forged Indorsements.

Banker not responsible for endorsement.

Bankers, that is, persons carrying on the business of bankers (*Halifax Union* v. *Wheelwright,* L. R. 10 Exp. 193), are not responsible for the genuineness of the indorsement on checks drawn payable to order on demand as they would be on an ordinary bill of exchange or on a letter of credit (*British Linen Co.* v. *Caledonian Insurance Co.,* 4 Macqueen 107). For 16 & 17 Vic. c. 59, s. 19, enacts that any draft or order drawn upon a banker for a sum of money payable to order on demand which shall, when presented for payment, purport to be indorsed by the person to whom the same shall be drawn payable, shall be a sufficient authority to such banker to pay the amount of such draft or order to the bearer thereof; and it shall not be incumbent on such banker to prove that such indorsement, or any subsequent indorsement was made by or under the direction or authority of the person

16 & 17 Vic. c. 59, s. 19.

to whom the said draft or order was or is made payable, either by the drawer or any indorser thereof.

Endorsement *per proc.*

An indorsement "per procuration" or "as agent" is within the meaning of this enactment (*Charles* v. *Blackwell*, 1 C. P. D. 548). But the enactment does not extend to protect any other person who takes the check or receives payment of a check upon the faith of an indorsement which turns out to be forged (*Ogden* v. *Benas*, L. R. 9 C. P. 513), and therefore money paid by the drawees to the person presenting the check is in reality the money of the lawful holder of the check, and may be recovered by him from the person so receiving it (*Ogden* v. *Benas*, *supra*; *Arnold* v. *The Cheque Bank*, 1 C. P. D. 578, 585).

Drawee alone protected.

Effect of forgery on subsequent holders.

Where the title to a bill or check is necessarily made through a forgery, even a *bonâ fide* holder for value cannot recover against any party prior to the forgery by suing on the bill or check (*Burchfield* v. *Moore*, 23 L. J. Q. B. 261), or even retain it (*Johnson* v. *Windle* 3 Bing. N. C. 225), and a forgery or alteration by an indorsee not only avoids the security as against all prior parties but also extinguishes the debt due to the indorsee from the indorser (*Alderson* v. *Langdale*, 3 B. & Ad. 660); but each *bonâ fide* holder can recover from his predecessor in title till the forger or holder with notice is reached, for, as in the case of bank notes or navy bills, the party negotiating them is answerable for their being what they purport to be (*Jones* v. *Ryde*, 5 Taunt. 488, 494).

Altered Check.

An alteration in a material part avoids a check (*Davidson* v. *Cooper*, 11 M. & W. 778; 13 M. & W. 343), like every other instrument made while it is in the custody of plaintiffs, although the alteration be by a stranger. The

CHECKS.

Material alteration after issue makes check void.

date (*Vance* v, *Lowther*, 1 Ex. D. 176), sum (*Hamelin* v. *Burch*, 9 Q. B. 306), or time of payment are all material parts.

Again an alteration in a material part makes the instrument void within the Stamp Laws: for after the alteration the instrument is a new instrument, and requires a new stamp.

But an alteration in a material part will not make void the instrument when the alteration is made before the check is issued or become available, where the check is altered to correct a mistake and in furtherance of the original intention of the parties (Byles on Bills—Alteration of Bill or Note).

The alteration by the drawer and payee of a check does not extinguish the debt between the parties, but an alteration by an endorsee avoids the instrument as against all parties and extinguishes the debt due to the indorsee from the indorser (*Alderson* v. *Langdale*, 3 B. & Ad. 660).

A *bonâ fide* transferee for value of an altered check or bill is in no better position as to his remedy on the check than his transferor (*Burchfield* v. *Moore*, 23 L. J. Q. B. 261).

Raised check.

Where an alteration has been made in the amount for which a check was originally drawn, increasing the apparent amount, and the banker has paid the larger amount, he cannot charge his customer with the excess (*Hall* v. *Fuller*, 5 B. & C. 750), unless the customer has been guilty of some neglect in the transaction itself, and the neglect has been the proximate cause of the banker being misled. Thus, the banker can charge his customer with the whole amount where the customer so negligently fills up a check as to invite forgery, or to allow forgery to be easily committed, as in a check for fifty pounds by writing fifty with a small f, and leaving a sufficient space before the "fifty," and the figures 50 at the bottom of the check to

Banker and customer.

allow the insertion of another figure before the 5 (*Young* v. *Grote*, 4 Bing. 253; *Halifax Union* v. *Wheelwright*, L. R. 10 Ex. 183; see too as to the rule, *Robarts* v. *Tucker*, 16 Q. B. 579; *Barker* v. *Union Bank*, 1 Macqueen 513; *Swan* v. *North British Australasian Cy.*, 32 L. J. Ex. 273; *Foster* v. *Mackinnon*, L. R. 4 C. P. 704, 712; *Arnold* v. *The Cheque Bank*, 1 C. P. D. 586—8). CHECKS.

No man, however, is bound to suspect that the person with whom he deals will commit forgery whenever the opportunity arises (*Société Générale* v. *Metropolitan Bank*, 27 L. T. 858), and, therefore, it is not necessary for a person drawing a check to exclude the possibility of any addition or alteration (*ibid*). It is apparently sufficient if he fill it up in the ordinary way.

More caution, according to Pothier, is expected of a banker from his position than from the rest of the world.

Banker must not be guilty of negligence.

Be that as it may, it appears that though a customer had been in some degree negligent, if the check when presented and paid bore marks which might be alterations, or which might fairly rouse suspicion, the banker would pay it in his own wrong.

Thus (*Scholey* v. *Ramsbottom*, 2 Camp. 485), a check which evidently had been torn in four pieces and pasted together on a sheet of paper was paid by the banker. The customer proved that after drawing it he had torn it up and thrown it away. It was held the bankers were not justified in paying it without inquiry, and having done so could not charge their customer with the payment (*Ingham* v. *Primrose*, 28 L. J. C. P. 295).

But the banker may recover from the payee or holder the amount paid by mistake on a fraudulently raised check if neither party have been in fault, as money paid without consideration; but where either party has been guilty of negligence or carelessness in the transaction by

CHECKS. which the other has been injured the negligent party must bear the loss (*Espy* v. *The Bank of Cincinnati*, 18 Wallace Rep. 604).

Where an alteration appears on the face of a bill or note it lies on the plaintiff to show that it was made under such circumstances as not to vitiate the instrument (*Johnson* v. *The Duke of Marlborough*, 2 Stark 313; *Henman* v. *Dickinson*, 5 Bing. 183; *Knight* v. *Clements*, 8 Ad. & E. 215).

Lost Checks.

By 17 & 18 Vic. c. 125, s. 87, in case of any action founded upon a bill of exchange or other negotiable instrument, the court or a judge has power to order that the loss of such instrument shall not be set up, provided an indemnity be given to the satisfaction of the court or judge or a master against the claims of any other person upon such negotiable instrument.

The party suing on the lost bill should offer an indemnity to the defendants before bringing the action, or pleas setting up the loss of the bill will not be struck out, except on payment of the defendant's costs of the action (*King* v. *Zimmerman*, L. R. 6 C. P. 466).

This enactment only applies to cases where an action has been begun on the lost check, and it would seem that where, after the loss of the check and before the commencement of the action, the bankers on whom the check was drawn, fail, the drawer is not liable for the amount of the check, at least where the ordinary time for presenting the check has elapsed (*Bevan* v. *Hill*, 2 Camp. 381).

Cashed Checks.

The custom of bankers is to return checks after cashing them to the drawer; and it has been said that a banker has no more right to retain a check which he has cashed than the payee a bill of exchange which has been paid (Per Wilde, C. J., *Reg.* v. *Watts*, 2 Den. C. C. 14, 21).

CHECKS.

To whom a cashed check belongs.

It is, however, obvious that a cashed check is the banker's only voucher for the payment with which he has charged his customer. On the other hand, a cashed check is evidence for the customer that money has been paid on his behalf to the payee. Probably, as between the banker and customer, the customer is only entitled to retain the checks after he has settled with the banker the account to which the checks refer. But, as regards third parties, the banker is taken to be in privity with his customer, and, therefore, where the drawer is one of the parties to an action, a notice to him to produce the check, whether it be in his actual possession or the banker's is sufficient to secure its production, or, failing that, the admission of secondary evidence (*Partridge* v. *Coals*, Ry. & M. 156 ; *Burton* v. *Payne*, 2 C. & P. 520).

Bankers not unfrequently in return for a loan obtain a check drawn by the borrower on them for the amount of the loan and in such a case the bankers retain the check as a voucher for the loan (*Other* v. *Ireson*, 24 L. J. Chanc. 654), and see Checks as Evidence, *infra*.

Checks as Payment.

The giving and taking a negotiable check on a banker for and on account of a debt is equivalent to payment, until it has been presented for payment and refused (Pearce v. *Davis*, 1 M. & Rob. 365 ; *Caine* v. *Coulson*, 32 L. J. Ex. 97).

But a check is no payment where it is not honored, though it may have been taken in preference to cash (*Everitt* v. *Collins*, 2 Camp. 515). A creditor may refuse to accept a check in payment, and it would appear may sue

CHECKS.

Payment by check.

for the original debt before returning the check (*Hough* v. *May*, 4 A. & E. 954; *Stuart* v. *Cawse*, 28 L. J. C. P. 193). The mere receipt of a check drawn in conditional terms is no payment (*Hough* v. *May, supra*).

Where a payment has been made by a check, the drawer is entitled to stop the payment of the check, and to resist an action on the check, on any grounds which would enable him at law to recover his money if he had paid in cash and not by check (*Mills* v. *Oddy*, 6 C. & P. 728; 2 C. M. & R. 103).

If a check be given on a condition which the drawer finds to be eluded or broken he is entitled to stop the payment of the check (*Wienholt* v. *Spitta*, 3 Camp. 376; *Spincer* v. *Spincer*, 2 M. & G. 295).

But if A., by means of a false pretence or promise, or a condition which he does not fulfil, procure B. to give him a check in favour of C., to whom he pays it, and who receives it *bonâ fide* for value, B. remains liable on the check, and if cashed by C., cannot recover the money from him (*Watson* v. *Russell*, 31 L. J. Q. B. 304; *Currie* v. *Misa*, L. R. 10 Ex. 163; 1 App. Ca. 554).

Where the acceptor or drawee of a bill proposes to pay by check, the holder should not in strictness give up the bill till the check is paid (*Ward* v. *Evans*, 2 Ld. Ray. 928). It has been held, where a country correspondent sent up to a London banker a bill for presentment, and the banker receiving a check in payment gave up the bill, and the check was afterwards dishonored, that the banker was not guilty of negligence (*Russell* v. *Hankey*, 6 T. R. 12).

Where a buyer pays for goods by a check which he knows, or has good reason to believe, will not be honored, though the goods be delivered, no property in them passes to him, and the seller may recover them in trover (*Noble* v. *Adams*, 7 Taunt. 59; *Earl of Bristol* v. *Willsmore*, 1 B. & C. 514).

Payment by an Agent by Check.

Where a creditor receives from a debtor's agent in payment of the debt the agent's own check, which is afterwards dishonored, whether the debtor is discharged or not, is more a question of fact than of law, depending on the answer to the question whether exclusive credit was given to the agent or not. Thus, where a debtor took his creditor to his agent, and the creditor, being offered by the agent either cash or the agent's check, took the check, which was afterwards dishonored, it was held that the debtor was not discharged, though the agent failed with a balance belonging to his principal in his hands to a larger amount than the amount of the check; because the agent's check was, considering all the circumstances, tantamount to the debtor's check, and no debtor is discharged by giving a check which produces nothing, though cash may have been previously tendered (*Everitt* v. *Collins,* 2 Camp. 515). But if the creditor, taking from the debtor's agent a check which is afterwards dishonored, give the agent a receipt as if the money were actually received, and the debtor, without notice of the dishonor, in consequence of such receipt deals with the agent on the footing that the debt has been satisfied, the debt will be deemed discharged as to the debtor (*Wyat* v. *Marquis of Hertford,* 3 East. 147; Story on Agency, s. 433—4). CHECKS.

Payment to an Agent by Check.

As a general rule, an agent authorised to receive payment has authority only to receive it in cash, therefore a debtor paying his creditor's agent in any other form than cash (as by bill) may have to pay again to the principal if the agent turn out a defaulter. But since it is the

CHECKS.

Payment of agent by check.

custom to pay in checks, it is a question for the jury whether payment by a check which is afterwards honored is, or is not, equivalent to a cash payment as against the principal (see judgment of Blackburn, J., in *Williams* v *Evans*, L. R. 1 Q. B. 352).

And where the agent has a higher authority, as where he is not bound to hand over the sum in specie, but to pay an equivalent sum, payment to him by a check crossed to his bankers and honored by the drawees is a good payment as against the principal (*Bridges* v. *Garrett*, L. R. 5 C. P. 451).

Checks as Evidence of a Debt.

No inference can be drawn from the fact *per se* of a man drawing a check in favour of another. Thus a check drawn but not presented is no evidence of a previous debt due from the drawee to the payee (*Pearce* v. *Davis*, 1 M. & R. 365; *Lloyd* v. *Sandelands*, as explained by Alderson, B., in *Mountford* v. *Harper*, 16 M. & W. 825). A check drawn and delivered to the payee, and crossed in the payee's handwriting, and produced by the drawer with other papers belonging to the payee, is no evidence of a loan by the drawer without proof of the payment of the check to the payee (*Bleasby* v. *Crossley*, 3 Bing. 430). A check shown to have been in circulation is evidence of a payment having been made to the payee on behalf of the drawer (*Thomson* v. *Pitman*, 1 F. & F. 339).

A check which has been cancelled by a banker is no evidence of money lent by the banker to the customer (*Fletcher* v. *Manning*, 12 M. & W. 571), but it is *primâ facie* evidence of a payment to the amount of the check by the banker of his debt to the customer (*ibid.*).

Of Payment.

To prove payment by a check it is not sufficient to prove delivery of a check by way of payment. It must be further shown that the circumstances were such as would make the check a payment by the debtor to the creditor. Therefore proof of the delivery of a check not unconditional, but drawn in these terms: Pay H. & Co. *balance account railing* or bearer, does not support a plea of payment (*Hough* v. *May*, 4 A. & E. 954). CHECKS.

A cashed check is not sufficient by itself to prove the payment of a debt to the payee of the check, but it must be further shown that a debt existed between the parties at the date of the check (*Aubert* v. *Walsh*, 4 Taunt, 293), and *either* the delivery of the check to the payee (*Mountford* v. *Harper*, 16 M. & W. 825; *Boswell* v. *Smith*, 6 C. & P. 60), *or* the receipt by the payee of the money for the check as evidenced by indorsement of the payee (*Egg* v. *Barrett*, 3 Esp. 196; *Boswell* v. *Smith*, 6 C. & P. 60). It is, therefore, prudent to cause the payee to write his name across the check or to indorse it.

In an action by A. to recover from B. a sum alleged to have been paid on B.'s behalf to C. by A., upon proof of a claim received by A. from C. of the sending of a check by A. to C., and of a receipt of a check by C., a receipt for the amount from C. to A. was held admissible in evidence against B., as a fact to prove the payment of the amount by A. without proving that the check was honored (*Carmarthen Ry.* v. *Manchester Ry.*, L. R. 8 C. P. 684).

Statute of Limitations.

Where a bill is given under such circumstances as to raise the implication of a promise to pay the balance, and

CHECKS. Statute of limitations.

so if necessary to revive the debt, the revived right of action dates from the delivery of the bill, whether it be subsequently honored or not (*Turney* v. *Dodwell*, 23 L. J. Q. B. 137).

The law seems to be the same where payment is made by check.

But when a loan is made by check the statute begins to run from the time of the payment of the check by the bankers on whom it is drawn (*Garden* v. *Bruce*, L. R. 3 C. P. 300).

A Check as a Gift.

A check drawn by A. in favour of B. and given to B. as a gift cannot be enforced by B. against A. (*Easton* v. *Pratchett*, 1 C. M. & R. 808).

A check drawn by the donor on his own banker and not presented before the death of the donor is not a valid donatio mortis causâ (*Hewett* v. *Kaye*, L. R. 6 Eq. 198), because the death of the donor is a revocation of the authority to pay. But where a check has been given inter vivos, and presented, but not paid on the ground that the signature differed from the usual signature of the drawer, and the drawer died before the check was paid, it was held that the gift was as complete as the donor could make it, and that the check must be paid out of the funds in the hands of the executors (*Bromley* v. *Brunton*, 6 Eq. 275); but the gift of a check and of the donor's pass-book when the donor died before presentment is not a good donatio mortis causâ (*Beak* v. *Beak*, L. R. 13 Eq. 489).

Check held by Stakeholder.

Where a stakeholder is intrusted with a check as representing the stakes, he does not necessarily commit a breach of trust by cashing the check before the occurrence of the event deciding the right to the stakes (*Wilkinson* v. *Godefroy*, 9 A. & E. 536).

Action on Check.

A check is within the provision of the "Bills of Exchange Act 1855" (18 & 19 Vic. c. 67), by which a summary mode of recovery is provided (*Eyre* v. *Waller*, 29 L. J. Ex. 246).

CHAPTER VII.

CROSSED CHECKS.

CROSSED CHECKS.

As the Act of 39 & 40 Vic. c. 81, begins by repealing the two previous Acts on the same subject, it is necessary to consider the state of the law before the passing of this Act.

History of practice of crossing.

Previous to the passing of the 19 & 20 Vic. c. 25, the first Act relating to crossed checks, it had long been the practice to write across the face of a check the name of a banker. This practice began at the clearing house; the clerks of the different bankers who did business there, having been accustomed to write across the checks the names of their employers, so as to enable the clearing-house clerks to make up the accounts. It then became a common practice to cross checks, which were not intended to go through the clearing house at all, with the name of a banker, or with the words "& Co." This crossing was made indifferently by the drawer or a subsequent holder of the check. The meaning given by usage to the crossing was that of a direction to the drawees to pay only to a banker: the object was to trace for whose use the money on the check was received, and thus invalidate the payment to a wrongful holder in case of loss; but it was held that, at common law, the crossing was a mere memorandum on the face of the instrument, formed no part of the instrument itself, and did not affect its negotiability; from which it followed that the direction attempted to be given in the crossing, being in fact a mere memorandum, was not one the banker was bound to obey as between himself and his customer; but, that the practice being where a check was crossed for a banker to refuse to pay it to anyone except a banker, a banker breaking through the practice did so at his peril; for the circumstance of his so paying would be strong evidence of negligence in an action against him by his customer for the amount paid on the check if the person presenting it turned out to be not the lawful holder (*Bellamy* v. *Majoribanks*, 7 Ex. 389; *Carlon* v. *Ireland*, 25 L. J., Q. B. 113). CROSSED CHECKS.

Upon this state of the law the Act of 19 & 20 Vic. c. 25 was passed, giving a crossing the force of a direction to the bankers that the check should only be paid to or through some banker, thus rendering payment otherwise than through a banker invalid. But it was shortly afterwards held (*Simmons* v. *Taylor*, 27 L. J., C. P. 45), that the crossing was no part of the check; that its unauthorized obliteration was no forgery of the check, and therefore, that the payment without negligence of a check, whose crossing had been obliterated, to a holder not a banker was as between the banker and his customer the drawer a good payment. 19 & 20 Vic. c. 25.

Thereupon 21 & 22 Vict. c. 79, ss. 1 & 3, made the crossing a part of the check, and the fraudulent obliteration or alteration of it felony; it gave a lawful holder power to cross a check, and provided in favour of the banker, that where a crossing had been so obliterated or altered as not plainly to appear, a wrong payment in consequence, if without the fraud or negligence of the banker, should not be questioned. 21 & 22 Vic. c. 79.

It was decided in 1875 (*Smith* v. *Union Bank of London*, L. R. 10 Q. B. 291, & 1 Q. B. D. 31) that the crossing did not restrain the negotiability of a check, and that the restriction of payment of a crossed check was for the

CROSSED CHECKS. direct benefit of the drawer, and indirectly only for the benefit of a holder of a check; therefore, that a plaintiff who had ceased to be the holder of a crossed check (the check having been lost and then come into the hands of a *bonâ fide* holder) could not sue the bank on whom the check was drawn for paying it through a banker, other than the one with whose name the check was crossed.

Crossed Checks Act. After this decision, "The Crossed Checks Act 1875" (39 & 40 Vic. c. 81) was passed, of which the following is the effect: It repeals all previous Acts, and after defining a check to mean a draft or order on a banker payable to bearer or to order on demand, and to include a Bank of England or Ireland dividend warrant, it creates four kinds of crossed checks.

I. A check generally crossed (sec. 4).
II. A check once specially crossed (sec. 4).
III. A check twice specially crossed (sec. 5).
IV. A check generally or specially crossed, and with the words "not negotiable" (sec. 5).

Check "generally crossed." I. A check is "generally crossed" (sec. 4) which bears across its face an addition of two parallel transverse lines, or of the words "& Company," or any abbreviation thereof, between two parallel transverse lines; that addition is a crossing, and may (sec. 5) be made by a lawful holder. When made (sec. 6) it is deemed a material part of the check and may not be obliterated. Such a check is payable by the banker on whom it is drawn only to a banker (sec. 7).

A variation of the old form of crossing is here introduced, *i.e.*, by an addition simply of two transverse parallel lines.

Check "specially crossed." II. A check is "specially crossed" (sec. 4) which bears across its face an addition of the name of a banker. That addition is a crossing. A lawful holder may (sec. 5) cross an uncrossed check specially, or convert a general into a special crossing. This special crossing is a material, part of the check, and may not be obliterated, added to or altered (except by a banker, see *infra*). The effect of a special crossing is (sec. 7) to make the check so crossed payable, by the banker on whom it is drawn, only to the banker to whom it is crossed, or his agent for collection.

CROSSED CHECKS.

The name of the "agent for collection" may appear on the face of this class of check, as when it is specially crossed to him by his principal (see *infra*); but unless after "his agent for collection" are to be read some such words as "where it is so crossed," a specially crossed check appears to be payable to the banker's agent for collection, though his name does not appear on the check.

III. A check twice specially crossed (sec. 5) arises lawfully where a banker to whom a check is specially crossed, again specially crosses it, as he may do, to another banker, his agent for collection. The second crossing, like the first, is a material part of the check, and must not be obliterated or altered (sec. 6).

Check "twice specially crossed."

This is a new kind of check apparently payable only to the agent for collection with whose name it is crossed. It would appear advisable, in some way, to show on the face of the check that one of the crossings is, in fact, a crossing to an agent for collection by the banker to whom the check was firstly crossed; for as a banker is prohibited by sec. 8 from paying a check specially crossed to more than one banker, he seems bound, for his own protection from a charge of negligence (sec. 9), to satisfy himself that the bank presenting is, *primâ facie* at all events, the agent for collection of the bank to whom the check is crossed.

IV. A check generally and specially crossed, and with the words "not negotiable."

CROSSED CHECKS.

Checks crossed generally or specially and "not negotiable."

A lawful holder may, in addition to crossing a check generally or specially, add (sec. 5) the words "not negotiable;" these words then form part of the crossing and may not be obliterated (secs. 4 & 6). The holder of such a check cannot give a better title than the person from whom he received it (sec. 12).

This is a new form of check; in some respects its incidents are like those of a forged or altered bill; that is, where there is a flaw in the title, the right of the holder for value is confined to a right to recover the consideration for the bill as between himself and the party from whom he received it. A similar remedy may be resorted to till the party is reached whose title was bad (*Burchfield* v. *Moore*, 23 L. J., Q. B. 261).

Who may cross a check.

A lawful holder (which expression includes the drawer) has power (sec. 5) to cross a check. The lawful holder may cross a check generally or specially, or add the words "not negotiable" to a crossing: a banker to whom a check is specially crossed may cross it specially again to his agent for collection.

Crossing may not be obliterated, altered, or added to.

A crossing may not be (sec. 6) obliterated, nor altered, or added to, except as above mentioned. There are no express words forbidding the cancellation of a crossing. The expression "to obliterate" means, it is suggested, to erase the marks of a crossing so as to make the check look as if it never had been crossed (*Simmonds* v. *Taylor*, 27 L. J., C. P. 249, & sec. 11), while "to alter" seems to refer either to the changing of a general into a special crossing, or to the recrossing spoken of in sec. 5. The drawer can probably, as under 21 & 22 Vict. c. 79 (the repealed Act), by which the crossing does not become material till the issue of the check, cancel the crossing by writing "pay cash," or equivalent words; but it has never been decided that a lawful holder has a similar power. Alteration of a check in a material point, such as the crossing, whether by obliteration, or addition, or alteration, by persons without power, avoids the instrument and releases the drawer.

Banker only may cross a check a second time, and only with agent's name.

A check cannot be a second time specially crossed, except (sec. 5) by the banker to whom it was first specially crossed, and by him only to his agent, being a banker for collection. The banker (sec. 8) to whom a check specially crossed more than once is presented for payment is commanded to refuse payment of such a check, except in the case where it is crossed to an agent for the purpose of collection.

Duty of banker to whom check bearing two crossings is presented for payment.

The banker to whom a check bearing more than one special crossing is presented for payment must apparently satisfy himself that of the two crossings on such a check, one, the first in point of time, had been placed on the check by a lawful holder when the check was paid into the banker, whose agent now presents it; for the banker, unless he is a lawful holder, has no right to cross it, and he does not become a lawful holder, until he has given value for it. And, as to the second crossing, that it was placed on the check by the banker to whom the check was first specially crossed, as an appointment of the person who presents it, to be his agent for collection. Except when the banker on whom the check is drawn is satisfied of this (sec. 8) he pays the check at his peril.

Banker liable to true owner for disobedience to crossing.

Section 10 provides that any banker paying a crossed check contrary to the directions of the crossing shall be liable to the true owner of the check for any loss he may sustain owing to the check having been so paid.

"The true owner" is a term as yet without interpretation. It would appear to be some one other than the person whose bankers have obtained payment on the check; and as the term "lawful holder" is already used in sec. 5, some one not necessarily the same as the lawful holder. Possibly a lawful holder who has been injured by a pay-

CROSSED CHECKS.

ment contrary to the provisions of a crossing may recover under this section.

The expression used with reference to the check is "crossed," and not "appearing to be crossed," as in sec. 11. It may be inferred that "crossed" means lawfully crossed, that is, by a lawful holder: if so, any one seeking to recover under this section must prove that the crossing was made by a lawful holder before he can make the banker liable under this section.

Provisions for protection of drawer.

It is then provided for the protection of the drawer (sec. 9), that where the banker on whom a crossed check is drawn has in good faith and without negligence paid such check, in accordance with the directions of the crossing, the drawer, in case such check has come to the hands of the payee, shall be entitled to the same rights and be placed in the same position in all respects, as if the amount of the check had been paid to and received by the true owner thereof.

The duty of the banker is considered below (p. 105), and here it is only necessary to consider what concerns the drawer himself.

The word "payee" presents some difficulty. Probably it includes not only persons named in the check (for this interpretation would limit the application of the section), but any person to whom the check is delivered in payment.

"Come to the hands of" implies necessarily only a bare receipt by the payee, irrespective of any acceptance in satisfaction. It appears sufficient for the drawer to prove a receipt of the check, followed by a payment by the drawer's bankers.

"The true owner," as has been said above, apparently is some person other than the one whose bankers have obtained payment on the check, and not necessarily the same person as the lawful holder.

The drawer appears still to have the power to decline to be charged with any payment made on a crossed check except to a banker (*Smith* v. *The Union Bank,* 1 Q. B. D. 31), or to adopt the payment and sue the person who received the money, if the latter had a bad title to the check (*Bobbett* v. *Pinkett,* 1 Ex. D. 368, 373).

Provisions for protection of banker presenting crossed check.

It is provided on behalf of the banker presenting the check (sec. 12)—

That a banker who has, in good faith and without negligence, received payment for a customer of a check crossed generally or specially to himself shall not, in case the title to the check prove defective, incur any liability to the true owner of the check by reason only of having received such payment.

"Customer" is a word as yet without interpretation. It would appear to mean a person on whose behalf the bank has undertaken to present a check; and not necessarily a person, therefore, keeping an account with the bank.

"In good faith and without negligence." The Act apparently casts on the banker the duty of satisfying himself that the person for whom he presents the check has a good title. It is difficult to say how far a jury might think a banker bound to push his researches. The appearance of the instrument would appear to be less a subject of consideration by the banker presenting, than by the banker who pays on the instrument.

"Check crossed generally or specially." If, as would seem by sec. 5, a crossing can only be effectually done by a lawful holder, the banker to avail himself of this section must prove that the check was crossed by a lawful holder. The banker himself has no right to cross the check to himself, until he has given value for it, and become a lawful holder.

"True owner." Here again the true owner is some one

CROSSED CHECKS.

other than the "customer," and may not necessarily be the lawful holder (see *ante*, p. 103).

"By reason only of having received such payment." The protection exists where the money has been received for—but not apparently where it has been paid away to—the customer. And the liability of the banker laid down in *Ogden* v. *Berras*, L. R. 9 C. P. 513, and *Arnold* v. *The Cheque Bank*, 1 C. P. D. 578, remains unaltered. That is, a banker, though he has paid away the money he obtained on the check to his customer, is liable for that amount to the lawful holder, if his customer turn out to have no title.

It is provided on behalf of the drawer's banker—

Provisions for protection of drawee.

I. (Sec. 9.) That where a banker on whom a check is drawn has, in good faith and without negligence, paid such check, if crossed generally, to a banker, and if crossed specially, to the banker to whom it is crossed, or his agent for collection, being a banker, the banker paying the check shall be entitled to the same rights and placed in the same position in all respects, as if the amount of the check had been paid to and received by the true owner thereof.

"In good faith and without negligence." The paying banker may not have to look beyond the banker presenting, or his agent for collection; but he would seem bound to consider the appearance of the instrument.

"Crossed," if it means "lawfully crossed," *i. e.*, by a lawful holder (sec. 5), makes the banker responsible for the genuineness of the crossing (see *ante*, p. 104).

"The true owner" seems to mean some person other than the one whose banker had procured payment of the check who may not be the lawful owner.

II. (Sec. 11.) Where a check is presented for payment which does not at the time of presentation appear to be crossed, or to have had a crossing which has been obliterated, or to have been added to or altered otherwise than as authorized by the Act, a banker paying the check in good faith and without negligence shall not be responsible or incur any liability, nor shall the payment be questioned by reason of the check having been otherwise than it appears.

This section is in effect the same as that of the repealed Act, 21 & 22 Vic. c. 79, s. 4, except that the latter Act makes it necessary that the check shall "plainly" appear to be crossed, &c.

There is no section in the 39 & 40 Vic. c. 81, making the obliteration, &c. of a crossing with intent to defraud a felony, as in the 21 & 22 Vic. c. 79.

CHAPTER VIII.

LETTERS OF CREDIT AND CIRCULAR NOTES.

LETTERS OF CREDIT AND CIRCULAR NOTES.

LETTERS of credit have been more considered in America than in this country, and the result of the decisions has been summarized in the Civil Code of the State of New York, § 1573—1581, from which much of the following matter is extracted (and see Story on Bills, § 459—464).

Letters of credit.

A letter of credit is a written request addressed by one person to another, requesting the latter to give credit to the person in whose favour it is drawn. It may be addressed to several persons in succession. The writer of a letter of credit is upon default of the debtor liable to those who gave credit in compliance with its terms.

A letter of credit is either general or special. When the request for credit in a letter is addressed to specified persons by name or description, the letter is special. All other letters of credit are general.

General letter of credit.

A general letter of credit gives any person to whom it may be shown authority to comply with its request, and by his so doing it becomes as to him of the same effect as if addressed to him by name. Thus (*In re Agra and Masterman's Bank; Ex parte Asiatic Banking Company*, L. R. 2 Ch. Ap. 391; 36 L. J. Ch. 222), a letter of credit was in the following form. It was addressed to D. T. & Co. in these words: "No. 394. You are hereby authorized to draw upon this bank to the extent of £15,000, and such drafts I undertake duly to honor on presentation. This credit will remain in force for twelve months from its date, and parties negotiating bills under it are requested to indorse particulars on the back hereof," and signed by the general manager and chief accountant of the Agra and Masterman's Bank. The court held this letter consisted of two parts, the first containing an authority to D. T. & Co. to draw the bills; the second, though not in terms, in substance addressed to the persons who were to negotiate the bills; that when the offer contained in the second part had been accepted and acted upon, there was probably at law a valid and binding legal contract against the bank issuing the letter of credit in favour of the parties who acted on it, either on the principles laid down in cases as to the offer of rewards (*Williams* v. *Carwardine*, 1 B. & Ad. 621), or on the principle that the holder of the letter of credit is the agent of the writer for the purpose of entering into the contract. But assuming the contract to have been at law with D. T. & Co. and with no other, such a contract was in equity assignable and must be taken to have been assigned to the parties who acted on the letter (The Asiatic Banking Company); and according to the meaning and essence of the contract, free from any equities between D. T. & Co. and the bank. In a later case (*Maitland* v. *The Chartered Mercantile Bank of India, London, and China*, 38 L. J. Ch. 363) it was held that the *bonâ fide* holder of a bill of exchange drawn under an open letter of credit, and taken by him on the faith of such letter of credit, has a right of action at law against the grantor of the letter of credit in case of the latter's refusal to accept the bill. In this case the letter of credit was of the kind known as a marginal letter of credit; that is, it was written on the margin of a draft form of bill of exchange for £2000, the date and signature to which were left to be inserted by the drawer. The letter of credit authorized certain named persons to

LETTERS OF CREDIT AND CIRCULAR NOTES.

Marginal letter of credit.

LETTERS OF CREDIT AND CIRCULAR NOTES.

draw the "annexed" bill of exchange, which would be honored by G. & Co. of London; and the suit was to restrain a *bonâ fide* holder from dealing with the bill.

Where the marginal letter of credit is an open one an indorsee is not bound to make inquiry as to the purposes for which the letter was granted; but he will be taken to have notice of all that appears on the face of the letter, as in the case of a document letter of credit which says on the face of it that it is only to be used for the purpose of obtaining produce (*Maitland* v. *The Chartered Bank of India, London, and China*, 2 H. & M. 440).

Several persons may successively give credit upon a general letter.

Letter of credit may be in nature of a continuing guarantee.

If the parties to a credit appear by its terms to contemplate a course of future dealing between the parties it is not exhausted by giving a credit, even to the amount limited by the letter, which is subsequently reduced or satisfied by payments made by the debtor, but it is to be deemed a continuing guarantee.

The writer of a letter of credit is liable for credit given upon it without notice to him, unless its terms express or imply the necessity of giving notice.

If a letter of credit prescribes the persons by whom or the mode in which the credit is to be given, or the term of credit, or limits the amount thereof, the writer is not bound except for transactions which in these respects conform strictly to the terms of the letter.

Terms of the letter must be followed.

Nor, on the other hand, can the writer discharge himself if money has been paid in against the issue of the note, nor charge the person on whose account the letter was issued except with payments in strict conformity to the terms of the letter (*British Linen Company* v. *The Caledonian Insurance Co.*, 4 Macqueen, H. L. C. 107).

Thus a letter of credit directing the payment to be made to A. B., or directing the addressee "to honor the drafts of A. B.," is not a negotiable instrument, and is only satisfied by the payment to the genuine A. B. or on his genuine order; payment on the forged order of A. B. is not a payment sufficient within the terms of the letter.

Letters of Credit and Circular Notes.

Payment must be made to the right person.

It is the duty of the person paying on the letter to pay to the right person; the mere possession of the letter of credit by the person demanding payment does not necessarily impart that he is the person entitled to draw for the amount mentioned in it, and the person paying is bound for his own safety to make further inquiries (*Orr* v. *The Union Bank of Scotland*, 1 Macqueen, H. L. C. 513, 523).

Therefore, where for a sum down a banker grants a letter of credit, he must show that it has been complied with or pay back the money (*Orr* v. *The Union Bank of Scotland*, *supra*); and in such case the banker cannot insist on the letter of credit being brought back to him as a condition precedent to the recovery of the money.

The 16 & 17 Vic. c. 59, s. 19, which absolves bankers from responsibility for the genuineness of the indorsement of a draft payable to order on demand, does not apply to a letter of credit couched in the words, "please to honor the drafts of A. B." (*British Linen Company* v. *Caledonian Insurance Company*, 4 Macqueen 107).

Where a bank has issued a letter of credit on the terms that the bills they agree to accept are to be covered by bills of lading, suspension of payment before there has been time for the letter of credit to be used is not a breach of the contract for which, under the Companies Act 1862, the holder of the letter can claim damages; for the court might have given permission to the liquidators to accept bills (*Ex parte Tondeur, In re The Agra Bank*, L. R. 5 Eq. 160).

A letter of credit granted in the United Kingdom authorizing drafts to be drawn out of the United Kingdom

LETTERS OF CREDIT AND CIRCULAR NOTES.

payable in the United Kingdom, is exempt from stamp duty (33 & 34 Vic. c. 97, schedule, tit. *B*ill of Exchange).

Every letter of credit issued by a limited company under the Companies Act 1862 must contain the full name of the company (25 & 26 Vic. c. 89, s. 42).

Circular notes.

Circular notes are somewhat in the nature of letters of credit; they are requests addressed to the correspondents of the bank issuing them to pay a certain named person the sum therein named. Each request generally refers to the letter of indication, stating that the bearer of the note should present a letter of indication in which his signature will be found.

The letter of indication is a letter addressed to the bank's correspondents, with a space for the signature of the payee of the notes, and signed by some official of the bank.

The circular notes are in general issued against a payment of money to the amount of the notes.

It is not obligatory (*Conflans Quarry Co.* v. *Parker*, L. R. 3 C. P. 1) upon the holder to cash the circular notes, though he purchases a right to do so if he thinks proper; in the event of his not requiring to use them abroad he may, after reasonable notice of his electing not to use them, require repayment at the banker's hands.

But he must present or return them to the banker, for the latter cannot be called upon to return the amount so long as the notes are outstanding and in existence, so that he may be called upon to pay a correspondent who has cashed them.

A correspondent who pays on a forged signature to a circular note cannot recover against the banker as upon a payment to the right person.

CHAPTER IX.

BILLS OF EXCHANGE PAYABLE AT A BANK.

Bills of Exchange Payable at a Bank.

THE bills of exchange which concern a banker in his trade of banker are those which are payable at his banking-house, whether those his customer has made payable at his banking-house, or those which he has agreed to accept for his customer.

Duty of banker when agent for presentment.

For where a customer employs his banker as agent for presentment the duties and liabilities of the latter do not differ from those of any other agent for a like purpose towards his principal. He is liable for any neglect of the duty he has undertaken to perform. Thus he should at once give notice to his principal of a refusal to accept or to pay, for he will be held liable for any injury to his principal arising from his neglect (*Van Wart* v. *Woolley*, 3 B. & C. 439).

His relations, then, are twofold, towards his customer and towards the presenter or holder of the bill.

Banker and customer.

First, to deal with the relations between the banker and his customer. A customer who makes an acceptance payable at a bank in effect orders the bank to pay the bill to the person who is according to the law merchant capable of giving a good discharge for the bill (*Robarts* v. *Tucker*, 16 Q. B. 570, 579; *Forster* v. *Clements*, 2 Camp. 17); therefore if the bill be payable to order, it is an authority to pay the bill to any person who becomes holder by a genuine indorsement, and if the bill is originally payable to bearer, or if there is afterwards a genuine indorsement in blank, it is an authority to pay the bill to the person who seems to be the holder. It follows that the banker is responsible to his customer for the title of the person to whom he pays the bill, for he cannot charge his customers with any payment made to a person not the lawful holder, nor with the difference in amount, where the bill has been altered and a larger sum inserted than the sum for which it was made payable by the customer (*Hall* v. *Fuller*, 5 B. & C. 750).

Banker and customer.

His duty is to pay the bill (*Kymer* v. *Laurie*, 18 L. J. Q.B. 218) on presentment during the hours of business out of funds belonging to the customer, if any have been in his hands a sufficient time to enable his clerks to know of their existence (*Whittaker* v. *Bank of England*, 1 C. M. & R. 744); and he is bound if he has received a sum of money for the express purpose of taking up a certain bill, to apply it to that purpose only (*Farley* v. *Turner*, 26 L. J. Chan. 710); and if he do not so apply it, his customer may recover the deposit, or may sue for damages for breach of his mandate to the banker (*Hill* v. *Smith*, 12 M. & W. 618; *Bell* v. *Carey*, 8 C. B. 887). He is entitled, if he has accepted bills for the accommodation of his customer, to retain a sum of money out of the customer's account sufficient to answer the outstanding bills which are due (*Morse* v. *Kempson*, 1 Camp. 12; but see *Jeffryes* v. *Agra Bank*, L. R. 2 Eq. 674), although the remedy on the bills be barred by the Statute of Limitations (*Morse* v. *Williams*, 3 Camp. 418).

Banker under acceptance for customer.

Banker's duty to mark bills as paid.

It is the duty of bankers to make some memorandum on bills and notes which have been paid; and if they do not, the holders of such securities cannot be affected by any payment made before they are due (per Lord Ellenborough, *Burbidge* v. *Manners*, 3 Camp. 193; *Attenborough* v. *Mackenzie*, 25 L. J. Ex. 244).

Next, as to the relations between the banker and presenter or holder.

Bills of Exchange Payable at a Bank.

Banker's duty to presenter.

The duty of the banker towards the presenter or holder of a bill is (*Warwick* v. *Rogers*, 5 M. & G. 340) to take good care of the bill, and if he do not choose to pay it, to return it uncancelled, unless it has been cancelled by mistake, and in that case to indicate the same by writing on the bill; if he wrongfully omits to return or defaces the bill he becomes liable to an action on the case, if the holder has sustained injury through his breach of duty.

Banker's remedy who pays holder of forged acceptance.

If he pay and afterwards find out the acceptance to be a forgery, it is doubtful on authority whether he can recover the money so paid from the holder. The point has come before the court in two cases (*Smith* v. *Mercer*, 6 Taunt. 76; *Cox* v. *Masterman*, 9 B. & C. 902; and see *Price* v. *Neal*, 3 Burr. 1354 & 1 W. Bl. 390); in *Smith* v. *Mercer* the majority of the court held that a banker, being bound to know his customer's signature, could not recover from the holder the money he had paid; but the court, in *Cox* v. *Masterman*, expressly refused to give an opinion on this point. In both cases a period elapsed between the payment and the discovery of the forgery—in *Smith* v. *Mercer* of seven days, and *Cox* v. *Masterman* of one day—sufficient to enable the court to decide against the banker, on the ground that by his delay in giving notice of the forgery the remedy of the holder against the antecedent parties had been lost or impaired. But a banker does not necessarily, by discounting for the indorsee a bill purporting to be accepted by his customer, warrant the signature to be genuine; he may therefore on discovering such an acceptance to be a forgery recover the money he paid on the bill (*Fuller* v. *Smith*, 1 Car. & P. 197).

Banker refusing to pay.

On the other hand, the banker may refuse to pay the presenter, either till he has more information whether the presenter is the holder or not, a course which he is justified in pursuing (*Robarts* v. *Tucker*, 16 Q. B. 578), or he may refuse unconditionally; in this latter case no action will lie against the banker by the holder, neither when the banker has agreed with the acceptor to apply certain moneys to the discharge of the bill, and has so appropriated them in the books of the bank (*Moore* v. *Bushell*, 27 L. J. Ex. 4; *Hill* v. *Royds*, L.R. 8 Eq. 290); nor where the banker has cancelled the signature of a bill presented to him through the clearing house by drawing lines across it in the way customary among bankers when they intend to pay a bill or check, and returned it with the statement that it was cancelled by mistake, and that he had orders not to pay (*Warwick* v. *Rogers*, 5 M. & G. 340); nor where the bankers having received funds to take up the bill called on the presenter in order to take it up at a period when the bill was not actually in the presenter's possession (*Stewart* v. *Fry*, 7 Taunton, 339).

No action lies against banker by holder of bill accepted by customer;

But under certain circumstances the acceptor's banker may be also the holder's agent for presentment, and if while he is agent for the holder the acceptor pay in a sum specifically for the discharge of the bill the holder can recover the amount of this sum from his agent the banker (*De Bernales* v. *Fuller*, 14 East, 590, 593).

unless banker be holder's agent for presentment.

Where a bank who have given credit in account for a bill to the drawer, their customer, receive directions from the acceptor, who is also a customer, to stop payment of the bill at the place of payment, and do so accordingly, they are not bound to give notice of this circumstance to the drawer, but may upon non-payment look to the drawer, and are not bound to apply the money of the acceptor in their hands in discharge of the bill (*Crosse* v. *Smith*, 1 M. & S. 545).

Where drawer and acceptor have same banker.

It sometimes happens that a banker, at whose house a bill is payable, is himself the holder of the bill when it

Where banker is

falls due; in such a case, to enable the banker to charge a previous indorser, it is a sufficient demand and sufficient refusal to find from his books that the customer has no effects in his hands (*Sanderson* v. *Judge*, 2 H. Bl. 509; *Bailey* v. *Porter*, 14 M. & W. 44). Again the banker may be the indorser of the bill; if he pay it on presentment it is a matter of inference, from the facts of the case, whether he paid it as agent for the acceptor or on his own account as indorser (*Pollard* v. *Ogden*, 2 E. & B. 459; 22 L. J. Q. B. 439). "The Stamp Acts, 1870, 1871," affix the following duties on—

BILLS OF EXCHANGE PAYABLE AT A BANK.

Banker holder, or indorser of bill payable by him.

Duties on bills.

	£	s.	d.
Bills of exchange payable at sight or on demand	0	0	1

Bills of exchange of any other kind whatsoever (except a bank note) and promissory note of any kind whatsoever (except a bank note), drawn, or expressed to be payable, or actually paid, or indorsed, or in any manner negotiated in the United Kingdom—

	£	s.	d.
Where the amount or value of the money for which the bill or note is drawn or made does not exceed £5	0	0	1
Exceeds £5 and does not exceed £10 . .	0	0	2
£10 „ „ £25 . .	0	0	3
£25 „ „ £50 . .	0	0	6
£50 „ „ £75 . .	0	0	9
£75 „ £100 . .	0	1	0
„ £100			
For every £100 and also for any fractional part of £100 of such amount or value .	0	1	0

51 (1). The ad valorem duties upon bills of exchange and promissory notes drawn or made out of the United Kingdom are to be denoted by adhesive stamps.

Bills drawn abroad.

Bills of Exchange Payable at a Bank.

(2). Every person into whose hands any such bill or note comes in the United Kingdom before it is stamped, shall, before he presents for payment or indorses, transfers, or in any manner negotiates or pays such bill or note, affix thereto a proper adhesive stamp or proper adhesive stamps of sufficient amount, and cancel every stamp so affixed thereto.

(3). Provided as follows:—

Provisos for protection of *bonâ fide* holders.

(*a*). If at the time when any such bill or note comes into the hands of any *bonâ fide* holder thereof there is affixed thereto an adhesive stamp effectually obliterated, and purporting and appearing to be duly cancelled, such stamp shall, so far as relates to such holder, be deemed to be duly cancelled, although it may not appear to have been so affixed or cancelled by the proper person.

(*b*). If at the time when any such bill or note comes into the hands of any *bonâ fide* holder thereof, there is affixed thereto an adhesive stamp not duly cancelled, it shall be competent for such holder to cancel such stamp as if he were the person by whom it was affixed, and upon his so doing such bill or note shall be deemed duly stamped, and as valid and available as if the stamp had been duly cancelled by the person by whom it was affixed.

Not to relieve any other persons.

(4). But neither of the foregoing provisos is to relieve any person from any penalty incurred by him for not cancelling any adhesive stamp.

Bills purporting to be drawn abroad.

52. A bill of exchange or promissory note purporting to be drawn or made out of the United Kingdom is, for the purposes of this Act, to be deemed to have been so drawn or made, although it may in fact have been drawn or made within the United Kingdom.

53 (1). Where a bill of exchange or promissory note

has been written on material bearing an impressed stamp of sufficient amount but improper denomination, it may be stamped with the proper stamp on payment of the duty, and a penalty of forty shillings if the bill or note be not then payable according to its tenor, and of ten pounds if the same be so payable.

Bills of Exchange Payable at a Bank.

Stamping after execution.

(2). Except as aforesaid, no bill of exchange or promissory note shall be stamped with an impressed stamp after the execution thereof.

54 (1). Every person who issues, indorses, transfers, negotiates, presents for payment, or pays any bill of exchange or promissory note liable to duty and not being duly stamped shall forfeit the sum of ten pounds, and the person who takes or receives from any other person any such bill or note not being duly stamped either in payment or as a security, or by purchase or otherwise, shall not be entitled to recover thereon, or to make the same available for any purpose whatever.

Penalty for issuing unstamped bills.

Bill is void.

(2). Provided that if any bill of exchange for the payment of money on demand, liable only to the duty of one penny, is presented for payment unstamped, the person to whom it is so presented may affix thereto a proper adhesive stamp and cancel the same, as if he had been the drawer of the bill, and may, upon so doing, pay the sum in the said bill mentioned, and charge the duty in account against the person by whom the bill was drawn, or deduct such duty from the said sum, and such bill is, so far as respects the duty, to be deemed good and valid.

Proviso as to fixed duty

(3). But the foregoing proviso is not to relieve any person from any penalty he may have incurred in relation to such bill.

BILLS OF EXCHANGE PAYABLE AT A BANK.

One bill only of a set need be stamped.

55. When a bill of exchange is drawn in a set according to the custom of merchants, and one of the set is duly stamped, the other or others of the set shall, unless issued or in some manner negotiated apart from such duly stamped bill, be exempt from duty; and upon proof of the loss or destruction of a duly stamped bill forming one of a set, any other bill of the set which has not been issued, or in any manner negotiated apart from such lost or destroyed bill, may, although unstamped, be admitted in evidence to prove the contents of such lost or destroyed bill.

Bills of exchange payable otherwise than at sight or on demand, purporting to be drawn in the United Kingdom, must be drawn on stamped paper (33 & 34 Vic. c. 97, s. 23).

Certain bankers may issue unstamped bills.

But bankers with a licence, carrying on business beyond three miles from the city of London, may issue unstamped bills payable to order on demand, or at any period not exceeding seven days after sight, or twenty-one days after date, provided such bills are drawn on bankers in London, Westminster, or Southwark, or are drawn at a place where the drawer is licensed to issue unstamped notes and bills (9 Geo. 4, c. 23, s. 1; and see *ante*, pp. 6, 9).

With regard to bills which the banker is directed by his customer to accept, if he is directed to accept bills which A. B. will draw against bills of lading, he is not bound to ascertain the genuineness of the bills of lading before accepting or paying the bills of exchange; and if the banker pays the bills, although the bills of lading should afterwards turn out to be forgeries, he will be entitled to recover from his customer what he may have paid in respect of the bills of exchange (*Woods* v. *Thiedman*, 1 H. & C. 478).

CHAPTER X.

CUSTOMER'S PASS-BOOK AND BANKER'S BOOKS.

Customer's Pass-book and Banker's Books.

The state of the customer's account is communicated to him, in London at least, by a book formerly known as a passage-book, and now more commonly called a pass-book. The course of dealing between banker and customer was the subject of inquiry in the Court of Chancery in the year 1816, and the master's report being still so applicable to present circumstances is set out below verbatim (*Devaynes* v. *Noble*, 1 Merivale, 530, 535).

"A book called a passage-book, is opened by the bankers, and delivered by them to the customer, in which at the head of the first folio, and there only the bankers by the name of their firm are described as the debtors, and the customer as the creditor, in the account; and on the debtor side, are entered all sums paid to or received by the bankers on account of the customer; and, on the creditor side, all sums paid by them to him, or on his account; and the said entries being summed up at the bottom of each page, the amount of each, or the balance between them, is carried over to the next folio without further mention of the names of the parties, until, from the passage-book being full, it becomes necessary to open and deliver out to the customer a new book of the same kind. For the purpose of having the passage-book made up by the bankers from their own books of account, the customer returns it to them from

CUSTOMER'S PASS-BOOK AND BANKER'S BOOKS.

time to time as he thinks fit; and, the proper entries being made by them up to the day on which it is left for that purpose, they deliver it again to the customer, who thereupon examines it, and if there appears any error or omission, brings or sends it back to be rectified, or if not, his silence is regarded as an admission that the entries are correct; but no other settlement, statement, or delivery of accounts; or any other transaction which can be regarded as the closing of an old, or opening of a new account, or as varying, renewing, or confirming (in respect of the persons of the parties mutually dealing) the credit given on either side takes place in the ordinary course of business, unless when the name or firm of one of the parties is altered, and a new account thereupon opened in the new name or firm. The course of business is the same between such bankers and their customers resident at a distance from the metropolis, except that, to avoid the inconvenience of sending in and returning the passage-book, accounts are, from time to time, made out by the bankers, and transmitted to the customer in the country when required by him, containing the same entries as are made in the passage-books; but with the names of the parties, debtor and creditor, at the head and with the balance struck at the foot of each account; on receipt of which accounts, the customer, if there appears to be any error or omission, points out the same by letter to the bankers; but, if not, his silence after the receipt of the account, is in like manner regarded as an admission of the truth of the account, and no other adjustment, statement, or allowance thereof usually takes place."

The pass-book, beginning with the name of the banking firm, is notice to the customer of the persons with whom he is dealing; and where dealings have taken place with a banking firm, a change in the title of that firm entered in the pass-book, and the entry therein of items, by which the customer is debited in account with the payment of interest on debts due by him to the old firm, is notice of the assignment to the new firm of the debts due by him to the old firm (*Cavendish* v. *Geaves*, 27 L. J. Ch. 314).

CUSTOMER'S PASS-BOOK AND BANKER'S BOOKS.

Entries in a pass-book.

The entries in a pass-book are binding on the banker so far as they admit receipts of money by him on behalf of his customer; but it is open to him to show that the entries are erroneous and have been made by mistake (*The Commercial Bank of Scotland* v. *Rhind*, 3 Macqueen, H. L. C. 643).

But he is bound by the entry where the customer has acted upon the faith of it, or altered his situation in consequence of it, as by drawing on his account and spending the money. And it is not competent to the banker, where this has taken place, to claim to set off sums subsequently received against the sums which he erroneously represented himself by the entries to have received on behalf of his customer (*Skyring* v. *Greenwood*, 4 B. & C. 281; *Shaw* v. *Picton*, 4 B. & C. 715).

The entries in a pass-book against the customer are, where the pass-book has been in custody of the customer and returned by him without remark, *primâ facie* evidence against him (*The Commercial Bank* v. *Rhind*, 3 Macqueen, H. L. C. 643).

The books of bankers, containing details from which the course of any mercantile transaction in which their customers were engaged could be followed, were frequently called for and produced under compulsion in legal proceedings to which the banker was no party. Much inconvenience being thereby caused to bankers and the public, "The Bankers' Books Evidence Act, 1876" (39 & 40 Vic. c. 48), was passed to remedy the general inconvenience caused by removing books from banks for the purpose of being produced in legal proceedings; and to

Customer's Pass-book and Banker's Books.

facilitate the proof of the transactions recorded in such books; it enacts—

Sec. 3, that the entries in the account-books of any bank are to be admissible in all legal proceedings as *primâ facie* evidence of the matters therein recorded, on proof—*F*irst, that the persons carrying on the business in which the books are used are a bank, by (sec. 9) producing a copy of the return made by them under 7 & 8 Vic. c. 32, s. 21, verified by affidavit or by the production of a copy of a newspaper purporting to contain a copy of such return published therein by the Commissioners of Inland Revenue; and on proof, Secondly (sec. 3), by affidavit that the books are the ordinary books of the bank, and the entries made in the usual course of business, and the books are in the custody of the bank.

By sec. 4, the originals need not be produced in any legal proceedings, but the entries may be proved by copies certified by affidavit of the person examining.

But (sec. 3) the above-mentioned enactments are not to apply in any legal proceedings to which a bank, whose books may be required to be produced in evidence, is a party.

Litigants (sec. 5) intending to avail themselves of this Act must give five days' notice in writing, or such other notice as may be ordered by the court of their intention. The notice must contain a copy of the entries proposed to be adduced, an expression of the intention to adduce the entries in evidence, and of permission to the opposite side to inspect the original entries.

Upon the receipt of such a notice (sec. 6), the other party may, under an order of court, inspect and copy any pertinent entries on giving the bank notice of the order three days before copies are required.

A judge (sec. 7) has power to order that copies shall not be admissible.

Customer's Pass-book and Banker's Books.

A special (sec. 8) order by a judge is necessary to compel a bank to produce their books in any legal proceeding.

CHAPTER XI.

APPROPRIATION OF PAYMENTS.

APPRO- PRIATION OF PAYMENTS.

THE appropriation of payments is governed by three rules (*Clayton's case*, Mer. 585).

1. The debtor has the option at the time of making the payment to appropriate it to any of the debts due from him to the creditor.
2. If the debtor do not make this appropriation, the creditor may do so at any time before action (*Mills* v. *Fowkes*, 5 Bing. N. C. 455).
3. Where neither party makes the appropriation, the law will appropriate the payment to the earlier debt.

It is this last rule which regulates ordinary banking accounts. All the sums paid in to the account form one blended fund, the parts of which have no longer any distinct existence. The presumption, therefore, is, that the sum first paid in is the sum first paid out, so that the first item of the debit side of the account is presumed to be discharged by the first item of the credit side (*Clayton's case*, 1 Mer. 608).

From this rule it follows that where an account, opened between a firm of bankers and a customer, has been continued through a change in the members of the firm, and the balances have been carried forward after each rest as before the change, payments made to or by the customer

Appropriation of Payments.

without specific appropriation by or to the new firm may affect the old firm alone. For where a balance in favour of the customer has been brought forward, of which the earlier items are of moneys received by the old firm, payments made by the new firm are applied under the above rule to those items, and discharge the debt of the old firm, leaving the new firm liable for moneys received by them since they were constituted (*Clayton's case; Brook* v. *Enderby*, 2 Brod. & Bing. 70; *Copland* v. *Toulmin*, 7 Cl. & F. 349; *Bank of Scotland* v. *Christie*, 8 Cl. & F. 214; *Hooper* v. *Keay*, 1 Q. B. D. 178).

In the same way if the balance on such an account is against the customer, a payment by him after the change of firm, being *pro tanto* a discharge of the earliest items of the balance against him, is a discharge of his debt to the old firm (*Bodenham* v. *Purchas*, 2 B. & Ald. 39), and not of any liabilities he may have come under to the new firm. And this rule is strictly applied even as against third parties, who have not been privy to the account, such as sureties (*Williams* v. *Rawlinson*, 3 Bing. 71). Similarly, where trust moneys have been paid into a bank by a trustee, together with his own moneys, to a general account, and checks have been drawn by him upon his account generally, the payments made by the bank will be attributed to the earlier items (*Pennell* v. *Deffell*, 4 De G. M. & G. 372; *Brown* v. *Adams*, L. R. 4 Ch. Ap. 764).

But if money has been paid in with a specific appropriation by the payor as to meet a bill, the direction must be obeyed (*Hill* v. *Smith*, 12 M. & W. 618; *Farley* v. *Turner*, 26 L. J. Chanc. 710). So, again, if there have been a stipulation between the parties, either express (*Henniker* v. *Wigg*, 4 Q. B. 792), or to be implied from a particular course of dealing (*Lysaght* v. *Walker*, 3 Bligh. N. R. 1; *City Discount Coy.* v. *Maclean*, L. R. 9 C. P. 693),

APPRO-PRIATION OF PAYMENTS.

as where within a reasonable time after a change in the partners of a firm two accounts, one showing the position of the old firm, and the other the transactions of the new firm since the change, are communicated to the customer and received by him without objection, the payments he has made will be taken to be appropriated, as shown in the accounts (*Simson* v. *Ingham*, 2 B. & C. 65); and the bankers will be bound by the accounts communicated to their customer, and not by the entries made in their books and not so communicated (*ibid.*).

CHAPTER XII.

BANK NOTES.

BANK NOTES.

BANK notes are of two sorts: bank notes issued by the Bank of England, and bank notes issued by other banks or bankers entitled to issue them, as pointed out in Chap. I., where the statutory definitions of bank notes and the stamp duties imposed on them will be found.

Legal tender

As has before been stated, the notes of the Bank of England are by 3 & 4 Will. 4, c. 98, s. 6, made legal tender so long as the Bank of England continue to pay on demand their notes in legal coin.

Country notes when legal tender.

Country bank notes are also a legal tender, unless at the time of the tender an objection is made to receiving them on the ground of their being notes, not cash. If no objection is raised, country notes are treated as cash (*Owenson* v. *Morse*, 7 T. R. 64; *Polglass* v. *Oliver*, 2 C. & J. 15). A banker's own notes are not a legal tender to himself: that is, proof of a tender to a banker of his own notes will not support a plea of tender, for a banker stands in the same position towards his own notes as any other person (*Forster* v. *Wilson*, 12 M. & W. p. 201). If after a transfer of a note the note turns out worthless by reason of the failure of the maker, though given and accepted in perfect good faith on either side, the transferer is not liable on the instrument to the transferee because the transfer has been one by mere delivery, and not by indorsement and delivery (Byles on Bills, p. 159).

Transferor not liable on note after transfer.

BANK NOTES.

Transferor not liable to refund consideration in the absence of fraud.

Nor is the transferor liable to refund the consideration. Because, in the first place, there is no guarantee implied by law in the party passing a note payable on demand to bearer that the maker of the note is solvent at the time it was so passed (per Littledale, J., in *Camidge* v. *Allenby*, 6 B. & C. 373). Of course, if the transferee could show any fraud or knowledge of the insolvency of the maker by the transferor, the transferor would be liable to refund (see Anonymous, 12 Mod. 517; judgment of Bayley, J., in *Camidge* v. *Allenby*).

In the second place, it has long been held that on the sale of a bill or note the party purchasing takes it with all risks and without any remedy against the party selling the note (*Fenn* v. *Harrison*, 3 T. R. 759).

Sale of a note.

A sale of a note is presumed to take place where, at the time of the transaction, it is delivered without indorsement, by way of exchange for goods or money transferred to the party delivering the note, for the transferee elects to take the note instead of cash, and does so at his peril and without recourse to the transferor (see *Camidge* v. *Allenby*, *supra*). But where a note is delivered without indorsement for a pre-existing debt, it is only a conditional payment to become absolute if, upon due presentment, it is paid (*Clark* v. *Mindall*, 1 Salk. 124; *Ex parte Blackburne*, 10 Ves. 206; *Belshaw* v. *Bush*, 11 C. B. 191, 22 L. J. C. P. 24).

Note delivered in payment of an existing debt.

Where goods were bought at 10 a.m., a payment by notes for the goods at 3 p.m. on the same day was held to be a payment of an existing debt (*Camidge* v. *Allenby*, 6 B. & C. 373; but see Campbell, C. J., in *Timmins* v. *Gibbins*, 21 L. J. Q. B. 403, 18 Q. B. 722).

Time for presentment.

The transferee is allowed a reasonable time (of at least one day) within which he may present the note to the bank, or circulate it. If the bank fail within that time, the transferee should at once redemand his money from the transferor, at the same time tendering him back the note (*Camidge* v. *Allenby*, 6 B. & C. 373; *Henderson* v. *Appleton*, 1 C. & M. 642; *Rogers* v. *Langford*, 1 C. & M. 637; *Litchfield Board of Guardians* v. *Greene*, 26 L. J. Ex. 140). It is not necessary, to give a right of action against the transferor, where the bank has actually stopped, to present the notes for payment, before having any recourse to the transferor (*Rogers* v. *Langford*, 1 C. & M. 637; *Sands* v. *Clarke*, 19 L. J. C. P. 84; Byles on Bills, p. 203, *k*). But in any case short of actual stoppage presentment is necessary to give a right against the makers, but as between the transferor and transferee notice that the notes have turned out valueless, with an offer to return them, seems to dispense with actual presentment (*Robson* v. *Oliver*, 10 Q. B. p. 717).

Duty of holder of note.

It is not apparently unreasonable where notes have to be presented at a distance to cut them in half, and send the two sets of halves by different channels, and even though the presentment be made later in consequence (*Williams* v. *Smith*, 2 B. & Ald. 496).

Notice of dishonor.

Notice of dishonor must be given with reasonable diligence, and this would seem to be before the departure of the post on the day after that on which the holder after exercising reasonable diligence is in a position to give the notice (per Martin, B., *Gladwell* v. *Turner*, L. R. 5 Ex. 61).

Need not be a sale of note.

The inference that a transfer of a note was a sale of the note without recourse to the transferor in case of dishonor may be rebutted. Thus, a person asking as a favour to receive change for a note would be bound to refund it, if the note were duly presented and dishonored and due notice given (*Rogers* v. *Langford*, 1 C. & M. 637, 641; *Woodland* v. *Fear*, 7 E. & B. p. 522, 26 L. J. Q. B. p. 202).

And it has been held that if a customer pay to his account with his bankers the notes of a bank that has failed, and the banker has not been guilty of laches, the

BANK NOTES.

loss falls on the customer (*Timmins* v. *Gibbons*, 18 Q. B. 722).

Remedy against maker.

If the transferor be the maker of the note the remedy of the holder is to prove against his estate (*Litchfield Guardians* v. *Greene*, L. J. 26 Ex. 140).

Where the payment by note has been only conditional, and the note is not paid with no laches by the holder, the remedy on the antecedent debt revives (*Ward* v. *Evans*, 2 Lord Ray. 928; *Moore* v. *Warren*, 1 Stra. 415).

Lost or Stolen Notes.

Bank notes, whether of the Bank of England or of other banks, being notes payable to bearer, are negotiable instruments (*Solomon* v. *Bank of England*, 13 East, 135; *Miller* v. *Race*, 1 Sm. L. C. 526), and the title to them rests in any person taking them for value and *bonâ fide*, *i.e.*, without knowledge of the loss or robbery, (*Raphael* v. *Bank of England*, 17 C. B. 161), whatever may be the defects in the title of the person transferring them.

In an action by the loser of a note against the holder to recover the value, the loser on proving the loss puts the holder to prove that he has given value for the note. If the latter is a holder for value, the presumption is that he took it *bonâ fide*, and his title is good, unless he can be fixed with knowledge, or the means of knowledge wilfully disregarded, of the loss or robbery (*Goodman* v. *Harvey*, 4 A. & E. 870; *Uther* v. *Rich*, 10 A. & E. 784; *Raphael* v. *Bank of England*, 17 C. B. 161); and the existence of gross negligence is unimportant, except so far as it may be evidence of *mala fides* (*Goodman* v. *Harvey*, *supra*).

Action on Lost Note.

It is both reasonable and customary for the bank to stop payment of the note on receiving an indemnity from the loser (*Miller* v. *Race*, 1 Burr. 460); and 17 & 18

Vic. c. 125, s. 7, which enacts that, in case of any action founded on a negotiable instrument, it shall be lawful for the court or judge to order that the loss of such instrument shall not be set up, providing an indemnity is given to the satisfaction of the court or judge, or master, against the claims of any other person upon such negotiable instrument, in effect enables the loser to recover the value of the note subject to the rights of any innocent holder. BANK NOTES.

It was held that where a note had been cut in half, no action could be maintained against the maker by the *bonâ fide* holder of one half, on the ground that there might be a *bonâ fide* holder of the other half, and the maker could not be liable to both parties (*Mayor* v. *Johnson*, 3 Camp. 324). See as to cutting notes in half for purposes of transmission, *Redmayne* v. *Burton*, 2 L. T., N. S. 324. Note cut in half.

It has been said that as any person taking a half note must take with notice, the bankers would be bound to pay without any indemnity (per Willes, J., *Redmayne* v. *Burton*, 2 L. T., N. S. 324); but it is submitted that in any case the loser of half a note could avail himself of the above statute.

The finder of bank notes which have been lost is entitled to them as against all the world (*Armory* v. *Delamirie*, 1 Stra. 504), (notwithstanding he may find them on property belonging to some one else, as in a shop, *Bridges* v. *Hawkesworth*, 21 L. J. Q. B. 75) except the lawful owner. Finder of lost note.

Forged Notes.

Payment in forged bank notes, whether purporting to be issued by the Bank of England or any other bank, though made in good faith, is no payment in law; that is, "the party negotiating them is answerable for the notes being such as they purport to be," and therefore, if they turn out to be forged, an action will lie to recover the

BANK NOTES. money paid for them as money paid under a mistake of fact (*Jones* v. *Ryde*, 5 Taunt. 488, 494; *Woodland* v. *Fear*, 26 L. J. Q. B. 204).

Bankruptcy of Banker Issuing Notes.

Stopping payment is not itself an act of bankruptcy by a banker; therefore a person may, on knowing a banker has stopped, industriously buy up that banker's notes, and set them off against a debt of his to the banker (*Hawkins* v. *Whitten*, 10 B. & C. 217); but notes taken with a knowledge of an act of bankruptcy committed by the banker, or by one of the partners of a firm of bankers, cannot be set off (*Dickson* v. *Cass*, 1 B. & Ad. 343), unless the holders of the notes at the time of the bankruptcy could have set them off (*Ex parte Rogers*, Buck, 490; and see *Forster* v. *Wilson*, 12 M. & W. 191).

Where a company issuing notes has gone into liquidation or become bankrupt, the holders of its notes will be allowed interest at the rate of £5 per cent. from the date on which they demand payment from the liquidator (*In re East of England Banking Company*, L. R. 4 Ch. Ap. 14).

CHAPTER XIII.

BANKER AS BAILEE OF DEPOSITS.

Banker as Bailee of Deposits.

It is customary, as has been said, for bankers to take charge of property of certain kinds for safe custody.

If the property is lost or destroyed while in the banker's hands his liability depends upon his contract. If he has been in the position of a gratuitous bailee, that is, if the deposit of the securities has been a mere naked bailment for the accommodation of the depositor without any advantage to the banker (*Foster* v. *The Essex Bank*, 17 Mass. Reports, 479), the banker is bound not to be guilty of gross negligence, but to exercise ordinary care, that is, such care as a reasonably prudent and careful man not being a banker might be expected to take of his own property. It is not necessarily sufficient for him to show that he keeps property deposited with him in the same manner as he keeps his own (*Doorman* v. *Jenkins*, 2 A. & E. 256).

Gratuitous bailee.

If the banker makes a charge for safe custody, he puts himself in the position of a bailee for hire, and is held liable for loss or injury occurring from a less degree of negligence.

Bailee for hire.

The difference between the care expected from a gratuitous bailee and a bailee for hire has been defined as follows. From the former is reasonably expected such care and diligence as persons ordinarily use in their own affairs, and such skill he has; from the latter is reasonably expected care and diligence such as are exercised in the

Care required of each class of bailee.

BANKER AS BAILEE OF DEPOSITS.

ordinary and proper course of similar business, and such skill as he ought to have, namely, the skill usual and requisite in the business for which he receives payment (*Beal* v. *South Devon Railway*, 3 H. & C. 337). The jury must decide whether the banker has brought himself within the rule applicable to the facts of each case.

When banker bailee for hire.

The profit gained by keeping the account of the depositor appears not to be sufficient by itself to make the banker a bailee for hire (*Giblin* v. *McMullen*, L. R. 2 P. C. 318), but receiving a commission for custody and realization apparently is (*In re United Service Company, Johnson's claim*, L. R. 6 Ch. Ap. 217; as to costs, *ibid.*).

Deposit must be restored to depositor.

The banker who has received property for safe custody must restore or account for it to him from whom he received it (*Buddle* v. *Bond*, 6 B. & S. 225), and it is not enough to excuse him from redelivery that he has become aware of the title of a third person, or that an adverse claim is made upon him so that he may be entitled to an interpleader (*Leese* v. *Martin*, L. R. 17 Eq. 224, 234).

A banker is a person known to have the goods of others in his possession, and therefore his trustee has no claim on his bankruptcy to property entrusted to him for safe custody (*Horn* v. *Baker*, 2 Sm. L. C. 205, 235, and notes).

CHAPTER XIV.

BANKER'S LIEN.

*B*ANKERS have a general lien on all securities deposited in their hands by their customers for their general balance, unless there be evidence to show that any particular security was received under special circumstances, which would take it out of the common rule (per Lord Kenyon, *Davis* v. *Bowsher*, 5 T. R. p. 491; *Brandao* v. *Barnett*, 12 Cl. & F. 787; *Bock* v. *Gorrisen*, 30 L. J. Ch. 39, 2 De G. F. & J. 434). BANKER'S LIEN.

This right of bankers is part of the law merchant, and is to be judicially noticed like the negotiability of bills of exchange (*Brandao* v. *Barnett*, *supra; Bock* v. *Gorrisen*, *supra*).

The right, though described as a lien, is more accurately described as a right similar to that of a pawnee over a pawn (*Donald* v. *Suckling*, L. R. 1 Q. B. 585, 604).

For a lien is strictly only a right to retain the subject matter of the lien until the demand is satisfied (*Hammond* v. *Barclay*, 2 East, p. 235). But the banker may realize the security over which his so-called lien exists: he may sue on it (*Holland* v. *Bygrave*, R. & M. 271, 6 M. & G. 653; *Bosanquet* v. *Dudman*, 1 Starkey 1), and recover so much as will cover the balance due to him from the customer (*Scott* v. *Franklin*, 15 East, 428); and it is said he may sell the security upon non-payment of the debt when a day has been fixed for the payment, but only after a

BANKER'S LIEN.

proper demand and notice where no day has been fixed (*Kemp* v. *Westbrook*, 1 Ves. sen. 278; *Martin* v. *Reid*, 31 L. J. C. P. 127, 11 Com. B. N. S. 730; *Piggott* v. *Cubley*, 15 Com. B. N. S. 701, 33 L. J. C. P. 134).

Lien arises when account overdrawn,

The right only arises where the customer is in debt to his banker, as on an overdrawn account (*Brandao* v. *Barnett, supra*); and whatever number of accounts are kept in the books the whole being really one account (*In re European Bank, Agra Bank claim*, L. R. 8 Ch. Ap. 44), even where the accounts are kept at two different branches (*Garnett* v. *McKewan*, L. R. 8 Ex. 10), the right cannot arise except the balance on the general account is against the customer.

or banker under acceptance.

The right also arises if the customer be in the banker's debt on bills accepted by the banker for the accommodation of his customer and already due (*Madden* v. *Kempster*, 1 Camp. 12; *Morse* v. *Williams*, 3 Camp. 418).

It may be doubted whether any right accrues before the bills are due (see *Jeffryes* v. *Agra and Masterman's Bank*, L. R. 2 Eq. 674, and *contra; Holland* v. *Bygrave*, 1 Ry. & M. 271, 6 M. & G. 653, 654).

Lien is on all securities.

The lien is on all securities in the banker's hands, so that no person can take any paper securities out of his banker's hands without paying him his general balance (*Davis* v. *Bowsher*, 5 T. R. p. 492).

What are securities.

The securities must be instruments for the payment of money or paper securities (*Davis* v. *Bowsher*, 5 T. R. 488), and have been said to include promissory notes, bills of exchange indorsed in blank or payable to bearer, exchequer bills (*Brandao* v. *Barnett, supra*), coupons, bonds of foreign governments (*Jones* v. *Peppercorne*, 28 L. J. Ch. 158; *Wylde* v. *Radford*, 33 L. J. Ch. 51, 53), certificates of shares (*In re United Service Company, Johnson's claim*, L. R. 6 Ch. Ap. 212), checks (*Scott and others* v. *Franklin*, 15 East, 428), marginal receipt notes (*Jeffryes* v.

Agra and Masterman's Bank, L. R. 2 Eq. 674), an order to purchaser of bills to pay the purchase money to a banker (*Currie* v. *Misa,* 1 App. Ca. 564).

BANKER'S LIEN.

Securities must be in possession of banker in the course of his trade.

The banker must further show that the securities came into his possession in the course of his trade of a banker, that is, a money factor, that he might perform some office which it is his duty as a banker to perform to such securities.

Thus one of the duties of a banker is to obtain acceptance of bills of exchange (*Brandao* v. *Barnett,* 6 M. & G. 630, 655), and the lien attaches on bills given him for that purpose.

On the other hand, some offices, such as taking care of plate of their customers, or receiving interest on exchequer bills for their customers, and exchanging the exchequer bills when such interest is paid, though customarily performed by bankers, are not part of their duty as bankers, and therefore no lien attaches to plate or bills entrusted to them under such circumstances. An office, for the performance of which remuneration is charged, is *primâ facie* one not within the duty of bankers to perform (*Brandao* v. *Barnett,* 12 Cl. & F. 809).

Thus it becomes a matter of importance in each case to determine in what character a banker has received a given bill from his customer, since each character is attended with different consequences. If the banker receives a bill as a purchase or takes it for value, and the property in the bill has once passed to him, the customer having no more interest in the bill, no question of lien or title to the note or its proceeds can arise between him and the banker.

If the banker receive it as a money factor to present for acceptance or payment, and to keep safely in the meanwhile, the banker has a lien on it for his general balance, and the customer can only claim the surplus remaining

BANKER'S LIEN.

after the banker is satisfied. Lastly, if the banker receive it for safe custody solely, he has no title to the proceeds, and no lien on it except for his reasonable charges for his care in keeping it safely, even though he has obtained judgment against the bailor for the balance of an account due to him from the bailor (see *Leese* v. *Martin*, L. R. 17 Eq. 224).

When property in bills has been held to pass to banker.

The courts have often had to decide the conflicting claims of the banker or his customer in cases arising generally on the bankruptcy of one of them, and the following, it is submitted, is the result of the decisions:

Bills paid in to a banker before they are due are *primâ facie* the property of the person paying them in (*Giles* v. *Perkins*, 9 East, 12). Where such bills are indorsed, the legal property in them passes to the banker, but they may be clothed with a trust in favour of the customer (*Ex parte Bond*, 1 M. D. & De G. 10; *Ex parte Brown*, 3 Deac. 91).

Bills which have been remitted to a banker are, on the bankruptcy of the banker, recoverable by the remitter, subject to the banker's right to lien, if they have been remitted to the banker for a special purpose which has not been fulfilled (*Ex parte Dumas*, 1 Atk. 232; *Zinck* v. *Walker*, 2 W. Bl. 1154; *Tooke* v. *Hollingworth*, 5 T. R. 215, 2 H. Bl. 501; *Bent* v. *Puller*, 5 T. R. 494; *Park* v. *Eliason*, 1 East, 544, 550; *Buchanan* v. *Findlay*, 9 B. & C. 738; *Ex parte Twogood*, 19 Vesey, 231); or to meet a contingency which might have arisen, but has not arisen, before the failure of the banker, as to discount when the customer's debit balance reached a certain figure (*Ex parte Wakefield*, 1 Rose, 243, 253); or to meet other bills which have not yet become due (*Jombart* v. *Woollett*, 2 My. & Cr. 389); or to be kept by the banker until they fall due, and in the meantime to be drawn against (*Ex parte Edwards*, 2 M. D. & De G. 625); or on deposit (*Ex parte Twogood*, 19 Vesey, 231).

If a bill be paid in to be discounted for the customer, the banker, until the bill is discounted, holds it as a deposit (*Ex parte Twogood,* 19 Vesey, 231).

BANKER'S LIEN.

If the banker discounts the bill he becomes the purchaser of the bill, and is entitled to sue upon it if necessary (*Carstairs* v. *Bates,* 3 Camp. 301; *Atwood* v. *Crowdie,* 1 Stark. 483). Indorsement on a bill is *primâ facie* evidence that it has been discounted (*Ex parte Twogood*). The taking of a banker's acceptance in exchange for another bill indorsed to the banker is equivalent to a discounting of a bill, and though the banker's acceptance be dishonored the bill will pass to his assignee (*Hornblower* v. *Proud,* 2 B. & Ald. 327).

If a bill has not been paid in expressly for immediate discount, it is in the absence of any special agreement to be inferred from the conduct of the parties what was the intention with which the bill was paid in.

Thus, bills sent up by a correspondent to his London banker "for account" were held to be received by the banker "for the floating account," and to be subject to the banker's lien as often as the balance of account turned against the correspondent (*Atwood* v. *Crowdie,* 1 Stark. 483).

It lies upon the banker who seeks to retain the bill against the customer to prove with what intention the bill has been paid in (*Ex parte Sargeant,* 1 Rose, 153; *Ex parte Barkworth,* 27 L. J. Bank. 5). And the entries in his books not communicated and assented to by his customer are not evidence in his favour, but may be evidence against him (*Ex parte Pease,* 1 Rose, 232, 239).

But it is against the inference that the property in the bills passed to the banker even where the bills are indorsed,—

If he entered the bills as short in his books (*Zinck* v. *Walker,* 2 W. Black. 1154); if he fail to prove the assent

BANKER'S LIEN.

of his customer to the bills being considered and entered as cash if so indorsed (*Ex parte Sargeant,* 1 Rose, 153; *Thompson* v. *Giles,* 2 B. & C. p. 430; *Ex parte Barkworth,* 27 L. J. Bank. 5); if in accounts sent by him to his customer the undue bills were described as property of the customer (*Ex parte Pease,* 1 Rose, 238); or if he have express permission given him by the customer to discount in some specified cases, as when the balance of the customer is unfavourable to a certain amount, since if the contract be that he is not to discount without the customer's permission, express or implied, the general contract applies where there is no such permission (*Ex parte Wakefield,* 1 Rose, 243, 253).

But it has been held (on the authority of *Ex parte Sargeant*) in *Ex parte Thomson,* (1 Mount. & Mac. 113), that the property in the bills did pass to the banker where the fund in the bank, against which the customer was in the habit of drawing, consisted almost wholly of bills paid in by him, and thus he gave the banker of necessity a right to deal with the bills as cash. Here, in an account of four years, there were but three entries of cash paid, the remaining entries being of bills.

In another case (*Thompson* v. *Giles,* 2 B. & C. 422), the banker had entered indorsed bills, paid in by the customer before they were due, as bills, but carried the full account into the cash column, and the customer was allowed to draw checks against that amount. This was held evidence of an undertaking by the banker to answer drafts in advance to the amount of the bills so entered, but not of a bargain that the bills were to be considered the property of the banker; and the customer's balance being in his favour at the time of the banker's failure, he was held entitled to recover such of the bills as remained in the banker's hands (*Ex parte Barkworth,* 27 L. J. Bank. 5, s. c. 2 De G. & J. 104).

The right to reclaim extends not only to the specific bills or securities deposited, but to the substitutes for, or proceeds of, them so long as they continue in the same hands and are ascertainable (*Vulliamy* v. *Noble*, 3 Mer. 593).

BANKER'S LIEN.

The banker can negotiate indorsed bills paid into him and give a good title to third parties who have obtained them *bonâ fide* and for value, although negotiated by the banker against good faith (*Ex parte Pease*, 1 Rose, 232; *Collins* v. *Martin*, 1 Bos. & Pull. 648; and *Bolton* v. *Puller*, 1 Bos. & Pull. p. 546; *Jones* v. *Peppercorne*, 28 L. J. Chan. 138). In the same way a banker can maintain his lien on negotiable instruments deposited by his customer, though the instruments should turn out to be the property of a stranger, provided the banker received the deposit in good faith (*Brandao* v. *Barnetto*, 12 Cl. & F.; *Wookey* v. *Pole*, 4 B. & Ald. 1).

No lien in certain cases.

Bankers have no lien on the deposit of a partner on his separate account for a balance due to the bank from a firm (*Watts* v. *Christie*, 11 Beav. 546; *Ex parte McKenna*, 30 L. J. Bank. p. 30).

Nor has a banker a lien on securities left by mistake or casually at the bank (*Lucas* v. *Dorrien*, 7 Taunt. 279).

Bankers are often said to have a lien where securities have been specifically pledged to secure the repayment of advances. The extent of such a lien depends on the terms of the agreement of pledge and the construction to be placed on the document, if any, containing the terms of such an agreement.

CHAPTER XV.

BRANCH BANKS.

BRANCH BANKS. THE head office of a bank having branches stands towards the branches in the relation of principal to agent, and on the rule that notice given to a principal is notice given to the agent, it was held (*Willis* v. *The Bank of England*, 4 A. & E. 21) that notice of an act of bankruptcy given to the Bank of England in London was as against the bank notice to the branches; at any rate, from the expiration of a reasonable time for the head office to communicate with the branches.

But the different branches as between themselves are considered distinct for several purposes: thus, payment by one branch of a check drawn on another branch is *primâ facie* a payment on the credit of the presenter of the check, and not on account of the drawer (*Woodland* v. *Fear*, 26 L. J. Q. B. 202). Again, the different branches of a bank may be indorsees of a bill of exchange one from the other, and are therefore each entitled to the usual notice of dishonor due to an indorser (*Clode* v. *Bayley*, 12 M. & W. 51).

As between a bank with branches and a customer having accounts at two or more branches, the accounts of the customer in the same right may, at the banker's discretion, be blended and treated by him as one account; and if the general result should be a balance against the customer, the banker may refuse to honor the customer's check drawn on a branch which holds a balance in favour of the customer; for a banker is not bound, apart from usage and contract, to honor checks drawn on one branch at that branch, because the customer has a credit there, if at another branch there is a countervailing debit (per *B*ramwell, B., L. R. 8 Ex. 10).

A limited banking company having branches must put up in a conspicuous part of the branches a copy of the statement of its capital, assets, and liabilities, as required by 25 & 26 Vic. c. 89, s. 44.

The stoppage of payment by a branch bank, if caused by the stoppage of the head office, dates from the receipt of the notice of the stoppage of the head office. *F*rom that date the branch ceased all functions; therefore, where a branch bank has received for the purpose of presentment a check drawn on another bank, at a time, in fact after the stoppage of the head office, but before notice of the stoppage reached the branch bank, the check, unless it has been cashed before the receipt of the notice of the stoppage, remains the property of the person who paid it in (*In re Agra and Masterman's Bank; Ex parte Waring*, 36 L. J. Ch. 151).

CHAPTER XVI.

BANKER AND CORRESPONDENT.

BANKER AND CORRESPONDENT.

BANKERS are often employed by their customers to transmit for collection, or to procure payment of, bills payable in different parts of the world, and are for this purpose obliged to employ agents or other bankers to act for them.

In case a loss arises from the conduct of the agents, Who is to bear the loss, the customer or the banker?

An agent, as a rule, has no right to delegate his authority to a sub-agent, without the assent of his principal (in which case the sub-agent becomes directly liable to the principal); but when from the nature of the agency or the course of business a sub-agent or sub-agents must necessarily be employed, the assent of the principal is implied, and if the agent in good faith chooses suitable agents for the purpose, he is not liable for the neglect or default of the sub-agent in the extension of the commission entrusted to him, but the sub-agent will be directly responsible to the principal (Paley on Agency, 17, 20; Story on Agency, § 201).

Thus it has been laid down in America (*Allen* v. *Merchant Bank*, 15 Wend. 482; *Bank of Washington* v. *Triplett*, 1 Peters, 25; *Fabens* v. *Mercantile Bank*, 23 Pick. 330; *Dorchester and Milton Bank* v. *New England Bank*, 1 Cush. 177; Story on Agency, § 14, n. 3; see *Daly* v. *The Butchers' and Drovers' Bank*, 17 The Am.

Rep. 663), that, where a bill is deposited with a bank for collection which is payable at another place, the whole duty of the bank so receiving the bill is seasonably to transmit the same to a suitable bank or other agent in the place of payment, and having transmitted the note to a bank or agent of good standing, the first bank is not responsible for the misfeasance or neglect of the corresponding bank or agent.

BANKER AND CORRESPONDENT.

Duty of bank undertaking collection.

But where a bank receives a bill or draft for collection against a drawer or maker resident at the place of the bank, or where the bank undertakes collection by their own officers, it will be liable for any loss that may occur from neglect (*Daly* v. *The Butchers' and Drovers' Bank*, *supra*).

Duty of agent for collection.

Where a bill has been transmitted to an agent to procure acceptance and payment, the duty of the agent is to obtain acceptance of the bill if possible, but not to press unduly for acceptance in such a way as to lead to a refusal, provided that the steps for obtaining acceptance or refusal are taken within that limit of time which will preserve the right of his principal against the drawer (*The Bank of Van Diemen's Land* v. *The Bank of Victoria*, L. R. 3 P. C. 526, 542).

Liability of bank for their agent for collection.

If the sub-agent employed to procure the payment of the bill does receive payment, the banker must answer to his customer for that amount; even though the sub-agent has failed or absconded after receiving the money and before remitting it. Thus, where bankers in England undertook for reward to procure payment of a bill payable in India, and their sub-agent, to whom the bill was transmitted for presentment, received the money from the acceptor, and credited the bankers with it in account, but failed shortly afterwards, so that the money never actually reached the bankers, the bankers were held bound to account to their customer for the

BANKER AND CORRESPONDENT.

amount, on the ground that the receipt of the money by the sub-agent was in law a receipt by the sub-agent's principal, the bankers (*Mackersy* v. *Ramsays*, 9 Cl. & F. 818).

Remittance.

Where a banker receives a sum of money to be transmitted by him to his correspondent for the purpose of meeting an acceptance payable in another place, and the money is debited and so transmitted in the customer's account, but before the acceptance falls due, the bank making the remittance stops payment, the amount transmitted belongs to the customer and not to the creditors of the bank (*Farley* v. *Turner*, 26 L. J. Ch. 710).

Bankruptcy of banker making remittance.

But if, before the money is transmitted, the bank fails, the payor cannot recover the money paid, but has merely a right of proof as a general creditor (*In re Barned's Banking Company, Massey's case*, 39 L. J. Eq. 635; see, too, *Ex parte Waring*, 36 L. J. Ch. 151).

Where the banker receives an allowance for commission, or commission for transacting business for his correspondent, his relation to his correspondent is that of factor, and bills sent to him by his correspondent are presumably remitted to him in the first place for collection, and on payment to be carried to account as cash. On the bankruptcy of the banker, those of such bills as remain in specie, or their proceeds, if realized by the assignees, can be recovered by the correspondent. The property also remains in the correspondent, where the banker in accounts sent by him to the correspondent has entered the bills as property of the correspondent, thus raising an express declaration of trust in his favour (*Ex parte Pease*, 1 Rose, 232; and see chapter on Banker's Lien).

There is no privity between a banker and the customer of his correspondent. Thus, a banker who receives bills from his correspondent receives them subject to the instructions given him by his correspondent, and not to the instructions given to his correspondent by the person paying them in (*Johnson* v. *Robarts,* L. R. 10 Ch. Ap. 505), and equity will not declare the banker a trustee for the customer on the instructions given by the latter to the correspondent (*ibid.*).

BANKER AND CORRESPONDENT.

Where money in pursuance of the creditor's order is paid by the debtor to a bank with directions to place it to the creditor's account with the bank's correspondent, no action will lie against the bank at the suit of the creditor after the money has been once carried by the bank to the account between it and its correspondent (*Williams* v. *Deacon,* 4 Ex. 397).

CHAPTER XVII.

PUBLIC OFFICER AND MANAGER.

PUBLIC OFFICER AND MANAGER.

THE 7 Geo. 4, c. 46, s. 4, authorized banking copartnerships, established under that Act, to appoint "two or more persons being members of such copartnership, and being resident in England, to be public officers of such copartnership, in the name of any one of whom such copartnership should sue and be sued." The names of these persons, "together with the title of office or other description of every such public officer," were to be included in the preliminary return to be made to the Stamp Office in London.

Banking companies established under 3 & 4 Wm. 4, c. 98, within a radius of sixty-five miles of London, have by 7 & 8 Vic. c. 113, s. 47 (re-enacted by 25 & 26 Vic. c. 89, Third Sched. Part III.), the privilege of suing or being sued by a public officer, provided they were established before May 6, 1844, on condition of their making out and delivering to the Stamp Commissioners similar accounts and returns to those delivered by banks under 7 Geo. 4, c. 46. Banking copartnerships discontinuing their issue of notes, commencing to carry on their business in London, preserve their privileges of suing and being sued by a public officer, and as to enforcement of decrees, orders, and judgments (27 & 28 Vic. c. 32, s. 1).

The duty of the public officer is to make out, verify on oath, and deliver the annual returns in the form prescribed by 7 Geo. 4, c. 46, as pointed out in Chap. II.

The appointment of a public officer may be proved by a copy of the return to the Stamp Office or by parol evidence.

The public officer can alone sue on behalf of a banking company under 7 Geo. 4, c. 46; even where the company has stopped payment, and continues for the sole purpose of winding up (*Davidson* v. *Cooper*, 11 M. & W. 778).

The public officer is the only person to be sued; it is not competent for creditors to waive that mode, and sue the individual members at common law (*Steward* v. *Greaves*, 10 M. & W. 711).

He is the proper person to sue and be sued on behalf of the company so long as they treat him and hold him out as their public registered officer (*Steward* v. *Dunn*, 12 M. & W. 655).

The public officer is the person to sue on a guarantee given to the copartnership, though the copartnership has gone through a partial change of members and total change of name since the guarantee was given (*Wilson* v. *Craven*, 8 M. & W. 584).

In suing a public officer under this Act, the statement should allege that the plaintiff at the time of the commencement of the suit (*Esdaile* v. *Maclean*, 15 M. & W. 277) had been named, and appointed nominal plaintiff (*Spiller* v. *Johnson*, 6 M. & W. 570; *Christie* v. *Peart*, 7 M. & W. 491), and that the copartnership was then carrying on business (*Fletcher* v. *Crosbie*, 9 M. & W. 252).

The public officer will not be allowed to plead that he has become bankrupt, as well as pleas to the merits (*Steward* v. *Dunn*, 11 M. & W. 63).

The public officer being a member of the company is personally liable on a judgment obtained against him, and therefore execution may be had against him without suing out a *sci. fa.* (*Harwood* v. *Law*, 7 M. & W. 203).

When a warrant of attorney is given to three trustees

of a bank to secure a debt due to the copartnership, the judgment thereon is properly entered up in the name of the public officer for the time being (*Bell* v. *Fisk,* 12 C. B. 493).

7 Geo. 4, c. 46, s. 9, enacts that the death, resignation, removal, or any act of a public officer shall not abate or prejudice any action, suit, indictment, information, prosecution, or other proceeding commenced against, or by or on behalf of a copartnership, but the same may be continued, prosecuted, and carried on in the name of any other of the public officers of such copartnership.

The name of the new public officer should be entered by suggestion on the record (*Barnewall* v. *Sutherland,* 19 L. J. C. P. 292).

The public officer in whose name any suit or action has been commenced, prosecuted, or defended, or against whom execution has been issued, is entitled to be indemnified and reimbursed by the other members of the copartnership (7 Geo. 4, c. 46, s. 14).

Manager.

Banking companies formed under 7 & 8 Vic. c. 113, are directed by that Act (sec. 4) to insert in their deed of partnership specific provisions for the appointment of a manager or other officer to perform the duties of manager. The duties and liabilities of this person were further regulated by the same Act. But the 7 & 8 Vic. c. 113, was repealed by 25 & 26 Vic. c. 89, and the general result appears to be that banking companies formed under 7 & 8 Vic. c. 113, are still bound to appoint a manager, but his duties are prescribed by 25 & 26 Vic. c. 89, and are the same as the duties of a manager when appointed by any company formed under that Act.

Speaking generally, the manager or directors of a company are subjected to penalties whenever the company of which he or they may be manager or directors omit to fulfil the statutory requirements. Thus penalties are imposed (sec. 25) for omitting to keep a register of members; for (sec. 27) not making out an annual list of shareholders, and forwarding a copy thereof to the registrar; for (sec. 32) not allowing inspection of the register; for (sec. 34) not giving notice of increase of capital to the registrar; for (sec. 42) omitting or neglecting, in the case of a limited company, the name of the company on the outside of its place of business; for (sec. 42) omitting to use the full name of the company, on the seal of the company, and on bills of exchange, promissory notes, checks, or orders for money or goods to which the company is a party. The manager is further made personally liable to the holder of any such bill of exchange, promissory note, check, or order for money or goods for the amount thereof, unless the same is duly paid by the company.

PUBLIC OFFICER AND MANAGER.

Under this section where a joint-stock company being duly registered with limited liability, a bill of exchange was addressed to the company as drawees by their name, omitting "limited," and the defendant, the secretary of the company, who had authority to accept bills for the company, accepted the bill in his own name, adding "secretary" to the said company, it was held that the acceptance was intended as the acceptance of the company, and the defendant, therefore, was personally liable to the holder of the bill under this section by reason of the omission of the word limited (*Penrose* v. *Martyn*, 28 L. J. Q. *B.* 28).

Penalties are also inflicted on every director or manager for (sec. 43) omitting to keep a register of mortgages, and to allow inspection thereof; for (sec. 44) omitting, in the

PUBLIC OFFICER AND MANAGER.

case of a limited banking company, to publish a statement of account in the statutory form on the first Monday in February and the first Monday in August, or to put it up in a conspicuous place in the registered office of the company; for (sec. 45), in the case of a company not having a capital divided into shares, omitting to send a list of the directors to the registrar; for (sec. 54) omitting, where articles of association have been registered, to annex a copy of any special resolution which may have been passed to every copy of the articles subsequently issued, or omitting to forward a copy of such resolution to any members demanding it; for (secs. 58 and 60) omitting to produce any book or document required to be produced, by or refusing to answer any of the questions of inspection appointed by the Board of Trade or by the company.

Powers of manager.

The manager of a bank is in the position towards his principals of a general agent for business. His principals are bound by, and are responsible for all his acts in the course of his business : that is, all acts which come within the scope of his employment; and his position being that of a general agent for business, he must be taken to be authorized to do all such acts which are necessary and proper for the carrying on the business of a bank (*Thompson* v. *Bell*, 10 Ex. 10), and his principals are bound by the results of such acts. Thus, where a manager who had received money from a depositor, in order that he, as manager, might dispose of it in a way within the scope of his authority, did not so dispose of it, but absconded, taking the money with him, the bank were held responsible for the money, because the money having been received by their agent for a purpose which was unfulfilled must be taken to be still in the bank's possession (*Thompson* v. *Bell*, *supra;* and *Melville* v. *Doidge*, 6 C. B. 450).

When bank responsible for his acts

It is a question of fact whether a particular act is or is not within the scope of a manager's authority.

and torts.

On the same principle the bank is responsible for every wrong committed by their manager which is committed in the course of the service and for the bank's benefit, though no express command or privity of the master be proved (*Barwick* v. *The English Joint-Stock Bank,* L. R. 2 Ex. 259), because, though a master may not have authorized a particular act, he has put the agent in his place to do that class of acts, and he must be answerable for the manner in which the agent has conducted himself in doing the business which it was the act of his master to place him in (per Willes, J., *Barwick* v. *The English Joint-Stock Bank*).

Thus, if a manager, to enable a debtor of a bank to obtain advances, gives on his behalf to a third party a guarantee apparently good (but which the manager knows and intends to be unavailing), and thereby obtains for his principals payment of part of the debtor's debt to the bank, his principals are liable for such fraudulent representation by their agent (*Barwick* v. *The English Joint-Stock Bank, supra*). An action of deceit may be maintained against a company, whether incorporated or unincorporated, in respect of the fraud of its agent. Where an officer of a banking corporation, whose duty it was to obtain the acceptance of bills of exchange in which the bank was interested, fraudulently, but without the knowledge of the president or directors of the bank, made a representation to A, which, by omitting a material fact, misled A and induced him to accept a bill in which the bank was interested, and A was compelled to pay the bill, it was held A could recover from the bank the amount so paid (*Mackay* v. *The Commercial Bank of New Brunswick,* L. R. 5 P. C. 394).

But the act, for which the principals are sought to be

PUBLIC OFFICER AND MANAGER.

made liable, must be done while the agent is acting within the scope of the agency, or if without the scope, must have been expressly authorized by the principal. The following case is an instance where principals were held not responsible for the act of their agent, on the ground that the agent in doing what he did was not acting as agent, but as a private person.

The defendant was surety for the payment of a debt due by a firm, A, B and C, to a company (the plaintiffs). The firm of A, B and C, besides being debtors to the plaintiffs, were debtors to the plaintiffs' manager, Christie, in his private capacity. Money, which the surety contended, ought, as between him and the firm, A, B and C, to the knowledge of the plaintiffs, to have been applied to the debt due from the firm to the company, was paid to Christie by B and C, and applied by him in payment of his own debt. The defendant claimed that under the circumstances it was inequitable in Christie to receive payment of his own debt out of the money which should have been applied to the debt due to the company, and claimed to set the payment up as one in effect to the company. But it was held that there was no reason for holding the company responsible for the manner in which Christie received payment of his own private debt, though he happened to be also their managing director; for that what he did was in his private capacity receiving payment of his own individual debt, and extensive as his authority was as manager, that act did not come within it (*McGowan* v. *Dyer*, L. R. 8 Q. B. 141).

Further question whether it is the duty of a manager to do a certain act.

A further distinction may be drawn after an act is decided to be within the scope of the authority of a manager, viz., has he merely the permission to do the act, or is it his duty as manager to do it? If the former, his principal will not, if the latter, his principals will be responsible.

Public Officer and Manager.

Thus, it is the custom among bankers to answer inquiries made as to the solvency of third parties by other bankers; and it is within the scope of a manager's authority to give the information asked for; and if the manager were to refuse to give it he would be doing a wrong to the bank which employed him, because he would be refusing a courtesy which it was their habit to show, in order that a corresponding courtesy might be shown to them; but in no other sense is it the duty of the manager, or within the scope of his authority, to do it. Therefore, where such inquiries are made, it is the duty of the manager towards his employers to answer them, but if he answers them falsely in a writing signed by himself, he alone is responsible thereon in an action against him (under 9 Geo. 4, c. 14, s. 6), for making a false representation as to the credit of another person, and his signature is not the signature of the bank, so as to make them responsible (*Swift* v. *Winterbotham*, L. R. 9 Q. B. 301, 315).

Principal cannot benefit by fraud of his agent.

Though a principal is liable for the wrongful acts of his agent committed in the course of his service and for his benefit, he cannot benefit by the fraud of his agent on the ground that he was not privy to the committal of the fraud.

Therefore, where a manager (*Collinson* v. *Lister*, 7 De G. Mac. & G. 634) of a banking company advances money of the banking company by way of loan, knowing at the time facts which render the loan an improper transaction, and would prevent the agent from sustaining it, were the transaction and the money his own—as in the instance of a trustee borrowing money in that character, who by the very act of so borrowing commits a breach of trust, having sought and obtained the money for the sole purpose of misapplying it, and the circumstances being all known at the time to the agent lending—the banking

PUBLIC OFFICER AND MANAGER.

company acquire no better title than the agent would have done had the case been his own.

Again, in *Foster* v. *Green*, 31 L. J. Ex. 158, the plaintiff was a banker whose cashier was a debtor of one C. C applied to the cashier for payment, and the cashier paid him out of the plaintiff's money, taking from him a document which the creditor believed to be a receipt, but which was, in fact, a check. The plaintiff brought an action on the check against C, and the jury found in effect, that the check was taken by the cashier to cover his fraud: the court held the plaintiff could not recover, because he could not relieve himself from the act of his agent.

Third parties dealing with the manager of a bank should always consider whether he is acting within his authority; if he draws, accepts, or indorses bills with the words *per procurationem*, he thereby gives an express intimation of a special and limited authority, and any person taking such bills is bound to inquire into the extent of the authority (*Alexander* v. *Mackenzie*, 6 C. B. 766; *Stagg* v. *Elliott*, 31 L. J. C. P. 260).

A note given "to the manager of" a banking company vests at law with the person who fills that office when the note is given, and the person filling that office can sue on it in his own name (*Robertson* v. *Sheward*, 1 M. & G. 511).

The manager, like any other *bonâ fide* holder, may sue in his own name on any bills indorsed in blank belonging to a banking company (*Law* v. *Parnell*, 29 L. J. C. P. 17).

It remains now to consider the relation of a manager to his employers.

Banking company and their manager.

A manager of a banking copartnership has no right to grant himself accommodation out of the funds of the bank without the consent of the directors, given with a full knowledge of the circumstances, and he will have to

PUBLIC OFFICER AND MANAGER.

refund advances otherwise made (*Gwatkin* v. *Campbell*, 1 Jur. N. S. 131).

Liability of manager to principal.

A manager who has in the legitimate course of banking business, and therefore within the scope of his authority, made advances, cannot be made liable for such advances by his principals unless bad faith or fraud is proved against him; he is not necessarily liable because the advances were made to an incorporate company, of which he was a shareholder and director; for a manager is appointed to manage the business of a bank in the midst of a community, consisting of individuals and of incorporated trading companies, in which it is always possible the manager may hold shares (*The Bank of Upper Canada* v. *Bradshaw*, L. R. 1 P. C. 479).

CHAPTER XVIII.

CRIMINAL LAW.

CRIMINAL LAW.

BANKERS are made criminally liable for improper conduct with regard to securities entrusted to their charge by the 24 & 25 Vic. c. 96, which enacts:

75. Whosoever, having been entrusted, either solely or jointly with any other person, as a banker, merchant, broker, attorney, or other agent, with any money or security for the payment of money, with any direction in writing to apply, pay, or deliver such money or security, or any part thereof respectively, or the proceeds or any part of the proceeds of such security, for any purpose, or to any person specified in such direction, shall, in violation of good faith, and contrary to the terms of such direction, in anywise convert to his own use or benefit, or the use or benefit of any person other than the person by whom he shall have been so entrusted, such money, security, or proceeds, or any part thereof respectively, and whosoever, having been entrusted either solely or jointly with any other person, as a banker, merchant, broker, attorney, or other agent, with any chattel or valuable security, or any power of attorney for the sale or transfer of any share or interest in any public stock or fund,

whether of the United Kingdom, or any part thereof, or of any foreign state, or in any stock or fund of any body corporate, company or society, for safe custody, or for any special purpose, without any authority to sell, negotiate, transfer, or pledge, shall, in violation of good faith, and contrary to the object or purpose for which such chattel, security, or power of attorney shall have been entrusted to him, sell, negotiate, transfer, pledge, or in any manner convert to his own use or benefit, or the use or benefit of any person other than the person by whom he shall have been so entrusted, such chattel, or security, or the proceeds of the same, or any part thereof, or in the share or interest in the stock or fund to which such power of attorney shall relate, or any part thereof, shall be guilty of a misdemeanour, and being convicted thereof, shall be liable, at the discretion of the court, to be kept in penal servitude for any term not exceeding seven years, and not less than three years, or to be imprisoned for any term not exceeding two years, with or without hard labour, and with or without solitary confinement; but nothing in this section contained relating to agents shall affect any trustee in or under any instrument whatsoever, or any mortgagee of any property, real or personal, in respect of any act done by such trustee or mortgagee in relating to the property comprised in, or affected by, any such trust or mortgage, nor shall restrain any banker, merchant, broker, attorney, or other agent from receiving any money which shall be or become actually due and payable, or by virtue of any valuable security according to the tenor and effect thereof, in such manner as he might have done if this Act had not been passed; nor from selling, transferring, or otherwise disposing of any securities or effects in his possession upon which he shall have any lien, claim, or demand entitling him by law so to do, unless such sale, transfer, or other disposal shall extend to a greater number or part of such securities or effects than shall be requisite for satisfying such lien, claim, or demand.

76. Whosoever, being a banker, merchant, broker, attorney, or agent, and being entrusted either solely or jointly with any other person with the property of any other person for safe custody, shall, with intent to defraud, sell, negotiate, transfer, pledge, or in any manner convert, or appropriate the same, or any part thereof, to, or for his own use or benefit, or the use or benefit of any person other than the person by whom he was so entrusted, shall be guilty of a misdemeanour, and being convicted thereof, shall be liable, at the discretion of the court, to any of the punishments which the court may award as hereinbefore last mentioned.

The 24 & 25 Vict. c. 98, s. 23, enacts that whosoever shall forge or alter, or shall offer, utter, dispose of, or put off, knowing the same to be forged or altered, any undertaking, warrant, order, authority, or request for the payment of money, or for the delivery or transfer of any goods or chattels, or of any note, bill, or other security for the payment of money, or for procuring or giving credit, or any indorsement on, or assignment of, any such undertaking, warrant, order, authority, request, or any accountable receipt, acquittance, or receipt for money, or for goods, or for any note, bill, or other security, for the payment of money, or any indorsement on, or assignment of any such accountable receipt, with intent in any of the cases aforesaid to defraud, shall be guilty of felony, &c.

Pass-book.

If a person with intent to defraud, and to cause it to be supposed contrary to the fact, that he has paid a certain sum into the bank, make in a book, purporting to be a pass-book of the bank, a false entry which denotes that the bank has received the sum, he is guilty of forging an accountable receipt for money (*R.* v. *Moody*, 31 L. J. M. C. 156; *R.* v. *Smith*, 31 L. J. M. C. 154).

Letter of Credit.

Where the defendant in England forged on a letter of credit, whereby a bank in Australia was required to "honor the draft of" R. T. for £50, an indorsement of R. T.'s name, this was held not to be the forging of an order for the payment of money, payment of the money on such an indorsement not being within the original mandate (*R.* v. *Wilton*, 1 F. & F. 391).

Check.

A forged draft on a banker in a fictitious name, or in the name of a person who never kept cash with the banker, is a warrant or order within the meaning of the Act (*R.* v. *Lockett*, 1 Leach, 94).

So a forged draft in the name of a person who does keep cash with the banker is an order within the Act, whatever be the state of his account at the time (*R.* v. *Carter*, 1 Den. C. C. 65).

Where a man obtains goods upon his own draft on a banker with whom he does not keep cash, the proper method of proceeding against him is by indictment for false pretences.

Thus obtaining goods from another upon giving him in payment his check upon a banker with whom, in fact, he has no account, is a false pretence within 24 & 25 Vict. c. 96, s. 88 (*R.* v. *Jackson*, 3 Camp. 370; *R.* v. *Parker*, 7 C. & P. 825).

To give a check on a bank for an amount exceeding the balance, after various checks have been refused, and with the knowledge that overdrawing will not be allowed, is a false pretence that the drawer has power to draw for the amount (*R.* v. *Hazelton*, L. R. 2 C. C. R. 134).

Stealing a check is felony, for 24 & 25 Vict. c. 96, s. 27, enacts, that to steal, or for any fraudulent purpose, to destroy, cancel, or obliterate the whole or any part of any valuable security, is felony.

So also is embezzling a check by any clerk or servant (24 & 25 Vict. c. 96, s. 68).

To alter or obliterate the crossing on a check is felony (24 & 25 Vict. c. 28, s. 25).

Bank Notes.

It is felony (24 & 25 Vict. c. 98, s. 6) to forge or utter forged bank notes, or (s. 13) to purchase or receive forged bank notes, or (s. 16) to engrave or possess any plate or paper for making forged bank notes.

CHAPTER XIX.

SCOTCH BANKS.

THE first notice of banking in Scotland which occurs in the statute book, is Will. 3, Parl. 1, sec. 5, passed in 1695, under which the Bank of Scotland was established with an exclusive privilege of banking for twenty-one years. This privilege was not renewed at the expiration of that period. The Bank of Scotland issued promissory notes first in the year 1704, and continued to be the only bank until the year 1727. In that year the Royal *B*ank was incorporated by charter. SCOTCH BANKS.

It is convenient to deal first with the history of the note issue. History of note issue.

In the year 1765, 5 Geo. 3, c. 49, was passed, being the first Act which regulated the issue of promissory notes in Scotland. It appears from the preamble that a practice had prevailed in Scotland of issuing notes which circulated as specie, and which were made payable to the bearer on demand, or payable at the option of the issuer at the end of six months with a sum equal to the legal interest, from the demand to that time. 5 Geo. 3, c. 49.

The Act prohibits the issue of such notes and requires that all notes, in the nature of a bank note and circulating like specie, should be paid on demand, and prohibits the issue of any promissory note of a sum less than twenty shillings.

But this Act does not interfere with or restrain the

SCOTCH BANKS. issue by any person of promissory notes payable to the bearer on demand.

55 Geo. 3, c. 184. In the year 1815, the 55 Geo. 3, c. 184, allowed (sec. 14) bankers and others who had issued stamped promissory notes payable to bearer on demand to reissue them without further duty, but (sec. 24) compelled all such bankers and others to take out a licence to issue stamped promissory notes. It was provided on behalf of the Scotch bankers that (sec. 25) no banker was to be obliged to take out more than four licences for any number of towns in Scotland. The Bank of Scotland, the Royal Bank of Scotland, and the British Linen Company were (sec. 23) authorized to issue small notes on unstamped paper, accounting for the duties.

8 & 9 Vic. c. 38. In the year 1845, the 8 & 9 Vict. c. 38 was passed, which now regulates the note issue in Scotland. After reciting that by 7 & 8 Vict. c. 32, s. 10 (*supra*, p. 4), no person, from the passing of the last-mentioned Act, other than a banker, who on May 6, 1844, was lawfully issuing his own bank notes, should make or issue bank notes in any part of the United Kingdom; the 8 & 9 Vict. c. 38 provides a means for ascertaining what bankers in Scotland were, on May 6, 1844, lawfully issuing notes and the amount of the issue; it then enacts that it shall be lawful for every such banker to continue to issue his own bank notes to the extent of that ascertained amount, and to the amount of the gold and silver coin held by such banker at the head office or principal place of issue of such banker.

Bank notes. All bank notes (sec. 5) are to be expressed for payment of a sum in pounds sterling without any fractional parts of a pound.

Weekly accounts. Accounts are (sec. 7) to be rendered weekly by such bankers to the Commissioners of Stamps of the amount of their respective note circulation and of the amount of the gold and silver in possession of each banker. (This return had already been, as to part, compulsory on bankers in Scotland under 4 & 5 Vic. c. 50, s. 1.) The commissioners are to make (sec. 9) monthly returns of the average amount of note circulation, and of the average amount of all the gold and silver coin held by each banker.

SCOTCH BANKS.

Notes for less than twenty shillings (sec. 16) are made void and of no effect.

Form of notes.

Certain forms are (sec. 17) prescribed for notes of twenty shillings and less than 5*l.*; and persons other than bankers authorized by the Act are (sec. 19) forbidden to utter notes or bills for the payment of twenty shillings or less than 5*l.*; but this does not prohibit (sec. 20) checks on bankers.

Bank note deferred.

The term "bank note" is defined (sec. 22) to extend and apply to all bills or notes for the payment of money to the bearer on demand other than bills or notes of the Governor and Company of the Bank of England.

Power to compound.

By a subsequent Act, 16 & 17 Vict. c. 63, s. 7, power is given to the Treasury to compound with bankers in Scotland for the stamp duties on their promissory notes and bills of exchange on such terms and conditions as the Treasury shall think fit and proper; and upon such composition being entered into such bankers may issue and reissue such notes, and may draw all such bills on unstamped paper.

Banker's licence.

The licences to bankers in Scotland are regulated by 55 Geo. 3, c. 184 (above cited), and 24 & 25 Vict. c. 91, s. 35. This last Act requires licences issued to joint stock companies to specify the names of not more than six persons.

Constitution of Scotch Banks.

The following has been the course of legislation in respect of the constitution of Scotch banks.

The 7 Geo. 4, c. 67 (sec. 1), enables all banking copartnerships in Scotland to sue and be sued in the name of

Scotch Banks.

their manager or cashier, provided (sec. 2) each copartnership delivers yearly to the stamp office, in Edinburgh, an account containing the name and style of the firm, the names of the partners, the name of the officer in whose name the copartnership is to sue and be sued, and the places where the copartnership issues notes. Other sections provide for the method of procedure by and against the officer thus appointed to sue and be sued.

By the 9 & 10 Vict. c. 75, and 19 & 20 Vict. c. 3, the Crown is enabled to grant letters patent of incorporation in perpetuity to any company of bankers in Scotland carrying on business before August 9, 1845. But by 17 & 18 Vict. c. 73, no clause in any charter granted under 7 & 8 Vict. c. 113, and 9 & 10 Vict. c. 75, was to take away the common law right of a company in Scotland of lien over the shares of its partners, and the provision made as to signing bills of exchange and promissory notes in 7 & 8 Vict. c. 113, was not to apply to any Scotch banks.

In 1857, banking companies formed under 9 & 10 Vict. c. 75, were compelled to register themselves under the Joint Stock Banking Companies Act, 1857 (20 & 21 Vict. c. 49, s. 4), and from that time banking companies in Scotland have been subject to the same regulations as those in England. These have been already discussed in Chapter II.

Bank of England notes are not a legal tender in Scotland, but their circulation is not prohibited (8 & 9 Vict. c. 38, s. 15).

CHAPTER XX.

IRISH BANKS.

THE first Act regulating or restricting the issue of promissory notes in Ireland was passed in the year 1799. Up to the year 1781 no restriction at all seems to have been placed upon their issue; but in that year the 21 & 22 Geo. 3, c. 16 (Irish), was passed constituting the Bank of Ireland. IRISH BANKS. History of note issue.

By this Act power was given to the Crown to incorporate the subscribers to a loan of £620,000 as a body politic and corporate. The bills (sec. 19) obligatory, and of credit under the seal of the corporation, were made assignable by indorsement, and the assignee was empowered to sue thereon in his or her own name. From the passing of the Act it became unlawful (sec. 14) "for any body, politic or corporate, erected or to be erected, other than the corporation created by the Act, or for any other persons whatever, united or to be united in covenants or partnership, exceeding the number of six persons, to borrow, owe, or take up any sum or sums of money on their bills or notes, payable at demand, or at any less time than six months from the borrowing thereof." 21 & 22 Geo. 3, c. 16.

In this way the issue of bank notes on the credit of a partnership of more than six persons was put an end to.

In the year 1799, during the suspension of cash payments by the Bank of Ireland, the issue of promissory notes under certain regulations was allowed. In the year

IRISH BANKS. 1805, the last-mentioned Act and some others, which had been passed in the interim, were repealed, and notes under twenty shillings which had been previously permitted under certain regulations by the Act of 1799 were declared void.

6 Geo. 4, c. 42. In the year 1825, by the 6 Geo. 4, c. 42, it was made lawful for any number of persons in copartnership, having houses of business at any place not less than fifty miles from *D*ublin, to carry on the business of bankers in like manner as copartnerships of not more than six persons might then lawfully do; and to borrow, owe, or take up any sums of money on their bills or notes payable on demand, or at any time after date, and to make and issue such bills or notes at any place in Ireland exceeding fifty miles from Dublin, on the liability of all the persons composing the partnership.

Accounts were to be rendered yearly (sec. 6) of the names of the firm, the several partners therein, and the public officers thereof. The partnership was to sue and be sued in the name of the public officer. In this and many other points the terms of this Act were followed by the Act passed the following year (7 Geo. 4, c. 46), for the regulation of banking copartnerships in England, and which has been already dealt with.

11 Geo. 4 & 1 Will. 4, c. 32. In 1830, by the 11 Geo. 4, and 1 Will. 4, c. 32, sec. 1, banking copartnerships of more than six persons, not having houses of business at any place less than fifty miles from Dublin, were allowed to pay their notes in *D*ublin for the purpose of withdrawing them from circulation; but (sec. 3) were not allowed to reissue them in Dublin.

In 1845, in consequence of the passing of 7 & 8 Vict. c. 32 (*supra*, Chapter II.), in the previous year, enacting that no person other than a banker, who on May 6, 1844, was lawfully issuing his own bank notes should make or issue bank notes in any part of the United Kingdom, the

8 & 9 Vict. c. 37 was passed, which now regulates the note issue of Ireland.

8 & 9 Vict. c. 37.

Banks (sec. 8) claiming to be entitled to issue notes in Ireland are to give notice to the commissioners, and similar methods to those provided in England and Scotland are provided for ascertaining the average amount of the issue of each bank, and settling the amount of such issue for the future upon the average so obtained.

Returns.

All bankers (sec. 22) in Ireland are to return their names, &c., once a year to the stamp office in Dublin.

Public officers.

Banking companies (sec. 30) within fifty miles of Dublin may sue and be sued in the names of their public officers in manner provided as to companies beyond that distance by 6 Geo. 4, c. 42.

Constitution of Irish banks.

The following are the Acts regulating the constitution of banks in Ireland in addition to those above cited (the 21 & 22 Geo. 3, c. 16 (Irish Act), and the 6 Geo. 4, c. 42).

The provisions of the 7 & 8 Vict. c. 113, enabling the Crown to incorporate English joint stock banks were extended by the 9 & 10 Vict. c. 75, and 19 & 20 Vict. c. 3, to Irish banks.

In 1857, banks which had been formed under these Acts were compelled to register under the 20 & 21 Vict. c. 49, and since that time banks in Ireland have been subject to the same laws as the banks in England.

Estates of bankrupt bankers in Ireland.

With the object of giving greater security for the payment of the promissory notes issued by bankers carrying on business in Ireland, special Acts were passed, regulating, in case of bankruptcy, the estates of bankers unable to pay their debts, viz., 8 Geo. 1, c. 14 (Irish); 33 Geo. 2, c. 14 (Irish); 40 Geo. 3, c. 22 (Irish). It has been held (*Copeland* v. *Davies*, L. R. 5 E. & I. 358) that these Acts apply to all bankers, and not only to those issuing notes in Ireland.

Bank of England notes are not a legal tender in Ireland;

IRISH BANKS.

but their circulation is not prohibited (8 & 9 Vict. c. 37, s. 6).

Banker's licences.

The licences to bankers in Ireland are now regulated by the following statutes: the 6 Geo. 4, c. 42 (*supra*, p. 176), compels banking copartnerships of more than six persons in number carrying on business more than fifty miles from Dublin, and issuing notes, to take out a certificate from the stamp office, chargeable with a duty of thirty pounds. The 9 Geo. 4, c. 80, s. 16, enacts that no such copartnership shall be obliged to take out more than four certificates. The same Act (9 Geo. 4, c. 80, s. 1) allows bankers to issue unstamped notes on obtaining a licence and giving security for the payment of the composition. The licence duty (sec. 2) is £30. The 5 & 6 Vict. c. 82, s. 2, enacts that the same composition is to be paid in respect of promissory notes on unstamped paper issued by any licensed banker in Ireland, or the notes of such banker in circulation as is payable by bankers in England under 9 Geo. 4, c. 23.

APPENDIX.

—o—

STATUTES.

[5 Geo. 3, c. 49.]

An Act to prevent the inconveniences arising from the present method of issuing Notes and Bills by the Banks, Banking Companies, and Bankers, in that part of Great Britain called Scotland. 5 Geo. 3, c. 49.

WHEREAS a practice has prevailed in that part of *Great Britain* called *Scotland* of issuing notes, commonly called *bank notes*, for sums of money payable to the bearer on demand, or, in the option of the issuer or grantor, payable at the end of six months, with a sum equal to the legal interest, from the demand to that time: and whereas notes, with such option as aforesaid, have been and are circulated in that part of the United Kingdom to a great extent, and do pass, from hand to hand, as specie, whereby great inconveniences have arisen: for remedy whereof, may it please your Majesty that it may be enacted; and be it enacted by the King's most excellent Majesty, by and with the advice and consent of the Lords spiritual and temporal, and Commons, in this present Parliament assembled, and by the authority of the same, That from and after the fifteenth day of *May* one thousand seven hundred and sixty-six, it shall not be lawful for any person or persons whatsoever, bodies politic or corporate, to issue or give, or cause to be issued or given, within that part of *Great Britain* called *Scotland*, any note, ticket, token, or other writing, for money, of the nature of a bank note, circulated, or to be circulated, as specie, but such as shall be payable, on demand, in lawful money of *Great Britain*, and without reserving any power, or option of delaying payment thereof for any time or term whatsoever; and that from and after the said fifteenth day of *May* one thousand seven hundred and sixty-six, all notes, tickets, tokens, or other writings, for money, of the nature of a bank note, issued previous to the said day, and circulated as specie in that part of the United Kingdom, shall, and they are hereby declared and adjudged to be payable, on demand, in lawful money aforesaid; any option, condition, or other clause therein contained to the contrary notwithstanding.

Preamble.

From and after 15 *May*, 1766, no notes to be issued in *Scotland*, and circulated as specie, but what shall be payable on demand; and notes issued, and circulated as specie, previous to the said day, shall be payable on demand, notwithstanding any optional clause to the contrary.

Provided always, That nothing contained in this Act shall prevent any person or persons, bodies politic or corporate, from issuing post

Post bills payable at

5 Geo. 3, c. 49.

bills, payable seven days after sight, in the same manner as they are at present issued by the Bank of *England*.

seven days' sight, excepted: and persons acting contrary hereto, forfeit 500*l*.,

And be it further enacted by the authority aforesaid, That all and every person or persons whatsoever, bodies politic or corporate, and the legal administrators of such person or persons, bodies politic or corporate, who shall, after the said fifteenth day of *May* one thousand seven hundred and sixty-six, issue, or cause to be issued, any note, ticket, token, or other writing, for money, of the nature of a bank note, circulated, or to be circulated, as specie, contrary to the directions of this Act before mentioned, and to the true meaning and intent thereof, shall, for every such offence, forfeit and pay to the person or persons who shall inform and prosecute for the same, five hundred pounds sterling, with full costs of suit; to be sued for and recovered, by way of complaint, before the Court of Session, upon fifteen days' notice to the person or persons, bodies politic or corporate, complained of; which complaint the said Court of Session is hereby authorized and required summarily to determine, without abiding the course of any roll.

with full costs of suit.

* * * * *

From and after 1 *June*, 1765, no note to be issued, and circulated as specie for a less sum than 20*s*. *ster*.,

And whereas a practice has of late prevailed in that part of the United Kingdom, of issuing and circulating notes as specie, of the nature of bank notes, for small sums less than twenty shillings lawful money of *Great Britain*, whereby great inconveniences have arisen: for remedy whereof, be it further enacted by the authority aforesaid, That from and after the first day of *June* one thousand seven hundred and sixty-five, no note, accepted bill, post bill, ticket, token, or other writing, circulated, or which may be circulated, as specie, in the manner of a bank or banker's note, shall be issued, reissued, or given out, as specie, by any person or persons, bodies politic or corporate, their servants or agents, in that part of the United Kingdom, for any sum or sums of money less than twenty shillings lawful money of *Great Britain;* any law, usage, or custom, to the contrary notwithstanding: and that the person or persons, bodies politic or corporate, their servants or agents, who shall, after the said first day of *June*, issue reissue, or give out, any note, accepted bill, post bill, ticket, token, or other writing aforesaid, for any sum less than twenty shillings, shall, for every such offence, forfeit and pay the sum of five hundred pounds sterling, with full costs of suit, to the person or persons who shall inform or prosecute for the same; to be sued for and revovered by way of summary complaint, before the Court of Session; to be proceeded in, in manner before directed.

on forfeiture of 500*l*. with full costs of suit.

Holders of small notes not prevented hereby from passing the same, until 1 *June*, 1766, or from demanding payment thereof at any time.

Provided always, That nothing herein contained shall be interpreted to prevent the holders of all such notes, accepted bills, post bills, tickets, tokens, or other writings aforesaid, for sums less than twenty shillings, from passing the same in payment until the first day of *June* one thousand seven hundred and sixty-six, or from demanding payment thereof from the person or persons, bodies politic or corporate, who issued the same, at any time.

[17 Geo. 3, c. 30.]*

An Act for further restraining the Negotiation of Promissory Notes and Inland Bills of Exchange, under a limited sum, within that part of Great Britain called England. 17 Geo. 3, c. 30.

"WHEREAS by a certain Act of Parliament passed in the fifteenth year of the reign of His present Majesty (intituled, *An Act to restrain the negotiation of Promissory Notes and Inland Bills of Exchange under a limited sum, within that part of* Great Britain *called* England), all negotiable promissory or other notes, bills of exchange, or draughts, or undertakings in writing, for any sum of money less than the sum of twenty shillings in the whole, and issued after the twenty-fourth day of *June* one thousand seven hundred and seventy-five, were made void, and the publishing or uttering and negotiating of any such notes, bills, draughts, or undertakings, for a less sum than twenty shillings, or on which less than that sum should be due, was, by the said Act, restrained under certain penalties or forfeitures therein mentioned; and all such notes, bills of exchange, draughts, or undertakings in writing, as had issued before the said twenty-fourth day of *June*, were made payable upon demand, and were directed to be recovered in such manner as is therein also mentioned; And whereas the said Act hath been attended with very salutary effects, and in case the provisions therein contained were extended to a further sum (but yet without prejudice to the convenience arising to the public from the negotiation of promissory notes and inland bills of exchange for the remittance of money in discharge of any balance of account or other debt), the good purposes of the said Act would be further advanced;" be it therefore enacted by the King's most excellent Majesty, by and with the advice and consent of the Lords Spiritual and Temporal, and Commons, in this present Parliament assembled, and by the authority of the same, That all promissory or other notes, bills of exchange, or draughts, or undertakings in writing, being negotiable or transferrable, for the payment of twenty shillings, or any sum of money above that sum and less than five pounds; or on which twenty shillings, or above that sum, and less than five pounds, shall remain undischarged, and which shall be issued, within that part of *Great Britain* called *England*, at any time after the first day of *January* one thousand seven hundred and seventy-eight, shall specify the names and places of abode of the persons respectively to whom, or to whose order, the same shall be made payable; and shall bear date before or at the time of drawing or issuing thereof, and not on any day subsequent thereto; and

15 Geo. 3. recited.

All negotiable promissory notes, &c., for 20*s*. and less than 5*l*. shall specify the names, &c. of the persons to whom payable.

* Made perpetual by 27 Geo. 3, c. 16, but repealed by 26 & 27 Vict. c. 105 and by 39 & 40 Vict. c. 69, till Dec. 31, 1877. By 17 & 18 Vict c. 83, s. 9, the Act does not extend to drafts on bankers.

17 Geo. 3, c. 30.

shall be made payable within the space of twenty-one days next after the day of the date thereof; and shall not be transferrable or negotiable after the time thereby limited for payment thereof; and that every indorsement to be made thereon shall be made before the expiration of that time, and to bear date at or not before the time of making thereof; and shall specify the name and place of abode of the person or persons to whom, or to whose order, the money contained in every such note, bill, draught, or undertaking is to be paid; and that the signing of every such note, bill, draught, or undertaking, and also of every such indorsement, shall be attested by one subscribing witness at the least; and which said notes, bills of exchange, or draughts, or undertakings in writing, may be made or drawn in words to the purport or effect as set out in the Schedule hereunto annexed, No. I. and II.: And that all promissory or other notes, bills of exchange, or draughts, or undertakings in writing, being negotiable or transferrable, for the payment of twenty shillings, or any sum of money above that sum and less than five pounds; or in which twenty shillings, or above that sum, and less than five pounds, shall remain undischarged, and which shall be issued, within that part of *Great Britain* called *England*, at any time after the said first day of *January*, one thousand seven hundred and seventy-eight, in any other manner than as aforesaid; and also every indorsement on any such note, bill, draught, or undertaking, to be negotiated under this Act, other than as aforesaid, shall, and the same are hereby declared to be, absolutely void; any law, statute, usage, or custom to the contrary thereof in anywise notwithstanding.

Signing of every such note, and indorsement to be attested by one witness.

Penalty.

II. And be it further enacted by the authority aforesaid, That the publishing, uttering, or negotiating, within that part of *Great Britain* called *England*, of any promissory or other note, bill of exchange, draught, or undertaking in writing, being negotiable or transferrable, for twenty shillings, or above that sum and less than five pounds, or on which twenty shillings, or above that sum and less than five pounds, shall remain undischarged, and issued or made in any other manner than notes, bills, draughts, or undertakings, hereby permitted to be published or negotiated as aforesaid; and also the negotiating of any of such last-mentioned notes, bills, draughts, or undertakings, after the time appointed for payment thereof, or before that time in any other manner than as aforesaid, by any act, contrivance, or means whatsoever, from and after the said first day of *January* one thousand seven hundred and seventy-eight, shall be, and the same is hereby declared to be, prohibited or restrained, under the like penalties or forfeitures, and to be recovered and applied in like manner as by the said Act is directed, with respect to the uttering, or publishing, or negotiating of notes, bills of exchange, draughts, or undertakings in writing, for any sum of money not less than the sum of twenty shillings, or on which less than that sum should be due.

All negotiable promissory notes, &c., between 20*s* and 5*l*. which shall be issued

III. And be it further enacted by the authority aforesaid, That, from and immediately after the passing of this Act, all promissory or other notes, bills of exchange, draughts, or undertakings in writing, for the payment of any greater sum of money than twenty shillings, and less than the sum of five pounds, or on which twenty shillings, and less than the sum of five pounds, shall remain undischarged, and being negotiable or transferrable, as shall be issued before the said first day of *January* one thousand seven hundred and seventy-eight, shall be, and the same are hereby declared and adjudged payable, within that part of *Great Britain* called *England*, on demand, any terms, restrictions, or conditions therein contained to the contrary thereof notwithstanding; and shall be recoverable in such manner, or by the like means, as is or are directed in or by the said Act with respect to notes, bills of exchange, or draughts, or undertakings in writing therein mentioned to have issued previous to the said twenty-fourth day of *June* one thousand seven hundred and seventy-five; and that all and every other the powers, provisoes, limitations, restrictions, penalties, clauses, matters and things whatsoever in the said former Act contained with respect thereto, and also with respect to all such notes, bills of exchange, draughts, or undertakings in writing, issued after the said twenty-fourth day of *June* one thousand seven hundred and seventy-five, shall be, and the same are hereby declared to be in force, within that part of *Great Britain* called *England*, as to all notes, bills of exchange, or draughts, or undertakings in writing, for twenty shillings, or any greater sum and less than the sum of five pounds, or on which twenty shillings, or above that sum and less than five pounds, shall remain undischarged, issued after the said first day of *January* one thousand seven hundred and seventy-eight, and previous thereto respectively, and in like manner as if the same respectively had been the object of the said Act at the time of making thereof, save so far as the same or any of them are altered or varied by this present Act.

17 Geo. 3, c. 30.

before Jan 1, 1778, shall be Payable on demand.

IV. And be it further enacted by the authority aforesaid, That the said former, and also this present Act, shall continue in force, not only for the residue of the term of five years in the said former Act mentioned, and from thence to the end of the then next session of Parliament, but also for the further term of five years, and from thence to the end of the then next session of Parliament.

Continuance of this, and former Act.

SCHEDULE, No. I.

[*Place*] [*Day*] [*Month*] [*Year*]

Twenty-one days after date, I promise to pay to *A. B.* of [*Place*] or his order, the sum of for value received by

Witness, *E. F.* *C. D.*

And the Indorsement, toties quoties.

[*Day*] [*Month*] [*Year*]

Pay the contents to *G. H.* of [*Place*] or his order.

Witness, *J. K.* *A. B.*

No. II.

[*Place*] [*Day*] [*Month*] [*Year*]

Twenty-one days after date, pay to *A. B.* of [*Place*] or his order, the sum of value received, as advised by

to *E. F.* of [*Place*] *C. D.*

Witness, *G. H.*

And the Indorsement, toties quoties.

[*Day*] [*Month*] [*Year*]

Pay the contents to *J. K.* of [*Place*] or his order.

Witness, *L. M.* *A. B.*

[39 & 40 Geo. 3, c. 28.]

39 & 40 G. 3, c. 28.

An Act for establishing an Agreement with the Governor and Company of the Bank of England, for advancing the Sum of Three Millions towards the Supply for the Service of the Year One thousand eight hundred.

[28*th March,* 1800.]

No other bank shall be erected by Parliament during the continuance of the said privilege;

nor shall any number of bankers in partnership exceeding six be allowed.

Conditions of redemption.

XV. And to prevent any doubts that may arise concerning the privilege or power given by former Acts of Parliament to the said governor and company of exclusive banking, and also in regard to the erecting any other bank or banks by Parliament, or restraining other persons from banking during the continuance of the said privilege granted to the Governor and Company of the Bank of *England* as before recited; it is hereby further enacted and declared, That it is the true intent and meaning of this Act that no other bank shall be erected, established, or allowed by Parliament; and that it shall not be lawful for any body politic or corporate whatsoever erected or to be erected, or for any other persons united or to be united in covenants or partnership, exceeding the number of six persons, in that part of *Great Britain* called *England*, to borrow, owe, or take up any sum or sums of money on their bills or notes payable on demand, or at any less time than six months from the borrowing thereof, during the continuance of the said privilege to the said governor and company, who are hereby declared to be and remain a corporation, with the privilege of exclusive banking as before recited, subject to redemption on the terms and conditions before mentioned; (that is to say), on one year's notice to be given after the first day of *August* one thousand eight hundred and thirty-three, and repayment of the said sum of three millions two hundred thousand pounds, and all arrears of the said one hundred thousand pounds *per annum;* and also upon repayment of the said sum of eight millions four hundred and eighty-six thousand and eight hundred pounds, and the interest or annuities payable thereon or in respect thereof, and all the principal and interest money that shall be owing on all such tallies, exchequer orders, exchequer bills, parliamentary funds, or other government securities, which the said governor and company or their successors shall have remaining in their hands or be entitled to at the time of such notice to be given as aforesaid, and not otherwise; any thing in this Act or any former Act or Acts of Parliament to the contrary in anywise notwithstanding.

[48 Geo. 3, c. 88.] *

An Act to restrain the Negotiation of Promissory Notes and Inland Bills of Exchange, under a limited Sum, in England. [23rd June, 1808.]

48 Geo. 3, c. 88.

Promissory notes for less than 20s. void.

II. And be it further enacted, That all promissory or other notes, bills of exchange or drafts, or undertakings in writing, being negotiable or transferable for the payment of any sum or sums of money, or any orders, notes, or undertakings in writing, being negotiable or transferable for the delivery of any goods, specifying their value in money, less than the sum of twenty shillings in the whole, heretofore made or issued, or which shall hereafter be made or issued, shall from and after the first day of *October* one thousand eight hundred and eight, be and the same are hereby declared to be absolutely void and of no effect; any law, statute, usage or custom, to the contrary thereof in anywise notwithstanding.

Persons uttering such notes or bills for less than 20s. &c., shall forfeit not exceeding 20*l.* nor less than 5*l.*

III. And be it further enacted, That if any person or persons shall after the first day of *July* one thousand eight hundred and eight, by any art, device, or means whatsoever, publish or utter any such notes, bills, drafts, or engagements as aforesaid, for a less sum than twenty shillings, or on which less than the sum of twenty shillings shall be due, and which shall be in anywise negotiable or transferable, or shall negotiate or transfer the same, every such person shall forfeit and pay, for every such offence, any sum not exceeding twenty pounds, nor less than five pounds, at the discretion of the justice of the peace who shall hear and determine such offence.

Justices empowered to hear and determine offences.

IV. And be it further enacted, That it shall be lawful for any justice or justices of the peace, acting for the county, riding, city or place within which any offence against this Act shall be committed, to hear and determine the same in a summary way, at any time within twenty days after such offence shall have been committed; and such justice or justices, upon any information exhibited or complaint made upon oath in that behalf, shall summon the party accused, and also the witnesses on either side, and shall examine into the matter of fact, and upon due proof made thereof, either by the voluntary confession of the party or by the oath of one or more credible witness or witnesses, or otherwise (which oath such justice or justices is or are hereby authorized to administer), shall convict the offender, and adjudge the penalty for such offence.

Penalty on witnesses not attending.

V. And be it further enacted, That if any person shall be summoned as a witness to give evidence before such justice or justices, either on the part of the prosecutor or the person accused, and shall neglect or refuse to appear at the time or place to be for that purpose appointed without a reasonable excuse for such his neglect or

* Ss. 1 and 11 repealed by 35 & 36 Vict. c. 97. The Act, except as to notes on demand, is repealed by 26 & 27 Vict. c. 105, and 39 & 40 Vict. c. 69, till Dec. 31, 1877. The Act does not extend to drafts on bankers (23 & 24 Vict. c. 111, s. 19).

48 Geo. 3, c. 88.

refusal, to be allowed by such justice or justices, then such person shall forfeit for every such offence, the sum of forty shillings, to be levied and paid in such manner and by such means as are directed for recovery of other penalties under this Act.

VI. And be it further enacted, That the justice or justices before whom any offender shall be convicted as aforesaid, shall cause the said conviction to be made out, in the manner and form following; (that is to say),

Form of conviction.

"Be it remembered, That on the day of in the year of our Lord *A. B.* having appeared before me [*or* us] one [or more] of His Majesty's justices of the peace [*as the case may be*] for the county, riding, city or place [*as the case may be*], and due proof having been made upon oath by one or more credible witness or witnesses, or by confession of the party [*as the case may be*] is convicted of . [*specifying the offence*]. Given under my hand and seal [*or*, our hands and seals] the day and year aforesaid."

Convictions to be returned to the quarter sessions.

Which conviction the said justice or justices shall cause to be returned to the then next general quarter sessions of the peace of the county, riding, city or place where such conviction was made, to be filed by the clerk of the peace, to remain and be kept among the records of such county, riding, city or place.

Clerks of the peace to give copies of convictions on payment of 1*s.*

VII. Provided always, and be it further enacted, That it shall be lawful for any clerk of the peace for any county, riding, city or place, and he is hereby required, upon application made to him by any person or persons for that purpose, to cause a copy or copies of any conviction or convictions filed by him under the directions of this Act, to be forthwith delivered to such person or persons upon payment of one shiliing for every such copy.

How penalties shall be levied and applied.

VIII. And be it further enacted, That the pecuniary penalties and forfeitures hereby incurred and made payable upon any conviction against this Act, shall be forthwith paid by the person convicted, as follows: One moiety of the forfeiture to the informer, and the other moiety to the poor of the parish or place where the offence shall be committed; and in case such person shall refuse or neglect to pay the same, or to give sufficient security to the satisfaction of such justice or justices to prosecute any appeal against such conviction, such justice or justices shall by warrant under his or their hand and seal or hands and seals, cause the same to be levied by distress and sale of the offender's goods and chattels, together with all costs and charges attending such distress and sale, returning the overplus (if any) to the owner; and which said warrant of distress the said justice or justices shall cause to be made out in the manner and form following; (that is to say),

Form of the warrant of distress.

To the constable, headborough, or tythingman of

Whereas *A. B.* of in the county of is this day convicted before me [*or*, us] one [or more] of His Majesty's justices of the peace [*as the case may be*] for the county of [or, for the riding of the county of *York*, or for the town, liberty, or district of [*as the case may be*] upon the oath of or a credible witness or witnesses [or, by confession of the party, *as the case may be*] for that the said *A. B.* hath [*here set forth the offence*] contrary to the statute in that case made and provided, by reason whereof the said *A. B.* hath forfeited the sum of to be distributed as herein is mentioned, which he hath refused to pay: These are therefore in His Majesty's name, to command you to levy the said sum of by distress of the goods and chattels of him the said *A. B.*, and if within the space of five days next after such distress by you taken, the said sum, together with the reasonable charges of taking the same, shall not be paid, then that you do sell the said goods and chattels so by you distrained, and out of the money arising by such sale, that you do pay one half of the said sum of to of who informed me [or, us, *as the case shall be*] of the said offence, and the other half of the said sum of to the overseer of the poor of the parish, township or place where the offence was committed, to be employed for the benefit of such poor, returning the overplus (if any) upon demand, to the said *A. B.*, the reasonable charges of taking, keeping, and selling the said distress being first deducted; and if sufficient distress cannot be found of the goods and chattels of the said *A. B.* whereon to levy the said sum of that then you certify the same to me [or, us, *as the case shall be*], together with this warrant. Given under my hand and seal [or, our hands and seals] the day of in the year of our Lord

48 Geo. 3, c. 88.

Security may be taken for appearance.

IX. And be it further enacted, That it shall be lawful for such justice or justices to order such offender to be detained in safe custody until return may conveniently be had and made to such warrant of distress, unless the party so convicted shall give sufficient security, to the satisfaction of such justice or justices, for his appearance before the said justice or justices on such day as shall be appointed by the said justice or justices for the day of the return of the said warrant of distress (such day not exceeding five days from the taking of such security); which security the said justice or justices is and are hereby empowered to take by way of recognizance or otherwise.

Offenders may be committed for want of distress.

X. And be it further enacted, That if upon such return no sufficient distress can be had, then and in such case the said justice or justices shall and may commit such offender to the common gaol or house of correction of the county, riding, division or place where the offence shall be committed, for the space of three calendar months, unless the money forfeited shall be sooner paid, or unless or until such offender thinking him or herself aggrieved by such conviction, shall give notice to the informer that he or she intends to appeal to the justices of the peace at the next general quarter sessions of the peace to be holden for the county, riding, or place wherein the offence shall be committed, and shall enter into recognizance before some justice or justices, with two sufficient sureties conditioned to try such appeal, and to abide the order of and pay such costs as shall

48 Geo. 3, c. 88.

be awarded by the justices at such quarter sessions (which notice of appeal, being not less than eight days before the trial thereof, such person so aggrieved is hereby empowered to give); and the said justices at such sessions, upon due proof of such notice being given as aforesaid, and of the entering into such recognizance, shall hear and finally determine the causes and matters of such appeals in a summary way, and award such costs to the parties appealing or appealed against as they the said justices shall think proper; and the determination of such quarter session shall be final, binding, and conclusive, to all intents and purposes.

Convictions not to be removed.

XII. Provided always, That no proceedings to be had, touching the conviction or convictions of any offender or offenders against this Act, shall be quashed for want of form, or be removed by writ of *certiorari* or any other writ or process whatsoever, into any of His Majesty's courts of record at *Westminster*.

General issue may be pleaded.

XIII. And be it further enacted, That if any action or suit shall be commenced against any person or persons for any thing done or acted in pursuance of this Act, then and in every such case such action or suit shall be commenced or prosecuted within three calendar months after the fact committed, and not afterwards; and the same and every such action or suit shall be brought within the county where the fact was committed, and not elsewhere; and the defendant or defendants in every such action or suit shall and may plead the general issue, and give this Act and the special matter in evidence at any trial to be had thereupon, and that the same was done in pursuance and by the authority of this Act; and if the same shall appear to have been so done, or if any such action or suit shall be brought after the time limited for bringing the same, or be brought or laid in any other place than as aforementioned, then the jury shall find for the defendant or defendants; or if the plaintiff or plaintiffs shall become nonsuit, or discontinue his, her, or their action after the defendant or defendants shall have appeared, or if upon demurrer judgment shall be given against the plaintiff or plaintiffs, the defendant or defendants shall and may recover treble costs, and have the like remedy for the recovery thereof as any defendant or defendants hath or have in any other cases by law.

[55 Geo. 3, c. 184.]

An Act for repealing the Stamp Duties on Deeds, Law Proceedings, and other written or printed Instruments, and the Duties on Fire Insurances, and on Legacies and Successions to Personal Estate upon Intestacies, now payable in Great Britain; and for granting other Duties in lieu thereof. [*11th July*, 1815.]

55 Geo. 3, c. 184.

XIV. And be it further enacted, That from and after the thirty-first day of *August* one thousand eight hundred and fifteen, it shall be lawful for any banker or bankers, or other person or persons, who shall have made and issued any promissory notes for the payment to the bearer on demand, of any sum of money not exceeding one hundred pounds each, duly stamped according to the directions of this Act, to reissue the same from time to time, after payment thereof, as often as he, she, or they shall think fit, without being liable to pay any further duty in respect thereof; and that all promissory notes, so to be reissued as aforesaid, shall be good and valid, and as available in the law, to all intents and purposes, as they were upon the first issuing thereof.

Promissory notes to bearer on demand, not exceeding 100*l.* may be reissued by the original makers, without further duty.

XXIII. And be it further enacted, That from and after the thirty-first day of *August* one thousand eight hundred and fifteen, it shall be lawful for the Governor and Company of the Bank of *Scotland*, and the Royal Bank of *Scotland*, and the *British* Linen Company in *Scotland* respectively, to issue their promissory notes for the sums of one pound, one guinea, two pounds, and two guineas, payable to the bearer on demand, on unstamped paper, in the same manner as they were authorized to do by the aforesaid Act of the forty-eighth year of His Majesty's reign; they the said Governor and Company of the Bank of *Scotland*, and the Royal Bank of *Scotland*, and *British* Linen Company, respectively giving such security, and keeping and producing true accounts of all the notes so to be issued by them respectively, and accounting for and paying the several duties payable in respect of such notes, in such and the same manner, in all respects, as is and are prescribed and required by the said last-mentioned Act, with regard to the notes thereby allowed to be issued by them on unstamped paper, and also to reissue such promissory notes respectively, from time to time after the payment thereof, as often as they shall think fit.

The Bank and Royal Bank of Scotland, and British Linen Company, may issue small notes on unstamped paper, accounting for the duties.

XXIV. And be it further enacted, That from and after the tenth day of *October* one thousand eight hundred and fifteen, it shall not be lawful for any banker or bankers, or other person or persons (except the Governor and Company of the Bank of *England*), to issue any promissory notes for money payable to the bearer on demand, hereby charged with a duty and allowed to be reissued as aforesaid, without taking out a licence yearly for that purpose;

Reissuable notes not to be issued by bankers or others without a licence

55 Geo. 3, c. 184.

Regulation respecting licences.

in that behalf by the said commissioners, or the major part of them, which licence shall be granted by two or more of the said Commissioners of Stamps for the time being, or by some person authorized on payment of the duty charged thereon in the Schedule hereunto annexed; and a separate and distinct licence shall be taken out, for or in respect of every town or place where any such promissory notes shall be issued by, or by any agent or agents for or on account of, any banker or bankers or other person or persons; and every such licence shall specify the proper name or names and place or places of abode of the person or persons, or the proper name and description of any body corporate, to whom the same shall be granted, and also the name of the town or place where, and the name of the bank, as well as the partnership, or other name, style, or firm under which such notes are to be issued; and where any such licence shall be granted to persons in partnership, the same shall specify and set forth the names and places of abode of all the persons concerned in the partnership, whether all their names shall appear on the promissory notes to be issued by them, or not; and in default thereof such licence shall be absolutely void; and every such licence which shall be granted between the tenth day of *October* and the eleventh day of *November* in any year, shall be dated on the eleventh day of *October;* and every such licence, which shall be granted at any other time, shall be dated on the day on which the same shall be granted; and every such licence respectively shall have effect and continue in force from the day of the date thereof until the tenth day of *October* following, both inclusive.

No banker to take out more than four licences for any number of towns in *Scotland.*

XXV. Provided always, and be it further enacted, That no banker or bankers, person or persons, shall be obliged to take out more than four licences in all for any number of towns or places in *Scotland;* and in case any banker or bankers, person or persons shall issue such promissory notes as aforesaid, by themselves or their agents, at more than four different towns or places in *Scotland,* then after taking out three distinct licences for three of such towns or places, such banker or bankers, person or persons shall be entitled to have all the rest of such towns or places included in a fourth licence.

Several towns in *England* may be included in one licence, in certain cases.

XXVI. Provided also, and be it further enacted, That where any banker or bankers, person or persons applying for a licence under this Act, would under the said Act of the forty-eighth year of His Majesty's reign have been entitled to have two or more towns or places in *England,* included in one licence, if this Act had not been made, such banker or bankers, person or persons, shall have and be entitled to the like privilege under this Act.

Persons applying for licences to deliver specimens of their notes.

Penalty for issuing notes without licence, 100*l.*

XXVII. And be it further enacted, That the banker or bankers, or other person or persons applying for any such licence as aforesaid, shall produce and leave with the proper officer, a specimen of the promissory notes proposed to be issued by him or them, to the intent that the licence may be framed accordingly; and if any banker or bankers, or other person or persons (except the said Governor and Company of the Bank of *England*) shall issue or cause to be issued by any agent, any promissory note for money payable to the bearer on demand, hereby charged with a duty, and allowed to be reissued as aforesaid, without being licensed so to do in the manner aforesaid, or at any other town or place, or under any other name, style, or firm, than shall be specified in his or their licence, the banker or bankers, or other person or persons so offending, shall for every such offence forfeit the sum of one hundred pounds. 55 Geo. 3, c 184.

Licences to continue in force notwithstanding alteration in partnerships.

XXVIII. And be it further enacted, That where any such licence as aforesaid shall be granted to any persons in partnership, the same shall continue in force for the issuing of promissory notes duly stamped, under the name, style, or firm therein specified, until the tenth day of *October* inclusive following the date thereof, notwithstanding any alteration in the partnership.

SCHEDULE, Part I.

LICENCE to be taken out *yearly* by any banker or bankers, or other person or persons who shall issue any promissory notes for money payable to the bearer on demand, and allowed to be re-issued	£30 0 0

[1 & 2 Geo. 4, c. 72.]

1 & 2 Geo. 4, c. 72.

An Act to establish an Agreement with the Governor and Company of the Bank of Ireland, for advancing the Sum of Five hundred thousand Pounds Irish Currency; and to empower the said Governor and Company to enlarge the Capital Stock or Fund of the said Bank to Three Millions. [2nd *July*, 1821.]

Persons in partnerships residing 50 miles from Dublin may borrow any sum of money on bills and notes payable on demand, without being liable to penalty.

VI. And be it further enacted, That from and after the passing of this Act, it shall and may be lawful for any number of persons in *Ireland*, united or to be united in societies or partnerships, and residing and having their establishments or houses of business at any place not less than fifty miles distant from *Dublin*, to borrow, owe, or take up any sum or sums of money on their bills or notes payable on demand, and to make and issue such notes or bills accordingly, payable on demand, at any place in *Ireland* exceeding the distance of fifty miles from *Dublin*, all the individuals composing such societies or copartnerships being liable and responsible for the due payment of such bills and notes; and such persons shall not be subject or liable to any penalty for the making or issuing such bills or notes; any thing in an Act made in the Parliament of *Ireland*, holden in the twenty-first and twenty-second years of the reign of His late Majesty King *George* the Third, intituled *An Act for establishing a bank by the name of the Governor and Company of the Bank of* Ireland, to the contrary notwithstanding.

21 & 22 G. 3. (I.)

No other privilege to be granted to partnerships.

VII. Provided always, and be it enacted, That no further or other power, privilege, or authority shall, previous to the said first day of *January* one thousand eight hundred and thirty-eight, nor until after payment to the said governor and company of all sum and sums of money which now are or hereafter shall or may become due to them from Government, be granted to any copartnership or society of persons whatsoever, contrary to the laws now in force for establishing and regulating the Bank of *Ireland*, save and except the power of enabling such societies and copartnerships as aforesaid, residing and carrying on their business not less than fifty miles from *Dublin*, to sue and be sued in the name of a public officer, should Parliament hereafter think fit to grant such a power.

[6 Geo. 4, c. 42.]

An Act for the better Regulation of Copartnerships of certain Bankers in Ireland. [*10th June*, 1825.]

6 Geo. 4, c. 42.

II. And whereas an Act was passed in the session of Parliament holden in the first and second year of His present Majesty's reign, intituled *An Act to establish an Agreement with the Governor and Company of the Bank of* Ireland, *for advancing the Sum of Five hundred thousand Pounds*, Irish *Currency, and to empower the said Governor and Company to increase the Capital Stock or Fund of the said Bank to Three Millions*, and it is expedient that the said last-recited Act should be altered and amended, be it further enacted, That from and after the passing of this Act, it shall and may be lawful for any number of persons, united or to be united in any society or copartnership in *Ireland*, consisting of more than six in number, and not having the establishments or houses of business of such society or copartnership at any place or places less than fifty miles distant from *Dublin*, to carry on the trade and business of bankers, in like manner as copartnerships of bankers, consisting of not more than six in number, may lawfully do; and to borrow, owe, or take up any sum or sums of money on their bills or notes, payable on demand, or at any time after date, or after sight, and to make and issue such notes or bills accordingly at any place in *Ireland*, exceeding the distance of fifty miles from *Dublin* all the individuals composing such societies or copartnerships being liable and responsible for the due payment of all such bills and notes, in manner hereinafter provided; any thing contained in an Act made in the Parliament of *Ireland*, in the twenty-first and twenty-second years of the reign of His late Majesty King *George* the Third, intituled *An Act for establishing a Bank, by the Name of the Governor and Company of the Bank of* Ireland, or in the hereinbefore recited Act of the first and second years of His present Majesty's reign, or in any other Act or Acts, or any law, usage, or custom to the contrary in anywise notwithstanding.

1 & 2 G. 4, c. 72.

Societies of persons more than six in number may be bankers in Ireland at places fifty miles from Dublin, and issue bills and notes, every member being responsible.

Notwithstanding 21 & 22 G. 3, c. 16 (I.) or 1 & 2 G. 4, c. 72.

III. And be it further enacted, That it shall and may be lawful for any such society or copartnership, from time to time to have, employ, or appoint any agent or agents to do and transact, on behalf of any such society or copartnership, all such business, matters, and things as such society or copartnership may lawfully do, and as are not contrary to any Act or Acts now in force, and to the provisions of this Act.

Societies or copartnerships may appoint agents.

V. Provided always, and be it further enacted, That nothing contained in this Act or in any other Act or Acts shall extend or be construed to prevent any person or persons whatever, whether resident in *Great Britain* or *Ireland*, from being or becoming a member or members of any such society or copartnership in *Ireland* as afore-

Persons resident in Great Britain, &c, may be members of such copartnerships.

6 Geo. 4 c. 42.

said, or from being or becoming a subscriber and contributor, or subscribers and contributors, to the stock and capital of any such society or copartnership; and that any such society or copartnership which shall or may have been formed or begun to be formed under or by virtue of the provisions contained in the hereinbefore recited Acts of the first and second years and the fifth year of the reign of His present Majesty, and of which any person or persons shall be or shall become a member or members, or to which any such person or persons shall become a subscriber or subscribers or contributor or contributors as aforesaid, shall be or be deemed and taken, to all intents and purposes, to be a society or copartnership of persons united in *Ireland*, within the true intent and meaning of this Act; any thing in this Act or in any other Act or Acts of Parliament, or any law, usage, or custom to the contrary notwithstanding.

Such banking partnerships shall deliver and register, at the Stamp Office in Dublin, an account of the names of the firm, the several partners therein, and the public officers thereof.

VI. And be it further enacted, That between the twenty-fifth day of *March* in any year, and the twenty-fifth day of *March* following, an account or return shall be made out by the secretary or some other officer of every such society or copartnership, and shall be signed by such secretary or other officer, and shall be verified by the oath of such officer taken before any justice of the peace, (and which oath any justice of the peace is hereby authorized and empowered to administer), according to the form contained in the Schedule Number One to this Act annexed; and in every such account or return there shall be set forth the true name or firm of such society or copartnership, and also the names and places of abode of all the partners concerned or engaged in such society or copartnership, as the same respectively appear on the books of such society or copartnership, and the firm and name of and every bank or banks established or to be established by such society or copartnership, and also the names of two or more individuals of such society or partnership who shall be resident in *Ireland*, each and every of whom shall respectively be considered as a public officer of such society or copartnership, and the title of office or other description of every such individual respectively, in the name of any one of whom such society or copartnership shall sue and be sued, as hereinafter provided, and also the name of every town and place where any such bills or notes shall be issued by any such society or copartnership, or by any agent or agents of any such society or copartnership; and every such account or return shall be produced at the Stamp Office in *Dublin*, and an entry and registry thereof shall be made in a book or books to be kept for that purpose at the said Stamp Office, by some person or persons to be appointed for that purpose by the Commissioners of Stamp Duties; and if, after the passing of this Act, any such society or copartnership shall omit or neglect to deliver at the Stamp Office in *Dublin* such account and return as is by this Act required, such society or copartnership shall, for each and every week they shall so neglect to make such account and return, forfeit the sum of five hundred pounds.

Stamp Office shall give certificates of such

VII. And be it further enacted, That whenever any entry and registry of the firm or name of any such society or copartnership shall be made at the Stamp Office, in manner aforesaid, at any time between the twenty-fifth day of *March* in any year, and the twenty-fifth day of *March* following, a certificate of such entry or registry shall be granted by the said Commissioners of Stamps or by some person deputed and authorized by the said commissioners for that purpose, to the society or copartnership by or on whose behalf such entry or registry shall be made, and such certificate shall be written on vellum, parchment, or paper, duly stamped with the stamp required by law for certificates to be taken out yearly by any banker or bankers in *Ireland;* and a separate and distinct certificate on a separate piece of vellum, parchment, or paper, with a separate and distinct stamp, shall be granted for and in respect of every town and place where any such bill or note shall be issued by any such society or copartnership, or by any agent or agents, for or on account of such society or copartnership; and every such certificate shall specify the proper firm, style, title, or name of such society or copartnership, under which such notes are to be issued, and also the name of the town or place, or the several towns or places where such notes are to be issued, and the Christian and surname and place of abode and title of office or other description of the several individuals named respectively, as the public officers of such society or copartnership in the name of any one of whom such society or copartnership shall sue and be sued; and every certificate shall be dated on the day on which the same shall be granted, and shall have effect and continue in force from the day of the date thereof, until the twenty-fifth day of *March* following, both inclusive, and no longer, and shall be sufficient evidence of the appointment and authority of such public officers respectively.

6 Geo. 4, c. 42.

entry, to be in force to 25th March ensuing.

Account and registry of new officers or members in the course of any year may be made without further certificate.

IX. Provided also, and be it enacted, That it shall and may be lawful for the secretary or other officer of any such society or copartnership, as occasion may require, from time to time, in the year ending on the twenty-fifth day of *March* one thousand eight hundred and twenty-six, and in any succeeding year, without obtaining any further certificate for such year, and without payment of any further stamp duty for such year, to make out upon oath, in manner hereinbefore directed, an account or return of the name or names of any new or additional public officer or public officers, and also the name or names of any person or persons who may have ceased to be members of such society or copartnership, and also the name or names of any person or persons who may have become a member or members of such society or copartnership, either in addition to or in the place or stead of any former member or members, in the form expressed in the Schedule hereunto annexed, marked Number Two; and such accounts or returns shall be from time to time produced and entered or registered at the Stamp Office in *Dublin*, in like manner as is hereinbefore required with respect to the original account or return to be made for any such year, in behalf of such society or copartnership.

Societies or partnerships shall sue and be sued in the name of their public officers.

X. And be it further enacted, That all actions and suits, and also all petitions to found any sequestration, or any commission of bankruptcy, against any person or persons who may be at any time indebted to any such society or copartnership, and all proceedings at law or in equity under any sequestration or commission of bank-

6 Geo. 4, c. 42.

ruptcy, and all other proceedings at law and in equity, to be commenced or instituted for or on behalf of any such society or copartnership, against any person or persons, bodies politic or corporate, or others, whereby members of such society or copartnership or otherwise, for recovering any debts or enforcing any claims or demands due to such society or copartnership, or for any other matter relating to the concerns of such society or copartnership, shall and lawfully may, from and after the passing of this Act, be commenced or instituted and prosecuted in the name of any one of the public officers nominated as aforesaid for the time being of such society or copartnership, as the nominal plaintiff or petitioner for and on behalf of such society or copartnership: and that all actions or suits and proceedings at law or in equity, to be commenced or instituted by any person or persons, bodies politic or corporate, or others, whether members of such society or copartnership or otherwise, against such society or copartnership, shall and lawfully may be commenced, instituted, and prosecuted against any one of the public officers nominated as aforesaid for the time being of such society or copartnership, as the nominal defendant for and on behalf of such society or copartnership; and that all indictments, informations, and prosecutions, by or on behalf of such society or copartnership, for any stealing or embezzlement of any money, goods, effects, bills, notes, securities, or other property of or belonging to such society or copartnership, or for any fraud, forgery, crime, or offence committed against or with intent to injure or defraud such society or copartnership, shall and lawfully may be had, preferred, and carried on in the name of any one of the public officers nominated as aforesaid for the time being of such society or copartnership; and that in all indictments and informations to be had or preferred by or on behalf of such society or copartnership, against any person or persons whomsoever, notwithstanding such person or persons may happen to be a member or members of such society or copartnership, it shall be lawful and sufficient to state the money, goods, effects, bills, notes, securities, or other property of such society or copartnership, to be the money, goods, effects, bills, notes, securities, or other property of any one of the public officers nominated as aforesaid for the time being of such society or copartnership; and that any forgery, fraud, crime, or other offence committed against or with intent to injure or defraud such society or copartnership, shall and lawfully may in such indictment or indictments, notwithstanding as aforesaid, be laid or stated to have been committed against or with intent to injure or defraud any one of the public officers nominated as aforesaid for the time being of such society or copartnership, and any offender or offenders may thereupon be lawfully convicted for any such forgery, fraud, crime, or offence; and that in all other allegations, indictments, informations or other proceedings of any kind whatsoever, in which it otherwise might or would have been necessary to state the names of the persons composing such society or copartnership, it shall and may be lawful and sufficient to state the name of any one of the public officers nominated as aforesaid for the time being of such society or copartnership; and the death, resignation, removal, or any act of such public officer shall not abate or prejudice any such action, suit, indictment, information, prosecution, or other proceeding commenced against or by or on behalf of such society or copartnership, but the same may be con-

6 Geo. 4, c. 42.

tinued, prosecuted, and carried on in the name of any other of the public officers of such society or copartnership for the time being.

Not more than one action for the recovery of one demand.

XI. And be it further enacted, That no person or persons, or body or bodies politic or corporate, having or claiming to have any demand upon or against any such society or corporation, shall bring more than one action or suit in respect of such demand; and the proceedings in any action or suit by or against any one of the public officers nominated as aforesaid for the time being of such society or copartnership, may be pleaded in bar of any other action or actions, suit or suits, for the same demand, by or against any other of the public officers of such society or copartnership.

Parties obtaining judgment in Ireland may authorize the acknowledgment of like judgment in Great Britain.

XII. And be it further enacted, That it shall and may be lawful for any person or persons obtaining a judgment in any of His Majesty's courts of record in *Dublin*, against any such public officer for the time being of any such society or copartnership; and such person or persons is and are hereby empowered, by warrant under hand and seal, reciting the effect of such judgment, to authorize any attorney or attorneys in *Great Britain* to appear for such public officer in an action of debt to be brought in any court of record in *Great Britain* against such public officer, at the suit of the person or persons obtaining such judgment in *Ireland*, and thereupon to confess judgment forthwith in such action for a sum equal to the sum for which judgment shall have been so obtained in *Ireland*, together with the costs of such proceeding; and such judgment shall be thereupon entered up of record in the said court in *Great Britain* against such public officer, and shall have the like effect in *Great Britain* against the members of such society or copartnership as the original judgment so obtained in *Ireland*.

And in like manner parties obtaining judgment in Great Britain may proceed thereon in Ireland.

XIII. And be it further enacted, That it shall and may be lawful for any person or persons obtaining a judgment in any court of law in *Great Britain* against any such public officer for the time being of any such society or copartnership in *Ireland*, and such person or persons is and are hereby empowered, by warrant under hand and seal, reciting the effect of such judgment, to authorize any attorney or attorneys in *Ireland* to appear for such public officer in an action of debt, to be brought in any court of record in *Ireland* against such public officer, at the suit of the person or persons obtaining such judgment in *Great Britain*, for a sum equal to the sum for which judgment shall have been so obtained in *Great Britain*, together with the costs of such proceeding; and such judgment shall be thereupon entered up of record in the said court in *Ireland* against such public officer, and shall have the same effect in *Ireland* against the members of such society or copartnership as the original judgment so obtained in *Great Britain*.

Decrees and orders of a court of equity against the public officer

XIV. And be further enacted, That all and every decree or decrees, order or orders, made or pronounced in any suit or proceeding in any court of equity, against any public officer of any such society or copartnership, shall have the like effect and operation

6 Geo. 4, c. 42.

to take effect against the society or copartnership.

upon and against the property and funds of such society or copartnership, and upon and against the persons and property of every member thereof, as if all the members of such society or copartnership were parties before the court to and in any such suit or proceeding; and it shall and may be lawful for any court in which such order or decree shall have been made, to cause such order and decree to be enforced against any, every, or any member of such society or copartnership, in like manner as if every member of such society or copartnership were parties before such court, to and in such suit or proceeding.

41 G. 3, and 5 G. 4, to extend to proceedings to which the public officer shall be a party.

XV. And be it further enacted, That an Act passed in the forty-first year of the reign of King *George* the Third, intituled *An Act for the more speedy and effectual Recovery of Debts due to His Majesty, His Heirs and Successors, in Right of the Crown of the United Kingdom of* Great Britain *and* Ireland, *and for the better Administration of Justice within the same*; and also an Act passed in the fifth year of His present Majesty, intituled *An Act to amend an Act of the Forty-first Year of the Reign of His late Majesty King* George *the Third, for the more speedy and effectual Recovery of Debts due to His Majesty, His Heirs and Successors, in Right of the Crown of the United Kingdom of* Great Britain *and* Ireland, *and for the better Administration of Justice within the same,* shall extend to all suits, matters, and proceedings in any court of equity in *England* or *Ireland*, in which any public officer of such society or copartnership shall be a party, in like manner as if all the members of such society or copartnership were parties before the court in such suits, matters, and proceedings.

Decrees, judgments, and orders to be registered, and have effect in Scotland.

XVI. And be it further enacted, That it shall and may be lawful for any person or persons obtaining any judgment in any court of law, or decree or order in any court of equity, against any public officer of any such society or copartnership, to produce an office copy of such judgment, decree or order, under the seal of the court in which judgment, decree, or order shall have been obtained, to one of the principal clerks in the Court of Session in *Scotland*, or his deputy, for registration there, and such judgment, decree, or order shall thereupon be registrable and registered there, in like manner as a bond executed according to the law of *Scotland*, with a clause of registration therein contained, and execution may and shall pass upon a decree to be interponed thereto, in like manner as execution passes upon a decree interponed to such bond, and shall have the like effect upon and against all and every or any of the members of such society or copartnership, as if such members had executed such bond.

Judgments against such public officer in such actions shall operate against the society or copartnership.

XVII. And be it further enacted, That all and every judgment and judgments which shall at any time after the passing of this Act be had or recovered or entered up as aforesaid in any action, suit, or proceedings in law or equity against any public officer of any such society or copartnership, shall have the like effect and operation upon and against the property of such society or copartnership, and upon and against the property of every member thereof, as if such judgment or judgments had been recovered or obtained against such society or copartnership themselves; and that the bankruptcy, insolvency, or stopping payment of any such public officer for the time being of such society or copartnership in his individual character or capacity, shall not be nor be construed to be the bankruptcy, insolvency, or stopping payment of such society or copartnership, and that such society or copartnership, and every member thereof, and the capital stock and effects of such society or copartnership, and the effects of every member of such society or copartnership, shall in all cases, notwithstanding the bankruptcy, insolvency, or stopping payment of any such public officer, be attached and attachable, and be in all respects liable to the lawful claims and demands of the creditor and creditors of such society or copartnership, as if no such bankruptcy, insolvency, or stooping payment of such public officer of such society or copartnership had happened or taken place.

6 Geo. 4, c. 42.

Execution upon judgment in any such action may be issued against any member of the society or copartnership.

XVIII. And be it further enacted, That execution upon any judgment in any action obtained against any public officer for the time being, of any such society or copartnership, whether as plaintiff or defendant, may be issued against any member or members for the time being of such society or copartnership; and that in case any such execution against any member or members for the time being of such society or copartnership shall be ineffectual for obtaining payment and satisfaction of the amount of such judgment, it shall be lawful for the party or parties so having obtained judgment against such public officer for the time being, to issue execution against any person or persons who was or were a member or members of such society or copartnership at the time when the contract or contracts, or engagement or engagements on which such judgment may have been obtained, was or were entered into: Provided always, that no such execution as last mentioned shall be issued without leave first granted, on motion in open court, by the court in which such judgment shall have been obtained, and which motion shall be made on notice to the person or persons sought to be charged, nor after the expiration of three years next after any such person or persons shall have ceased to be a member or members of such society or copartnership.

Officer, &c., in such cases indemnified.

XIX. Provided always, and be it enacted, That every such public officer, in whose name any such suit or action shall have been commenced, prosecuted, or defended, and every person or persons against whom execution upon any judgment obtained or entered up as aforesaid in any such action shall be issued as aforesaid, shall always be reimbursed and fully indemnified for all loss, damages, costs and charges, without deduction, which any such officer or person may have incurred by reason of such execution, out of the funds of such society or copartnership, or in failure thereof, by contribution from the other members of such society or copartnership, as in the ordinary cases of copartnerships.

Members may be indicted for fraud on societies or copartnerships.

XX. And be it further enacted, That if any person or persons being a member or members of any copartnership of bankers in *Ireland*, shall steal or embezzle any money, goods, effects, bills, notes, securities, or other property of or belonging to such society or copartnership, or shall commit any fraud, forgery, crime, or offence

6 Geo. 4, c. 42,

against or with intent to injure or defraud such society or copartnership, such member or members shall be liable to indictment, information, prosecution, or other proceeding, in the name of any one of the public officers nominated for the time being of such society or copartnership, for every such fraud, forgery, crime, or offence, and may thereupon be lawfully convicted, as if such person or persons had not been, or was or were not a member or members of such society or copartnership; any law, usage, or custom to the contrary notwithstanding.

Act extended to existing partners for the time being.

XXI. And be it further enacted, That this Act and the powers and provisions herein contained shall extend and be at all times construed to extend to any society or copartnership for banking in *Ireland*, consisting of more than six persons in number, and to the members thereof for the time being, during the continuance of such society or copartnership, whether the same do or shall consist of all or some only of the persons who originally were, or at the time of the passing of this Act may have subscribed to, or may be members of any such society or copartnership, or of all or some only of those persons, together with some other persons, or entirely of some other persons, all of whom became or may become members of such society or copartnership, at any time after the original institution thereof, or subsequent to the passing of this Act.

Members of societies or copartnerships may transfer shares, and such transfers shall be registered at the Stamp Office;

XXII. And be it further enacted, That it shall and may be lawful for any and every member of any and every such society or copartnership, their respective executors, administrators, and assigns, to sell and transfer any share or shares, orportion or portions of, or the entire stock or interest which any such member respectively is or may be respectively entitled to or possessed of in such society or copartnership, and the property and funds thereof, subject to such regulations and under such restrictions as may be required by the constitution of such society or copartnership; and whenever any such sale and transfer shall be made, a return or account thereof, in the form set forth in the Schedule, marked Number Three, to this Act annexed, shall be made upon oath, in manner hereinbefore directed by the secretary or other officer of such society or copartnership, and shall be from time to time produced, entered, and registered at the Stamp Office in *Dublin*, in the book containing the then last register of such society or copartnership; and the person or persons to whom such transfer shall be made shall be and stand, in all respects and to all intents and purposes, in the place and stead of the person or persons making such transfer: Provided always, that nothing herein contained shall be deemed, taken, or construed to discharge or release any member or members making any such transfer as aforesaid, of or from the being liable to or responsible for the due payment of the bills, notes, and other engagements of such society or copartnership, existing at the time of the entry or register of such transfer, or of or from any action, suit, judgment, or execution in respect of the same, according to the provisions of this Act: Provided always, that no such transfer as aforesaid shall take place without the consent of the directors for the time being of any such society or copartnership;

but not to affect their liability while members.

nor shall any transfer be valid unless signed by one or more of such directors, as the court of directors for the time being of such society or copartnership may from time to time determine, in testimony of the court of directors having consented to such transfer. 6 Geo. 4, c. 42.

Clerks of bankers embezzling money, &c., felony.

XXIII. And be it further enacted, That if any cashier or clerk of any banker or bankers, or of any society or copartnership or bankers, or of any merchant or merchants, or of any officer or officers intrusted with the receipt or custody of public money in *Ireland*, shall without the consent of such banker or bankers, or society or copartnership, or merchant or merchants, or officer or officers, embezzle or take away money, cash, notes, or securities for money to the value of fifty pounds sterling belonging to such banker or bankers, or society or copartnership, or merchant or merchants, or intrusted to the care of such officer or officers with an intent to defraud such banker or bankers, or society or copartnership, or merchant or merchants, or officer or officers, such cashier or clerk shall, upon conviction thereof, be adjudged to be guilty of felony, and shall be transported for life or for any term of years as the court before whom such offender shall be convicted shall think fit to order and adjudge; and every person who shall receive such money, notes, or securities for money, from such cashier or clerk, knowing them to be so taken away with intent to defraud such banker or bankers, or society or copartnership, or merchant or merchants, or officer or officers, shall be likewise adjudged to be guilty of felony, and shall be transported for life, or for any term of years as the court before whom such offender shall be convicted shall think fit to order and adjudge.

Recovery of penalties.

XXIV. And be it further enacted, That every penalty, forfeiture, and sum of money to be forfeited under this Act, by reason of any omission or neglect of any of the regulations hereinbefore enacted, may be sued for and recovered in any of His Majesty's courts of record at *Dublin* by any person, by action of debt, bill, plaint, or information, provided such action be commenced within twelve calendar months next after such offence committed, in which action there shall not be any essoign, or wager of law, nor more than one imparlance allowed; and all sums to be recovered shall be applied, one moiety thereof to the use of the person who shall sue for the same, and the other moiety to the use of His Majesty, his heirs and successors.

Irish Act 19 & 20 G. 3, c. 25, declared not to extend to bankers.

XXV. And be it declared and enacted, That so much of an Act made in the Parliament of *Ireland* in the nineteenth and twentieth years of the reign of His late Majesty King *George* the Third, intituled *An Act to explain an Act, intituled 'An Act to prevent Frauds committed by Bankrupts,'* whereby it is enacted, that all mercantile companies or partnerships shall set forth in their several invoices, bills of parcels, promissory notes, and custom-house entries, the names of the several individuals of which such partnership or company doth consist, doth not and shall not be construed to extend to any society or copartnership of bankers in *Ireland*; any custom or usage to the contrary in anywise notwithstanding.

6 Geo. 4, c. 42.

This Act not to affect matters otherwise legal.

XXVI. Provided always and be it enacted, That nothing in this Act contained shall be construed to prevent any such society or copartnership from doing any act, matter, or thing which, but for the express provision of this Act, they would by law be entitled to do.

SCHEDULE, No. 2.

Return or Account, to be entered at the Stamp Office in Dublin, on behalf of [*name the society or copartnership*], in pursuance of an Act passed in the sixth year of the reign of King *George* the Fourth, intituled [*insert the title of this Act*], viz.

Names of any and every new or additional public officer of the said society or copartnership, viz.

A. B. in the room of *C. D.* deceased or removed, [*as the case may be*], [*set forth every name*].

Names of any and every person who may have ceased to be a member of such society or copartnership, viz. [*set forth every name*].

Names of any and every person who may have become a new member of such society or copartnership [*set forth every name*].

A. B. of [*Secretary or other officer*] of the above-named society or copartnership, maketh oath and saith, That the above doth contain the name and place of abode of any and every person who hath become or been appointed a public officer of the above society or copartnership, and also the name and place of abode of any and every person who hath ceased to be a member of the said society or copartnership, and of any and every person who hath become a member of the said society or copartnership since the registry of the said society or copartnership on the day of last, as the same respectively appear on the books of the said society or copartnership, and to the best of the information, knowledge, and belief of this deponent.

Sworn, &c.

[7 Geo. 4, c. 6.]

7 Geo. 4 c. 6.

An Act to limit, and after a certain Period to prohibit, the issuing of Promissory Notes under a limited Sum in England. [*22nd March*, 1826.]

Penalty 20*l.* on issuing, &c. before 5th April, 1829, any notes under 5*l.* payable on demand, except such as are

III. And be it further enacted, That if any body politic or corporate, or any person or persons, shall from and after the passing of this Act, and before the fifth day of *April* one thousand eight hundred and twenty-nine, make, sign, issue, or reissue in *England* any promissory note payable on demand to the bearer thereof, for any sum of money less than the sum of five pounds, except such promissory note or form of note as aforesaid, of any banker or bankers, or banking companies, or person or persons duly licensed in that behalf, which shall have been duly stamped before the fifth day of *February* one thousand eight hundred and twenty-six; and except such promissory note of the Governor and Company of the Bank of *England* as shall have been or shall be made out and bear date before the said tenth day of *October* one thousand eight hundred and twenty-six; or if any body politic or corporate, or person or persons, shall, after the said fifth day of *April* one thousand eight hundred and twenty-nine, make, sign, issue, or reissue in *England* any promissory note in writing, payable on demand to the bearer thereof, for any sum of money less than five pounds, then and in either of such cases every such body politic or corporate, or person or persons, so making, signing, issuing, or reissuing any such promissory note as aforesaid, except as aforesaid, shall for every such note so made, signed, issued, or reissued, forfeit the sum of twenty pounds.

7 Geo. 4, c. 6.

allowed by this Act; or on issuing any note whatever on demand for less than 5*l.* after 5th April, 1829.

IV. And be it further enacted, That if any body politic or corporate, or person or persons, in *England*, shall, from and after the passing of this Act, publish, utter, or negotiate any promissory or other note (not being a note payable to bearer on demand, as is hereinbefore mentioned), or any bill of exchange, draft, or undertaking in writing, being negotiable or transferable for the payment of twenty shillings, or above that sum and less than five pounds, or on which twenty shillings, or above that sum, and less than five pounds, shall remain undischarged, made, drawn, or indorsed in any other manner than as is directed by the said Act passed in the seventeenth year of the reign of His late Majesty; every such body politic or corporate, or person or persons, so publishing, uttering, or negotiating any such promissory or other note (not being such note payable to bearer on demand as aforesaid), bill of exchange, draft, or undertaking in writing as aforesaid; shall forfeit and pay the sum of twenty pounds.

Penalty 20*l.* on uttering, &c. any notes payable to order or bills of exchange under 5*l.* (not payable on demand), otherwise than according to the directions of 17 G. 3, c. 30.

V. And be it further enacted, That the penalties, which shall or may be incurred under any of the provisions of this Act, and which are in lieu of the penalties imposed by the said Act of the seventeenth year of His late Majesty, may be sued for, recovered, levied, mitigated, and applied in such and the same manner as any other penalties imposed by any of the laws now in force relating to the duties under the management of the Commissioners of Stamps.

Penalties may be recovered under the Stamp Acts.

VI. And be it further enacted, That the Governor and Company of the Bank of *England* shall and they are hereby required, from time to time, from and after the passing of this Act, on the fifteenth day of each month in each and every year preceding the fifth of *April* one thousand eight hundred and twenty-nine (or if such days or any of them, shall happen on a *Sunday*, then on the sixteenth day of any such month respectively), to cause a true and perfect account in writing to be taken and attested by the proper officer, of the total number of notes of the said governor and company, under the value of five pounds, which shall have been issued during each and every week of the preceding month, ending on the *Saturday* next preceding such days respectively, from *Monday* until *Saturday* in each and every week, both inclusive, distinguishing the respective denominations and values of such notes, and also stating the total amount actually in circulation at the close of business on every such *Saturday*, and

Bank of England shall deliver to Treasury, monthly accounts of their notes under 5*l.* in circulation during each week of every such month.

7 Geo. 4, c. 6.

shall cause such account to be transmitted and delivered within three days after such fifteenth day of each and every such *Saturday*, and shall cause such account to be transmitted and delivered within three days after such fifteenth day of each and every such month as aforesaid, to one of the secretaries of the Commissioners of His Majesty's Treasury, who shall and they are hereby required to cause the same to be published forthwith in the *London Gazette*, and shall also, and are hereby required to cause a copy of such account to be laid before both Houses of Parliament at each and every of the periods above mentioned, if Parliament shall at such times be sitting, or otherwise, within ten days after the next meeting of Parliament.

Such Accounts to be published in the 'Gazette,' and laid before Parliament, if sitting.

Commissioners of Stamps shall not stamp notes under 5*l.* payable on demand.

VII. And be it further enacted, That from and after the passing of this Act, the Commissioners of Stamps shall not be empowered to provide any stamp or stamps for expressing or denoting the duty or duties payable in *England* upon any promissory note for the payment to the bearer on demand of any sum of money less than the sum of five pounds; nor shall it be lawful for the said commissioners, or any of their officers, to stamp any promissory note, or the form of any promissory note, for the payment to the bearer on demand of any sum of money less than five pounds.

Indemnity.

VIII. And whereas the said Commissioners of Stamps did, in pursuance of directions in that behalf from the Commissioners of His Majesty's Treasury of the United Kingdom of *Great Britain* and *Ireland*, on the third day of *February* last past, order their officers not to stamp any more promissory notes for circulation in *England* of less value than five pounds; and it is expedient that the said Commissioners of the Treasury and the Commissioners of Stamps, and all persons acting under their authority in that behalf, should be indemnified for having so respectively acted without the authority of Parliament; be it therefore enacted, That the said Commissioners of His Majesty's Treasury, and the said Commissioners of Stamps respectively, and all persons who shall by their order, in pursuance of the said directions, have refused to stamp any such notes, or to do any matter or thing relating thereto, shall be and are and is hereby saved harmless, indemnified, and discharged in respect thereof, as well against the King's Majesty, his heirs and successors, as against all and every other persons and person; and that all suits and proceedings whatsoever touching or concerning any matter discharged by this Act, shall be and the same are hereby made void and of no effect, to all intents and purposes; any law, statute, or usage to the contrary notwithstanding.

Act not to extend to orders drawn by any person on his banker.

IX. Provided always, and be it further enacted, That nothing herein contained shall extend to any draft or order drawn by any person or persons on his, her, or their banker or bankers, or on any person or persons acting as such banker or bankers, for the payment of money held by such banker or bankers, person or persons, to the use of the person or persons by whom such draft or order shall be drawn.

Notes under 20*l.* to be payable at the bank where issued.

X. And be it further enacted, That every promissory note payable to bearer on demand, for any sum of money under the sum of twenty pounds, which shall be made and issued after the fifth day of *April* one thousand eight hundred and twenty-nine, shall be made payable at the bank or place where the same shall be so made and issued as aforesaid: Provided always, that nothing herein contained shall extend to prevent any such promissory note from being made payable at several places, if one of such places shall be the bank or place where the same shall be so issued as aforesaid. 7 Geo. 4, c. 6.

[7 Geo. 4, c. 46.]

An Act for the better regulating Copartnerships of certain Bankers in England; and for amending so much of an Act of the Thirty-ninth and Fortieth Years of the Reign of His late Majesty King George the Third, intituled An Act for establishing an agreement with the Governor and Company of the Bank of England, for advancing the sum of three millions towards the supply for the service of the year one thousand eight hundred, as relates to the same. [26*th May*, 1826.] 7 Geo. 4, c. 46.

Whereas an Act was passed in the thirty-ninth and fortieth years of the reign of His late Majesty King *George* the Third, intituled *An Act for establishing an agreement with the Governor and Company of the Bank of* England, *for advancing the sum of three millions towards the supply for the service of the year one thousand eight hundred:* And whereas it was, to prevent doubts as to the privilege of the said governor and company, enacted and declared in the said recited Act, that no other bank should be erected, established, or allowed by Parliament; and that it should not be lawful for any body politic or corporate whatsoever, erected or to be erected, or for any other persons united or to be united in covenants or partnership, exceeding the number of six persons, in that part of *Great Britain* called *England*, to borrow, owe, or take up any sum or sums of money on their bills or notes payable on demand, or at any less time than six months from the borrowing thereof, during the continuance of the said privilege to the said governor and company, who were thereby declared to be and remain a corporation, with the privilege of exclusive banking, as before recited; but subject nevertheless to redemption on the terms and conditions in the said Act specified: And whereas the Governor and Company of the Bank of *England* have consented to relinquish so much of their exclusive privilege as prohibits any body politic or corporate, or any number of persons exceeding six, in *England*, acting in copartnership, from borrowing, owing, or taking up any sum or sums of money on their bills or notes payable on demand, or at any less time than six months from the borrowing thereof; provided that such body politic or corporate, or persons united in covenants or partnerships, exceeding the number of six persons in each copartnership, shall have the whole of their banking establishments and carry on their business as bankers at any place or places in *England* exceeding the distance of sixty- 39 & 40 Geo. 3, c. 28.

7 Geo. 4, c. 46.

five miles from *London*, and that all the individuals composing such corporations or copartnerships, carrying on such business, shall be liable to and responsible for the due payment of all bills and notes issued by such corporations or copartnerships respectively: Be it therefore enacted by the King's most excellent Majesty, by and with the advice and consent of the Lords spiritual and temporal, and Commons, in this present Parliament assembled, and by the authority of the same, That from and after the passing of this Act it shall and may be lawful for any bodies politic or corporate erected for the purposes of banking, or for any number of persons united in covenants or copartnership, although such persons so united or carrying on business together shall consist of more than six in number, to carry on the trade or business of bankers in *England*, in like manner as copartnerships of bankers consisting of not more than six persons in number may lawfully do; and for such bodies politic or corporate, or such persons so united as aforesaid, to make and issue their bills or notes at any place or places in *England* exceeding the distance of sixty-five miles from *London*, payable on demand, or otherwise at some place or places specified upon such bills or notes, exceeding the distance of sixty-five miles from *London*, and not elsewhere, and to borrow, owe, or take up any sum or sums of money on their bills or notes so made and issued at any such place or places as aforesaid: Provided always, that such corporations or persons carrying on such trade or business of bankers in copartnership shall not have any house of business or establishment as bankers in *London*, or at any place or places not exceeding the distance of sixty-five miles from *London;* and that every member of any such corporation or copartnership shall be liable to and responsible for the due payment of all bills and notes which shall be issued, and for all sums of money which shall be borrowed, owed, or taken up by the corporation or copartnership of which such person shall be a member, such person being a member at the period of the date of the bills or notes, or becoming or being a member before or at the time of the bills or notes being payable, or being such member at the time of the borrowing, owing, or taking up of any sum or sums of money upon any bills or notes by the corporation or copartnership, or while any sum of money on any bills or notes is owing or unpaid, or at the time the same became due from the corporation or copartnership; any agreement, covenant, or contract to the contrary notwithstanding.

Copartnerships of more than six in number may carry on business as bankers in England, 65 miles from London, provided they have no establishment as bankers in London, and that every member shall be liable for the payment of all bills, &c.

II. Provided always, and be it further enacted, That nothing in this Act contained shall extend or be construed to extend to enable or authorize any such corporation, or copartnership exceeding the number of six persons, so carrying on the trade or business of bankers as aforesaid, either by any member of or person belonging to any such corporation or copartnership, or by any agent or agents, or any other person or persons on behalf of any such corporation or copartnership, to issue or reissue in London, or at any place or places not exceeding the distance of sixty-five miles from *London*, any bill or note of such corporation or copartnership, which shall be payable to bearer or demand, or any bank post bill; nor to draw upon any partner or agent, or other person or persons who may be resident in *London*, or at any place or places not exceeding the distance of sixty-five miles from *London*, any bill of exchange which shall be payable on demand, or which shall be for a less

This Act not to authorize copartnerships to issue, within the limits mentioned, any bills payable on demand; nor to draw bills upon any partner, &c., so resident, for less than 50*l.*;

amount than fifty pounds: Provided also, that it shall be lawful, notwithstanding any thing herein or in the said recited Act contained, for any such corporation or copartnership to draw any bill of exchange for any sum of money amounting to the sum of fifty pounds or upwards, payable either in *London* or elsewhere, at any period after date or after sight.

7 Geo. 4, c. 46.

III. Provided also, and be it further enacted, That nothing in this Act contained shall extend or be construed to extend to enable or authorize any such corporation, or copartnership exceeding the number of six persons, so carrying on the trade or business of bankers in *England* as aforesaid, or any member, agent or agents of any such corporation or copartnership, to borrow, owe, or take up in *London*, or at any place or places not exceeding the distance of sixty-five miles from *London*, any sum or sums of money on any bill or promissory note of any such corporation or copartnership payable on demand, or at any less time than six months from the borrowing thereof, nor to make or issue any bill or bills of exchange or promissory note or notes of such corporation or copartnership contrary to the provisions of the said recited Act of the thirty-ninth and fortieth year of King *George* the Third, save as provided by this Act in that behalf: Provided also, that nothing herein contained shall extend or be construed to extend to prevent any such corporation or copartnership, by any agent or person authorized by them, from discounting in *London*, or elsewhere, any bill or bills of exchange not drawn by or upon such corporation or copartnership, or by or upon any person on their behalf.

nor to borrow money, or take up or issue bills of exchange, contrary to the provisions of the recited Act, except as herein provided.

IV. And be it further enacted, That before any such corporation, or copartnership exceeding the number of six persons, in *England*, shall begin to issue any bills or notes, or borrow, owe, or take up any money, on their bills or notes, an account or return shall be made out, according to the form contained in the Schedule marked (A.) to this Act annexed, wherein shall be set forth the true names, title, or firm of such intended or existing corporation or copartnership, and also the names and places of abode of all the members of such corporation, or of all the partners concerned or engaged in such copartnership, as the same respectively shall appear on the books of such corporation or copartnership, and the name or firm of every bank or banks established or to be established by such corporation or copartnership, and also the names and places of abode of two or more persons, being members of such corporation or copartnership, and being resident in *England*, who shall have been appointed public officers of such corporation or copartnership, together with the title of office or other description of every such public officer respectively, in the name of any one of whom such corporation shall sue and be sued as hereinafter provided, and also the name of every town and place where any of the bills or notes of such corporation or copartnership shall be issued by any such corporation, or by their agent or agents; and every such amount or return shall be delivered to the Commissioners of Stamps, at the Stamp Office in *London*, who shall cause the same to be filed and kept in the said Stamp Office, and an entry and registry thereof to be made in a book or books to be there kept for that purpose by some person or persons to be appointed by the said commissioners in that behalf, and which book or books any

Such copartnerships shall, before issuing any notes, &c., deliver at the Stamp Office in London an account containing the name of the firm, &c.

7 Geo. 4, c. 46. person or persons shall from time to time have liberty to search and inspect on payment of the sum of one shilling for every search.

Account to be verified by secretary.

V. And be it further enacted, That such account or return shall be made out by the secretary or other person, being one of the public officers appointed as aforesaid, and shall be verified by the oath of such secretary or other public officer, taken before any justice of the peace, and which oath any justice of the peace is hereby authorized and empowered to administer; and that such account or return shall, between the twenty-eighth day of *February* and the twenty-fifth day of *March* in every year after such corporation or copartnership shall be formed, be in like manner delivered by such secretary or other public officer as aforesaid, to the Commissioners of Stamps, to be filed and kept in the manner and for the purposes as hereinbefore mentioned.

Certified copies of returns to be evidence of the appointment of the public officers, &c.

VI. And be it further enacted, That a copy of any such account or return so filed or kept and registered at the Stamp Office, as by this Act is directed, and which copy shall be certified to be a true copy under the hand or hands of one or more of the Commissioners of Stamps for the time being, upon proof made that such certificate has been signed with the handwriting of the person or persons making the same, and whom it shall not be necessary to prove to be a commissioner or commissioners, shall in all proceedings, civil or criminal, and in all cases whatsoever, be received in evidence as proof of the appointment and authority of the public officers named in such account or return, and also of the fact that all persons named therein as members of such corporation or copartnership were members thereof at the date of such account or return.

Commissioners of Stamps to give certified copies of affidavits, on payment of 10*s*.

VII. And be it further enacted, That the said Commissioners of Stamps for the time being shall and they are hereby required, upon application made to them by any person or persons requiring a copy certified according to this Act, of any such account or return as aforesaid, in order that the same may be produced in evidence or for any other purpose, to deliver to the person or persons so applying for the same such certified copy, he, she, or they paying for the same the sum of ten shillings and no more.

Account of new officers or members in the course of any year to be made.

VIII. Provided also, and be it further enacted, That the secretary or other officer of every such corporation or copartnership shall and he is hereby required, from time to time, as often as occasion shall render it necessary, make out upon oath, in manner hereinbefore directed, and cause to be delivered to the Commissioners of Stamps as aforesaid, a further account or return according to the form contained in the Schedule marked (B.) to this Act annexed, of the name or names of any person or persons who shall have been nominated or appointed a new or additional public officer or public officers of such corporation or copartnership, and also of the name or names of any person or persons who shall have ceased to be members of such corporation or copartnership, and also of the name or names of any person or persons who shall have become a member or members of such corporation or copartnership, either in addition to or in the place or stead of any former member or members thereof, and of the name or names of any new or additional town or towns, place or places, where such bills or notes are or are intended to be issued, and where the same are to be made payable; and such further accounts or returns shall from time to time be filed and kept, and entered and registered at the Stamp Office in *London*, in like manner as is hereinbefore required with respect to the original or annual account or return hereinbefore directed to be made.

7 Geo. 4, c. 46.

Copartnerships shall sue and be sued in the name of their public officers.

IX. And be it further enacted, That all actions and suits, and also all petitions to found any commission of bankruptcy against any person or persons, who may be at any time indebted to any such copartnership carrying on business under the provisions of this Act, and all proceedings at law or in equity under any commission of bankruptcy, and all other proceedings at law or in equity to be commenced or instituted for or on behalf of any such copartnership against any person or persons, bodies politic or corporate, or others, whether members of such copartnership or otherwise, for recovering any debts or enforcing any claims or demands due to such copartnership, or for any other matter, relating to the concerns of such copartnership, shall and lawfully may, from and after the passing of this Act, be commenced or instituted and prosecuted in the name of any one of the public officers nominated as aforesaid for the time being of such copartnership, as the nominal plaintiff or petitioner for and on behalf of such copartnership; and that all actions or suits, and proceedings at law or in equity, to be commenced or instituted by any person or persons, bodies politic or corporate, or others, whether members of such copartnership or otherwise, against such copartnership, shall and lawfully may be commenced, instituted, and prosecuted against any one or more of the public officers nominated as aforesaid for the time being of such copartnership, as the nominal defendant for and on behalf of such copartnership; and that all indictments, informations, and prosecutions by or on behalf of such copartnership, for any stealing or embezzlement of any money, goods, effects, bills, notes, securities, or other property of or belonging to such copartnership, or for any fraud, forgery, crime, or offence committed against or with intent to injure or defraud such copartnership, shall and lawfully may be had, preferred, and carried on in the name of any one of the public officers nominated as aforesaid for the time being of such copartnership; and that in all indictments and informations to be had or preferred by or on behalf of such copartnership against any person or persons whomsoever, notwithstanding such person or persons may happen to be a member or members of such copartnership, it shall be lawful and sufficient to state the money, goods, effects, bills, notes, securities, or other property of such copartnership, to be the money, goods, effects, bills, notes, securities, or other property of any one of the public officers nominated as aforesaid for the time being of such copartnership; and that any forgery, fraud, crime, or other offence committed against or with intent to injure or defraud any such copartnership, shall and lawfully may in such indictment or indictments, notwithstanding as aforesaid, be laid or stated to have been committed against or with intent to injure or defraud any one of the public officers nominated as aforesaid for the time being of such copartnership; and any offender or offenders may thereupon be lawfully convicted for any such forgery, fraud, crime, or offence; and that in all other allegations, indictments, informations, or other proceedings of any kind

7 Geo. 4, c. 46.

whatsoever, in which it otherwise might or would have been necessary to state the names of the persons composing such copartnership, it shall and may be lawful and sufficient to state the name of any one of the public officers nominated as aforesaid for the time being of such copartnership; and the death, resignation, removal, or any act of such public officer, shall not abate or prejudice any such action, suit, indictment, information, prosecution, or other proceeding commenced against or by or on behalf of such copartnership, but the same may be continued, prosecuted, and carried on in the name of any other of the public officers of such copartnership for the time being.

Not more than one action for the recovery of one demand.

X. And be it further enacted, That no person or persons, or body or bodies politic or corporate, having or claiming to have any demand upon or against any such corporation or copartnership, shall bring more than one action or suit, in case the merits shall have been tried in such action or suit, in respect of such demand; and the proceedings in any action or suit, by or against any one of the public officers nominated as aforesaid for the time being of any such copartnership, may be pleaded in bar of any other action or actions, suit or suits, for the same demand, by or against any other of the public officers of such copartnership.

Decrees of a court of equity against the public officer to take effect against the copartnership.

XI. And be it further enacted, That all and every decree or decrees, order or orders, made or pronounced in any suit or proceedings in any court of equity against any public officer of any such copartnership carrying on business under the provisions of this Act, shall have the like effect and operation upon and against the property and funds of such copartnership, and upon and against the persons and property of every or any member or members thereof, as if every or any such members of such copartnership were parties members before the court to and in any such suit or proceeding; and that it shall and may be lawful for any court in which such order or decree shall have been made, to cause such order and decree to be enforced against every or any member of such copartnership, in like manner as if every member of such copartnership were parties before such court to and in such suit or proceeding, and although all such members are not before the court.

Judgments against such public officer shall operate against the copartnership.

XII. And be it further enacted, That all and every judgment and judgments, decree or decrees, which shall at any time after the passing of this Act be had or recovered or entered up as aforesaid, in any action, suit, or proceedings in law or equity against any public officer of any such copartnership, shall have the like effect and operation upon and against the property of such copartnership, and upon and against the property of every such member thereof as aforesaid, as if such judgment or judgments had been recovered or obtained against such copartnership; and that the bankruptcy, insolvency, or stopping payment of any such public officer for the time being of such copartnership, in his individual character or capacity, shall not be nor be construed to be the bankruptcy, insolvency, or stopping payment of such copartnership; and that such copartnership and every member thereof, and the capital stock and effects of such copartnership, and the effects of every member of such copartnership, shall in all cases, notwithstanding the bankruptcy, insolvency, or

7 Geo. 4, c. 46.

stopping payment of any such public officer, be attached and attachable, and be in all respects liable to the lawful claims and demands of the creditor and creditors of such copartnership, or of any member or members thereof, as if no such bankruptcy, insolvency, or stopping payment of such public officer of such copartnership had happened or taken place.

Execution upon judgment may be issued against any member of the copartnership.

XIII. And be it further enacted, That execution upon any judgment in any action obtained against any public officer for the time being of any such corporation or copartnership carrying on the business of banking under the provisions of this Act, whether as plaintiff or defendant, may be issued against any member or members for the time being of such corporation or copartnership; and that in case any such execution against any member or members for the time being of any such corporation or copartnership shall be ineffectual for obtaining payment and satisfaction of the amount of such judgment, it shall be lawful for the party or parties so having obtained judgment against such public officer for the time being, to issue execution against any person or persons who was or were a member or members of such corporation or copartnership at the time when the contract or contracts or engagement or engagements in which such judgment may have been obtained was or were entered into, or became a member at any time before such contracts or engagements were executed, or was a member at the time of the judgment obtained: Provided always, that no such execution as last mentioned shall be issued without leave first granted, on motion in open court, by the court in which such judgment shall have been obtained, and when motion shall be made on notice to the person or persons sought to be charged, nor after the expiration of three years next after any such person or persons shall have ceased to be a member or members of such corporation or copartnership.

Officer, &c., in such cases indemnified.

XIV. Provided always, and be it further enacted, That every such public officer in whose name any such suit or action shall have been commenced, prosecuted, or defended, and every person or persons against whom execution upon any judgment obtained or entered up as aforesaid in any such action shall be issued as aforesaid, shall always be reimbursed and fully indemnified for all loss, damages, costs, and charges, without deduction, which any such officer or person may have incurred by reason of such execution, out of the funds of such copartnership, or in failure thereof, by contribution from the other members of such copartnership, as in the ordinary cases of copartnership.

Governor and Company of the Bank of England may empower agents to carry on banking business at any place in England.

XV. And to prevent any doubts that might arise whether the said governor and company, under and by virtue of their charter, and the several Acts of Parliament which have been made and passed in relation to the affairs of the said governor and company, can lawfully carry on the trade or business of banking, otherwise than under the immediate order, management, and direction of the court of directors of the said governor and company; be it therefore enacted, That it shall and may be lawful for the said governor and company to authorize and empower any committee or committees, agent or agents, to carry on the trade and business of bank-

7 Geo. 4 c. 46.

ing, for and on behalf of the said governor and company, at any place or places in that part of the United Kingdom called *England*, and for that purpose to invest such committee or committees, agent or agents, with such powers of management and superintendence, and such authority to appoint cashiers and other officers and servants as may be necessary or convenient for carrying on such trade and business as aforesaid; and for the same purpose to issue to such committee or committees, agent or agents, cashier or cashiers, or other officer or officers, servant or servants, cash, bills of exchange, bank post bills, bank notes, promissory notes, and other securities for payment of money: Provided always, that all such acts of the said governor and company shall be done and exercised in such manner as may be appointed by any bye-laws, constitutions, orders, rules, and directions from time to time hereafter to be made by the general court of the said governor and company in that behalf, such bye-laws not being repugnant to the laws of that part of the United Kingdom called *England;* and in all cases where such bye-laws, constitutions, orders, rules, or directions of the said general court shall be wanting, in such manner as the governor, deputy governor, and directors, or the major part of them assembled, whereof the said governor or deputy governor is always to be one, shall or may direct, such directions not being repugnant to the laws of that part of the United Kingdom called *England;* any thing in the said charter or Acts of Parliament, or other law, usage, matter, or thing to the contrary thereof notwithstanding: Provided always, that in any place where the trade and business of banking shall be carried on for and on behalf of the said Governor and Company of the Bank of *England*, any promissory note issued on their account in such place shall be made payable in coin in such place as well as in *London*.

Copartnerships may issue unstamped notes, on giving bond.

XVI. And be it further enacted, That if any corporation or copartnership carrying on the trade or business of bankers under the authority of this Act, shall be desirous of issuing and reissuing notes in the nature of bank notes, payable to the bearer on demand, without the same being stamped as by law is required, it shall be lawful for them so to do on giving security by bond to His Majesty, his heirs and successors, in which bond two of the directors, members, or partners of such corporation or copartnership shall be the obligors, together with the cashier or cashiers, or accountant or accountants employed by such corporation or copartnership, as the said Commissioners of Stamps shall require; and such bonds shall be taken in such reasonable sums as the duties may amount unto during the period of one year, with condition to deliver to the said Commissioners of Stamps, within fourteen days after the fifth day of *January*, the fifth day of *April*, the fifth day of *July*, and the tenth day of *October* in every year, whilst the present stamp duties shall remain in force, a just and true account, verified upon the oaths or affirmations of two directors, members, or partners of such corporation or copartnership, and of the said cashier or cashiers, accountant or accountants, or such of them as the said Commissioners of Stamps shall require, such oaths or affirmations to be taken before any justice of the peace, and which oaths or affirmations any justice of the peace is hereby authorized and empowered to administer, of the amount or value of all their promissory notes in circulation on some given day in every week, for the space of one quarter of a year prior to the quarter day immediately preceding the delivery of such account, together with the average amount or value thereof according to such account; and also to pay or cause to be paid into the hands of the receivers general of stamp duties in *Great Britain*, as a composition for the duties which would otherwise have been payable for such promissory notes issued within the space of one year, the sum of seven shillings for every one hundred pounds, and also for the fractional part of one hundred pounds of the said average amount or value of such notes in circulation, according to the true intent and meaning of this Act; and on due performance thereof such bond shall be void; and it shall be lawful for the said commissioners to fix the time or times of making such payment, and to specify the same in the condition to every such bond; and every such bond may be required to be renewed from time to time, at the discretion of the said commissioners or the major part of them, and as often as the same shall be forfeited, or the party or parties to the same, or any of them, shall die, become bankrupt or insolvent, or reside in parts beyond the seas.

7 Geo. 4, c. 46.

No corporation compelled to take out more than four licences.

XVII. Provided always, and be it further enacted, That no such corporation or copartnership shall be obliged to take out more than four licences for the issuing of any promissory notes for money payable to the bearer on demand, allowed by law to be reissued in all for any number of towns or places in *England;* and in case any such corporation or copartnership shall issue such promissory notes as aforesaid, by themselves or their agents, at more than four different towns or places in *England*, then after taking out three distinct licences for three of such towns or places, such corporation or copartnership shall be entitled to have all the rest of such towns or places included in a fourth licence.

Penalty on copartnership neglecting to send returns, 500*l.*

XVIII. And be it further enacted, That if any such corporation or copartnership exceeding the number of six persons in *England*, shall begin to issue any bills or notes, or to borrow, owe, or take up any money on their bills or notes, without having caused such account or return as aforesaid to be made out and delivered in the manner and form directed by this Act, or shall neglect or omit to cause such account or return to be renewed yearly and every year, between the days or times hereinbefore appointed for that purpose, such corporation or copartnership so offending shall, for each and every week they shall so neglect to make such account and return, forfeit the sum of five hundred pounds; and if any secretary or other officer of such corporation or copartnership shall make out or sign any false account or return, or any account or return which shall not truly set forth all the several particulars by this Act required to be contained or inserted in such account or return, the corporation or copartnership to which such secretary or other officer so offending shall belong shall for every such offence forfeit the sum of five hundred pounds, and the said secretary or other officer so offending shall also for every such offence forfeit the sum of one hundred pounds; and if any such secretary or other officer making out or signing any such account or return as aforesaid, shall knowingly and wilfully make a false oath of or concerning any of the

Penalties for making false returns.

7 Geo. 4, c. 46.

False oath perjury.

matters to be therein specified and set forth, every such secretary or other officer so offending, and being thereof lawfully convicted, shall be subject and liable to such pains and penalties as by any law now in force persons convicted of wilful and corrupt perjury are subject and liable to.

Penalty on copartnership for issuing bills payable on demand; or drawing bills of exchange payable on demand, or for less than 50*l.*; or borrowing money on bills, except as herein provided.

XIX. And be it further enacted, That if any such corporation or copartnership exceeding the number of six persons, so carrying on the trade or business of bankers as aforesaid, shall, either by any member of or person belonging to any such corporation or copartnership, or by any agent or agents, or any other person or persons on behalf of any such corporation or copartnership, issue or reissue in *London*, or at any place or places not exceeding the distance of sixty-five miles from *London*, any bill or note of such corporation or copartnership which shall be payable on demand; or shall draw upon any partner or agent, or other person or persons who may be resident in *London*, or at any place or places not exceeding the distance of sixty-five miles from *London*, any bill of exchange which shall be payable on demand, or which shall be for a less amount than fifty pounds; or if any such corporation or copartnership, exceeding the number of six persons, so carrying on the trade or business of bankers in *England* as aforesaid, or any member, agent or agents of any such corporation or copartnership, shall borrow, owe, or take up in *London*, or at any place or places not exceeding the distance of sixty-five miles from *London*, any sum or sums of money on any bill or promissory note of any such corporation or copartnership payable on demand, or at any less time than six months from the borrowing thereof, or shall make or issue any bill or bills of exchange or promissory note or notes of such corporation or copartnership contrary to the provisions of the said recited Act of the thirty-ninth and fortieth years of King *George* the Third, save as provided by this Act, such corporation or copartnership so offending, or on whose account or behalf any such offence as aforesaid shall be committed, shall for every such offence forfeit the sum of fifty pounds.

Not to affect the rights of Bank of England, except as herein specially altered.

XX. Provided also, and be it further enacted, That nothing in this Act contained shall extend or be construed to extend to prejudice, alter, or affect any of the rights, powers, or privileges of the said Governor and Company of the Bank of *England;* except as the said exclusive privilege of the said governor and company is by this Act specially altered and varied.

Act may be altered.

XXII. And be it further enacted, That this Act may be altered, amended, or repealed by any Act or Acts to be passed in this present session of Parliament.

SCHEDULE (B).

Return or account to be entered at the Stamp Office in London, on behalf of [*name the corporation or copartnership*] in pursuance of an Act passed in the seventh year of the reign of King *George* the Fourth, intituled [*insert the title of this Act*], *viz.*

Names of any and every new or additional public officer of the said corporation or copartnership; *viz.* 7 Geo. 4, c. 46.

A. B. in the room of *C. D.* deceased or removed [*as the case may be*] [*set forth every name*].

Names of any and every person who may have ceased to be a member of such corporation or copartnership; *viz.* [*set forth every name*].

Names of any and every person who may have become a new member of such corporation or copartnership [*set forth every name*].

Names of any additional towns or places where bills or notes are to be issued, and where the same are to be made payable.

A. B. of secretary [*or other officer*] of the above named corporation or copartnership, maketh oath and saith, That the above doth contain the name and place of abode of any and every person who hath become or been appointed a public officer of the above corporation or copartnership, and also the name and place of abode of any and every person who hath ceased to be a member of the said corporation or copartnership, and of any and every person who hath become a member of the said copartnership since the registry of the said corporation or copartnership on the day of last, as the same respectively appear on the books of the said corporation or copartnership, and to the best of the information, knowledge, and belief of this deponent.

Sworn before me, the day of at in the county of

C. D. justice of the peace in and for the said county.

[7 Geo. 4, c. 67.]

An Act to regulate the Mode in which certain Societies or Copartnerships for Banking in Scotland may sue and be sued. [26*th May*, 1826.] 7 Geo. 4, c. 67.

Whereas the practice has prevailed in *Scotland* of instituting societies possessing joint stocks, the shares of which are either conditionally or unconditionally transferable, for the purpose of carrying on the business of banking; and it is expedient that every such society or copartnership should be enabled to sue and be sued in the name of its manager, cashier, or other principal officer; be it therefore enacted by the King's most excellent Majesty, by and with the advice and consent of the Lords spiritual and temporal, and Commons, in this present Parliament assembled, and by the authority of the same, That it shall and may be lawful for every such joint stock society or copartnership, already established or that may hereafter be established in *Scotland* for the purposes of banking, to sue and be sued in the name of the manager, cashier, or other principal

Banking copartnerships in Scotland may sue and be sued in

7 Geo. 4, c. 67.

officer of such society or copartnership, provided that such joint stock society or copartnership shall observe the regulations prescribed by this Act.

the name of their manager, &c.

Such societies shall yearly deliver, at the Stamp Office in Edinburgh, an account, containing the name of the firm, &c.

II. And be it further enacted, That every such joint stock society or copartnership already formed shall, between the twenty-fifth day *May* and the twenty-fifth day of *July* in this and each succeeding year, and every such joint stock society or copartnership hereafter to be formed, shall, before such joint stock society or copartnership shall begin to carry on business, and thereafter in each succeeding year, between the said twenty-fifth day of *May* and the twenty-fifth day of *July*, cause an account or return to be made out according to the form contained in the schedule marked A to this Act annexed, wherein shall be set forth the true names, title, or firm of such intended or existing society or copartnership, and also the names and places of abode of all the members of such society, or of all the partners concerned or engaged in such copartnership, as the same respectively shall appear on the books of such society or copartnership, and the name or firm of every bank or banks established or to be established by such society or copartnership, and also the name and place of abode of the manager, cashier, or other principal officer, in the name of whom such society or copartnership shall sue and be sued, as hereinafter provided, and also the name of every town and place where any of the bills or notes of such society or copartnership shall be issued by any such society or copartnership, or by their agent or agents ; and every such account or return shall be delivered to the head collector of stamp duties at the Stamp Office in *Edinburgh*, who shall cause the same to be filed and kept in the Stamp Office there, and an entry and registry thereof to be made in a book or books to be there kept for that purpose, and which book or books any person or persons shall from time to time have liberty to search and inspect, on payment of the sum of one shilling for every search.

Accounts to be verified on oath.

III. And be it further enacted, That such account or return shall be made out by the officer named as aforesaid, and shall be verified by the oath of such officer taken before any justice of the peace, and which oath any justice of the peace is hereby authorized and empowered to administer, and that such account or return shall, between the twenty-fifth day of *May* and the twenty-fifth day of *July* in every year, be in like manner delivered by such officer as aforesaid to the said collector, to be filed and kept in the manner and for the purposes as hereinbefore mentioned.

Certified copies of such returns to be evidence of the appointment of the public officers, &c.

IV. And be it further enacted, That a copy of any such account or return, so filed or kept and registered at the Stamp Office, as by this Act is directed, and which copy shall be certified to be a true copy, under the hand of the said collector, or of the comptroller of the stamp duties at *Edinburgh*, shall in all proceedings, civil or criminal, and in all cases whatsoever, be received in evidence as proof of the appointment and authority of the officer named in such account or return, and also of the fact that all persons named therein as members of such society or copartnership were members thereof at the date of such account or return.

V. And be it further enacted, That the said collector or comptrollor for the time being shall, and he is hereby required, upon application made to him by any person or persons requiring a copy certified according to this Act, of any such account or return as aforesaid, in order that the same may be produced inevidence, or for any other purpose, to deliver to the person or persons so applying for the same such certified copy, he, she, or they paying for the same the sum of ten shillings and no more.

7 Geo. 4, c. 67.

Commissioners of Stamps to give certified copies of affidavits.

VI. Provided also, and be it further enacted, That the manager or other officer of every such society or copartnership shall, and he is hereby required from time to time, as often as occassion shall render it necessary, make out upon oath, in manner hereinbefore directed, and cause to be delivered to the said collector as aforesaid, a further account or return according to the form contained in the schedule marked (B) to this Act annexed, of the name of any person who shall have been nominated or appointed a new or additional officer of such society or copartnership, in whose name the same shall sue and be sued, and also of the name or names of any person or persons who shall have ceased to be members of such society or copartnership, and also of the name or names of person or persons who shall have become a member or members of such society or copartnership, either in addition to or in the place or stead of any former member or members thereof, and of the name or names of any new or additional town or towns, place or places, where such bills or notes are or are intended to be issued, and where the same are to be made payable; and such furthur accounts or returns shall from time to time be filed and kept, and entered and registered at the Stamp Office in *Edinburgh* in like manner as is hereinbefore required with respect to the original or annual account or return hereinbefore directed to be made.

Account of new officers or members in the course of any year to be made.

VII. And be it further enacted, That all actions and suits and also all petitions to found any sequestration in *Scotland*, or commission of bankruptcy in *England*, against any person or persons who may be at any time indebted to any such copartnership carrying on business under the provisions of this Act, and all proceedings at law or in equity under any sequestration or commission of bankruptcy, and all other proceedings at law or in equity to be commenced or instituted for or on behalf of any such copartnership, against any person or persons, bodies politic or corporate, or others, whether members of such copartnership or otherwise, for recovering any debts or enforcing any claims or demands due to such copartnership, or for any other matter relating to the concerns of such copartnership, shall and lawfully may, from and after the passing of this Act, be commenced or instituted and prosecuted in the name of the officer named as aforesaid for the time being of such copartnership, as the nominal pursurer, plaintiff, or petitioner, for and on behalf of such copartnership, and that all actions or suits, and proceedings at law or in equity, to be commenced or instituted by any person or persons, bodies politic or corporate, or others, whether members of such copartnership or otherwise, against such copartnership, shall and lawfully may be commenced, instituted, and prosecuted against the officer named as aforesaid for the time being of such copartnership, as the nominal defender or defendant for and on

Copartnerships shall sue and be sued in the name of their officer.

7 Geo. 4, c. 67.

behalf of such copartnership; and that all indictments, informations, and prosecutions by or on behalf of such copartnership, for any stealing or embezzlement of any money, goods, effects, bills, notes, securities, or other property of or belonging to such copartnership, or for any fraud, forgery, crime, or offence committed against or with intent to injure or defraud such copartnership, may be had, preferred, and carried on in the name of the officer named as aforesaid for the time being of such copartnership; and that in all indictments and informations to be had or preferred by or on behalf of such copartnership against any person or persons whomsoever, it shall be lawful and sufficient to state the money, goods, effects, bills, notes, securities, or other property of such copartnership to be the money, goods, effects, bills, notes, securities, or other property of the officer named as aforesaid, for the time being, of such copartnership; and that any forgery, fraud, crime, or other offence committed against or with intent to injure or defraud any such copartnership, shall and lawfully may in such indictment or indictments, notwithstanding as aforesaid, be laid or stated to have been committed against or with intend to injure or defraud the officer named as aforesaid, for the time being, of such copartnership; and any offender or offenders may thereupon be lawfully convicted for any such forgery, fraud, crime, or offence; and that in all other allegations, indictments, informations, or other proceedings of any kind whatsoever, in which it otherwise might or would have been necessary to state the names of the persons composing such copartnership, it shall and may be lawful and sufficient to state the name of the officer named as aforesaid, for the time being, of such copartnership; and the death, resignation, removal, or any act of such officer shall not abate or prejudice any such action, suit, indictment, information, prosecution, or other proceeding commenced against, or by or on behalf of such copartnership, but the same may be continued, prosecuted, and carried on in the name of any other manager, cashier, or other principal officer of such copartnership for the time being.

Not more than one action for the recovery of one demand.

VIII. And be it further enacted, That no person or persons, or body or bodies politic or corporate, having or claiming to have any demand upon or against any such society or copartnership, shall bring more than one action or suit, in case the merits shall have been tried in such action or suit, in respect of such demand; and the proceedings in any action or suit by or against the officer named as aforesaid for the time being, of any such copartnership, may be pleaded in bar of any other action or actions, suit or suits, for the same demand, by or against such copartnership.

Decrees of a court of equity against the officer to take effect against the copartnership.

IX. And be it further enacted, That all and every decree or decrees, order or orders, interlocutor or interlocutors, made or pronounced in any suit or proceeding in any court of law or equity against the officer named as aforesaid of any such copartnership carrying on business under the provisions of this Act, shall have the like effect and operation upon and against the property and funds of such copartnership, and upon and against the persons and property of every or any member or members thereof, as if every or any such members of such copartnership were parties before the court to and in any such suit or proceeding; and such order, interlocutor, and decree shall be enforced against every or any member of such copartnership, in like manner as if every such member of such copartnership was a party before such court to and in such suit or proceeding. 7 Geo. 4, c. 67.

X. And be it further enacted, That all and every judgment and judgments, decree or decrees, in any action, suit or proceedings in law or equity against the officer named as aforesaid of any such copartnership, shall have the like effect and operation upon and against the property of such copartnership, and upon and against the property of every such member thereof as aforesaid, as if such judgment or judgments had been recovered or obtained against such copartnership; and that the bankruptcy, insolvency, or stopping payment of such officer for the time being of such copartnership, in his individual character or capacity, shall not be nor be construed to be the bankruptcy, insolvency, or stopping payment of such copartnership; and that such copartnership and every member thereof, and the capital stock and effects of such copartnership, and the effects of every member of such copartnership, shall in all cases, notwithstanding the bankruptcy, insolvency, or stopping payment of any such officer, be attached and attachable, and be in all respects liable to the lawful claims and demands of the creditor and creditors of such copartnership, or of any member or members thereof, as if no such bankruptcy, insolvency, or stopping payment of such officer had happened or taken place. Judgments against officer shall operate against the copartnership.

XI. Provided always, and be it further enacted, That such officer in whose name any such suit or action shall have been commenced, prosecuted, or defended, and every person or persons against whom execution upon any judgment obtained or entered up as aforesaid in any such action shall be issued as aforesaid, shall always be reimbursed and fully indemnified for all loss, damages, costs, and charges which such officer or person may have incurred by reason of such execution, out of the funds of such copartnership, or in failure thereof, from the funds of the other members of such copartnership, as in the ordinary cases of copartnership. Officer, &c. in such cases indemnified.

XIII. Provided always, and be it further enacted, That no such society or copartnership shall be obliged to take out more than four licences for the issuing of any promissory notes for money payable to the bearer on demand, allowed by law to be reissued, in all, for any number of towns or places in *Scotland;* and in case any such society or copartnership shall issue such promissory notes as aforesaid, by themselves or their agents, at more than four different towns or places in *Scotland,* then after taking out three distinct licences for three of such towns or places, such society or copartnership shall be entitled to have all the rest of such towns or places included in a fourth licence. Limiting the number of licences to be taken out for branches.

XIV. And be it further enacted, That if any such society or copartnership, carrying on the business of bankers under the authority of this Act, shall issue any bills or notes, or to borrow or owe or take up any money on their bills or notes, without having caused such account or return as aforesaid to be made out and delivered in the manner and form directed by this Act, or shall neglect or omit to cause such account or return to be renewed yearly and every year Penalty on copartnership neglecting to send returns, and penalties for making false returns.

7 Geo. 4, c. 67.

between the days or times hereinbefore appointed for that purpose, such society or copartnership so offending shall, for each and every week they shall so neglect to make such account and return forfeit the sum of five hundred pounds; and if any officer of such society or copartnership shall make out or sign any false account or return, or any account or return which shall not truly set forth all the several particulars by this Act required to be contained or inserted in such account or return, the society or copartnership to which such officer so offending shall belong, shall for every such offence forfeit the sum of five hundred pounds, and the said officer so offending shall also for every such offence forfeit the sum of one hundred pounds; and if any such officer making out or signing any such account or return as aforesaid, shall knowingly and wilfully make a false oath of or concerning any of the matters to be therein specified and set forth, every such officer so offending, and being thereof lawfully convicted, shall be subject and liable to such pains and penalties as by any law now in force persons convicted of wilful and corrupt perjury are subject and liable to.

Penalties, how to be recovered.

XV. And be it further enacted, That all pecuniary penalties and forfeitures imposed by this Act shall and may be sued for and recovered in His Majesty's Court of Exchequer at *Edinburgh*, in the same manner as penalties incurred under any Act or Acts relating to stamp duties may be sued for and recovered in such court.

Act may be altered this session.

XVI. And be it further enacted, That this Act may be altered, amended, or repealed by any Act or Acts to be passed in this present session of Parliament.

SCHEDULE (B).

Return or Account to be entered at the Stamp Office in Edinburgh, on behalf of [*name the society or copartnership*], in pursuance of an Act passed in the seventh year of the reign of King George the Fourth, intituled [*insert the title of this Act*]; *videlicet*,

Name of any new or additional officer of the said society or copartnership in whose name the same shall sue and be sued; *videlicet*, *A. B.* in the room of *C. D.* deceased or removed [*as the case may be*].

Names of any and every person who may have ceased to be a member of such society or copartnership; *videlicet* [*set forth every name*].

Names of any and every person who may have become a new member of such society or copartnership [*set forth every name*].

Names of any additional towns or places where bills or notes are to be issued, and where the same are to be made payable.

A. B. of manager [*or other officer*] of the above-named society or copartnership, maketh oath and saith, That the above doth contain the name and place of abode of any person who hath become or been appointed an officer of the above society or copartnership, in whose name the same may sue and be sued, and also the name and place of abode of any and every person who hath ceased to be a member of the said society or copartnership, and of any and every person who hath become a member of the said copartnership, since the registry of the said society or copartnership on the day of last, as the same respectively appear on the books of the said society or copartnership, and to the best of the information, knowledge, and belief of this deponent.

7 Geo. 4, c. 67.

Sworn before me, the day of at in the county of

C. D. justice of the peace in and for the said county.

[9 Geo. 4, c. 23.]

An Act to enable Bankers in England to issue certain unstamped Promissory Notes and Bills of Exchange, upon Payment of a Composition in lieu of the Stamp Duties thereon. [19*th June*, 1828.]

9 Geo. 4, c. 23.

WHEREAS it is expedient to permit all persons carrying on the business of bankers in *England* (except within the city of *London*, or within three miles thereof), to issue their promissory notes payable to bearer on demand, or to order within a limited period after sight, and to draw bills of exchange payable to order on demand, or within a limited period after sight or date, on unstamped paper, upon payment of a composition in lieu of the stamp duties which would otherwise be payable upon such notes and bills respectively, and subject to the regulations hereinafter mentioned; be it therefore enacted by the King's most excellent Majesty, by and with the advice and consent of the Lords spiritual and temporal, and Commons, in this present Parliament assembled, and by the authority of the same, That from and after the first day of *July* one thousand eight hundred and twenty-eight, it shall be lawful for any person or persons carrying on the business of a banker or bankers in *England* (except within the city of *London*, or within three miles thereof), having first duly obtained a licence for that purpose, and given security by bond in manner hereinafter mentioned, to issue, on unstamped paper, promissory notes for any sum of money amounting to five pounds or upwards, expressed to be payable to the bearer on demand, or to order at any period not exceeding seven days after sight; and also to draw and issue, on unstamped paper, bills of exchange, expressed to be payable to order on demand, or at any period not exceeding seven days after sight, or twenty-one days after the date thereof; provided such bills of exchange be drawn upon a person or persons carrying on the business of a banker or bankers in *London*, *Westminster*, or the borough of *Southwark*, or provided such bills of exchange be drawn by any banker or bankers, at a town or place where he or they shall be duly licensed to issue unstamped notes and bills under the authority of this Act, upon himself or themselves, or

Certain bankers may issue unstamped promissory notes and bills of exchange, subject to the regulations herein mentioned.

9 Geo. 4, c. 23.

his or their copartner or copartners, payable at any other town or place where such banker or bankers shall also be duly licensed to issue such notes and bills as aforesaid.

Commissioners of Stamps may grant licences to issue unstamped notes and bills.

II. And be it enacted, That it shall be lawful for any two or more of the Commissioners of Stamps, to grant to all persons carrying on the business of bankers in *England* (except as aforesaid), who shall require the same, licences authorizing such persons to issue such promissory notes, and to draw and issue such bills of exchange as aforesaid, on unstamped paper; which said licences shall be and are hereby respectively charged with a stamp duty of thirty pounds for every such licence.

A separate licence to be taken for every place where such notes or bills shall be issued, but not to exceed four licences for any number of such places.

III. And be it further enacted, That a separate licence shall be taken out in respect of every town or place where any such unstamped promissory notes or bills of exchange as aforesaid shall be issued or drawn: Provided always, that no person or persons shall be obliged to take out more than four licences in all for any number of towns or places in *England;* and in case any person or persons shall issue or draw such unstamped notes or bills as aforesaid, at more than four different towns or places, then, after taking out three distinct licences for three of such towns or places, such person or persons shall be entitled to have all the rest of such towns or places included in a fourth licence.

Regulations respecting licences.

IV. And be it further enacted, That every licence granted under the authority of this Act shall specify all the particulars required by law to be specified in licences to be taken out by persons issuing promissory notes payable to bearer on demand, and allowed to be reissued; and every such licence which shall be granted between the tenth day of *October* and the eleventh day of *November* in any year shall be dated on the eleventh day of *October*, and every such licence which shall be granted at any other time shall be dated on the day on which the same shall be granted; and every such licence shall (notwithstanding any alteration which may take place in any copartnership of persons to whom the same shall be granted) have effect and continue in force from the day of the date thereof until the tenth day of *October* then next following, both inclusive, and no longer.

Commissioners may cancel licences already taken out, and grant licences under this Act in lieu thereof.

V. Provided always, and be it further enacted, That where any banker or bankers shall have obtained the licence required by law for issuing promissory notes payable to bearer on demand, at any town or place in *England*, and during the continuance of such licence shall be desirous of taking out a licence to issue at the same town or place unstamped promissory notes and bills of exchange under the provisions of this Act, it shall be lawful for the Commissioners of Stamps to cancel and allow as spoiled the stamp upon the said first-mentioned licence, and in lieu thereof to grant to such banker or bankers a licence under the authority of this Act; and every such last-mentioned licence shall also authorize the issuing and reissuing of all promissory notes papable to the bearer on demand, which such banker or bankers may by law continue to issue or reissue at the same town or place, on paper duly stamped.

VI. Provided always, and be it further enabled, That if any banker or bankers, who shall take out a licence under the authority of this Act, shall issue, under the authority either of this or any other Act, any unstamped promissory notes for payment of money to the bearer on demand, such banker or bankers shall, so long as he or they shall continue licenced as aforesaid, make and issue on unstamped paper all his or their promissory notes for payment of money to the bearer on demand, of whatever amount such notes may be; and it shall not be lawful for such banker or bankers, during the period aforesaid, to issue for the first time any such promissory note as aforesaid on stamped paper.

9 Geo. 4, c. 23.

Bankers while licensed under this Act shall not issue, for the first time, notes on stamped paper.

VII. And be it further enacted, That before any licence shall be granted to any person or persons to issue or draw any unstamped promissory notes or bills of exchange under the authority of this Act, such person or persons shall give security, by bond, to His Majesty, his heirs and successors, with a condition, that if such person or persons do and shall from time to time enter or cause to be entered in a book or books to be kept for that purpose, an account of all such unstamped promissory notes and bills of exchange as he or they shall so as aforesaid issue or draw, specifying the amount or value thereof respectively, and the several dates of the issuing thereof; and in like manner, also, a similar account of all such promissory notes as, having been issued as aforesaid, shall have been cancelled, and the dates of the cancelling thereof, and of all such bills of exchange as, having been drawn or issued as aforesaid, shall have been paid, and the dates of the payment thereof; and do and shall from time to time, when thereunto requested, produce and show such accounts to, and permit the same to be examined and inspected by, the said Commissioners of Stamps, or any officer of stamps appointed under the hands and seals of the said commissioners for that purpose; and also do and shall deliver to the said Commissioners of Stamps half-yearly (that is to say), within fourteen days after the first day of *January* and the first day of *July* in every year, a just and true account in writing, verified upon the oaths or affirmations (which any justice of the peace is hereby empowered to administer), to the best of the knowledge and belief of such person or persons, and of his or their cashier, accountant, or chief clerk, or of such of them as the said commissioners shall require, of the amount or value of all unstamped promissory notes and bills of exchange, issued under the provisions of this or any former Act, in circulation within the meaning of this Act on a given day (that is to say), on *Saturday* in every week, for the space of half a year prior to the half-yearly day immediately preceding the delivery of such account, together with the average amount or value of such notes and bills so in circulation, according to such account; and also do and shall pay or cause to be paid to the Receiver General of Stamp Duties in *Great Britain*, or to some other person duly authorized by the Commissioners of Stamps to receive the same, as a composition for the duties which would otherwise have been payable for such promissory notes and bills of exchange issued or in circulation during such half year, the sum of three shillings and sixpence for every one hundred pounds, and also for the fractional part of one hundred pounds, of the said average amount or value of such notes and bills in circulation, according to the true intent and meaning of this Act; and on

Bankers licensed to issue unstamped notes or bills shall give security, by bond, for the due performance of the conditions herein contained.

9 Geo. 4, c. 23.

due performance thereof such bond shall be void, but otherwise the same shall be and remain in full force and virtue.

For what period notes and bills are to be deemed in circulation.

VIII. And be it further enacted, That every unstamped promissory note payable to the bearer on demand, issued under the provisions of this Act, shall, for the purpose of payment of duty, be deemed to be in circulation from the day of the issuing to the day of the cancelling thereof, both days inclusive, excepting nevertheless the period during which such note shall be in the hands of the banker or bankers who first issued the same, or by whom the same shall be expressed to be payable; and that every unstamped promissory note payable to order, and every unstamped bill of exchange so as aforesaid issued, shall for the purpose aforesaid, be deemed to be in circulation from the day of the issuing to the day of the payment thereof, both days inclusive: Provided always, that every such promissory note payable to order, and bill of exchange as aforesaid, which shall be paid in less than seven days from the issuing thereof, shall, for the purpose aforesaid, be included in the account of notes and bills in circulation on the *Saturday* next after the day of the issuing thereof as if the same were then actually in circulation.

Regulations respecting the bonds to be given pursuant to this Act.

IX. And be it further enacted, That in every bond to be given pursuant to the directions of this Act the person or persons intending to issue or draw any such unstamped promissory notes and bills of exchange as aforesaid, or such and so many of the said persons as the Commissioners of Stamps shall require, shall be the obligors; and every such bond shall be taken in the sum of one hundred pounds, or in such larger sum as the said Commissioners of Stamps may judge to be the probable amount of the composition or duties that will be payable from such person or persons, under or by virtue of this Act, during the period of one year; and it shall be lawful for the said commissioners to fix the time or times of payment of the said composition or duties, and to specify the same in the condition to every such bond; and every such bond may be required to be renewed from time to time, at the discretion of the said commissioners, and as often as the same shall be forfeited, or the parties to the same, or any of them, shall die, become bankrupt or insolvent, or reside in parts beyond the seas.

Fresh bonds to be given on alterations of copartnerships.

X. And be it further enacted, That if any alteration shall be made in any copartnership of persons who shall have given any such security by bond as by this Act is directed, whether such alteration shall be caused by the death or retirement of one or more of the partners of the firm, or by the accession of any additional or new partner or partners, a fresh bond shall be given by the remaining partner or partners, or the persons composing the new copartnership, as the case may be, which bond shall be taken as a security for the duties which may be due and owing, or may become due and owing, in respect of the unstamped notes and bills which shall have been issued by the persons composing the old copartnership, and which shall be in circulation at the time of such alteration, as well as for duties which shall or may be or become due or owing in respect of the unstamped notes and bills issued or to be issued by the persons composing the new copartnership; provided that no such fresh bond shall be rendered necessary by any such alteration as aforesaid in any copartnership of persons exceeding six in number, but that the bonds to be given by such last-mentioned copartnerships shall be taken as securities for all the duties they may incur so long as they shall exist, or the persons composing the same, or any of them, shall carry on business in copartnership together, or with any other person or persons, notwithstanding any alteration in such copartnership; saving always the power of the said Commissioners of Stamps to require a new bond in any case where they shall deem it necessary for better securing the payment of the said duties. 9 Geo. 4, c. 23.

XI. And be it further enacted, That if any person or persons who shall have given security, by bond, to His Majesty, in the manner hereinbefore directed, shall refuse or neglect to renew such bond when forfeited, and as often as the same is by this Act required to be renewed, such person or persons so offending shall for every such offence forfeit and pay the sum of one hundred pounds. Penalty on bankers neglecting to renew their bonds.

XII. And be it further enacted, That if any person or persons who shall be licensed under the provisions of this Act shall draw or issue, or cause to be drawn or issued, upon unstamped paper, any promissory note payable to order, or any bill of exchange which shall bear date subsequent to the day on which it shall be issued, the person or persons so offending shall, for every such note or bill so drawn or issued, forfeit the sum of one hundred pounds. Penalty for post-dating unstamped notes or bills.

XIII. Provided always, and be it further enacted, That nothing in this Act contained shall extend or be construed to extend to exempt or relieve from the forfeitures or penalties imposed by any Act or Acts now in force, upon persons issuing promissory notes or bills of exchange not duly stamped as the law requires, any person or persons who under any colour or pretence whatsoever shall issue any unstamped promissory note or bill of exchange, unless such person or persons shall be duly licensed to issue such note or bill under the provisions of this Act; and such note or bill shall be drawn and issued in strict accordance with the regulations and restrictions herein contained. This Act not to exempt from penalties any persons issuing unstamped notes or bills not in accordance herewith.

XIV. And be it further enacted, That all pecuniary forfeitures and penalties which may be incurred under any of the provisions of this Act shall be recovered for the use of His Majesty, his heirs and successors, in His Majesty's Court of Exchequer at *Westminster*, by action of debt, bill, plaint, or information, in the name of His Majesty's Attorney or Solicitor General in *England*. Recovery of penalties.

XV. Provided always, and be it further enacted, That nothing in this Act contained shall extend or be construed to extend to prejudice, alter, or affect any of the rights, powers, or privileges of the Governor and Company of the Bank of *England*. Not to affect the privileges of the of the Bank of England.

[9 Geo. 4, c. 65.]

9 Geo. 4, c. 65.

An Act to restrain the Negotiation, in England, of Promissory Notes and Bills under a limited Sum, issued in Scotland or Ireland. [15*th July*, 1828.]

7 G. 4, c. 6.

WHEREAS an Act was passed in the seventh year of His present Majesty's reign, intituled *An Act to limit, and after a certain Period to prohibit, the issuing of Promissory Notes under a limited Sum in* England; and doubts may arise how far the provisions of the said Act may be effectual to restrain the circulating in *England* of certain notes, drafts, or undertakings made or issued in *Scotland* or *Ireland*: Be it therefore enacted by the King's most excellent Majesty, by and with the advice and consent of the Lords spiritual and temporal, and Commons, in this present Parliament assembled, and by the authority of the same, That if any body politic or corporate, or person or persons, shall, after the fifth day of *April* one thousand eight hundred and twenty-nine, by any art, device, or means whatsoever, publish, utter, negotiate, or transfer, in any part of *England*, any promissory or other note, draft, engagement, or undertaking in writing, made payable on demand to the bearer thereof, and being negotiable or transferable, for the payment of any sum of money less than five pounds, or on which less than the sum of five pounds shall remain undischarged, which shall have been made or issued, or shall purport to have been made or issued, in *Scotland* or *Ireland*, or elsewhere out of *England*, wheresoever the same shall or may be payable, every such body politic or corporate, or person or persons, so publishing, uttering, negotiating, or transferring any such note, bill, draft, engagement, or undertaking, in any part of *England*, shall forfeit and pay for every such offence any sum not exceeding twenty pounds nor less than five pounds, at the discretion of the justice of the peace who shall hear and determine such offence.

After 5th April 1829, no corporation or person shall utter in England notes or bills under 5*l.* which have been made or issued in Scotland or Ireland, under penalty of 20*l.*

Mode of recovering penalties.

II. And be it further enacted, That the penalties which may be incurred under the provisions of this Act shall and may be recovered in a summary way, by information on complaint, before a justice or justices of the peace, and shall be levied and applied in the manner directed by an Act passed in the forty-eighth year of the reign of His late Majesty King *George* the Third, intituled *An Act to restrain the Negotiation of Promissory Notes and Inland Bills of Exchange under a limited Sum in* England, with respect to the penalties by the said last-mentionod Act imposed; and all and every the clauses and provisions in the said last-mentioned Act contained, relating to the recovery and application of the penalties thereby imposed, shall be applied and put in execution for the recovery and application of the penalties by this Act imposed, as fully and effectually, to all intents and purposes, as if such clauses and provisions had been herein repeated and expressly re-enacted.

48 G. 3, c. 88.

III. Provided always, and be it enacted, That it shall and may be lawful for the Lord High Treasurer, or for the Commissioners of His Majesty's Treasury, or any three or more of them, to order and direct that the whole or any part of any penalty which shall be incurred under this Act shall and may be remitted, or mitigated or abated to such amount, and in such manner and upon such conditions as to such Lord High Treasurer or Commissioners of the Treasury may seem fit and proper.

9 Geo 4, c. 65

The Treasury may order a remission or mitigation of penalties.

IV. Provided always, and be it further enacted, That nothing herein contained shall extend to any draft or order drawn by any person or persons on his, her, or their banker or bankers, or on any person or persons acting as such banker or bankers, for the payment of money held by such banker or bankers, person or persons, to the use of the person or persons by whom such draft or order shall be drawn.

Not to extend to drafts on bankers for the use of the drawer.

[9 Geo. 4, c. 80.]

An Act to enable Bankers in Ireland to issue certain unstamped Promissory Notes, upon Payment of a Composition in lieu of the Stamp Duties thereon. [*25th July*, 1828.]

9 Geo. 4, c. 80.

WHEREAS it is expedient to permit all persons carrying on the business of bankers in *Ireland* to issue their promissory notes payable to bearer on demand on unstamped paper, upon payment of a composition in lieu of the stamp duties which would otherwise be payable upon such notes, and subject to the regulations hereinafter mentioned; be it therefore enacted by the King's most excellent Majesty, by and with the advice and consent of the Lords spiritual and temporal, and Commons, in this present Parliament assembled, and by the authority of the same, that from and after the first day of *September* one thousand eight hundred and twenty-eight, it shall be lawful for any person or persons carrying on the business of a banker or bankers in *Ireland*, who shall have duly registered the firm of his or their house according to law, and who shall have obtained a licence and given security by bond in manner hereinafter mentioned, to make and issue on unstamped paper his or their promissory notes, for payment to the bearer on demand of any sum of money not exceeding the sum of one hundred pounds.

Bankers in Ireland may issue certain promissory notes on unstamped paper

II. And be it further enacted, That it shall be lawful for any two or more of the Commissioners of Stamps, or any officer of stamps duly authorized by the said commissioners in that behalf, to grant licences to all persons carrying on the business of bankers in *Ireland* who shall have duly registered the firm of their house according to law, and who shall require such licences authorizing such persons to issue such promissory notes as aforesaid on unstamped paper; which said licences shall be and are hereby respectively charged with a stamp duty of thirty pounds for every such licence.

The Commissioners of Stamps or their officers may grant licences to issue unstamped promissory notes

9 Geo. 4, c. 80.

Bankers to take out a separate licence for every place where unstamped notes shall be issued, but not to take out more than four licences for any number of such places.

III. And be it further enacted, That a separate licence shall be taken out in respect of every town or place where any such unstamped promissory notes as aforesaid shall be issued: Provided always, that no person or persons shall be obliged to take out more than four licences in all for any number of towns or places in *Ireland;* and in case any person or persons shall issue such unstamped notes as aforesaid at more than four different towns or places, then after taking out three distinct licences for three of such towns or places, such person or persons shall be entitled to have all the rest of such towns or places included in a fourth licence; and that if any person or persons, after having taken out four distinct licences under the authority of this Act, shall begin to issue such unstamped notes as aforesaid at any other town or place not named in any of the said four licences, it shall not be necessary to include such last-mentioned town or place in any licence until the twenty-fourth day of *March* next following the beginning to issue thereat such notes as aforesaid.

Regulations respecting licences.

IV. And be it further enacted, That every licence granted under the authority of this Act shall specify all the particulars required by law to be specified in the certificates to be taken out by persons in *Ireland* issuing promissory notes payable to bearer on demand, and allowed to be reissued; and every such licence which shall be granted between the twenty-fourth day of *March* and the twenty-fifth day of *April* in any year, shall be dated on the twenty-fifth day of *March;* and every such licence which shall be granted at any other time, shall be dated on the day on which the same shall be granted; and every such licence shall (notwithstanding any alteration which may take place in any copartnership of persons to whom the same shall be granted) have effect and continue in force from the day of the date thereof until the twenty-fourth day of *March* then next following, both inclusive, and no longer.

Commissioners of Stamps to cancel certificates taken out for issuing promissory notes payable to bearer on demand, and to grant licences under this Act in lieu thereof.

V. Provided always, and be it further enacted, That where any banker or bankers shall have taken out the certificate required by law for issuing promissory notes payable to bearer on demand at any town or place in *Ireland,* and during the period for which such certificate shall have been granted, shall be desirous of taking out a licence to issue at the same town or place unstamped promissory notes under the provisions of this Act, it shall be lawful for the Commissioners of Stamps, or their officers, to cancel and allow as spoiled the stamp upon such certificate, and in lieu thereof to grant to such banker or bankers a licence under the authority of this Act; and every such licence shall, during its continuance in force, also authorize the reissuing of all promissory notes payable to the bearer on demand, which such banker or bankers may have previously issued on paper duly stamped, until the twenty-fourth day of *March* inclusive then next following, provided such notes may so long be lawfully reissued.

Bankers licensed under this Act to issue all their promissory notes for

VI. Provided always, and be it further enacted, That if any banker or bankers who shall take out a licence under the authority of this Act shall issue, under the authority either of this or any other Act, any unstamped promissory notes for payment of money to the bearer on demand, such banker or bankers shall, so long as he

9 Geo. 4, c. 80.

or they shall continue licensed as aforesaid, make and issue on unstamped paper all his or their promissory notes for payment of money to the bearer on demand, of whatever amount or value (not exceeding the sum of one hundred pounds) such notes may be; and it shall not be lawful for such banker or bankers, during the period aforesaid, to issue, for the first time, any such promissory note as aforesaid on stamped paper.

payment of money to the bearer on demand on unstamped paper.

Bankers issuing unstamped notes to give security by bond for the due performance of the conditions herein contained.

VII. And be it further enacted, That before any licence shall be granted to any person or persons to issue any unstamped promissory notes under the authority of this Act, such person or persons shall give security by bond to His Majesty, his heirs and successors, with a condition that if such person or persons do and shall from time to time enter or cause to be entered, in a book or books to be kept for that purpose, an account of all such unstamped promissory notes as he or they shall so as aforesaid issue, specifying the amount or value thereof respectively, and the several dates of the issuing thereof, and in like manner also a similar account of all such promissory notes as, having been issued as aforesaid, shall have been cancelled, and the dates of the cancelling thereof; and do and shall from time to time, when thereunto requested, produce and show such accounts to and permit the same to be examined and inspected by the said Commissioners of Stamps, or any officer of stamps appointed under the hands and seals of the said commissioners for that purpose; and also do and shall deliver to the said Commissioners of Stamps half-yearly (that is to say), within fourteen days after the first day of *January* and the first day of *July* in every year, a just and true account in writing, verified upon the oaths or affirmation (which any justice of the peace is hereby empowered to administer), to the best of the knowledge and belief of such person or persons, and of his or their cashier, accountant, or chief clerk, or of such of them as the said commissioners shall require, of the amount or value of all unstamped promissory notes issued under the provisions of this Act in circulation, within the meaning of this Act, on a given day, that is to say, on *Saturday* in every week, for the space of half a year prior to the half-yearly day immediately preceding the delivery of such account, together with the average amount or value of such promissory notes so in circulation according to such account; and also do and shall pay or cause to be paid to the Receiver General of Stamp Duties in *Ireland*, or to some other person duly authorized by the Commissioners of Stamps to receive the same, as a composition for the duties which would otherwise have been payable for such promissory notes issued or in circulation during such half year, the sum of one shilling and sixpence for every one hundred pounds, and also for the fractional part of one hundred pounds of the said average amount or value of such notes in circulation, according to the true intent and meaning of this Act; and on due performance thereof such bond shall be void, but otherwise the same shall be and remain in full force and virtue.

For what period notes are to be deemed in circulation

VIII. And be it further enacted, That every unstamped promissory note issued under the provisions of this Act shall, for the purpose of payment of duty, be deemed to be in circulation from the day of the issuing to the day of the cancelling thereof, both days inclusive, excepting nevertheless the period during which such note

9 Geo. 4, c. 80.

shall be in the hands of the banker or bankers who first issued the same, or by whom the same shall be expressed to be payable, or, in case of copartnerships of more than six persons, which shall be in the hands of the public officers of such copartnership.

Regulations respecting the bonds to be given pursuant to this Act.

IX. And be it further enacted, That in every bond to be given pursuant to the directions of this Act, the person or persons intending to issue any such unstamped promissory notes as aforesaid, or such and so many of the said persons as the Commissioners of Stamps, or their proper officer in that behalf, shall require, shall be the obligors; and every such bond shall be taken in the sum of one hundred pounds, or in such larger sums as the said Commissioners of Stamps, or such officer as aforesaid, may judge to be the probable amount of the composition or duties that will be payable from such person or persons under or by virtue of this Act during the period of one year; and it shall be lawful for the said commissioners, or such officer as aforesaid, to fix the time or times of payment of the said composition or duties, and to specify the same in the condition to every such bond; and every such bond may be required to be renewed from time to time, at the discretion of the said commissioners, or of such officer as aforesaid, and as often as the same shall be forfeited, or the parties to the same, or any of them, shall die, become bankrupt or insolvent, or reside in parts beyond the seas.

Fresh bonds to be given on alterations of copartnerships.

X. And be it further enacted, That if any alteration shall be made in any copartnership of persons who shall have given any such security by bond as by this Act is directed, whether such alteration shall be caused by the death or retirement of one or more of the partners of the firm, or by the accession of any additional or new partner or partners, a fresh bond shall, within one calendar month after any such alteration, be given by the remaining partner or partners, or the persons composing the new copartnership, as the case may be, which bond shall be taken as a security for the duties which may be due and owing or may become due and owing in respect of the unstamped promissory notes which shall have been issued by the persons composing the old copartnership, and which shall be in circulation at the time of such alteration, as well as for duties which shall or may be or become due or owing in respect of the unstamped promissory notes issued or to be issued by the persons composing the new copartnership: Provided that no such fresh bond shall be rendered necessary by any such alteration as aforesaid in any copartnership of persons exceeding six in number, but that the bonds to be given by such last-mentioned copartnerships shall be taken as securities for all the duties they may incur so long as they shall exist, or the persons composing the same or any of them shall carry on business in copartnership together, or with any other person or persons, notwithstanding any alteration in such copartnership; saving always the power of the said Commissioners of Stamps to require a new bond in any case where they shall deem it necessary for better securing the payment of the said duties.

Penalty on bankers refusing to renew their bonds.

XI. And be it further enacted, That if any person or persons, who shall have given security by bond to His Majesty in the manner hereinbefore directed, shall refuse or neglect, for the space of one calendar month, to renew such bond when forfeited, and as often as the same is by this Act required to be renewed, such person or persons so offending shall for every such offence forfeit and pay the sum of one hundred pounds. 9 Geo. 4, c. 80.

XII. Provided always, and be it further enacted, That nothing in this Act contained shall extend or be construed to extend to exempt or relieve, from the forfeitures or penalties imposed by any Act or Acts now in force upon persons issuing promissory notes not duly stamped as the law requires, any person or persons who, under any colour or pretence whatsoever, shall issue any unstamped promissory note, unless such person or persons shall be duly licensed to issue such promissory note under the provisions of this Act, and such note shall be drawn and issued in strict accordance with the regulations and restrictions herein contained.

This Act not to exempt from penalties any persons issuing unstamped notes not in accordance herewith.

XIII. And be it further enacted, That all pecuniary forfeitures and penalties which may be incurred under any of the provisions of this Act, shall be recovered for the use of His Majesty, his heirs and successors, in any of His Majesty's courts of record, by action of debt, bill, plaint, or information, in the name of His Majesty's Attorney or Solicitor General in *Ireland*.

Penalties, how and by whom to be recovered.

XIV. Provided always, and be it further enacted, That nothing in this Act contained shall extend or be construed to extend to prejudice, alter, or affect any of the rights, powers, or privileges of the Governor and Company of the Bank of *Ireland*.

Not to affect the privileges of the Bank of Ireland.

XV. And whereas it may happen that bankers who may be desirous to issue unstamped promissory notes payable to bearer on demand, under the provisions of this Act, may have provided themselves with stamps for such notes, which may not have been issued, and which may by this Act be rendered useless or unnecessary, and it is expedient to enable the Commissioners of Stamps and their officers to cancel and allow such stamps in manner hereinafter mentioned; be it therefore enacted, That where any banker or bankers who shall take out a licence under the authority of this Act shall have in his or their possession stamps for reissuable promissory notes payable to the bearer on demand, which shall be rendered useless or unnecessary in consequence of such banker or bankers electing to issue such notes on unstamped paper, under the provisions of this Act, it shall be lawful for the said Commissioners of Stamps or their officers, and they are hereby authorized and empowered, to cancel and allow such stamps so as aforesaid rendered useless or unnecessary, and to repay the amount or value thereof in money, deducting therefrom the sum of one pound ten shillings for every one hundred pounds, and so in proportion for any greater or less sum than one hundred pounds of such amount or value, provided proof be made, by affidavit or affirmation, to the satisfaction of the said commissioners, that such stamps have not been issued, and provided application be made for such allowance within six calendar months next after the passing of this Act.

Commissioners of Stamps to cancel reissuable promissory note stamps rendered unnecessary and to repay the amount.

XVI. And whereas by an Act passed in the sixth year of the reign of His present Majesty, intituled *An Act for the better Regulation of Copartnerships of certain Bankers in* Ireland, any certificate 6 G. 4, c. 42.

9 Geo. 4, c. 80.

granted by the Commissioners of Stamps in *Ireland*, to any society or copartnership of bankers in *Ireland* exceeding six in number, of the registry of the firm and name of such society, is liable to the stamp duty payable by law on certificates to be taken out yearly by any banker or bankers in *Ireland*, that is to say, a stamp duty of thirty pounds: And whereas it is provided by the said recited Act, that a separate and distinct certificate, with a separate and distinct stamp, shall be granted for and in respect of every town or place where any such bills or notes as in the said Act are mentioned shall be issued by any such society or copartnership: And whereas it is expedient that no such society or copartnership should be required to take out more than four certificates in any one year, although it should issue such notes or bills as aforesaid at more than four towns or places in *Ireland;* be it therefore further enacted, That no society or copartnership of bankers in *Ireland* exceeding six in number, and carrying on the trade or business of bankers under the authority of the said recited Act, shall be obliged to take out more than four certificates in any one year of the entry and registry of the firm or name of such society or copartnership; and in case any such society or copartnership shall issue such bills or notes as aforesaid, by themselves or their agents, at more than four different towns or places in *Ireland*, then after taking out three distinct certificates for three of such towns or places, such society or copartnership shall be entitled to have all the remainder of such towns or places included in a fourth certificate; any thing in the said Act of the sixth year of the reign of His present Majesty to the contrary notwithstanding.

No society or copartnership of bankers shall be obliged to take out more than four certificates in one year.

XVII. And be it further enacted, That every certificate which hath been or shall at any time hereafter be taken out by any such last-mentioned society or copartnership as aforesaid, shall continue in force, for the issuing of such bills and notes as aforesaid at the town or place or the several towns or places therein named, until the twenty-fifth day of *March* next following the date of such certificate, notwithstanding any fresh entry or registry of the name or firm of such society or copartnership; and that if any fresh entry or registry shall be made from any cause whatever, after any such society or copartnership shall have taken out four such distinct certificates as aforesaid, such society or copartnership shall not be required to take out any further certificate, in respect of any town or place not included in any of such four certificates until the twenty-fourth day of *March* next following such fresh entry or registry.

Certificates to continue in force notwithstanding any fresh registry.

XVIII. And be it further enacted, That this Act may be altered, amended, or repealed by any Act or Acts to be passed in this present session of Parliament.

Act may be altered.

[9 Geo. 4, c. 81.]

An Act for making Promissory Notes payable, issued by Banks, Banking Companies, or Bankers, in Ireland, at the Places where they are issued. 9 Geo 4, c. 81.

[25*th July*, 1828.]

WHEREAS divers banks, banking companies, and bankers, in *Ireland*, have made and issued promissory notes, without making the same payable in coin of the realm at the several places respectively where such notes have been issued or reissued: And whereas it is expedient that in future all such promissory notes, and all bank post bills, issued by such banks, banking companies, or bankers, should be made payable at the places where the same shall be issued or reissued; be it therefore enacted by the King's most excellent Majesty, by and with the advice and consent of the Lords spiritual and temporal, and Commons, in this present Parliament assembled, and by the authority of the same, that from and after the first day of *April* one thousand eight hundred and twenty-nine, no bank, banking company, or banker, in *Ireland*, shall, by themselves, or by any agent or agents, partner or partners, or other person or persons whomsoever on their or his behalf, or on their or his account, make, issue, or reissue, in any place in *Ireland* where such bank, banking company, or banker shall have any house or establishment for business, or any authorized resident agent or agents, any promissory note or bank post bill of any denomination whatsoever, being or purporting to be the note or notes, bank post bill or bank post bills of the bank, banking company, or banker, making, issuing, or reissuing the same, which shall not be payable at the places respectively where the same shall be made, issued, or reissued by or on behalf of such bank, banking company, or banker; and in every such note the place where the same shall have been issued or reissued shall be expressly mentioned: Provided nevertheless, that if any such promissory note or bank post bill shall be issued or reissued contrary to the provisions of this Act, the same shall nevertheless not only be valid against the bank, banking company, or banker issuing or reissuing the same by any of the ways or means aforesaid, but such bank, banking company, or banker shall be liable and bound to pay, in the lawful coin of the realm, double the amount of the sum specified in each such note or bank post bill (to be sued for and recovered by the holder thereof in any of His Majesty's courts for the recovery of debts in *Ireland*, by action of debt, bill, plaint, or information), either at the place where the same shall have been issued or reissued by or on behalf of such bank, banking company, or banker, or at any other place where such bank, banking company, or banker shall have any house or establishment for business, notwithstanding such note or bank post bill shall not be expressed to be so payable, or shall be or expressed to be otherwise payable: Provided always, that nothing herein contained shall extend to prevent any such promissory note or bank post bill from being made payable at several places, if one of such places shall be the bank or place where the same shall be so issued as aforesaid.

No banker in Ireland to issue notes which shall not express to be payable at the place where issued.

Notes issued contrary hereto shall be valid against the party issuing; who shall also be liable in double the amount.

Not to prevent notes being made payable at several places.

[1 Will. 4, c. 32.]

1 Will. 4, c. 32. *An Act to explain Two Acts of His present Majesty, for establishing an Agreement with the Governor and Company of the Bank of Ireland, for advancing the Sum of Five hundred thousand Pounds, Irish Currency, and for the better Regulation of Copartnerships of certain Bankers in Ireland.* [16*th July*, 1830.]

Whereas by an Act passed in the Parliament in *Ireland* in the twenty-first and twenty-second years of the reign of His late Majesty King *George* the Third, intituled *An Act for establishing a Bank by*
21 & 22 G. 3, c. 16. *the Name of the Governor and Company of the Bank of* Ireland, it was amongst other things enacted, that from and after the passing of the said Act it should not be lawful for any body politic or corporate, erected or to be erected, other than the corporation thereby intended to be created into a national bank, or for any other persons whatsoever united or to be united in covenants or partnerships exceeding the number of six persons, to borrow, owe, or take up any sum or sums of money on their bills or notes payable at demand, or at any less time than six months from the borrowing thereof, under a penalty or forfeiture by such persons, bodies politic or corporate, of treble the sum or sums so to be borrowed or taken up on such bill or bills, note or notes, one moiety thereof to be paid to the informer, and the other to the use of His said Majesty, his heirs and successors, to be recovered by action of debt, bill, plaint, or information in any of His Majesty's courts of record at *Dublin:* And whereas by another Act, passed in the first and second years of the reign of His present Majesty King *George* the Fourth, intituled *An Act to establish*
1 & 2 G. 4. *an Agreement with the Governor and Company of the Bank of* Ireland *for advancing the Sum of* Five *hundred thousand pounds*, Irish *Currency, and to empower the said Governor and Company to enlarge the capital Stock or* Fund *of the said Bank to Three Millions*, it was amongst other things enacted, that from and after the passing the same Act it should and might be lawful for any number of persons in *Ireland*, united or to be united in societies or partnerships, and residing and having their establishments or houses of business at any place not less than fifty miles distant from *Dublin*, to borrow, owe, or take up any sum or sums of money on their bills or notes payable on demand, and to make and issue such notes or bills accordingly payable on demand at any place in *Ireland* exceeding the distance of fifty miles from *Dublin*, the individuals composing such societies or copartnerships being liable and responsible for the due payment of such bills or notes; and such persons should not be subject or liable to any penalty for the making or issuing such bills or notes, any thing in an Act made in the Parliament of *Ireland* holden in the twenty-first and twenty-second years of the reign of His late Majesty King *George*
21 & 22 G. 3, c. 16 the Third, intituled *An Act for establishing a Bank by the Name of the Governor and Company of the Bank of* Ireland, to the contrary notwithstanding: provided always, and it was by the now reciting Act

further enacted, that no further or other power, privilege, or authority should, previous to the first day of *January* one thousand eight hundred and thirty-eight, nor until after payment to the said governor and company of all sum and sums of money which then were or thereafter should or might become due to them from Government, be granted to any copartnership or society of persons whatsoever, contrary to the laws then in force for establishing or regulating the Bank of *Ireland*, save and except the power of enabling such societies or copartnerships as aforesaid, residing and carrying on their business not less than fifty miles from *Dublin*, to sue and be sued in the name of a public officer, should Parliament thereafter think fit to grant such power; and it was by the now reciting Act lastly enacted, that nothing therein contained should extend or be construed to extend to authorize any persons exceeding six in number, or any bodies politic or corporate, residing or having their establishments or house of business within the distance of fifty miles from *Dublin*, to make or issue any bill or bills of exchange, or any promissory note or notes, contrary to the provisions of the said in part recited Act of the twenty-first and twenty-second years of the reign of King *George* the Third: And whereas by an Act passed in the sixth year of the reign of His said present Majesty, intituled *An Act for the better Regulation of Copartnerships of certain Bankers in* Ireland, reciting the lastly hereinbefore recited Act made and passed in the first and second years of His said present Majesty's reign, and that it was expedient that the said last-recited Act should be altered and amended, it was amongst other things enacted, that from and after the passing of the said Act of the sixth year of His said present Majesty's reign it should and might be lawful for any number of persons united or to be united in any society or copartnership in *Ireland*, consisting of more than six in number, and not having the establishments or houses of business of such society or copartnerships at any place or places less than fifty miles distant from *Dublin*, to carry on the trade and business of bankers in like manner as copartnerships of bankers consisting of not more than six in number might lawfully do, and to borrow, owe, or take up any sum or sums of money on their bills or notes payable on demand, or at any time after date or after sight, and to make and issue such notes or bills accordingly at any place in *Ireland* exceeding the distance of fifty miles from *Dublin*, all the individuals composing such societies or copartnerships being liable and responsible for the due payment of all such bills or notes in manner thereinafter provided, any thing contained in the said Act made in the Parliament of *Ireland* in the twenty-first and twenty-second years of the reign of His late Majesty King *George* the Third, hereinbefore recited, or in the hereinbefore recited Act of the first and second years of His present Majesty's reign, or in any other Act or Acts, or any law, usage, or custom, to the contrary in anywise notwithstanding; and it was by the same Act further enacted that it should and might be lawful for any such society or copartnership from time to time to have, employ, or appoint any agent or agents to do or transact, on behalf of any such society or copartnership, all such business, matters, and things as such society or copartnership might lawfully do, and as were not contrary to any Act or Acts then in force, and to the provisions of the now reciting Act: provided always, and it was by the same Act further enacted, that nothing therein contained should extend or be construed to extend to enable

1 Will. 4, c. 32.

6 G. 4, c. 42.

1 Will. 4, c. 32. or authorize any such society or copartnership, either by any member or members thereof, or by their agent or any other person on behalf of any such society or copartnership, to pay, issue, or reissue at at *Dublin*, or within fifty miles thereof, any bill or note of such society or copartnership which should be payable to bearer on demand, or any bank post bill, nor to draw upon any partner or agent who might be resident in *Dublin*, or within fifty miles thereof, any bill of exchange which should be payable on demand, or which should be for less amount than fifty pounds, nor to borrow, owe, or take up in *England* or in *Dublin*, or within fifty miles thereof, any sum or sums of money on any promissory note or bill of any such society or copartnership payable on demand, or at any less time than six months from the borrowing thereof, or to make or issue any bill or bills of exchange or promissory note or notes of any such society or copartnership contrary to the provisions of the said recited Act of the twenty-first and twenty-second years of the reign of King *George* the Third, or of the first and second years of the reign of His present Majesty, save as aforesaid, save as provided by the now reciting Act in that behalf; provided always, and it was by the now reciting Act further enacted, that nothing contained in that Act or any other Act or Acts should extend or be construed to prevent any person or persons whatever, whether resident in *Great Britain* or *Ireland*, from being or becoming a member or members of any such society or copartnership in *Ireland* as aforesaid, or from being or becoming a subscriber and contributor or subscribers and contributors to the stock and capital of any such society or copartnership; and that any such society or copartnership which should or might have been formed or begun to be formed under or by virtue of the provisions contained in the hereinbefore recited Acts of the first and second years, and an Act, therein recited, made and passed in the fifth year of the reign of His present Majesty, and of which any person or persons should be or should become a member or members, or to which any such person or persons should become a subscriber or subscribers or contributor or contributors as aforesaid, should be or be deemed and taken to all intents and purposes to be a society or copartnership of persons united in *Ireland* within the true intent and meaning of the now reciting Act, any thing in the now reciting Act, or in any other Act or Acts, or any law, usage, or custom, to the contrary notwithstanding; provided always, and it was by the now reciting Act lastly enacted, that nothing in the said now reciting Act contained should be construed to prevent any such society or copartnership from doing any act, matter, or thing which, but for the express provision of the now reciting Act, they would by law be entitled to do: And whereas it hath been doubted whether such banking societies or copartnerships, consisting of more than six in number, already created or to be created, and not having their establishments or houses of business not less than fifty miles late *Irish* measurement from *Dnblin*, might lawfully pay in *Dublin* their notes or bills payable to bearer on demand, for the purpose of withdrawing the same from circulation in *Dublin*, or within fifty miles late *Irish* measurement thereof; and it is expedient that such doubt should be removed: Be it therefore enacted and also declared by the King's most excellent Majesty, by and with the advice and consent of the Lords spiritual and temporal, and Commons, in this present Parliament assembled, and by the authority of the same, That it is and

shall be lawful for any number of persons united or to be united in any society or copartnership in *Ireland* as in and by the said Acts or either of them is mentioned or provided, consisting of more than six in number, and not having the establishments or houses of business of such society or copartnership at any place or places less than fifty miles of the late *Irish* measurement distant from *Dublin*, to pay in *Dublin*, for the purpose of withdrawing them from circulation in *Dublin*, or within fifty miles of the late *Irish* measurement thereof, by any bankers, agents, or correspondents, or any other person or persons on behalf of such society or copartnership, whether such bankers, agents, correspondents, or other person or persons shall be members or a member of such society or copartnership, any bills and notes of such society or copartnership made payable to bearer on demand, yet so nevertheless that all such bills and notes so paid in *Dublin* and withdrawn from circulation as aforesaid may be reissued at the place where such bills or notes were originally issued: Provided always, that such bills or notes are and shall be originally issued and made payable at some place or places, specified in such bills or notes, exceeding the distance of fifty miles of the late *Irish* measurement from *Dublin*, and not elsewhere, and shall not be reissued within fifty miles of the last *Irish* measurement of *Dublin*.

1 Will. 4, c. 32.

Copartnership bankers, within a certain distance may pay their notes in Dublin.

VI. And whereas by the said recited Act passed in the sixth year of the reign of His present Majesty, it was amongst other things further enacted, that between the twenty-fifth day of *March* in any year and the twenty-fifth day of *March* following, an account or return should be made out by the secretary or some other officer of every such society or copartnership, and should be signed by such secretary or other officer, and should be verified by the oath of such officer taken before any justice of the peace (and which oath any justice of the peace was thereby authorized and empowered to administer) according to the form contained in the Schedule to that Act annexed, and in every such account or return there should be set forth the true name or firm of such society or copartnership, and also the names and places of abode of all the partners concerned or engaged in such society or copartnership, as the same respectively appear on the books of such society or copartnership, and the firm and name of and every bank or banks established or to be established by such society or copartnership, and also the names of two or more individuals of such society or copartnership who should be resident in *Ireland*, each and every of whom should respectively be considered as a public officer of such society or copartnership, and the title of office or other description of every such individual respectively in the name of any one of whom such society or copartnership should sue and be sued as thereinafter provided, and also the name of every town and place where any such bills or notes should be issued by any such society or copartnership, or by any agent or agents of any such society or copartnership; and every such account or return should be produced at the Stamp Office in *Dublin*, and an entry and registry thereof should be made in a book or books to be kept for that purpose at the said Stamp Office by some person or persons to be appointed for that purpose by the Commissioners of Stamp Duties; and if, after the passing of that Act, any such society or copartnership should omit or neglect to deliver at the Stamp Office

Account of new officers or places of banking in the course of any year to be made out.

1 Will. 4, c. 32.

in *Dublin* such account and return as was by that Act required, such society or copartnership should, for each and every week they should so neglect to make such account and return, forfeit the sum of five hundred pounds; and it was further enacted, that whenever any entry and registry of the firm or name of any such society or copartnership should be made at the Stamp Office, in manner aforesaid, at any time between the twenty-fifth day of *March* in any year and the twenty-fifth day of *March* following, a certificate of such entry or registry should be granted by the said Commissioners of Stamps, or by some person deputed and authorized by the said commissioners for that purpose, to the society or copartnership by or on whose behalf such entry or registry should be made, and such certificate should be written on vellum, parchment, or paper duly stamped with a stamp required by law for certificates to be taken out yearly by any banker or bankers in *Ireland*, and a separate and distinct certificate on a separate piece of vellum, parchment, or paper, with a separate and distinct stamp, should be granted for and in respect of every town and place where any such bill or note should be issued by any such society or copartnership, or by any agent or agents for or on account of such society or copartnership, and every such certificate should specify the proper firm, style, title, or name of such society or copartnership under which such notes were to be issued, and also the name of the town or place or the several towns or places where such notes were to be issued, and the Christian and surname and place of abode and title of office or other description of the several individuals named respectively as the public officers of such society or copartnership, in the name of any one of whom such society or copartnership should sue and be sued; and every certificate should be dated on the day on which the same should be granted, and should have effect and continue in force from the day of the date thereof until the twenty-fifth day of *March* following, both inclusive, and no longer, and should be sufficient evidence of the appointment and authority of such public officers respectively: And whereas by the said last-recited Act no provision is made for adding to the registry, between the twenty-fifth day of *March* in any year and the twenty-fifth day of *March* in the succeeding year, the name or names of any additional public officer or public officers, or of any additional place or places where such societies or copartnerships may establish a bank or banks, or issue the bills or notes thereby authorized; be it therefore further enacted, That from and after the passing of this Act it shall and may be lawful to and for such societies or copartnerships from time to time, and at any times between the twenty-fifth day of *March* in any year and the twenty-fifth day of *March* in the succeeding year, to make out upon oath, and cause to be delivered to the Commissioners of Stamps, in manner mentioned in the said last-recited Act of the sixth year of the reign of King *George* the Fourth, a further account or return or further accounts or returns, according to the form contained in the Schedule of this Act annexed, of the name or names of any person or persons who shall have been nominated or appointed a new or additional public officer or public officers of such society or copartnership, or of the name of any new or additional town or towns, or place or places, where such bills or notes are or are intended to be issued, and where the same are to be made payable, or of both or either of the above matters together or separately;

and such further accounts or returns shall from time to time be filed and kept and entered and registered at the Stamp Office in *Dublin* in like manner as is by the said Act of the sixth year of the reign of King *George* the Fourth required with respect to the original or annual account or return thereby directed to be made, and that thereupon an additional certificate or additional certificates of such account and return or accounts and returns shall be granted by the persons, and in the same manner, and upon the same stamps, and containing the same particulars as in the said recited Act of the sixth year of the reign of His present Majesty particularly mentioned; and which additional certificate or certificates shall have effect and continue in force from the day of the date thereof until the twenty-fifth day of *March* following, and no longer, and shall be sufficient evidence of the appointment and authority of the public officers respectively.

1 Will. 4, c. 32.

Additional certificates to be granted.

VII. And be it further enacted, That a copy of any such account or return so filed or kept and registered at the Stamp Office as by the said recited Act of the sixth year of the reign of His present Majesty and by this Act is directed, and which copy shall be certified to be a true copy under the hand or hands of one or more of the Commissioners of Stamps, or other officer or officers of the Stamp Office in *London* or *Dublin* for the time being, upon proof made that such certificate has been signed with the handwriting of the person or persons making the same, and whom it shall not be necessary to prove to be a commissioner or commissioners, officer or officers, shall in all proceedings, civil or criminal, and in all cases whatsoever, be received in evidence as proof of the appointment and authority of the public officers named in such account or return, and also of the fact that all persons named therein as members of such society or copartnership were members thereof at the date of such account or return.

Certified copies of returns to be evidence of the appointment of the public officers, &c.

VIII. And be it further enacted, That the said Commissioners of Stamps or other officers of the Stamp Office for the time being shall and they are hereby required, upon application made to them by any person or persons requiring a copy, certified according to this Act, of any such account or return as aforesaid, in order that the same may be produced in evidence, or for any other purpose, to deliver to the person or persons so applying for the same such certified copy, he, she, or they paying for the same the sum of ten shillings, and no more.

Commissioners of Stamps to give certified copies of returns, on payment of 10*s*.

IX. And whereas doubts have arisen as to the mode and times at which the societies or copartnerships authorized by the said recited Act of the sixth year of the reign of King *George* the Fourth, by the terms of the said Act, are required to make a return or account of the sales and transfers of their shares; be it therefore further enacted and declared, That it is and shall be the true intent and meaning of the said recited Act of the sixth year of the reign of King *George* the Fourth, that such societies and copartnerships are not and shall not be liable or obliged to make any return or account to the Stamp Office in *Dublin* of any sale or transfer of their shares which shall take place between the twenty-fifth day of *March* in any year and the twenty-fifth day of *March* in the succeeding year; but the said

Explaining the time at which societies are to make returns to the Stamp Office.

1 Will 4, c. 32. societies or copartnerships shall only be liable and obliged to make an account or return to the Stamp Office in *Dublin* once in every year in the manner and containing the particulars in the said Act mentioned.

SCHEDULE.

RETURN or Account to be entered at the Stamp Office in Dublin, on behalf of [*name society or copartnership*], in pursuance of an Act passed in the year of the reign of King George the Fourth, intituled [*insert the title of this Act*]; videlicet,

Names of any and every new or additional public officer of the said society or copartnership; videlicet,

A. B. in room of *C. D.* deceased *or* removed, *or* in addition to *C. D.* and *E. F.* [*as the case may be; set forth every name*].

Names of any additional town or place or towns or places where bills or notes are to be issued, and where the same are to be made payable

[*Set forth the names*].

A. B. of secretary [*or other officer*] of the above-named society or copartnership, maketh oath and saith, That the above doth contain the name and place of abode of every person who hath become or been appointed a public officer of the above society or copartnership since the registry [*or* last account or return] of the said society or copartnership, on the day of last, as the same respectively appear on the books of the said society or copartnership, and to the best of the information, knowledge, and belief of this deponent.

Sworn before me, the day of
in the county of

C. D. justice of the peace in and for the said county.

[3 & 4 Will. 4, c. 83.]

3 & 4 Will. 4, c. 83. *An Act to compel Banks issuing Promissory Notes payable to Bearer on Demand to make Returns of their Notes in Circulation, and to authorize Banks to issue Notes payable in London for less than Fifty Pounds.* [28*th August*, 1833].

WHEREAS it is expedient that all corporations, copartnerships, and persons carrying on banking business, and making and issuing promissory notes payable to bearer on demand, should make returns of the amount of such notes in circulation: Be it therefore enacted by the King's most excellent Majesty, by and with the advice and consent of the Lords spiritual and temporal, and Commons, in this present Parliament assembled, and by the authority of the same,

That all corporations and copartnerships carrying on banking business under the provisions of an Act passed in the seventh year of the reign of His late Majesty King *George* the Fourth, intituled *An Act for the better regulating Copartnerships of certain Bankers in* England, *and of amending so much of an Act of the Thirty-ninth and Fortieth Years of the Reign of His late Majesty King* George *the Third, intituled 'An Act for establishing an Agreement with the Governor and Company of the Bank of* England *for advancing the Sum of Three Millions towards the Supply for the Service of the Year One Thousand eight hundred,' as relates to the same*, and all other persons carrying on banking business, and making and issuing promissory notes payable to bearer on demand, shall respectively keep weekly accounts from the passing of this Act of the average amount of notes in circulation at the end of each week of the corporation, copartnership, or persons or person so carrying on banking business and keeping such weekly account; and shall, within one month after the thirty-first day of *December* after the passing of this Act, make up from such weekly account an average account of the amount of such notes in circulation during the period between the passing of this Act and the making up such account; and shall also make up a like account at the end of each quarter ending on the first day of *April*, the first day of *July*, the first day of *October*, and the first day of *January* in the year one thousand eight hundred and thirty-four and every subsequent year, of the average amount of notes in circulation in the preceding quarter, and shall return and deliver such account to the Commissioners of Stamps at the Stamp Office in *London;* and such accounts and returns shall be verified upon the oath of the secretary or accountant or some officer of the corporation, company, or copartnership, or persons or person so carrying on banking business and making such return, which oath shall be taken before any justice of the peace, and which oath any justice of the peace is hereby authorized to administer; and if any corporation, company, or copartnership, or persons or person so carrying on banking business, shall neglect to keep such weekly accounts, or to make out or to return or deliver such averages to the Commissioners of Stamps at the Stamp Office in *London*, or if any secretary, accountant, or other person verifying any such account or average shall return or deliver to the Commissioners of Stamps any false account or return of such averages, the corporation, company, or copartnership, or persons or person to whom any such account or averages, or such secretary, accountant, or person verifying the account, shall belong, shall forfeit for every such offence the sum of five hundred pounds, and the secretary or other person so offending shall also forfeit for every such offence the sum of one hundred pounds; and any secretary, accountant, or other person who shall knowingly and wilfully take any false oath as to any such account or averages shall be subject to such pains and penalties as are by any law in force at the time of taking such oath enacted as to persons convicted of wilful and corrupt perjury.

3 & 4 Will. 4, c. 83.

Partnerships and persons carrying on banking business, and issuing promissory notes, to keep accounts of the amount in circulation, and make periodical returns therefrom to the Stamp Office in London.

Such returns to be verified on oath.

Penalty for default, 500*l*.

False swearing punished as perjury.

II. And be it further enacted, That it shall be lawful for any body politic or corporate whatsoever, erected or to be erected, and for any other persons united or to be united in covenants or partnership, exceeding the number of six persons, carrying on business as bankers, to make any bill of exchange or promissory note of such corporation

Banks of more than six persons may draw on agent in London, on

3 & 4 Will. 4, c. 83.

demand or otherwise, for less than 50*l*., notwithstanding the Act 7 G. 4, c. 46.

or copartnership payable in *London* by any agent of such corporation or copartnership in *London*, or to draw any bill of exchange or promissory note upon any such agent in *London*, payable on demand or otherwise in *London*, and for any less amount than fifty pounds, any thing in the said recited Act of the seventh year of the reign of His late Majesty King *George* the Fourth, or in any other Act, to the contrary notwithstanding.

Act may be altered this session.

III. And be it further enacted, That this Act may be amended, altered, or repealed by any Act or Acts to be passed in this present session of Parliament.

[3 & 4 Will. 4, c. 98.]

3 & 4 Will. 4, c. 98.

An Act for giving to the Corporation of the Governor and Company of the Bank of England certain Privileges, for a limited Period, under certain Conditions. [29*th August*, 1833.]

39 & 40 Geo. 3, c. 28.

7 Geo. 4, c. 46.

WHEREAS an Act was passed in the thirty-ninth and fortieth years of the reign of His Majesty King *George* the Third, intituled *An Act for establishing an Agreement with the Governor and Company of the Bank of* England *for advancing the Sum of Three Millions towards the Supply for the Service of the Year One thousand eight hundred:* And whereas it was by the said recited Act declared and enacted, that the said governor and company should be and continue a corporation, with such powers, authorities, emoluments, profits, and advantages, and such privileges of exclusive banking as are in the said recited Act specified, subject nevertheless to the powers and conditions of redemption, and on the terms in the said Act mentioned: And whereas an Act passed in the seventh year of the reign of His late Majesty King *George* the Fourth, intituled *An Act for the better regulating Copartnerships of certain Bankers in* England, *and for amending so much of an Act of the Thirty-ninth and Fortieth Years of the Reign of His late Majesty King* George *the Third, intituled 'An Act for establishing an Agreement with the Governor and Company of the Bank of* England *for advancing the Sum of Three Millions towards the Supply for the Service of the Year One thousand eight hundred,' as relates to the same:* And whereas it is expedient that certain privileges of exclusive banking should be continued to the said governor and company for a further limited period, upon certain conditions: And whereas the said Governor and Company of the Bank of *England* are willing to deduct and allow to the public, from the sums now payable to the said governor and company for the charges of management of the public unredeemed debt, the annual sum hereinafter mentioned, and for the period in this Act specified, provided the privilege of exclusive banking specified in this Act is continued to the said governor and company for the period specified in this Act: May it therefore please your Majesty that it may be enacted; and be it enacted by the King's most excellent Majesty, by and with the advice and consent of the Lords spiritual and temporal, and Commons, in this present Parliament assembled, and by the authority of the same, That the said Governor and Company of the Bank of *England* shall have and enjoy such exclusive privilege of banking as is given by this Act, as a body corporate, for the period and upon the terms and conditions hereinafter mentioned, and subject to termination of such exclusive privilege at the time and in the manner in this Act specified.

3 & 4 Will. 4, c 98.

Bank of England to enjoy an exclusive privilege of banking upon certain conditions.

II. And be it further enacted, That during the continuance of the said privilege, no body politic or corporate, and no society or company, or persons united or to be united in covenants or partnerships, exceeding six persons, shall make or issue in *London*, or within sixty-five miles thereof, any bill of exchange or promissory note, or engagement for the payment of money on demand, or upon which any person holding the same may obtain payment on demand: Provided always, that nothing herein or in the said recited Act of the seventh year of the reign of His late Majesty King *George* the Fourth contained shall be construed to prevent any body politic or corporate, or any society or company, or incorporated company or corporation, or copartnership, carrying on and transacting banking business at any greater distance than sixty-five miles from *London*, and not having any house of business or establishment as bankers in *London*, or within sixty-five miles thereof (except as hereinafter mentioned), to make and issue their bills and notes, payable on demand or otherwise, at the place at which the same shall be issued, being more than sixty-five miles from *London*, and also in *London*, and to have an agent or agents in *London*, or at any other place at which such bills or notes shall be made payable for the purpose of payment only, but no such bill or note shall be for any sum less than five pounds, or be reissued in *London*, or within sixty-five miles thereof.

During such privilege, no banking company of more than six persons to issue notes payable on demand within London, or sixty-five miles thereof.

III. And whereas the intention of this Act is, that the Governor and Company of the Bank of *England* should, during the period stated in this Act (subject nevertheless to such redemption as is described in this Act), continue to hold and enjoy all the exclusive privileges of banking given by the said recited Act of the thirty-ninth and fortieth years of the reign of His Majesty King *George* the Third aforesaid, as regulated by the said recited Act of the seventh year of His late Majesty King *George* the Fourth, or any prior or subsequent Act or Acts of Parliament, but no other or further exclusive privilege of banking: And whereas doubts have arisen as to the construction of the said Acts, and as to the extent of such exclusive privilege; and it is expedient that all such doubts should be removed, be it therefore declared and enacted, That any body politic or corporate, or society, or company, or partnership, although consisting of more than six persons, may carry on the trade or business of banking in *London*, or within sixty-five miles thereof, provided that such body politic or corporate, or society, or company, or partnership do not borrow, owe, or take up in *England* any sum or sums of money on their bills or notes payable on demand, or at any less time than six months from the borrowing thereof, during the continuance of the privileges granted by this Act to the said Governor and Company of the Bank of *England*.

Any company or partnership may carry on business of banking in London, or within sixty-five miles thereof, upon the terms hereinmentioned.

3 & 4 Will. 4, c. 98.

All notes of the Bank of England payable on demand which shall be issued out of London shall be payable at the place where issued, &c.

IV. Provided always, and be it further enacted, That from and after the first day of *August* one thousand eight hundred and thirty-four all promissory notes payable on demand of the Governor and Company of the Bank of *England* which shall be issued at any place in that part of the United Kingdom called *England* out of *London*, where the trade and business of banking shall be carried on for and on behalf of the said Governor and Company of the Bank of *England*, shall be made payable at the place where such promissory notes shall be issued; and it shall not be lawful for the said governor and company, or any committee, agent, cashier, officer, or servant of the said governor and company, to issue, at any such place out of *London*, any promissory note payable on demand which shall not be made payable at the place where the same shall be issued, any thing in the said recited Act of the seventh year aforesaid to the contrary notwithstanding.

Exclusive privileges hereby given to end upon one year's notice given at the end of ten years after August 1834.

V. And be it further enacted, That upon one year's notice given within six months after the expiration of ten years from the first day of *August* one thousand eight hundred and thirty-four, and upon repayment by Parliament to the said governor and company, or their successors, of all principal money, interest, or annuities which may be due from the public to the said governor and company at the time of the expiration of such notice, in like manner as is hereinafter stipulated and provided, in the event of such notice being deferred until after the first day of *August* one thousand eight hundred and fifty-five, the said exclusive privileges of banking granted by this Act shall cease and determine at the expiration of such year's notice; and any vote or resolution of the House of Commons, signified by the speaker of the said house in writing, and delivered at the public office of the said governor and company, or their successors, shall be deemed and adjudged to be a sufficient notice.

What shall be deemed sufficient notice.

Bank notes to be a legal tender, except at the bank and branch banks.

VI. And be it further enacted, That from and after the first day of *August* one thousand eight hundred and thirty-four, unless and until Parliament shall otherwise direct, a tender of a note or notes of the Governor and Company of the Bank of *England*, expressed to be payable to bearer on demand, shall be a legal tender, to the amount expressed in such note or notes, and shall be taken to be valid as a tender to such amount for all sums above five pounds on all occasions on which any tender of money may be legally made, so long as the Bank of *England* shall continue to pay on demand their said notes in legal coin: Provided always, that no such note or notes shall be deemed a legal tender of payment by the Governor and Company of the Bank of *England*, or any branch bank of the said governor and company; but the said governor and company are not to become liable or be required to pay and satisfy, at any branch bank of the said governor and company, any note or notes of the said governor and company not made specially payable at such branch bank; but the said governor and company shall be liable to pay and satisfy at the Bank of *England* in *London* all notes of the said governor and company, or of any branch thereof.

Accounts of bullion, &c. and of notes

VIII. And be it further enacted, That an account of the amount of bullion and securities in the Bank of *England* belonging to the said governor and company, and of notes in circulation, and of deposits in the said bank, shall be transmitted weekly to the Chancellor of the Exchequer for the time being, and such accounts shall be consolidated at the end of every month, and an average state of the bank accounts of the preceding three months, made from such consolidated accounts as aforesaid, shall be published every month in the next succeeding *London Gazette*.

3 & 4 Will. 4, c. 98.

in circulation to be sent weekly to the Chancellor of the Exchequer, &c.

IX. And be it further enacted, That one fourth part of the debt of fourteen million six hundred and eighty-six thousand eight hundred pounds, now due from the public to the Governor and Company of the Bank of *England*, shall and may be repaid to the said governor and company.

Public to pay the bank one fourth part of the debt of 14,686,800*l.*

X. And be it further enacted, That a general court of proprietors of the said Governor and Company of the Bank of *England* shall be held at some time between the passing of this Act and the fifth day of *October* one thousand eight hundred and thirty-four, to determine upon the propriety of dividing and appropriating the sum of three million six hundred and thirty-eight thousand two hundred and fifty pounds, out of or by means of the sum to be repaid to the said governor and company as hereinbefore mentioned, or out of or by means of the fund to be provided for that purpose, amongst the several persons, bodies politic or corporate, who may be proprietors of the capital stock of the said governor and company on the said fifth day of *October* one thousand eight hundred and thirty-four, and upon the manner and the time for making such division and appropriation, not inconsistent with the provisions for that purpose herein contained; and in case such general court, or any adjourned general court, shall determine that it will be proper to make such division, then, but not otherwise, the capital stock of the said governor and company shall be and the same is hereby declared to be reduced from the sum of fourteen million five hundred and fifty-three thousand pounds, of which the same now consists, to the sum of ten million nine hundred fourteen thousand seven hundred and fifty pounds, making a reduction or difference of three million six hundred and thirty-eight thousand two hundred and fifty pounds capital stock, and such reduction shall take place from and after the said fifth day of *October* one thousand eight hundred and thirty-four; and thereupon, out of or by means of the sum to be repaid to the said governor and company as hereinbefore mentioned, or out of or by means of the fund to be provided for that purpose, the sum of three million six hundred and thirty-eight thousand two hundred and fifty pounds sterling, or such proportion of the said fund as shall represent the same, shall be appropriated and divided amongst the several persons, bodies politic or corporate, who may be proprietors of the said sum of fourteen million five hundred and fifty-three thousand pounds bank stock on the said fifth day of *October* one thousand eight hundred and thirty-four, at the rate of twenty-five pounds sterling for every one hundred pounds of bank stock which such persons, bodies politic and corporate, may then be proprietors of or shall have standing in their respective names in the books kept by the said governor and company for the entry and transfer of such stock, and so in proportion for a greater or lesser sum.

Capital stock of the bank may be reduced.

3 & 4 Will. 4, c. 98.

Governor, deputy governor, or directors not to be disqualified by reduction of their share of the capital stock.

XI. Provided always, and be it enacted, That the reduction of the share of each proprietor of and in the capital stock of the said Governor and Company of the Bank of *England*, by the repayment of such one fourth part thereof, shall not disqualify the present governor, deputy governor, or director, or any or either of them, or any governor, deputy governor, or director who may be chosen in the room of the present governor, deputy governor, or directors at any time before the general court of the said governor and company to be held between the twenty-fifth day of *March* and the twenty-fifth day of *April* one thousand eight hundred and thirty-five: Provided that at the said general court, and from and after the same, no governor, deputy governor, or director of the said corporation shall be capable of being chosen such governor, deputy governor, or director, or shall continue in his or their respective offices, unless he or they respectively shall at the time of such choice have, and during such his respective office continue to have, in his and their respective name, in his and their own right, and for his and their own use, the respective sums or shares of and in the capital stock of the said corporation in and by the charter of the said governor and company prescribed as the qualification of governor, deputy governor, and directors respectively.

Proprietors not to be disqualified.

XII. Provided also, and be it enacted, That no proprietor shall be disqualified from attending and voting at any general court of the said governor and company, to be held between the said fifth day of *October* one thousand eight hundred and thirty-four and the twenty-fifth day of *April* one thousand eight hundred and thirty-five, in consequence of the share of such proprietor of and in the capital stock of the said governor and company having been reduced by such repayment as aforesaid below the sum of five hundred pounds of and in the said capital stock ; provided such proprietor had in his own name the full sum of five hundred pounds of and in the said capital stock on the said fifth day of *October* one thousand eight hundred and thirty-four ; nor shall any proprietor be required, between the said fifth day of *October* one thousand eight hundred and thirty-four and the twenty-fifth day of *April* one thousand eight hundred and thirty-five, to take the oath of qualification in the said charter.

Bank to deduct the annual sum of 120,000*l.* from sum allowed for management of national debt.

XIII. And be it further enacted, That from and after the said first day of *August* one thousand eight hundred and thirty-four the said governor and company, in consideration of the privileges of exclusive banking given by this Act, shall, during the continuance of such privileges, but no longer, deduct from the sums now payable to the said governor and company, for the charges of management of the public unredeemed debt, the annual sum of one hundred and twenty thousand pounds, any thing in any Act or Acts of Parliament or agreement to the contrary notwithstanding : Provided always, that such deduction shall in no respect prejudice or affect the right of the said governor and company to be paid for the management of the public debt at the rate and according to the terms provided in an Act passed in the forty-eighth year of His late Majesty King *George* the Third, intituled *An Act to authorize the advancing for the public Service, upon certain Conditions, a Proportion of the Balance remaining in the Bank of* England *for Payment of Unclaimed*

48 Geo. 3, c. 4.

Dividends, Annuities, and Lottery Prizes, and for regulating the Allowances to be made for the Management of the National Debt. 3 & 4 Will. 4, c. 98.

XIV. And be it further enacted, That all the powers, authorities, franchises, privileges, and advantages given or recognized by the said recited Act of the thirty-ninth and fortieth years aforesaid, as belonging to or enjoyed by the Governor and Company of the Bank of *England*, or by any subsequent Act or Acts of Parliament, shall be and the same are hereby declared to be in full force and continued by this Act, except so far as the same are altered by this Act, subject nevertheless to such redemption upon the terms and conditions following; (that is to say,) that at any time, upon twelve months' notice to be given after the first day of *August* one thousand eight hundred and fifty-five, and upon repayment by Parliament to the said governor and company or their successors of the sum of eleven million fifteen thousand one hundred pounds, being the debt which will remain due from the public to the said governor and company after the payment of the one fourth of the debt of fourteen million six hundred and eighty-six thousand eight hundred pounds as hereinbefore provided, without any deduction, discount, or abatement whatsoever, and upon payment to the said governor and company and their successors of all arrears of the sum of one hundred thousand pounds *per annum* in the said Act of the thirty-ninth and fortieth years aforesaid mentioned, together with the interest or annuities payable upon the said debt or in respect thereof, and also upon repayment of all the principal and interest which shall be owing unto the said governor and company and their successors upon all such tallies, exchequer orders, exchequer bills, or parliamentary funds which the said governor and company or their successors shall have remaining in their hands or be entitled to at the time of such notice to be given as last aforesaid, then and in such case, and not till then (unless under the proviso hereinbefore contained), the said exclusive privileges of banking granted by this Act shall cease and determine at the expiration of such notice of twelve months. Provisions of Act of 39 & 40 Geo. 3 to remain in force, except as altered by this Act.

XV. And be it further enacted, That this Act may be altered, amended, or repealed by any Act to be passed in this session of Parliament. Act may be amended this session.

[1 & 2 Vict. c. 96.]*

An Act to amend, until the End of the next Session of Parliament, the Law relative to Legal Proceedings by certain Joint Stock Banking Companies against their own Members, and by such Members against the Companies. [14*th August*, 1838.] 1 & 2 Vict. c. 96.

Whereas by an Act passed in the seventh year of the reign of His late Majesty King *George* the Fourth, intituled *An Act for the better* 7 Geo. 4, c. 46.

* Made perpetual by 5 & 6 Vict. c. 85.

1 & 2 Vict. c. 96.

regulating Copartnerships of certain Bankers in England, *and for amending so much of an Act of the Thirty-ninth and Fortieth Years of the Reign of His late Majesty King* George *the Third, intituled 'An Act for establishing an Agreement with the Governor and Company of the Bank of* England *for advancing the Sum of Three Millions towards the Supply of the Service of the Year Eighteen hundred,' as relates to the same,* it was amongst other things enacted, that it should be lawful for any bodies politic or corporate erected for the purposes of banking, or for any number of persons united in covenants or copartnerships, although such persons so united or carrying on business together should consist of more than six in number, to carry on (subject to certain provisions therein contained) the trade or business of bankers in *England,* in like manner as copartnerships of bankers consisting of not more than six persons in number might lawfully do; and it was further enacted, that all actions and suits against any persons who might be at any time indebted to any such copartnership carrying on business under the provisions of the said Act, and all other proceedings at law and in equity to be instituted on behalf of any such copartnership against any persons, bodies politic or corporate, or others, whether members of such copartnership or otherwise, for recovering any debts or enforcing any claims or demands due to such copartnership, or for any other matter relating to the concerns of such copartnership, might be commenced and prosecuted in the name of any one of the public officers for the time being of such copartnership, to be nominated as therein is mentioned, as the nominal party on behalf of such copartnership, and that actions or suits, and proceedings at law or in equity, to be instituted by any persons, bodies politic or corporate, or others, whether members of such copartnership or otherwise, against such copartnership, should be commenced and prosecuted against any one or more of the public officers for the time being of such copartnership as the nominal defendant on behalf of such copartnership, and that the death, resignation, removal, or any act of such public officer should not abate or prejudice any such action, suit, or other proceeding commenced against or on behalf of such copartnership, but that the same might be continued in the name of any other of the public officers of such copartnership for the time being: And whereas an Act was passed in the sixth year of the reign of His said late Majesty, intituled *An Act for the better Regulation of Copartnerships of certain Bankers in* Ireland: And whereas it is expedient that the said Acts should for a limited time be amended so far as relates to the powers enabling any such copartnership, not being a body corporate, to sue any of its own members, and the powers enabling any member of any such copartnership, not being a body corporate, to sue the said copartnership: Be it therefore enacted by the Queen's most excellent Majesty, by and with the advice and consent of the Lords spiritual and temporal, and Commons, in this present Parliament assembled, and by the authority of the same,

6 Geo. 4, c. 42.

Banking copartnerships may sue and be sued.

That any person now being or having been or who may hereafter be or have been a member of any copartnership now carrying on or which may hereafter carry on the business of banking under the provisions of the said recited Acts may, at any time during the continuance of this Act, in respect of any demand which such person may have, either solely or jointly with any other person, against the said copartnership, or the funds or property thereof, commence and prosecute, either solely or jointly with any other person (as the case may require), any action, suit, or other proceeding at law or in equity against any public officer appointed or to be appointed under the provisions of the said Acts to sue and be sued on the behalf of the said copartnership; and that any such public officer may in his own name commence and prosecute any action, suit, or other proceeding at law or in equity against any person being or having been a member of the said copartnership, either alone or jointly with any other person, against whom any such copartnership has or may have any demand whatsoever; and that every person being or having been a member of any such copartnership shall, either solely or jointly with any other person (as the case may require), be capable of proceeding against any such copartnership by their public officer, and be liable to be proceeded against, by or for the benefit of the said copartnership, by such public officer as aforesaid, by such proceedings and with the same legal consequences as if such person had not been a member of the said copartnership; and that no action or suit shall in anywise be affected or defeated by reason of the plaintiffs or defendants or any of them respectively, or any other person in whom any interest may be averred, or who may be in anywise interested or concerned in such action, being or having been a member of the said copartnership; and that all such actions, suits, and proceedings shall be conducted and have effect as if the same had been between strangers. 1 & 2 Vict. c. 96.

II. And be it enacted, That in case the merits of any demand by or against any such copartnership shall have been determined in any action or suit by or against any such public officer, the proceedings in such action or suit may be pleaded in bar of any other action or suit by or against the public officer of the same copartnership for the same demand. Proceedings in an action may be pleaded in bar of any other action.

III. And be it enacted, That all the provisions of the said recited Acts relative to actions, suits, and proceedings commenced or prosceuted under the authority thereof, shall be applicable to actions, suits, and proceedings commenced or prosecuted under the authority of this Act. Extending provisions of recited Acts to present Act.

IV. And be it enacted, That no claim or demand which any member of any such copartnership may have in respect of his share of the capital or joint stock thereof, or of any dividends, interest, profits, or bonus payable or apportionable in respect of such share, shall be capable of being set off, either at law or in equity, against any demand which such copartnership may have against such member on account of any other matter or thing whatsoever; but all proceedings in respect of such other matter or thing may be carried on as if no claim or demand existed in respect of such capital or joint stock, or of any dividends, interest, profits, or bonus payable or apportionable in respect thereof. A member's share in capital of copartnership not to be set off against any demand which such copartnership may have against him

V. And be it enacted, That this Act shall continue in force until the end of the next session of Parliament; and that any such action, suit, or other proceeding as aforesaid, which during the continuance of this Act may have been commenced or instituted, shall (notwith- Continuance of Act.

1 & 2 Vict. c. 96. standing this Act may have expired) be carried on in all respects whatsoever as if this Act had continued in force.

Act may be amended this session. VI. And be it enacted, That this Act may be amended or repealed by any Act to be passed in this present session of Parliament.

[3 & 4 Vict. c. 111.] *

3 & 4 Vict. c. 111. *An Act to continue until the Thirty-first Day of August One thousand eight hundred and Forty-two, and to extend, the Provisions of an Act of the First and Second Years of Her present Majesty, relating to Legal Proceedings by certain Joint Stock Banking Companies against their own Members, and by such Members against the Companies.* [11*th August*, 1840.]

1 & 2 Vict. c. 96. WHEREAS an Act was passed in the first and second years of the reign of Her present Majesty, intituled *An Act to extend, until the End of the next Session of Parliament, the Law relative to Legal Proceedings by certain Joint Stock Banking Companies against their own Members, and by such Members against the Companies:* and whereas the said Act has been continued until the thirty-first day of *August* one thousand eight hundred and forty by an Act passed in the last session of Parliament, and it is expedient that the same should be further continued: Be it therefore enacted by the Queen's most excellent Majesty, by and with the advice and consent of the Lords spiritual and temporal, and Commons, in this present Parliament assembled, and by the authority of the same, That the said first recited Act shall be further continued until the thirty-first day of *August* one thousand eight hundred and forty-two.

Recited Act continued.

Punishing members of banking companies embezzling notes, &c. II. And whereas it is expedient to extend the provisions of the said Act hereby continued in manner hereinafter stated; be it enacted, That if any person or persons, being a member or members of any banking copartnership within the meaning of the said Act, or of any other banking copartnership consisting of more than six persons, formed under or in pursuance of an Act passed in the third and fourth years of the reign of King *William* the Fourth, intituled *An Act for giving to the Corporation of the Governor and Company of the Bank of* England *certain Privileges, for a limited Period, under certain Conditions,* shall steal or embezzle any money, goods, effects, bills, notes, securities, or other property of or belonging to any such copartnership, or shall commit any fraud, forgery, crime, or offence against or with attempt to injure or defraud any such copartnership, such member or members shall be liable to indictment, information, prosecution, or other proceeding in the name of any of the officers for the time being of any such copartnership, in whose name any

3 & 4 Will. 4, c. 98.

* Made perpetual by 5 & 6 Vict. c. 85.

action or suit might be lawfully brought against any member or members of any such copartnership for every such fraud, forgery, crime, or offence, and may thereupon be lawfully convicted, as if such person or persons had not been or was or were not a member or members of such copartnership; any law, usage, or custom to the contrary notwithstanding.

3 & 4 Vict. c. 111.

[4 Vict. c. 14.]

An Act to make good certain Contracts which have been or may be entered into by certain Banking and other Copartnerships. [*18th May*, 1841.]

4 Vict. c. 14.

Whereas divers associations and copartnerships consisting of more than six members or shareholders have from time to time been formed, for the purpose of being engaged in and carrying on the business of banking, and divers other trades and dealings, for gain and profit, and have accordingly for some time past been and are now engaged in carrying on the same, by means of boards of directors or managers, committees, or other officers acting on behalf of all the members or shareholders of or persons otherwise interested in such associations or copartnerships: And whereas divers spiritual persons having or holding dignities, prebends, canonries, benefices, stipendiary curacies, or lectureships have been members or shareholders of or otherwise interested in divers of such associations and copartnerships: And whereas it is expedient to render legal and valid all contracts entered into by such associations or copartnerships, although the same may now be void by reason of such spiritual persons being or having been such members or shareholders or otherwise interested as aforesaid; be it therefore enacted by the Queen's most excellent Majesty, by and with the advice and consent of the Lords spiritual and temporal, and Commons, in this present Parliament assembled, and by the authority of the same, That no such association or copartnership already formed, or which may be hereafter formed, nor any contract either as between the members, partners, or shareholders composing such association or copartnership for the purposes thereof, or as between such association or copartnership and other persons, heretofore entered into or which shall be entered into by any such association or copartnership already formed or hereafter to be formed, shall be deemed or taken to be illegal or void, or to occasion any forfeiture whatsoever, by reason only of any such spiritual person as aforesaid being or having been a member, partner, or shareholder of or otherwise interested in the same; but all such associations and copartnerships shall have the same validity, and all such contracts shall and may be enforced in the same manner, to all intents and purposes, as if no such spiritual person had been or was a member, partner, or shareholder of or interested in such association or copartnership: Provided always, that it shall not be lawful for any spiritual person holding any cathedral preferment, benefice, curacy, or lectureship, or who shall be licensed or allowed

No association or copartnership, or contract entered into by any of them, to be illegal or void by reason only of spiritual persons being members thereof.

No spiritual person beneficed or performing ec-

4 Vict. c. 14.

clesiastical duty to act as a director.

to perform the duties of any ecclesiastical office, to act as a director or managing partner, or to carry on such trade or dealing as aforesaid in person.

In all actions and suits by copartnerships established since the session of 2 & 3 Vict., the defendant to be entitled to taxed costs, and the Court to make order for further costs.

II. And be it enacted, That in all actions and suits which shall have been brought or instituted by or on behalf of any such association or copartnership which may have been formed since the end of the session of Parliament held in the second and third years of the reign of Her present Majesty, in case any defendant therein shall, before the twenty-ninth day of *March* one thousand eight hundred and thirty-eight, by plea or otherwise, have insisted on the invalidity of any contract thereby sought to be enforced, by reason of any such spiritual person as aforesaid being or having been a member or shareholder in such association or copartnership, such defendant shall be entitled to the full costs of such plea or other defence, to be paid by the plaintiff, and to be taxed as the Court in which the said action or suit shall be depending, or any judge thereof, shall direct; and in order fully to indemnify such defendant it shall be lawful for such Court or judge to order the plaintiff to pay to him such further costs (if any) of the said action or suit as the justice of the case may require.

Act may be amended this session.

III. And be it enacted, That this Act may be amended or repealed by any Act to be passed in this present session of Parliament.

[4 & 5 Vict. c. 50.]

4 & 5 Vict. c. 50.

An Act to make further Provision relative to the Returns to be made by Banks of the Amount of their Notes in Circulation. [21*st June*, 1841.]

3 & 4 Will. 4, c. 83.

Whereas by an Act passed in the third and fourth years of the reign of His late Majesty King *William* the Fourth, intituled *An Act to compel Banks issuing Promissory Notes payable to Bearer on Demand to make Returns of their Notes in Circulation, and to authorize Banks to issue Notes payable in* London *for less than Fifty Pounds*, all corporations and copartnerships carrying on banking business, under the provisions of a certain Act therein recited, passed in the seventh year of the reign of King *George* the Fourth, and all other persons carrying on banking business, and making and issuing promissory notes payable to bearer on demand, are required respectively to keep certain weekly accounts of the amount of notes in circulation, and to make up a quarterly account of the average amount of such notes in circulation, and to return and deliver such quarterly account to the Commissioners of Stamps, at the Stamp Office in *London*, at the times and in the manner by the said first-recited Act directed: And whereas it is expedient to amend the said first-recited Act, and to require all such corporations, copartnerships, and persons carrying on banking business in any part of the United Kingdom to render more frequent returns of the amount of their notes in circulation: Be it therefore enacted by the Queen's most excellent Majesty, by and with the advice and consent of the Lords spiritual and temporal, and Commons, in this present Parliament assembled, and by the authority of the same, That from and after the first day of *July* one thousand eight hundred and forty-one, all corporations and copartnerships carrying on banking business under the provisions of the said Act passed in the seventh year of the reign of King *George* the Fourth, and all other persons carrying on banking business in *England* and *Wales*, and making and issuing promissory notes payable to bearer on demand, and all corporations, copartnerships, and persons carrying on such business, and making and issuing such promissory notes as aforesaid, in *Scotland*, and also the Governor and Company of the Bank of *Ireland*, and all corporations, copartnerships, and persons carrying on such business, and making and issuing such promissory notes as aforesaid, in *Ireland*, shall severally keep just and true accounts of the amount of notes in circulation at the close of the business in each week, and shall, at the end of every four weeks, make up from such weekly accounts a just and true account of the average amount of such notes in circulation during such four weeks; and shall also, within seven days after the conclusion of such four weeks, return and deliver such last-mentioned account for the four weeks immediately preceding, and so on every successive four weeks, such accounts being always verified in the manner hereinafter directed, to the Commissioners of Stamps and Taxes, at their head office in *Westminster*, upon pain that any corporation, company, copartnership, or persons or person, who shall neglect or omit to keep, or to return and deliver, any such account in the manner directed by this Act, shall for every such neglect or omission forfeit the sum of fifty pounds, to be recovered, with full costs of suit, in the name of Her Majesty's Attorney or Solicitor General in *England* or *Ireland*, or of Her Majesty's Advocate General in *Scotland*.

4 & 5 Vict. c 50.

Bankers in England, Scotland, and Ireland, respectively, issuing promissory notes payable to bearer on demand, to keep accounts of the amount in circulation, and to make returns thereof every four weeks.

Penalty for default, 50*l*.

II. And be it enacted, That every such account so to be returned and delivered to the Commissioners of Stamps and Taxes as aforesaid shall be verified by the affidavit or affirmation of the secretary, accountant, cashier, or other chief clerk or officer of the corporation, company, or copartnership, or persons or person, so carrying on banking business and making such return; and such affidavit or affirmation shall be made before any justice of the peace in any part of the United Kingdom, or before a master extraordinary in Chancery, or any person authorized to take affidavits by any of the superior courts in *England* or *Ireland*; and no such affidavit or affirmation shall be liable to any stamp duty.

Accounts to be verified by affidavit or affirmation.

III. And be it enacted, That from the accounts which shall be rendered by the Governor and Company of the Bank of *England* in pursuance of the Act in that behalf, and also from the accounts which shall be rendered in pursuance of this Act, there shall be made up an account of the average aggregate amount of promissory notes payable to bearer on demand which have been in circulation in the United Kingdom during the preceding four weeks, and so on every successive four weeks, distinguishing those circulated by the Bank of *England*, by private banks, and by joint stock banks in *England* and *Wales*, by the banks in *Scotland*, by the Bank of *Ireland*, and by all other banks in *Ireland*, and of the average amount of the bullion

An account to be made up every four weeks from the accounts to be rendered by the Bank of England, and by other bankers under this Act, and to be published in the 'London

4 & 5 Vict. c. 50.

Gazette' every four weeks.

in the Bank of *England* during the preceding four weeks; and such account shall be published in the *London Gazette* in every four weeks as soon as the same can conveniently be prepared for that purpose.

[5 & 6 Vict. c. 82.]

5 & 6 Vict. c. 82.

An Act to assimilate the Stamp Duties in Great Britain and Ireland, and to make Regulations for collecting and managing the same, until the Tenth Day of October One thousand eight hundred and forty-five.
[*5th August,* 1842.]

New duties

On deeds, &c., the same as in England granted by 55 Geo. 3, c. 184.

On gold and silver plate the same as by 55 Geo. 3, c, 185.

On licences to deal in plate the same as by

II. And be it enacted, That (save and except for or in respect of the articles, matters, and things mentioned or specified in the Schedule to this Act annexed) there shall be granted, raised, levied, collected, and paid, in *Ireland*, unto and for the use of Her Majesty, her heirs and successors, in lieu of the duties and composition for duties hereby repealed, the several sums of money, and duties and composition for duties, following; (that is to say), for and in respect of the several instruments, articles, matters, and things mentioned, enumerated, and described, *mutatis mutandis*, in the Schedule to an Act passed in the fifty-fifth year of the reign of King *George* the Third, intituled *An Act for repealing the Stamp Duties on Deeds, Law Proceedings, and other written or printed Instruments, and the Duties on* Fire *Insurances, and on Legacies and Successions to Personal Estate upon Intestacies, now payable in* Great Britain; *and for granting other Duties in lieu thereof* (except those standing under the head of exemptions), or for or in respect of all instruments, articles, matters, and things of the like nature, kind, and description, respectively, in *Ireland*, or of the vellum, parchment, or paper upon which such instruments, articles, matters, and things, or any of them, shall be written or printed, such and the like duties as by or under the said last-mentioned Act, or by or under any subsequent Act, are now payable in *England* for or in respect of the said instruments, articles, matters, and things respectively mentioned, enumerated, and described in the said Schedule to the said Act of the fifty-fifth year of the reign of King *George* the Third annexed, or for or in respect of the vellum, parchment, or paper whereon such instruments, articles, matters, or things respectively are written or printed; and also for and in respect of plate of gold and silver made or wrought in *Ireland*, the several duties or sums of money respectively by another Act passed in the fifty-fifth year of the reign of King *George* the Third, intituled *An Act for repealing the Stamp Office Duties on Advertisements, Almanacks, Newspapers, Gold and Silver Plate, Stage Coaches, and Licences for keeping Stage Coaches, now payable in* Great Britain; *and for granting new Duties in lieu thereof*, granted for or in respect of plate of gold and silver respectively made or wrought in *Great Britain;* and also for or in respect of licences to persons to sell or make gold or silver plate in *Ireland*, the several duties or sums of money respectively by an Act passed in the forty-third year of the reign of King *George* the Third, intituled *An Act to repeal the Duties of Excise payable in* Great Britain, *and to grant other Duties in lieu thereof*, granted for and upon licences to persons trading in, vending, or selling gold or silver plate; and also for and in respect of the promissory notes on unstamped paper issued by any licensed banker in *Ireland*, or such notes of such banker in circulation, the same composition as is payable by bankers in *England* in pursuance of an Act passed in the ninth year of the reign of King *George* the Fourth, intituled *An Act to enable Bankers in* England *to issue certain unstamped Promissory Notes and Bills of Exchange, upon Payment of a Composition in lieu of the Stamp Duties thereon;* and that the said Schedule annexed to the said first-mentioned Act passed in the fifty-fifth year of the reign of King *George* the Third shall, for the purposes of this Act, be read and taken and considered as if the same was annexed to and was a part of this Act, and all the instruments, articles, matters, and things (except as aforesaid) therein mentioned, enumerated, and described respectively were, *mutatis mutandis* mentioned, enumerated, and described as instruments, articles, matters, and things in or relating to *Ireland*, and not in or relating to *Great Britain* or *England;* and that wherever in the said Schedule the words "United Kingdom," "United Kingdom of *Great Britain* and *Ireland*," "in *Great Britain*," "in *England*," "at *Westminster*," or "in *Doctors' Commons*," are used, the word "*Ireland*," or the words "in *Ireland*," as the case may be or require, shall be substituted and read in lieu thereof, save and except where any of such words in the said Schedule shall be consistent with the object and true intent and meaning of this Act, and shall be applicable to the purposes thereof: Provided always, that the duties on policies of insurance from loss or damage by fire, and the yearly percentage duties for and in respect of such insurances, not expressly exempted from duty, shall be charged and paid respectively upon and for and in respect of all such policies and such insurances in *Ireland* as shall or may be granted and made by any person licensed, or who ought to be licensed, in pursuance of any Act of Parliament for that purpose, and upon and for and in respect of all and every policy and insurance respectively that can or may and shall be lawfully granted or made in *Ireland* by any corporation, company, or person, whether licensed or not: Provided always, that where any deed or other instrument mentioned or described in the said Schedule, or in the said Act passed in the third year of the reign of King *George* the Fourth, is declared to be exempt from *ad valorem* duty, by reason of the payment for or in respect of any other deed or instrument of any *ad valorem* duty specified in the said Schedule, or granted by any former Act, such exemption shall be deemed to extend in like manner to all deeds and instruments of the same description executed after the commencement of this Act, in all cases where any *ad valorem* duty of the like kind respectively granted by the said Act passed in the fifty-sixth year of the reign of King *George* the Third, or any Act in that behalf therein mentioned, or this Act, shall have been paid for or in respect of any such other deed or instrument: Provided also, that in the cases of sub-sales mentioned in the said Schedule under the head "Conveyance," the sub-purchasers, and the persons immediately selling to them, shall be deemed and taken to be purchasers and sellers within the intent and meaning of the provisions and

5 & 6 Vict. c. 82.

43 Geo. 3. c. 69.

On composition for bankers' notes the same as by 9 Geo. 4. c. 23

The duties on fire insurance to be charged on policies granted by persons licensed in Ireland.

Exceptions not to extend to bills or notes of the Bank of Ireland.

5 & 6 Vict. c. 82.

Where any of the duties in England have been repealed, the same not to be charged in Ireland; and where new duties granted in lieu, the same to be payable in Ireland.

regulations of the said Act passed in the fifty-sixth year of the reign of King *George* the Third: Provided also, that nothing herein or in the said Schedule contained shall exempt, or be deemed to exempt, from any of the duties hereby charged, any of the bills or promissory notes of the Bank of *Ireland*, except under or by virtue of any contract or agreement authorized by the laws in force to be made between the governor and company of the said bank and the Commissioners of Her Majesty's Treasury in that behalf: Provided also, that nothing in this Act contained shall be deemed or construed to make payable in *Ireland* any of the duties or sums of money specified and set forth in the said Schedule annexed to the said Act of the fifty-sixth year of the reign of King *George* the Third, which shall have been repealed, or shall have ceased to be payable in *England;* and that in all cases where any of the said duties have been repealed, and any reduced or other duties have been granted and are now payable in lieu thereof, under or by virtue of any subsequent Act, such last-mentioned duties shall be deemed to be and shall be the duties payable and to be paid in *Ireland* for and in respect of the articles, matters, and things to which the same shall respectively relate: Provided also, that the releases and other conveyances of annuities or rent-charges made in the original grant thereof subject to be redeemed or repurchased, shall on the reconveyance thereof be exempted from the *ad valorem* duty imposed on conveyances on the sale of property by the said Act of the fifty-fifth year of the reign of King *George* the Third, and the said Schedule thereto annexed, and shall be charged only with the ordinary duty on deeds or instruments of the like kind not upon a sale.

Releases and conveyances of annuities, &c., exempted from ad valorem duty on repurchase.

[7 & 8 Vict. c. 32.]

7 & 8 Vict. c. 32.

An Act to regulate the Issue of Bank Notes, and for giving to the Governor and Company of the Bank of England certain Privileges for a limited Period.

[19*th July*, 1844].

Whereas it is expedient to regulate the issue of bills or notes payable on demand: And whereas an Act was passed in the fourth year of the reign of His late Majesty King *William* the Fourth, intituled *An Act for giving to the Corporation of the Governor and Company of the Bank of* England *certain Privileges for a limited Period, under certain Conditions;* and it is expedient that the privileges of exclusive banking therein mentioned should be continued to the said Governor and Company of the Bank of *England*, with such alterations as are herein contained, upon certain conditions: May it therefore please your Majesty that it may be enacted; and be it enacted by the Queen's most excellent Majesty, by and with the advice and consent of the Lords spiritual and temporal, and Commons, in this present Parliament assembled, and by the authority of the same, That from and after the thirty-first day of *August* one thousand

3 & 4 Will. 4, c. 98.

7 & 8 Vict. c. 32.

Bank to establish a separate department for the issue of notes.

eight hundred and forty-four the issue of promissory notes of the Governor and Company of the Bank of *England*, payable on demand, shall be separated and thenceforth kept wholly distinct from the general banking business of the said governor and company; and the business of and relating to such issue shall be thenceforth conducted and carried on by the said governor and company in a separate department, to be called "The Issue Department of the Bank of *England*," subject to the rules and regulations hereinafter contained; and it shall be lawful for the court of directors of the said governor and company, if they shall think fit, to appoint a committee or committees of directors for the conduct and management of such Issue Department of the Bank of *England*, and from time to time to remove the members, and define, alter, and regulate the constitution and powers of such committee, as they shall think fit, subject to any bye-laws, rules, or regulations which may be made for that purpose: Provided nevertheless, that the said issue department shall always be kept separate and distinct from the banking department of the said governor and company.

Management of the issue by Bank of England.

II. And be it enacted, That upon the thirty-first day of *August* one thousand eight hundred and forty-four there shall be transferred, appropriated, and set apart by the said governor and company to the Issue Department of the Bank of *England* securities to the value of fourteen million pounds, whereof the debt due by the public to the said governor and company shall be and be deemed a part; and there shall also at the same time be transferred, appropriated, and set apart by the said governor and company to the said issue department so much of the gold coin and gold and silver bullion then held by the Bank of *England* as shall not be required by the banking department thereof; and thereupon there shall be delivered out of the said issue department into the said banking department of the Bank of *England* such an amount of Bank of *England* notes as, together with the bank of *England* notes then in circulation, shall be equal to the aggregate amount of the securities, coin, and bullion so transferred to the said Issue Department of the Bank of *England;* and the whole amount of Bank of *England* notes then in circulation, including those delivered to the banking department of the Bank of *England* as aforesaid, shall be deemed to be issued on the credit of such securities, coin, and bullion so appropriated and set apart to the said issue department; and from thenceforth it shall not be lawful for the said governor and company to increase the amount of securities for the time being in the said issue department, save as hereinafter is mentioned, but it shall be lawful for the said governor and company to diminish the amount of such securities, and again to increase the same to any sum not exceeding in the whole the sum of fourteen million pounds, and so from time to time as they shall see occasion; and from and after such transfer and appropriation to the said issue department as aforesaid it shall not be lawful for the said governor and company to issue Bank of *England* notes, either into the banking department of the Bank of *England*, or to any persons or person whatsoever, save in exchange for other Bank of *England* notes, or for gold coin or for gold or silver bullion received or purchased for the said issue department under the provisions of this Act, or in exchange for securities acquired and taken in the issue department under the provisions

7 & 8 Vict. c. 32

herein contained: Provided always, that it shall be lawful for the said governor and company in their banking department to issue all such bank of *England* notes as they shall at any time receive from the said issue department or otherwise, in the same manner in all respects as such issue would be lawful to any other person or persons.

Proportion of silver bullion to be retained in the issue department.

III. And whereas it is necessary to limit the amount of silver bullion on which it shall be lawful for the issue department of the Bank of *England* to issue Bank of *England* notes; be it therefore enacted, That it shall not be lawful for the Bank of *England* to retain in the issue department of the said bank at any one time an amount of silver bullion exceeding one fourth part of the gold coin and bullion at such time held by the Bank of *England* in the issue department.

All persons may demand of the issue department notes for gold bullion.

IV. And be it enacted, That from and after the thirty-first day of *August* one thousand eight hundred and forty-four all persons shall be entitled to demand from the issue department of the Bank of *England* Bank of *England* notes in exchange for gold bullion, at the rate of three pounds seventeen shillings and ninepence *per* ounce of standard gold: Provided always, that the said governor and company shall in all cases be entitled to require such gold bullion to be melted and assayed by persons approved by the said governor and company at the expense of the parties tendering such gold bullion.

Power to increase securities in the issue department, and issue additional notes.

V. Provided always, and be it enacted, That if any banker who on the sixth day of *May* one thousand eight hundred and forty-four was issuing his own bank notes shall cease to issue his own bank notes, it shall be lawful for Her Majesty in council at any time after the cessation of such issue, upon the application of the said governor and company, to authorize and empower the said governor and company to increase the amount of securities in the said issue department beyond the total sum or value of fourteen million pounds, and thereupon to issue additional Bank of *England* notes to an amount not exceeding such increased amount of securities specified in such order in council, and so from time to time: Provided always, that such increased amount of securities specified in such order in council shall in no case exceed the proportion of two thirds the amount of bank notes which the banker so ceasing to issue may have been authorized to issue under the provisions of this Act; and every such order in council shall be published in the next succeeding *London Gazette*.

Account to be rendered by the Bank of England.

VI. And be it enacted, That an account of the amount of Bank of *England* notes issued by the issue department of the Bank of *England*, and of gold coin and of gold and silver bullion respectively, and of securities in the said issue department, and also an account of the capital stock, and the deposits, and of the money and securities belonging to the said governor and company in the banking department of the Bank of *England*, on some day in every week to be fixed by the Commissioners of Stamps and Taxes, shall be transmitted by the said governor and company weekly to the said commissioners in the form prescribed in the Schedule hereto annexed marked (A), and shall be published by the said commissioners in the next succeeding *London Gazette* in which the same may be conveniently inserted. 7 & 8 Vict. c. 32.

VII. And be it enacted, That from and after the said thirty-first day of *August* one thousand eight hundred and forty-four the said Governor and Company of the Bank of *England* shall be released and discharged from the payment of any stamp duty, or composition in respect of stamp duty, upon or in respect of their promissory notes payable to bearer on demand; and all such notes shall thenceforth be and continue free and wholly exempt from all liability to any stamp duty whatsoever. Bank of England exempted from stamp duty upon their notes.

VIII. And be it enacted, That from and after the said thirty-first day of *August* one thousand eight hundred and forty-four the payment or deduction of the annual sum of one hundred and twenty thousand pounds, made by the said governor and company under the provisions of the said Act passed in the fourth year of the reign of His late Majesty King *William* the Fourth, out of the sums payable to them for the charges of management of the public unredeemed debt, shall cease, and in lieu thereof the said governor and company, in consideration of the privileges of exclusive banking, and the exemption from stamp duties, given to them by this Act, shall, during the continuance of such privileges and such exemption respectively, but no longer, deduct and allow to the public, from the sums now payable by law to the said governor and company for the charges of management of the public unredeemed debt, the annual sum of one hundred and eighty thousand pounds, any thing in any Act or Acts of Parliament, or in any agreement, to the contrary notwithstanding: Provided always, that such deduction shall in no respect prejudice or affect the rights of the said governor and company to be paid for the management of the public debt at the rate and according to the terms provided in an Act passed in the forty-eighth year of the reign of His late Majesty King *George* the Third, intituled *An Act to authorize the advancing for the Public Service, upon certain Conditions, a Proportion of the Balance remaining in the Bank of* England, *for the Payment of Unclaimed Dividends, Annuities, and Lottery Prizes, and for regulating the Allowances to be made for the Management of the National Debt.* Bank to allow 180,000*l* per annum. 48 Geo. 3, c. 4.

IX. And be it enacted, That in case, under the provisions hereinbefore contained, the securities held in the said issue department of the Bank of *England* shall at any time be increased beyond the total amount of fourteen million pounds, then and in each and every year in which the same shall happen, and so long as such increase shall continue, the said governor and company shall, in addition to the said annual sum of one hundred and eighty thousand pounds, make a further payment or allowance to the public, equal in amount to the net profit derived in the said issue department during the current year from such additional securities, after deducting the amount of the expenses occasioned by the additional issue during the same period, which expenses shall include the amount of any and every composition or payment to be made by the said governor and company to any banker in consideration of the discontinuance at any time hereafter of the issue of bank notes by such banker; Bank to allow the public the profits of increased circulation.

7 & 8 Vict. c. 32.

and such further payment or allowance to the public by the said governor and company shall, in every year while the public shall be entitled to receive the same, be deducted from the amount by law payable to the said governor and company for the charges of management of the unredeemed public debt, in the same manner as the said annual sum of one hundred and eighty thousand pounds is hereby directed to be deducted therefrom.

No new bank of issue.

X. And be it enacted, That from and after the passing of this Act no person other than a banker who on the sixth day of *May* one thousand eight hundred and forty-four was lawfully issuing his own bank notes shall make or issue bank notes in any part of the United Kingdom.

Restriction against issue of bank notes.

XI. And be it enacted, That from and after the passing of this Act it shall not be lawful for any banker to draw, accept, make, or issue, in *England* or *Wales*, any bill of exchange or promissory note or engagement for the payment of money payable to bearer on demand, or to borrow, owe, or take up, in *England* or *Wales*, any sums or sum of money on the bills or notes of such banker payable to bearer on demand, save and except that it shall be lawful for any banker who was on the sixth day of *May* one thousand eight hundred and forty-four carrying on the business of a banker in *England* or *Wales*, and was then lawfully issuing, in *England* or *Wales*, his own bank notes, under the authority of a licence to that effect, to continue to issue such notes to the extent and under the conditions hereinafter mentioned, but not further or otherwise; and the right of any company or partnership to continue to issue such notes shall not be in any manner prejudiced or affected by any change which may hereafter take place in the personal composition of such company or partnership, either by the transfer of any shares or share therein, or by the admission of any new partner or member thereto, or by the retirement of any present partner or member therefrom: Provided always, that it shall not be lawful for any company or partnership now consisting of only six or less than six persons to issue bank notes at any time after the number of partners therein shall exceed six in the whole.

Bankers ceasing to issue notes may not resume.

XII. And be it enacted, That if any banker in any part of the United Kingdom who after the passing of this Act shall be entitled to issue bank notes shall become bankrupt, or shall cease to carry on the business of a banker, or shall discontinue the issue of bank notes, either by agreement with the Governor and Company of the Bank of *England* or otherwise, it shall not be lawful for such banker at any time thereafter to issue any such notes.

Existing banks of issue to continue under certain limitations.

XIII. And be it enacted, That every banker claiming under this Act to continue to issue bank notes in *England* or *Wales* shall, within one month next after the passing of this Act, give notice in writing to the Commissioners of Stamps and Taxes at their head office in *London* of such claim, and of the place and name and firm at and under which such banker has issued such notes during the twelve weeks next preceding the twenty-seventh day of *April* last; and thereupon the said commissioners shall ascertain if such banker was on the sixth day of *May* one thousand eight hundred and forty-four carrying on the business of a banker, and lawfully issuing his own bank notes in *England* or *Wales*, and if it shall so appear then the said commissioners shall proceed to ascertain the average amount of the bank notes of such banker which were in circulation during the said period of twelve weeks preceding the twenty-seventh day of *April* last, according to the returns made by such banker in pursuance of the Act passed in the fourth and fifth years of the reign of Her present Majesty, intituled *An Act to make further Provision relative to the Returns to be made by Banks of the Amount of their Notes in Circulation;* and the said commissioners or any two of them shall certify under their hands to such banker the said average amount, when so ascertained as aforesaid; and it shall be lawful for every such banker to continue to issue his own bank notes after the passing of this Act: Provided nevertheless, that such banker shall not at any time after the tenth day of *October* one thousand eight hundred and forty-four have in circulation upon the average of a period of four weeks, to be ascertained as hereinafter mentioned, a greater amount of notes than the amount so certified.

6 & 7 Vict. c. 32.

4 & 5 Vict. c. 50.

Provision for united banks.

XIV. Provided always, and be it enacted, That if it shall be made to appear to the Commissioners of Stamps and Taxes that any two or more banks have, by written contract or agreement (which contract or agreement shall be produced to the said commissioners), become united within the twelve weeks next preceding such twenty-seventh day of *April* as aforesaid, it shall be lawful for the said commissioners to ascertain the average amount of the notes of each such bank in the manner hereinbefore directed, and to certify the average amount of the notes of the two or more banks so united as the amount which the united bank shall thereafter be authorized to issue, subject to the regulations of this Act.

Duplicate certificate to be published in the 'Gazette.'

'Gazette' to be evidence

XV. And be it enacted, That the Commissioners of Stamps and Taxes shall, at the time of certifying to any banker such particulars as they are hereinbefore required to certify, also publish a duplicate of their certificate thereof in the next succeeding *London Gazette* in which the same may be conveniently inserted; and the Gazette in which such publication shall be made shall be conclusive evidence in all courts whatsoever of the amount of bank notes which the banker named in such certificate or duplicate is by law authorized to issue and to have in circulation as aforesaid.

In case banks become united commissioners to certify the amount of bank notes which each bank was authorized to issue.

XVI. And be it enacted, That in case it shall be made to appear to the Commissioners of Stamps and Taxes, at any time hereafter, that any two or more banks, each such bank consisting of not more than six persons, have, by written contract or agreement (which contract or agreement shall be produced to the said commissioners), become united subsequently to the passing of this Act, it shall be lawful to the said commissioners, upon the application of such united bank, to certify, in manner hereinbefore mentioned, the aggregate of the amount of bank notes which such separate banks were previously authorized to issue, and so from time to time; and every such certificate shall be published in manner hereinbefore directed; and from and after such publication the amount therein stated shall be and be deemed to be the limit of the amount of bank

7 & 8 Vict. c. 32.

notes which such united bank may have in circulation: Provided always, that it shall not be lawful for any such united bank to issue bank notes at any time after the number of partners therein shall exceed six in the whole.

Penalty on banks issuing in excess.

XVII. And be it enacted, That if the monthly average circulation of bank notes of any banker, taken in the manner hereinafter directed, shall at any time exceed the amount which such banker is authorized to issue and to have in circulation under the provisions of this Act, such banker shall in every such case forfeit a sum equal to the amount by which the average monthly circulation, taken as aforesaid, shall have exceeded the amount which such banker was authorized to issue and to have in circulation as aforesaid.

Issuing banks to render accounts.

XVIII. And be it enacted, That every banker in *England* and *Wales* who, after the tenth day of *October* one thousand eight hundred and forty-four, shall issue bank notes shall on some one day in every week after the nineteenth day of *October* one thousand eight hundred and forty-four (such day to be fixed by the Commissioners of Stamps and Taxes) transmit to the said commissioners an account of the amount of the bank notes of such banker in circulation on every day during the week ending on the next preceding *Saturday*, and also an account of the average amount of the bank notes of such banker in circulation during the same week; and on completing the first period of four weeks, and so on completing each successive period of four weeks, every such banker shall annex to such account the average amount of bank notes of such banker in circulation during the said four weeks, and also the amount of bank notes which such banker is authorized to issue under the provisions of this Act; and every such account shall be verified by the signature of such banker or his chief cashier, or, in the case of a company or partnership, by the signature of a managing director or partner or chief cashier of such company or partnership, and shall be made in the form to this Act annexed marked (B); and so much of the said return as states the weekly average amount of the notes of such bank shall be published by the said commissioners in the next succeeding *London Gazette* in which the same may be conveniently inserted; and if any such banker shall neglect or refuse to render any such account in the form and at the time required by this Act, or shall at any time render a false account, such banker shall forfeit the sum of one hundred pounds for every such offence.

Mode of ascertaining the average amount of bank notes of each banker in circulation during the first four weeks after 10th Oct. 1844.

XIX. And be it enacted, That for the purpose of ascertaining the monthly average amount of bank notes of each banker in circulation the aggregate of the amount of bank notes of each such banker in circulation on every day of business during the first complete period of four weeks next after the tenth day of *October* one thousand eight hundred and forty-four, such period ending on a *Saturday*, shall be divided by the number of days of business in such four weeks, and the average so ascertained shall be deemed to be the average of bank notes of each such banker in circulation during such period of four weeks, and so in each successive period of four weeks, and such average is not to exceed the amount certified by the Commissioners of Stamps and Taxes as aforesaid.

7 & 8 Vict. c. 32.

Commissioners of Stamps and Taxes empowered to cause the books of bankers containing accounts of their bank notes in circulation to be inspected.

XX. And whereas, in order to insure the rendering of true and faithful accounts of the amount of bank notes in circulation, as directed by this Act, it is necessary that the Commissioners of Stamps and Taxes should be empowered to cause the books of bankers issuing such notes to be inspected, as hereinafter mentioned; be it therefore enacted, That all and every the book and books of any banker who shall issue bank notes under the provisions of this Act, in which shall be kept, contained, or entered any account, minute, or memorandum of or relating to the bank notes issued or to be issued by such banker, or of or relating to the amount of such notes in circulation from time to time, or any account, minute, or memorandum the sight or inspection whereof may tend to secure the rendering of true accounts of the average amount of such notes in circulation, as directed by this Act, or to test the truth of any such account, shall be open for the inspection and examination, at all seasonable times, of any officer of stamp duties authorized in that behalf by writing, signed by the Commissioners of Stamps and Taxes or any two of them; and every such officer shall be at liberty to take copies of extracts from any such book or account as aforesaid; and if any banker or other person keeping any such book, or having the custody or possession thereof, or power to produce the same, shall, upon demand made by any such officer, showing (if required) his authority in that behalf, refuse to produce any such book to such officer for his inspection and examination, or to permit him to inspect and examine the same, or to take copies thereof or extracts therefrom, or of or from any such account, minute, or memorandum as aforesaid kept, contained, or entered therein, every such banker or other person so offending shall for every such offence forfeit the sum of one hundred pounds: Provided always, that the said commissioners shall not exercise the powers aforesaid without the consent of the Commissioners of Her Majesty's Treasury.

Penalty for refusing to allow such inspection.

All bankers to return names once a year to the Stamp Office.

XXI. And be it enacted, That every banker in *England* and *Wales* who is now carrying on or shall hereafter carry on business as such shall on the first day of *January* in each year, or within fifteeen days thereafter, make a return to the Commissioners of Stamps and Taxes at their head office in *London* of his name, residence, and occupation, or, in the case of a company or partnership, of the name, residence, and occupation of every person composing or being a member of such company or partnership, and also the name of the firm under which such banker, company, or partnership carry on the business of banking, and of every place where such business is carried on; and if any such banker, company, or partnership shall omit or refuse to make such return within fifteen days after the said first day of *January*, or shall wilfully make other than a true return of the persons as herein required, every banker, company, or partnership so offending shall forfeit and pay the sum of fifty pounds; and the said Commissioners of Stamps and Taxes shall on or before the first day of *March* in every year publish in some newspaper circulating within each town or county respectively a copy of the return so made by every banker, company, or partnership carrying on the business of bankers within such town or county respectively, as the case may be.

7 & 8 Vict. c. 32.

Bankers to take out a separate licence for every place at which they issue notes or bills.

Proviso in favour of bankers who had four such licences in force on the 6th of May, 1844.

XXII. And be it enacted, That every banker who shall be liable by law to take out a licence from the Commissioners of Stamps and Taxes to authorize the issuing of notes or bills shall take out a separate and distinct licence for every town or place at which he shall, by himself or his agent, issue any notes or bills requiring such licence to authorize the issuing thereof, any thing in any former Act contained to the contrary thereof notwithstanding: Provided always, that no banker who on or before the sixth day of *May* one thousand eight hundred and forty four had taken out four such licences, which on the said last-mentioned day were respectively in force, for the issuing of any such notes or bills at more than four separate towns or places, shall at any time hereafter be required to take out or to have in force at one and the same time more than four such licences to authorize the issuing of such notes or bills at all or any of the same towns or places specified in such licence in force on the said sixth day of *May* one thousand eight hundred and forty-four, and at which towns or places respectively such bankers had on or before the said last mentioned day issued such notes or bills in pursuance of such licences or any of them respectively.

Compensation to certain bankers named in the Schedule.

XXIII. And whereas the several bankers named in the Schedule hereto annexed marked (C) have ceased to issue their own bank notes under certain agreements with the Governor and Company of the Bank of *England;* and it is expedient that such agreements should cease and determine on the thirty-first day of *December* next, and that such bankers should receive by way of compensation such composition as hereafter mentioned; and a list of such bankers, and a statement of the maximum sums in respect of which each such banker is to receive compensation, hath been delivered to the Commissioners of Stamps and Taxes, signed by the chief cashier of the Bank of *England;* be it therefore enacted, That the several agreements subsisting between the said governor and company and the several bankers mentioned in the Schedule hereto relating to the issue of Bank of *England* notes shall cease and determine on the thirty-first day of *December* next; and from and after that day the said governor and company shall pay and allow to the several bankers named in the Schedule hereto marked (C), so long as such bankers shall be willing to receive the same, a composition at and after the rate of one pound *per centum per annum* on the average amount of the Bank of *England* notes issued by such bankers respectively and actually remaining in circulation, to be ascertained as follows (that is to say); on some day in the month of *April* one thousand eight hundred and forty-five, to be determined by the said governor and company, an account shall be taken of the Bank of *England* notes delivered to such bankers respectively by the said governor and company within three months next preceding, and of such of the said Bank of *England* notes as shall have been returned to the Bank of *England*, and the balance shall be deemed to be the amount of the Bank of *England* notes issued by such bankers respectively and kept in circulation; and a similar account shall be taken at intervals of three calendar months; and the average of the balances ascertained on taking four such accounts shall be deemed to be the average amount of Bank of *England* notes issued by such bankers respectively and kept in circulation during the year one thousand eight hundred and forty-five, and on which amount such bankers are respectively to receive the aforesaid composition of one *per centum* for the year one thousand eight hundred and forty-five; and similar accounts shall be taken in each succeeding year; but in each year such accounts shall be taken in different months from those in which the accounts of the last preceding year were taken, and on different days of the month, such months and days to be determined by the said governor and company; and the amount of the composition payable as aforesaid shall be paid by the said governor and company out of their own funds; and in case any difference shall arise between any of such bankers and the Governor and Company of the Bank of *England* in respect of the composition payable as aforesaid, the same shall be determined by the Chancellor of the Exchequer for the time being, or by some person to be named by him, and the decision of the Chancellor of the Exchequer, or his nominee, shall be final and conclusive: Provided always, that it shall be lawful for any banker named in the Schedule hereto annexed marked (C) to discontinue the receipt of such composition as aforesaid, but no such banker shall by such discontinuance as aforesaid thereby acquire any right or title to issue bank notes.

7 & 8 Vict. c. 32.

Bank of England to be allowed to compound with issuing bauks.

XXIV. And be it enacted, That it shall be lawful for the said governor and company to agree with every banker who, under the provisions of this Act, shall be entitled to issue bank notes, to allow to such banker a composition at the rate of one *per centum per annum* on the amount of Bank of *England* notes which shall be issued and kept in circulation by such banker, as a consideration for his relinquishment of the privilege of issuing his own bank notes; and all the provisions herein contained for ascertaining and determining the amount of composition payable to the several bankers named in the Schedule hereto marked (C) shall apply to all such other bankers with whom the said governor and company are hereby authorized to agree as aforesaid; provided that the amount of composition payable to such bankers as last aforesaid shall in every case in which an increase of securities in the issue department shall have been authorized by any order in council be deducted out of the amount payable by the said governor and company to the public under the provisions herein contained: Provided always, that the total sum payable to any banker, under the provisions herein contained, by way of composition as aforesaid, in any one year, shall not exeeed, in case of the bankers mentioned in the Schedule hereto marked (C), one *per centum* on the several sums set against the names of such bankers respectively in the list and statement delivered to the Commissioners of Stamps as aforesaid, and in the case of other bankers shall not exceed one *per centum* on the amount of bank notes which such bankers respectively would otherwise be entitled to issue under the provisions herein contained.

Limitation of compositions.

Compositions to cease on 1st August 1856.

XXV. And be it enacted, That all the compositions payable to the several bankers mentioned in the Schedule hereto marked (C), and such other bankers as shall agree with the said governor and company to discontinue the issue of their own bank notes as aforesaid, shall, if not previously determined by the Act of such banker as hereinbefore provided, cease and determine on the first day of *August* one thousand eight hundred and fifty-six, or on

7 & 8 Vict. c. 32.

any earlier day on which Parliament may prohibit the issue of bank notes.

Banks within sixty-five miles of London may accept, &c., bills.

XXVI. And be it enacted, That from and after the passing of this Act it shall be lawful for any society or company or any persons in partnership, though exceeding six in number, carrying on the business of banking in *London*, or within sixty-five miles thereof, to draw, accept, or indorse bills of exchange, not being payable to bearer on demand, any thing in the hereinbefore-recited Act passed in the fourth year of the reign of His said Majesty King *William* the Fourth, or in any other Act, to the contrary, notwithstanding.

Bank to enjoy privileges, subject to redemption.

XXVII. And be it enacted, That the said Governor and Company of the Bank of *England* shall have and enjoy such exclusive privilege of banking as is given by this Act, upon such terms and conditions and subject to the termination thereof at such time and in such manner as is by this Act provided and specified; and all and every the powers and authorities, franchises, privileges, and advantages, given or recognized by the said recited Act passed in the fourth year of the reign of His Majesty King *William* the Fourth, as belonging to or enjoyed by the said Governor and Company of the Bank of *England*, or by any subsequent Act or Acts of Parliament, shall be and the same are hereby declared to be in full force, and continued by this Act, except so far as the same are altered by this Act; subject nevertheless to redemption upon the terms and conditions following (that is to say); at any time upon twelve months' notice to be given after the first day of *August* one thousand eight hundred and fifty-five, and upon repayment by Parliament to the said governor and company or their successors of the sum of eleven million fifteen thousand and one hundred pounds, being the debt now due from the public to the said governor and company, without any deduction, discount, or abatement whatsoever, and upon payment to the said governor and company and their successors of all arrears of the sum of one hundred thousand pounds *per annum*, in the last-mentioned Act mentioned, together with the interest or annuities payable upon the said debt or in respect thereof, and also upon repayment of all the principal and interest which shall be owing unto the said governor and company and their successors upon all such tallies, exchequer orders, exchequer bills, or parliamentary funds which the said governor and company or their successors shall have remaining in their hands or be entitled to at the time of such notice to be given as last aforesaid, then and in such case, and not till then, the said exclusive privileges of banking granted by this Act shall cease and determine at the expiration of such notice of twelve months; and any vote or resolution of the House of Commons, signified under the hand of the speaker of the said house in writing, and delivered at the public office of the said governor and company, shall be deemed and adjudged to be a sufficient notice.

Interpretation clause.

XXVIII. And be it enacted, That the term "bank notes" used in this Act shall extend and apply to all bills or notes for the payment of money to the bearer on demand other than bills or notes of the Governor and Company of the Bank of *England;* and that the term "Bank of *England* notes" shall extend and apply to the promissory notes of the Governor and Company of the Bank of *England* payable to bearer on demand; and that the term "banker" shall extend and apply to all corporations, societies, partnerships, and persons, and every individual person carrying on the business of banking, whether by the issue of bank notes or otherwise, except only the Governor and Company of the Bank of *England;* and that the word "person" used in this Act shall include corporations; and that the singular number in this Act shall include the plural number, and the plural number the singular, except where there is any thing in the context repugnant to such construction; and that the masculine gender in this Act shall include the femine, except where there is any thing in the context repugnant to such construction. 7 & 8 Vict. c. 32

XXIX. And be it enacted, That this Act may be amended or repealed by any Act to be passed in the present session of Parliament. Act may be amended.

SCHEDULE (B).

Name and title as set forth in the licence - -	________________	bank.
Name of the firm - -	________________	firm.
Insert head office, or principal place of issue -	________________	place.

An account pursuant to the Act 7 & 8 Vict. cap. of the notes of the said bank in circulation during the week ending Saturday the day of 18

Monday - - -
Tuesday - - - -
Wednesday - - - -
Thursday - - -
Friday - - - -
Saturday - - -

6)

Average of the week

[*To be annexed to this account at the end of each period of four weeks.*]

Amount of notes authorized by law - - £
Average amount in circulation during the four weeks ending as above - - - £

I, being [the banker, chief cashier, managing director, *or* partner of the bank, *as the case may be*], do hereby certify, that the above is a true account of the notes of the said bank in circulation during the week above written.

(Signed)

Dated the day of 18 .

[7 & 8 Vict. c. 113.]

7 & 8 Vict. c. 113.

An Act to regulate Joint Stock Banks in England. [*5th September*, 1844.]

No joint stock bank established after 6th May last to carry on business unless by virtue of letters patent granted according to this Act; but companies previously established not restrained from carrying on business until letters patent have been granted.

WHEREAS the laws in force for the regulation of copartnerships of bankers in *England* need to be amended: Be it enacted by the Queen's most excellent Majesty, by and with the advice and consent of the *L*ords spiritual and temporal, and Commons, in this present Parliament assembled, and by the authority of the same, that it shall not be lawful for any company of more than six persons to carry on the trade or business of bankers in *England*, after the passing of this Act, under any agreement or covenant of copartnership made or entered into on or after the sixth day of *May* last passed, unless by virtue of letters patent to be granted by Her Majesty according to the provisions of this Act; but nothing herein contained shall be construed to restrain any such company established before the said sixth day of *May*, for the purpose of carrying on the said trade or business of bankers in *England*, from continuing to carry on the same trade and business as legally as they might have done before the passing of this Act, until letters patent shall have been granted to them severally on their application, as hereinafter provided, to be made subject to the provisions of this Act.

Company to petition for charter.

II. And be it enacted, That before beginning to exercise the said trade or business every such company shall present a petition to Her Majesty in council, praying that Her Majesty will be graciously pleased to grant to them letters patent under this Act; and every such petition shall be signed by seven at least of the said company, and shall set forth the following particulars; (that is to say),

First, the names and additions of all the partners of the company, and the name of the street, square, or other place where each of the said partners reside:

Second, the proposed name of the bank:

Third, the name of the street, square, or other local description of the place or places where the business of the bank is to be carried on:

Fourth, the proposed amount of the capital stock, not being in any case less than one hundred thousand pounds, and the means by which it is to be raised:

Fifth, the amount of capital stock then paid up, and where and how invested:

Sixth, the proposed number of shares in the business:

Seventh, the amount of each share, not being less than one hundred pounds each.

Charter to be granted on report of Board of Trade.

III. And be it enacted, That every such petition shall be referred by Her Majesty to the committee of Privy Council for Trade and Plantations, and so soon as the *L*ords of the said committee shall have reported to Her Majesty that the provisions of this Act have been complied with on the part of the said company, it shall thereupon be lawful for Her Majesty, if Her Majesty shall so think fit, with the advice of her privy council, to grant the said letters patent.

7 & 8 Vict c. 113

Deed of settlement.

IV. And be it enacted, That the deed of partnership of every such banking company shall be prepared according to a form to be approved by the *Lords* of the said committee, and shall in addition to any other provisions which may be contained therein, contain specific provisions for the following purposes; (that is to say),

First, for holding ordinary general meetings of the company once at least in every year, at an appointed time and place:

Second, for holding extraordinary general meetings of the company, upon the requisition of nine shareholders or more, having in the whole at least twenty-one shares in the partnership business:

Third, for the management of the affairs of the company, and the election and qualification of the directors:

Fourth, for the retirement of at least one fourth of the directors yearly, and for preventing the re-election of the retiring directors for at least twelve calendar months:

Fifth, for preventing the company from purchasing any shares or making advances of money, or securities for money, to any person on the security of a share or shares in the partnership business:

Sixth, for the publication of the assets and liabilities of the company once at least in every calendar month:

Seventh, for the yearly audit of the accounts of the company by two or more auditors chosen at a general meeting of the shareholders, and not being directors at the time:

Eighth, for the yearly communication of the auditors' report, and of a balance sheet, and profit and loss account, to every shareholder:

Ninth, for the appointment of a manager or other officer to perform the duties of manager:

And such deed, executed by the holders of at least one half of the shares in the said business, on which not less than ten pounds on each such share of one hundred pounds, and in proportion for every share of larger amount, shall have been then paid up, shall be annexed to the petition; and the provisions of such deed, with such others as to Her Majesty shall seem fit, shall be set forth in the letters patent.

No company to commence business till deed executed and all the shares subscribed for, and at least half the amount paid up.

V. Provided always, and be it enacted, That it shall not be lawful for any such company to commence business until all the shares shall have been subscribed for, and until the deed of partnership shall have been executed, personally or by some person duly authorized by warrant of attorney to execute the same on behalf of such holder or holders, by the holders of all the shares in the said business, and until a sum of not less than one half of the amount of each share shall have been paid up in respect of each such share; and it shall not be lawful for the company to repay any part of the sum so paid up without leave of the *Lords* of the said committee.

Company to

VI. And be it enacted, That it shall be lawful for Her Majesty in

7 & 8 Vict. c. 113.

be incorporated.

and by such letters patent to grant that the persons by whom the said deed of partnership shall have been executed, and all other persons who shall thereafter become shareholders in the said banking business, their executors, administrators, successors, and assigns respectively, shall be one body politic and corporate, by such name as shall be given to them in and by the said letters patent, for the purpose of carrying on the said banking business, and by that name shall have perpetual succession and a common seal, and shall have power to purchase and hold lands of such annual value as shall be expressed in such letters patent; and such letters patent shall be granted for a term of years, not exceeding twenty years, and may be made subject to such other provisions and stipulations as to Her Majesty may seem fit.

Incorporation not to limit the liability of the shareholders.

VII. Provided always, and be it enacted, That notwithstanding such incorporation the several shareholders for the time being in the said banking business, and those who shall have been shareholders therein, and their several executors, administrators, successors, and assigns, shall be and continue liable for all the dealings, covenants, and undertakings of the said company, subject to the provisions hereinafter contained, as fully as if the said company were not incorporated.

Actions by or against shareholders.

VIII. And be it enacted, That no action or suit by or against the company shall be in anywise affected by reason of the plaintiff or defendant therein being a shareholder or former shareholder of the company; but any such shareholder, either alone or jointly with another person as against the company, or the company as against any such shareholder, either alone or jointly with any other person, shall have the same action and remedy in respect of any cause of action or suit whatever which such shareholder or company might have had if such cause of action or suit had arisen with a stranger.

Decree or judgment to be enforced against company and shareholders.

IX. And be it enacted, That every judgment, decree, or order of any court of justice in any proceeding against the company may be lawfully executed against, and shall have the like effect on, the property and effects of the company, and also subject to the provisions hereinafter contained, upon the person, property, and effects of every shareholder and former shareholder thereof, as if every individual shareholder and former shareholder had been by name a party to such proceeding.

Execution against company to precede execution against present or former shareholders.

X. And be it enacted, That it shall be lawful for the plaintiff to cause execution upon any judgment, decree, or order obtained by him in any such action or suit against the company to be issued against the property and effects of the company; and if such execution shall be ineffectual to obtain satisfaction of the sums sought to be recovered thereby, then it shall be lawful for him to have execution in satisfaction of such judgment, decree, or order against the person, property, and effects of any shareholder, or, in default of obtaining satisfaction of such judgment, decree, or order from any shareholder, against the person, property, and effects of any person who was a shareholder of the company at the time when the cause of action against the company arose: Provided always, that no person having ceased to be a shareholder of the company shall be

Extent of liability of

7 & 8 Vict. c. 113.

liable for the payment of any debt for which any such judgment, decree, or order shall have been so obtained, for which he would not have been liable as a partner in case a suit had been originally brought against him for the same, or for which judgment shall have been obtained, after the expiration of three years from the time when he shall have ceased to be a shareholder of such company; nor shall this Act be deemed to enable any party to a suit to recover from any individual shareholder of the company, or any other person whomsoever, any other or greater sum than might have been recovered if this Act had not been passed.

former shareholders.

XI. And be it enacted, That every person against whom or against whose property or effects any such execution shall have issued shall be reimbursed out of the property and effects of the company for all moneys paid, and for all damages, costs, and expenses incurred by him by reason of such execution, or of the action or suit in which the same shall have issued, or, in default of such reimbursement, by contribution from the other shareholders of the company.

Reimbursement of individual shareholders.

XII. And be it enacted, That if any such execution be issued against any present or former shareholder of the company, and if, within fourteen days next after the levying of such execution, he be not reimbursed, on demand, out of the property and effects of the company, all such moneys, damages, costs, and expenses as he shall have paid or incurred in consequence of such execution, it shall be lawful for such shareholder, or his executors or administrators, to have execution against the property and effects of the company in satisfaction of such moneys, damages, costs, and expenses; and the amount of such moneys, damages, costs, and expenses shall be ascertained and certified by one of the masters or other officer of the court out of which such execution shall issue.

Individuals paying under execution to recover against the company.

XIII. And be it enacted, That in the cases provided by this Act for execution on any judgment, decree, or order in any action or suit against the company, to be issued against the person or against the property and effects of any shareholder or former shareholder of such company, or against the property and effects of the company at the suit of any shareholder or former shareholder, in satisfaction of any moneys, damages, costs, and expenses paid or incurred by him as aforesaid in any action or suit against the company, such execution may be issued by leave of the court, or of a judge of the court in which such judgment, decree, or order shall have been obtained, upon motion or summons for a rule to show cause, or other motion or summons consistent with the practice of the court, without any suggestion or scire facias in that behalf, and that it shall be lawful for such court or judge to make absolute or discharge such rule, or allow or dismiss such motion (as the case may be), and to direct the costs of the application to be paid by either party, or to make such order therein as to such court or judge shall seem fit; and in such cases such form of writs of execution shall be sued out of the courts of law and equity respectively, for giving effect to the provision in that behalf aforesaid, as the judges of such courts respectively shall from time to time think fit to order, and the

How such execution is to be had.

7 & 8 Vict. c. 113.

execution of such writs shall be enforced in like manner as writs of execution are now enforced; provided that any order made by a judge as aforesaid may be discharged or varied by the court, on application made thereto by either party dissatisfied with such order; provided also, that no such motion shall be made nor summons granted for the purpose of charging any shareholder or former shareholder until ten days' notice thereof shall have been given to the person sought to be charged thereby.

Contribution to be recovered from other shareholders.

XIV. And be it enacted, That if such shareholder be not by the means aforesaid fully paid all such moneys, with interest, damages, costs, and expenses, as he shall have paid or incurred by reason of any such execution, it shall be lawful for him, his executors or administrators, to divide the amount thereof, or so much thereof as he shall not have been reimbursed, into as many equal parts as there shall then be shares in the capital stock of the company (not including shares then under forfeiture); and every shareholder for the time being of the company, and the executors or administrators of every deceased shareholder, shall, in proportion to the number of shares which they may hold in the company, pay one or more of such parts, upon demand, to the shareholder against whom such execution shall have been issued, or to his executors or administrators; and upon neglect or refusal so to pay, it shall be lawful for such shareholder, his executors or administrators, to sue for and recover the same against the shareholder, or the executors or administrators of any shareholder, who shall so neglect or refuse as aforesaid, in any of Her Majesty's courts of record at *Westminster*, or in any other court having jurisdiction in respect of such demand.

Further remedy in case of bankruptcy, &c., of company's shareholders.

XV. And be it enacted, That if the shareholder or former shareholder against whom any such execution shall have issued, his executors or administrators, shall, by reason of the bankruptcy or insolvency of any shareholder, or from any other cause, but without any neglect or wilful default on his own part, be prevented from recovering any proportion of the moneys, costs, or expenses which he shall have so paid, it shall be lawful for him, his executors or administrators, again to divide the amount of all such moneys, costs, and expenses as shall not have been recovered by him or them into as many equal parts as there shall then be shares in the capital stock of the company (not including the shares then under forfeiture), except the shares in respect of which such default shall have happened; and every shareholder for the time being of the company, and the executors or administrators of every deceased shareholder, except as aforesaid, shall rateably, according to the number of shares which they shall hold in the company, upon demand, pay one or more such last-mentioned parts to the shareholder against whom such execution shall have issued, his executors or administrators; and in default of payment he or they shall have the same remedies in all respects for the recovery thereof as under the provisions hereinbefore mentioned are given in respect of the original proportions of such moneys, damages, costs, and expenses; and if any proportion of the said moneys, damages, costs, and expenses shall remain unpaid by reason of any such bankruptcy, insolvency, or other cause as aforesaid, such shareholder, his executors or administrators, shall have in like manner, from time to time, and by way of accumulative remedy, the same powers, according to the circumstances of the case, of again dividing and enforcing payment of the amount of such proportion, until he or they shall, in the end, if a former shareholder, be fully reimbursed the whole of the said moneys, costs, and expenses, and if then a shareholder, the whole, excepting the portions belonging to the shares held by him. 7 & 8 Vict. c. 113.

XVI. And be it enacted, That within three months after the grant of the said letters patent, and before the company shall begin to carry on their business as bankers, an account or memorial shall be made out, according to the form contained in the Schedule marked (A) to this Act annexed, wherein shall be set forth the true title or firm of the company, and also the names and places of abode of all the members of such company as the same respectively shall appear on the books of such company, and also the name and place of abode of every director and manager or other like officer of the company, and the name or firm of every bank or banks established or to be established by such company, and also the name of every town or place where the business of the said company shall be carried on; and a new account or memorial of the same particulars shall be made by the said company in every year, between the twenty-eighth day of *February* and the twenty-fifth day of *March*, while they shall continue to carry on their business as bankers; and every such memorial shall be delivered to the Commissioners of Stamps and Taxes at the Stamp Office in *London*, who shall cause the same to be filed and kept in the said Stamp Office, and an entry or registry thereof to be made in a book or books to be there kept for that purpose by some person or persons to be appointed by the said commissioners in that behalf, which book or books any person or persons shall from time to time have liberty to search and inspect on payment of the sum of one shilling for every search; and the company shall from time to time cause to be printed and kept, in a conspicuous place accessible to the public in their office or principal place of business, a list of the registered names and places of abode of all the members of such company for the time being. Memorial to be registered.

XVII. Provided also, and be it enacted, That the manager or one of the directors of every such company shall, from time to time as occasion shall require, make out in manner hereinbefore directed, and cause to be delivered to the Commissioners of Stamps and Taxes as aforesaid, a further account or memorial, according to the form contained in the Schedule marked (B) to this Act annexed, of the name and place of abode of every new director, manager, or other like officer of such company, and also of the name or names of any person or persons who shall have ceased to be members of such company, and also of the name or names of any person or persons who shall have become a member or members of such company, either in addition to or instead of any former member or members thereof, and of the name or names of any new or additional town or towns, place or places, where the business of the said company is carried on; and such further account or memorial shall from time to time be filed, and kept and entered and registered at the Stamp Memorials of occasional changes.

7 & 8 Vict. c. 113.

Office in *London*, in like manner as is hereinbefore required with respect to the original or annual account or memorial hereinbefore directed to be made.

Form of memorials.

XVIII. And be it enacted, That the several memorials as aforesaid shall be signed by the manager or one of the directors of the company, and shall be verified by a declaration of such manager or director before a justice of the peace, or a master or master extraordinary of the High Court of Chancery, made pursuant to the provisions of an Act passed in the sixth year of His late Majesty's reign, intituled *An Act to repeal an Act of the present Session of Parliament, intituled 'An Act for the more effectual Abolition of Oaths and Affirmations taken and made in various Departments of the State, and to substitute Declarations in lieu thereof, and for the more entire Suppression of voluntary and extra-judicial Oaths and Affidavits,' and to make other Provisions for the Abolition of unnecessary Oaths;* and if any declaration so made shall be false in any material particular the person wilfully making such false declaration shall be guilty of a misdemeanor.

5 & 6 W. 4, c. 62.

Evidence of memorials.

XIX. And be it enacted, That a true copy of any such memorial, certified under the hand of one of the Commissioners of Stamps and Taxes for the time being, upon proof made that such certificate has been signed with the handwriting of the person certifying the same, whom it shall not be necessary to prove to be a Commissioner of Stamps and Taxes, shall be received in evidence as proof of the contents of such memorial, and proof shall not be required that the person by whom the memorial shall purport to be verified was, at the time of such verification, the manager or one of the directors of the company.

Commissioners of Stamps to give certified copies on payment of ten shillings.

XX. And be it enacted, That the said Commissioners of Stamps and Taxes for the time being shall, upon application made to them by any person or persons requiring a copy, certified according to this Act, of any such account or memorial as aforesaid, in order that the same may be produced in evidence, or for any other purpose, deliver to the person or persons so applying for the same such certified copy, he, she, or they paying for the same the sum of ten shillings and no more.

Existing liabilities to continue till new memorials.

XXI. And be it enacted, That the persons whose names shall appear from time to time in the then last delivered memorial, and their legal representatives, shall be liable to all legal proceedings under this Act, as existing shareholders of the company, and shall be entitled to be reimbursed, as such existing shareholders only, out of the funds or property of the company, for all losses sustained in consequence thereof.

Bills and notes to be signed by one director or manager.

XXII. And be it enacted, That all bills of exchange or promissory notes made, accepted, or indorsed on behalf of the said company may be made, accepted, or indorsed (as the case may be) in any manner provided by the deed of partnership, so that they be signed by one of the managers or directors of the company, and be by him expressed to be so made, accepted, or indorsed by him on behalf of such company: Provided always, that nothing herein contained

Manager not

shall be deemed to make any such manager or director liable upon any such bill of exchange or promissory note to any greater extent or in a different manner than upon any other contract signed by him on behalf of any such company; and that every such company, on whose behalf any bill of exchange or promissory note shall be made, accepted, or indorsed in manner and form as aforesaid, may sue and be sued thereon as fully as in the case of any contract made and entered into under their common seal.

7 & 8 Vict. c. 113.

personally liable.

XXIII. And be it enacted, That, subject to the regulations herein contained, and to the provisions of the deed of settlement, every shareholder may sell and transfer his shares in the said company by deed duly stamped, in which the consideration shall be truly stated; and such deed may be according to the form in the Schedule marked (C) annexed to this Act, or to the like effect; and the same (when duly executed) shall be delivered to the secretary, and be kept by him; and the secretary shall enter a memorial thereof in a book, to be called the "Register of Transfers," and shall indorse such entry on the deed of transfer, and for every such entry and indorsement the company may demand any sum not exceeding two shillings and sixpence; and until such transfer have been so delivered to the secretary as aforesaid the purchaser of the share shall not be entitled to receive any share of the profits of the said business, or to vote in respect of such share.

Transfers of shares to be registered, &c.

XXIV. And be it enacted, That no shareholder shall be entitled to transfer any share until he shall have paid all calls for the time being due on every share held by him.

Transfer not to be made until all calls paid.

XXV. And be it enacted, That the directors may close the register of transfers for a period not exceeding fourteen days previous to each ordinary meeting, and may fix a day for the closing of the same, of which seven days' notice shall be given by advertisement in some newspaper as after mentioned; and any transfer made during the time when the transfer books are so closed shall as between the company and the party claiming under the same, but not otherwise, be considered as made subsequently to such ordinary meeting.

Closing of transfer books.

XXVI. And with respect to the registration of shares the interest in which may have become transmitted in consequence of the death or bankruptcy or insolvency of any shareholder, or in consequence of the marriage of a female shareholder, or by any other legal means than by a transfer according to the provisions of this Act, be it enacted, That no person claiming by virtue of any such transmission shall be entitled to receive any share of the profits of the said business, or to vote in respect of any such share as the holder thereof, until such transmission have been authenticated by a declaration in writing as hereinafter mentioned, or in such other manner as the directors shall require; and every such declaration shall state the manner in which and the party to whom such share shall have been so transmitted, and shall be made and signed by some credible person before a justice of the peace, or before a master or master extraordinary in the High Court of Chancery; and such declaration shall be left with the secretary, and thereupon he shall enter the name of the person entitled under such transmission in

Transmission of shares by other means than transfer to be authenticated by a declaration.

7 & 8 Vict. c. 113.

the register book of shareholders of the company; and for every such entry the company may demand any sum not exceeding two shillings and sixpence.

Proof of transmission by marriage, will, &c.

XXVII. And be it enacted, That if such transmission be by virtue of the marriage of a female shareholder, the said declaration shall contain a copy of the register of such marriage, or other particulars of the celebration thereof, and shall declare the identity of the wife with the holder of such share; and if such transmission have taken place by virtue of any testamentary instrument, or by intestacy, the probate of the will or letters of administration, or an official extract therefrom, shall, together with such declaration, be produced to the secretary; and upon such production, in either of the cases aforesaid, the secretary shall make an entry of the declaration in the said register of transfers.

Notices to joint proprietors of shares.

XXVIII. And be it enacted, That with respect to any share to which several persons may be jointly entitled, all notices directed to be given to the shareholders shall be given to such of the said persons whose name shall stand first in the register of shareholders; and notice so given shall be sufficient notice to all the proprietors of such share.

Receipts for money payable to minors, &c.

XXIX. And be it enacted, That if any money be payable to any shareholder, being a minor, idiot, or lunatic, the receipt of the guardian of such minor, or the receipt of the committee of such idiot or lunatic, shall be a sufficient discharge to the company for the same.

Company not bound to regard trusts.

XXX. And be it enacted, That the company shall not be bound to see to the execution of any trust, whether express, implied, or constructive, to which any of the said shares may be subject; and the receipt of the party in whose name any such share shall stand in the books of the company shall from time to time be a sufficient discharge to the company for any dividend or other sum of money payable in respect of such share, notwithstanding any trusts to which such share may then be subject, and whether or not the company have had notice of such trusts; and the company shall not be bound to see to the application of the money paid upon such receipt.

Power to make calls.

XXXI. And be it enacted, That from time to time the directors may make such calls of money upon the respective shareholders, in respect of the amount of capital stock respectively subscribed by them, as they shall think fit; and whenever execution upon any judgment against the company shall have been taken out against any shareholder, the directors, within twenty-one days next after notice shall have been served upon the company of the payment of any money by such shareholder, his executor or administrators, in or toward satisfaction of such judgment, shall make such calls upon all the shareholders as will be sufficient so reimburse to such shareholder, his executors or administrators, the money so paid by him or them, and all his or their damages, costs, and expenses by reason of such execution, and shall apply the proceeds of such calls accordingly; and every shareholder shall be liable to pay the amount of every call, in respect of the shares held by him, to the persons, and at the times and places, from time to time appointed by the directors. 7 & 8 Vict. c. 113.

XXXII. And be it enacted, That if, before or on the day appointed for payment, any shareholder do not pay the amount of any call to which he may be liable, then such shareholder shall be liable to pay interest for the same at the yearly rate of five pounds in the hundred from the day appointed for the payment thereof to the time of the actual payment. Interest on calls unpaid.

XXXIII. And be it enacted, That if at the time appointed by the directors for the payment of any call the holder of any share fail to pay the amount of such call, the company may sue such shareholder for the amount thereof in any court of law or equity having competent jurisdiction, and may recover the same, with interest at the yearly rate of five pounds in the hundred from the day on which such call may have been payable. Enforcement of calls by action.

XXXIV. And be it enacted, That in any action to be brought by the company against any shareholder to recover any money due for any call it shall not be necessary to set forth the special matter, but it shall be sufficient for the company to declare that the defendant is a holder of one share or more in the company (stating the number of shares), and is indebted to the company in the sum of money to which the calls in arrears shall amount, in respect of one call or more upon one share or more (stating the number and amount of each of such calls), whereby an action hath accrued to the company by virtue of this Act. Declaration in action for calls.

XXXV. And be it enacted, That on the trial of such action it shall not be necessary to prove the appointment of the directors who made such call, or any other matter, except that the defendant at the time of making such call was a holder of one share or more in the company, and that such call was in fact made, and such notice thereof given, as is directed by this Act; and thereupon the company shall be entitled to recover what shall be due upon such call, with interest thereon. Matter to be proved in action for calls.

XXXVI. And be it enacted, That the production of the register book of shareholders of the company shall be evidence of such defefendant being a shareholder, and of the number and amount of his shares. Proof of proprietorship.

XXXVII. And be it enacted, That if the holder of any share fail to pay a call payable by him in respect thereof, with the interest, if any, that shall have accrued thereon, the directors, at any time after the expiration of six calendar months from the day appointed for payment of such call, may declare such share forfeited, and that whether the company have sued for the amount of such call or not; but the forfeiture of any such share shall not relieve any shareholder, his executors or administrators, from his and their liability to pay the calls made before such forfeiture. Forfeiture of shares for nonpayment of calls.

7 & 8 Vict. c. 113.

Notice of forfeiture to be given before declaration thereof.

XXXVIII. And be it enacted, That before declaring any share forfeited the directors shall cause notice of such intention to be left at the usual or last place of abode of the person appearing by the register book of shareholders to be the proprietor of such share; and if the holder of any such share be not within the United Kingdom, or if the interest in any such share shall be known by the directers to have become transmitted otherwise than by transfer, as hereinbefore mentioned, but a declaration of such transmission shall not have been registered as aforesaid, and so the address of the parties to whom the same may have been transmitted shall not be known to the directors, the directors shall give public notice of such intention in the *London Gazette;* and the several notices aforesaid shall be given twenty-one days at least before the directors shall make such declaration of forfeiture.

Forfeiture to be confirmed by a general meeting.

XXXIX. And be it enacted, That such declaration of forfeiture shall not take effect, so as to authorize the sale or other disposition of any share, until such declaration have been confirmed at some general meeting of the company, to be held after the expiration of two calendar months at the least from the day on which such notice of intention to make such declaration of forfeiture shall have been given; and it shall be lawful for the company to confirm such forfeiture at any such meeting, and by an order at such meeting, or at any subsequent general meeting, to direct the share so forfeited to be sold or otherwise disposed of; and after such confirmation the directors shall sell the forfeited share, either by public auction or private contract, within six calendar months next after the confirmation of the forfeiture, and if there be more than one such forfeited share, then either separately or together, as to them shall seem fit; and any shareholder may purchase any forfeited share so sold.

Sale of forfeited shares.

Evidence as to forfeiture of shares.

XL. And be it enacted, That a declaration in writing by some credible person not interested in the matter, made before any justice of the peace, or before any master or master extraordinary in the High Court of Chancery, that the call in respect of a share was made, and notice thereof given, and that default in payment of the call was made, and that the forfeiture of the share was declared and confirmed in manner hereinbefore required, shall be sufficient evidence of the facts therein stated; and such declaration, and the receipt of a director or manager of the company for the price of such share, shall constitute a good title to such share, and thereupon such purchaser shall be deemed the holder of such share discharged from all calls made prior to such purchase; and a certificate of proprietorship shall be delivered to such purchaser, and he shall not be bound to see to the application of the purchase money, nor shall his title to such share be affected by any irregularity in the proceedings in reference to any such sale.

No more shares to be sold than sufficient for payment of calls.

XLI. And be it enacted, That the company shall not sell or transfer more of the shares of any such defaulter than will be sufficient, as nearly as can be ascertained at the time of such sale, to pay the arrears then due from such defaulter on account of any calls, together with interest, and the expenses attending such sale and declaration of forfeiture; and if the money produced by the sale of any such forfeited share be more than sufficient to pay all arrears of calls, and interest thereon, due at the time of such sale, and the expenses attending the declaration of forfeiture and sale thereof, the surplus shall, on demand, be paid to the defaulter.

7 & 8 Vict. c. 113.

On payment of call, forfeited shares to revert.

XLII. And be it enacted, That if payment of such arrears of calls, and interest and expenses, be made before any share so forfeited and vested in the company shall have been sold, such share shall revert to the party to whom the same belonged before such forfeiture, in such manner as if such calls had been duly paid.

Service of notice on the company.

XLIII. And be it enacted, That in all cases wherein it may be necessary for any person to serve any notice, writ, or other proceeding at law or in equity, or otherwise, upon the company, service thereof respectively on the manager or any director for the time being of the company, by leaving the same at the principal office of the company, or, if the company have suspended or discontinued business, by serving the same personally on such manager or director, or by leaving the same with some inmate at the usual or last abode of such manager or director, shall be deemed good service of the same on the company.

Existing companies may continue their trades until twelve months after the passing of this Act.

XLIV. Provided always, and be it enacted, That every company of more than six persons, for the formation or establishment of which proceedings had been begun or taken before the sixth day of *May* last, and which before the fourth day of *July* then next following was registered at the Stamp Office, and on the fourth day of *July* actually carried on the said trade or business of bankers in *England*, although under a covenant or agreement of copartnership made or entered into on or after the sixth day of *May* last, may continue to carry on the said trade or business under any such agreement or covenant of copartnership for any time not exceeding twelve calendar months next after the passing of this Act, in the same manner in all respects as they legally might have done before the passing of this Act, and after the expiration of the said twelve calendar months, in case the company shall not be incorporated under this Act, shall have, for the purpose of closing their trade or business, but for no other purpose, the same powers and privileges which they would have had if this Act had not been passed.

Existing companies may be brought under this Act.

XLV. And be it enacted, That it shall be lawful for any company of more than six persons carrying on the trade or business of bankers in *England* before the said sixth day of *May*, or any company which by the provision hereinbefore in that behalf contained is enabled to carry on the said trade or business of bankers in *England* for a time not exceeding twelve calendar months next after the passing of this Act, to present a petition to Her Majesty, praying that Her Majesty will be pleased to grant to them letters patent under this Act; and if, upon their compliance with the provisions hereinbefore contained with respect to companies formed after the said sixth day of *May*, Her Majesty shall be pleased to grant to them letters patent under this Act as aforesaid, it shall be lawful for them thereafter to carry on their trade and business of bankers as aforesaid according to this Act, and not otherwise: Provided always, that a majority of the directors of any such company for the time

7 & 8 Vict. c. 113.

being, with the consent of three fourths in number and value of the shareholders present at a general meeting of the company, to be specially called for the purpose, may resolve to make any alterations in the constitution of such company, or otherwise, which may be deemed necessary or expedient for enabling such company to come within the provisions of this Act; and the majority of the directors of such company may, in pursuance of the resolution of such meeting as aforesaid, execute a new deed of partnership on behalf of such company, and it shall not be necessary for such deed to be executed by any other shareholder of such company; and it shall thereupon be lawful for such company to present such petition as aforesaid, and a copy of such resolution and of such new deed of partnership so executed by a majority of the directors of the company as aforesaid shall be annexed to such petition; and if Her Majesty shall thereupon grant letters patent to such company under this Act, all the shareholders of such company at the time of the grant of such letters patent shall be deemed to be incorporated under such letters patent, and to be the first shareholders in such incorporated company; and the said new deed of partnership so executed by a majority of the directors as aforesaid shall have such and the same effect, to all intents and purposes, as if it had been executed by all the shareholders.

Agreements entered into with companies after their incorporation to be enforced as if made before incorporation.

XLVI. And be it enacted, That notwithstanding the incorporation of any company under this Act all contracts and agreements entered into by and with such company shall continue in force as between such incorporated company and the parties with which the company entered into such contracts and agreements before the incorporation thereof, and may be enforced in like manner as if the company had been incorporated before the making of any such contract or agreement, and that no suit at law or in equity by or against such company shall be abated by reason of such incorporation; but on the application of either of the parties to such suit to the court in which such suit is pending, at any time before execution on any judgment in such suit shall have issued, it shall be lawful for the court to order that the corporate name of such company be entered on the record, instead of the name of the plaintiff or defendant representing such company before the incorporation thereof, and thereupon such suit may be prosecuted and defended in the same manner as if the same had been originally instituted by or against the said incorporated company; and where execution on any judgment in such suit shall have issued before such application, execution of such judgment may be had as if such company were not incorporated as if this Act had not been passed.

Existing companies to have the powers of suing and being sued.

XLVII. And be it enacted, That after the passing of this Act every company of more than six persons established on the said sixth day of *May* for the purpose of carrying on the said trade or business of bankers within the distance of sixty-five miles from *London*, and not within the provisions of this Act, shall have the same powers and privileges of suing and being sued in the name of any one of the public officers of such copartnership as the nominal plaintiff, petitioner, or defendant on behalf of such copartnership; and that all judgments, decrees, and orders, made and obtained in any such suit may be enforced in like manner as is provided with respect to such companies carrying on the said trade or business at any place in *England* exceeding the distance of sixty-five miles from *London* under the provisions of an Act passed in the seventh year of the reign of King *George* the Fourth, intituled *An Act for the better regulating Copartnerships of certain Bankers in* England; *and for amending so much of an Act of the Thirty-ninth and* Fortieth *Years of the Reign of His late Majesty King* George *the Third, intituled 'An Act for establishing an Agreement with the Governor and Company of the Bank of England, for advancing the Sum of Three Millions towards the Supply for the Service of the Year One thousand eight hundred,' as relates to the same;* provided that such first-mentioned company shall make out and deliver from time to time to the Commissioners of Stamps and Taxes the several accounts or returns required by the last-mentioned Act; and all the provisions of the last-recited Act as to such accounts or returns shall be taken to apply to the accounts or returns so made out and delivered by such first-mentioned companies, as if they had been originally included in the provisions of the last-recited Act.

7 & 8 Vict. c. 113.

7 G. 4, c. 46.

XLVIII. And be it declared and enacted, That every company of more than six persons carrying on the trade or business of bankers in *England* shall be deemed a trading company within the provisions of an Act passed in this session of Parliament, intituled *An Act for facilitating the winding up the Affairs of Joint Stock Companies unable to meet their pecuniary Engagements.*

Banking companies to be deemed trading companies.

XLIX. And be it enacted, That in this Act the following words and expressions shall have the several meanings hereby assigned to them, unless there be something in the subject or context repugnant to such construction; (that is to say),

Interpretation of Act.

Words importing the singular number shall include the plural number, and words importing the plural number shall include the singular number:
Words importing the masculine gender shall include females:
The word "plaintiff" shall include pursuer and petitioner:
The word "defendant" shall include defender and respondent:
The word "execution" shall include diligence or other proceeding proper for giving effect to any judgment, decree, or order of a court of justice.

L. And be it enacted, That this Act may be amended or repealed by any Act to be passed in this session of Parliament.

Act may be amended.

SCHEDULES REFERRED TO BY THE FOREGOING ACT.

SCHEDULE (A).

Memorial or Account to be entered at the Stamp Office in London in pursuance of an Act passed in the eighth year of the reign of Queen Victoria, intituled [*here insert the title of this Act*]; viz.,

7 & 8 Vict. c. 113.

Firm or name of the banking company; viz. [*set forth the firm or name*].

Names and places of abode of all the members of the company; viz. [*set forth all the names and places of abode*].

Names and places of the bank or banks established by such company; viz. [*set forth all the names and places*].

Names and places of abode of the directors, managers, and other like officers of the said banking company; viz. [*set forth all the names and places of abode*].

Names of the several towns and places where the business of the said company is to be carried on; viz. [*set forth the names of all the towns and places*].

A. B. of manager [*or other officer, describing the office*] of the above-mentioned company, maketh oath and saith, That the above-written account doth contain the name, style, and firm of the said company, and the names and places of the abode of the several members thereof, and of the banks established by the said company, and the names, titles, and descriptions of the directors, managers, and other like officers of the said company, and the names of the towns and places where the business of the company is carried on, as the same respectively appear in the books of the said company, and to the best of the information, knowledge, and belief of this deponent.

Sworn before me, the day of at in the county of

C. D., justice of the peace in and for the county of [*or* master *or* master extraordinary in Chancery].

SCHEDULE (B).

MEMORIAL or Account to be entered at the Stamp Office in London on behalf of [*name of the company*], in pursuance of an Act passed in the eighth year of the reign of Queen Victoria, intituled [*insert the title of this Act*]; viz.

Names and places of abode of every new or additional director, manager, or other like officer of the said company; viz. *A. B.* in the room of *C. D.*, deceased *or* removed [*as the case may be*] [*set forth every name and place of abode*].

Names and places of abode of every person who has ceased to be a member of such company; viz. [*set forth every name and place of abode*].

Names and places of abode of every person who has become a new member of such company; viz. [*set forth every name and place of abode*].

Names of any additional towns or places where the business of the company is carried on; viz. [*set forth the names of all the towns and places*].

A. B. of manager [*or other officer*] of the above-named company, maketh oath and saith, That the above-written account doth contain the name and place of abode of every person who hath become or been appointed a director, manager, or other like officer of the above company, and also the name and place of abode of any and every person who hath ceased to be a member of the said company, and of every person who hath become a member of the said company since the registry of the said company on the day of last, as the same respectively appear on the books of the said company, and to the best of the information, knowledge, and belief of this deponent. 7 & 8 Vict. c. 113.

Sworn before me, the day of at in the county

C. D., justice of the peace in and for the county of [*or* master *or* master extraordinary in Chancery].

SCHEDULE (C).

Form of Transfer of Shares.

I of in consideration of the sum of paid to me by of do hereby transfer to the said share [*or* shares], numbered in the business called "The Banking Company," to hold unto the said his executors, administrators, and assigns [*or* successors and assigns], subject to the several conditions on which I held the same at the time of the execution hereof. And I the said do hereby agree to take the said share [*or* shares], subject to the same conditions. As witness our hands and seals, the day of

---

[8 & 9 Vict. c. 37.]

An Act to regulate the Issue of Bank Notes in Ireland, and to regulate the Repayment of certain Sums advanced by the Governor and Company of the Bank of Ireland for the Public Service. 8 & 9 Vict. c. 37.

[21*st July*, 1845.]

WHEREAS by an Act passed in the Parliament of *Ireland* in the twenty-first and twenty-second years of the reign of His Majesty King *George* the Third, intituled *An Act for establishing a Bank by the Name of the Governors and Company of the Bank of* Ireland, it was amongst other things enacted, that from and after the passing of that Act it should not be lawful for any body politic or corporate 21 & 22 G. 3. (I.)

8 & 9 Vict. c. 37. erected or to be erected, other than the corporation thereby intended to be created and erected into a national bank, or for any other persons whatsoever united or to be united in covenants or partnership exceeding the number of six persons, to borrow, owe, or take up any sum or sums of money on their bills or notes payable at demand, or at any less time than six months from the borrowing thereof, under a penalty or forfeiture by such persons, bodies politic or corporate, of treble the sum or sums so to be borrowed or taken upon such bill or bills, note or notes, one moiety thereof to be paid to the informer, and the other to the use of His Majesty, his heirs and successors, to be recovered by action of debt, bill, plaint, or information in any of His Majesty's courts of record at *Dublin:* And whereas, in pursuance of the powers in the said Act of Parliament contained, a charter of incorporation was granted to certain persons, by the name of the Governor and Company of the Bank of *Ireland:* And whereas by an Act passed in the first and second years of the
1 & 2 G. 4, c. 72. reign of His Majesty King *George* the Fourth, intituled *An Act to establish an Agreement with the Governor and Company of the Bank of* Ireland *for advancing the Sum of Five hundred thousand Pounds* Irish *Currency, and to empower the said Governor and Company to enlarge the Capital Stock or Fund of the said Bank to Three million Pounds*, it was enacted, that it might be lawful for any number of persons in *Ireland* united or to be united in society or partnership, and residing and having their establishments or houses of business at any place not less fifty miles distant from *Dublin*, to borrow, owe, or take up any sum or sums of money on their bills or notes payable on demand, and to make and issue such notes or bills accordingly, payable on demand at any place in *Ireland* exceeding the distance of fifty miles from *Dublin*, all the individuals composing such societies or partnerships being liable and responsible for the due payment of such bills or notes; but nothing therein contained was to extend or be construed to extend to authorize any persons exceeding six in number, or any bodies politic or corporate, residing or having their establishment or house of business within the distance of fifty miles from *Dublin*, to make or issue any bill or bills of exchange, or any promissory note or notes, contrary to the provisions of the said in part recited Act of the twenty-first and twenty-second years of the reign of King *George* the Third: And whereas by another Act passed
6 G. 4, c. 42. in the sixth year of the reign of His Majesty King *George* the Fourth, intituled *An Act for the better Regulation of Copartnerships of certain Bankers in* Ireland, and by another Act passed in the first year of the reign of His late Majesty King *William* the Fourth, intituled
11 G. 4, & 1 W. 4, c. 32. *An Act to explain Two Acts of His present Majesty, for establishing an Agreement with the Governor and Company of the Bank of* Ireland *for advancing the Sum of Five hundred thousand Pounds* Irish *Currency, and for the better Regulation of Copartnerships of certain Bankers in* Ireland, such copartnerships of bankers established at places beyond the distance of fifty miles from *Dublin* were authorized to transact certain matters of business by agents in *Dublin* or within the distance of fifty miles thereof: And whereas the said governor and company at different times advanced, for the public service, to His Majesty King *George* the Third, the several sums of six hundred thousand pounds, five hundred thousand pounds, and one million two hundred and fifty thousand pounds, late *Irish* currency, and in respect thereof the said governor and company were entitled to

certain annuities payable at the receipt of the Exchequer in *Dublin:* And whereas by an Act passed in the forty-eighth year of the reign of His said Majesty King *George* the Third, intituled *An Act for further extending the Provisions of several Acts for establishing the Bank of* Ireland, *and for empowering the Governor and Company of the said Bank to advance the Sum of One million two hundred and fifty thousand Pounds* Irish *Currency towards the Service of the Year One thousand eight hundred and eight,* it was amongst other things enacted, that at any time after the first day of *January* in the year of our Lord one thousand eight hundred and thirty-seven, upon twelve months' notice, to be published in the *Dublin Gazette* by order of the Lord Lieutenant or other chief governor or governors of *Ireland,* the said corporation of the bank was to be dissolved; and upon repayment by Parliament to the said Governor and Company of the Bank of *Ireland,* or their successors, of the said several sums of six hundred thousand pounds, five hundred thousand pounds, and one million two hundred and fifty thousand pounds, and also of all arrears of the several annuities payable in respect of the said three several capital sums, if any such arrear should then be due, or at any time previous to the said first day of *January* one thousand eight hundred and thirty-seven, upon like repayment by and with the desire and consent of the said governor and company, to be signified by them by their petition in writing sealed with their common seal, and addressed to the Lord Lieutenant or other chief governor or governors of *Ireland* for the time being, then and in such case the said several annuities should from and after the expiration of twelve months after such notice published, cease and determine, and the said corporation should be dissolved: And whereas in pursuance of the said recited Act passed in the first and second years of the reign of His Majesty King *George* the Fourth, intituled *An Act to establish an Agreement with the Governor and Company of the Bank of* Ireland *for advancing the Sum of Five hundred thousand Pounds* Irish *Currency, and to empower the said Governor and Company to enlarge the Capital Stock or Fund of the said Bank to Three millions,* the said Governor and Company of the Bank of *Ireland* advanced for the public service, to His Majesty King *George* the Fourth, the sum of five hundred thousand pounds late *Irish* currency, at interest, making, with the said three several sums of six hundred thousand pounds, five hundred thousand pounds, and one million two hundred and fifty thousand pounds, late *Irish* currency, previously advanced, the sum of two million eight hundred and fifty thousand pounds, equal to two million six hundred and thirty thousand seven hundred and sixty-nine pounds four shillings and eightpence sterling money of the United Kingdom of *Great Britain* and *Ireland:* And whereas by an Act passed in the third and fourth years of the reign of Her present Majesty, intituled *An Act to regulate the Repayment of certain Sums advanced by the Governor and Company of the Bank of* Ireland *for the Public Service,* it was amongst other things enacted, that from and after the passing of the said Act there should be paid and payable, but subject to the condition of redemption thereinafter contained, at the receipt of Her Majesty's Exchequer in *Dublin,* to the Governor and Company of the said Bank of *Ireland,* out of the Consolidated Fund of the United Kingdom of *Great Britain* and *Ireland,* an interest or annuity of one hundred and fifteen thousand three hundred and

8 & 9 Vict. c 37

48 G. 3, c. 103, s. 10.

1 & 2 G. 4, c. 72.

3 & 4 Vict. c. 75.

8 & 9 Vict. c. 37. eighty-four pounds twelve shillings and fourpence, money of the United Kingdom, being a sum equal to the several annuities and interest theretofore payable in respect of the principal money due to the said governor and company as aforesaid, by two equal half-yearly payments, without any defalcation or abatement, on the fifth day of *January* and the fifth day of *July* in each year, the first payment of the said interest or annuity to be made on the fifth day of *January* in the year one thousand eight hundred and forty-one; and it was by the last-mentioned Act further provided, that the said last-mentioned annuity should be redeemable at any time after the first day of *January* one thousand eight hundred and forty-one, on six months' notice to the said governor and company, and on repayment to them of the said several sums of six hundred thousand pounds, five hundred thousand pounds, one million two hundred and fifty thousand pounds, and five hundred thousand pounds, late *Irish* currency, together with all arrears of the said annuity of one hundred and fifteen thousand three hundred and eighty-four pounds twelve shillings and fourpence: And whereas the last-mentioned annuity has, by consent of the said governor and company, been reduced to an annuity of ninety-two thousand and seventy-six pounds eighteen shillings and fivepence of *British* currency: And whereas it is expedient that the exclusive privilege of banking granted to the said governor and company by the said recited Act of the Parliament of *Ireland*, or by any other Act or Acts of Parliament now in force, should cease, but that the said governor and company should continue a corporation, with full power and authority to carry on the business of bankers, subject to the regulations hereinafter contained; and the said Governor and Company of the Bank of *Ireland* have agreed to continue the management in *Ireland* of so much of the public debt of the United Kingdom as shall for the time being require to be transacted in *Ireland*, and of all loans and other creations of stock which shall at any time be made in *Ireland*, and of any public annuities for lives or for years which may be payable in *Ireland*, free of all charge and expense whatever for such management, or for their trouble in the payment of the interest of the said public debt or annuities from time to time during the continuance of the said corporation under the provisions of this Act; and it hath been further agreed that the said governor and company shall continue to receive the said annuity of ninety-two thousand and seventy-six pounds eighteen shillings and fivepence, being an annual interest at and after the rate of three and a half *per centum per annum*, for and in respect of the said capital sum of two million six hundred and thirty thousand seven hundred and sixty-nine pounds four shillings and eightpence, and that the repayment of the last-mentioned sum shall be postponed till the expiration of six months after notice to be given by the Commissioners of Her Majesty's Treasury of the United Kingdom of *Great Britain* and *Ireland* to the said governor and company of their intention to pay off the same, or by the said governor and company to the said Commissioners of Her Majesty's Treasury requiring payment thereof, such notice not to be given by either party before the first day of *January* one thousand eight hundred and fifty-five: And whereas by an Act passed in the seventh and eighth years of the reign of Her Majesty, intituled

7 & 8 Vict. c. 32, s. 10. *An Act to regulate the Issue of Bank Notes, and for giving to the*

Governor and Company of the Bank of England *certain Privileges for a limited Period*, it was enacted, that from and after the passing of that Act no person, other than a banker who on the sixth day of *May* one thousand eight hundred and forty-four was lawfully issuing his own bank notes, should make or issue bank notes in any part of the United Kingdom : And whereas it is expedient to regulate the issue of bank notes by the said Governor and Company of the Bank of *Ireland*, and by such other bankers as are now by law authorized to issue bank notes in *Ireland:* Be it therefore enacted by the Queen's most excellent Majesty, by and with the advice and consent of the Lords spiritual and temporal, and Commons, in this present Parliament assembled, and by the authority of the same, That from and after the sixth day of *December*, one thousand eight hundred and forty-five, so much of the said recited Act of the Parliament of *Ireland* of the twenty-first and twenty-second years of the reign of His Majesty King *George* the Third as prohibits any body politic or corporate erected or to be erected, other than the Governor and Company of the Bank of *Ireland*, or for any other persons whatsoever united or to be united in covenants or partnership exceeding the number of six persons, to borrow, owe, or take up any sum or sums of money on their bills or notes payable at demand, or at any less time than six months from the borrowing thereof, shall be and the same is hereby repealed; and that from and after the said sixth day of *December* one thousand eight hundred and forty-five, it shall and may be lawful for any persons exceeding six in number united or to be united in societies or partnerships, or for any bodies politic or corporate, to transact or carry on the business of bankers in *Ireland* at *Dublin*, and at every place within fifty miles thereof, as freely as persons exceeding six in number united as aforesaid may lawfully carry on the same business at any place in *Ireland* beyond the distance of fifty miles from *Dublin:* Provided always, that every member of any such society, partnership, bodies politic or corporate, shall be liable and responsible for the due payment of all the debts and liabilities of the corporation or copartnership of which such person shall be a member, any agreement, covenant, or contract to the contrary notwithstanding.

8 & 9 Vict. c. 37.

Restriction on bankers by 21 & 22 G. 3 (Ireland), repealed.

Authorizing certain banking copartnerships to carry on business in Dublin or within 50 miles thereof.

II. And be it enacted, That from and after the passing of this Act the repayment of the said sum of two millions six hundred and thirty thousand seven hundred and sixty-nine pounds four shillings and eightpence shall be and the same is hereby made chargeable upon the Consolidated Fund of the United Kingdom of *Great Britain* and *Ireland* until Parliament shall otherwise provide, and there shall be paid and payable, but subject to the condition of redemption hereinafter contained, at the receipt of Her Majesty's Exchequer in *Dublin*, to the Governor and Company of the said Bank of *Ireland*, out of the Consolidated Fund of the United Kingdom of *Great Britain* and *Ireland*, in respect of the said capital sum of two million six hundred and thirty thousand seven hundred and sixty-nine pounds four shillings and eightpence so now due by the public to the said governor and company, the aforesaid annuity of ninety-two thousand and seventy-six pounds eighteen shillings and fivepence, being an interest or annuity at and after the rate of three pounds ten shillings *per centum per annum*, in the now lawful currency of the United Kingdom, by two equal half-yearly payments, without

Interest at the rate of three and a half per centum per annum made payable to the Bank.

8 & 9 Vict. c. 37.

any defalcation or abatement, on the fifth day of *January* and the fifth day of *July* in each year.

Bank shall manage the public debt of Ireland, and pay dividends without expense to Government.

III. And be it enacted, That from and after the passing of this Act the said Governor and Company of the Bank of *Ireland* shall from time to time and at all times during the continuance of their charter, and until the said corporation shall be dissolved pursuant to the provisions of this Act, continue to manage and to pay all interest, annuities, and dividends payable at the said bank in respect of such part of the public debt as shall for the time being require to be transacted in *Ireland*, or in respect of any fund or stock created or to be created in consequence of any public loan, or funding of exchequer bills, or conversion of stock in *Ireland*, or of any public annuities, whether for lives or for years, without making any charge to Her Majesty, her heirs or successors, or to the Lord High Treasurer or the Commissioners of Her Majesty's Treasury, for their trouble or expense in so doing, any law, usage, or custom to the contrary notwithstanding.

Bank corporation may be dissolved on notice after 1st of January 1855.

IV. And be it enacted, That at any time after the first day of *January* which will be in the year of our Lord one thousand eight hundred and fifty-five, upon twelve months' notice, to be published in the *Dublin Gazette* by order of the Lord Lieutenant or other chief governor or governors of *Ireland*, that the said corporation of the bank is to be dissolved, and upon repayment by Parliament to the said Governor and Company of the Bank of *Ireland*, or their successors, of the said sum of two million six hundred and thirty thousand seven hundred and sixty-nine pounds four shillings and eightpence, together with all arrears of interest or annuity due in respect thereof, then and in such case the said interest or annuity shall, from and after the expiration of twelve months after such notice published, cease and determine, and the said corporation shall be dissolved.

Repeal of so much of 33 G. 2, c. 14, s. 15 (I.), as prohibits public officers from being partners in banks.

V. And whereas by an Act passed in the Parliament of *Ireland* in the thirty-third year of His late Majesty King *George* the Second, intituled *An Act for repealing an Act passed in this Kingdom in the Eighth Year of the Reign of King* George *the First, intituled 'An Act for the better securing the payment of Bankers' Notes, and for providing a more effectual Remedy for the Security and Payment of Debts due by Bankers,'* it was among other things enacted, that no person who by reason of any office, employment, deputation, or clerkship was then or should at any time thereafter be entrusted with the receipt, custody, or payment of public money, or any part of the public revenue of that kingdom, should, either singly or in partnership, so long as such person should continue in such office, employment, deputation, or clerkship, follow the trade or business of a banker, or by himself, or by any person authorized by him, issue or give any note or accountable receipt as a banker or in partnership with any banker, or for profit or reward discount any promissory note, or foreign or inland bill of exchange: And whereas it is expedient to repeal the said enactment; be it therefore enacted, That from and after the passing of this Act so much of the last-mentioned Act as is herein recited shall be and the same i hereby repealed.

VI. And whereas by an Act passed in the third and fourth years of the reign of His late Majesty King *William* the Fourth, intituled *An Act for giving to the Corporation of the Governor and Company of the Bank of* England *certain Privileges for a limited Period, under certain Conditions*, it was enacted, that from and after the first day of *August* one thousand eight hundred and thirty-four, unless and until Parliament should otherwise direct, a tender of a note or notes of the Governor and Company of the Bank of *England* expressed to be payable to bearer on demand should be a legal tender to the amount expressed in such note or notes, and should be taken to be valid as a tender to such amount for all sums above five pounds, on all occasions on which any tender of money may be legally made, so long as the Bank of *England* should continue to pay on demand their said notes in legal coin; provided always, that no such note or notes should be deemed a legal tender of payment by the Governor and Company of the Bank of *England*, or any branch bank of the said governor and company: And whereas doubts have arisen as to the extent of the said enactment; for removal whereof, be it enacted and declared, That nothing in the said last-recited Act contained shall extend to be construed to extend to make the tender of a note or notes of the Governor and Company of the Bank of *England* a legal tender in *Ireland*: Provided also, that nothing in this Act shall be construed to prohibit the circulation in *Ireland* of the notes of the Governor and Company of the Bank of *England* as heretofore.

8 & 9 Vict. c. 37.

Bank of England notes not a legal tender in Ireland.

Proviso.

VII. And be it enacted, That from and after the passing of this Act it shall not be necessary for any governor, deputy governor, or director of the said bank, before acting in the said several offices or trusts, to make and subscribe the declaration pursuant to the Act of Parliament passed in the kingdom of *Ireland*, intituled *An Act to prevent the further Growth of Popery*, nor to take any other oaths than the oath of allegiance, the oath of qualification by possession of stock, and the oath of fidelity to the corporation prescribed in and by the charter of incorporation of the governor and company of the said bank, and that it shall not be necessary for any member of the said corporation, before voting in any general court, to make and subscribe the aforesaid declaration, nor to take any other oaths than the oaths of allegiance, the oath of qualification by the possession of stock, and the oath of fidelity to the said corporation provided in the said charter of incorporation: Provided always, that in case any of the persons called Quakers shall at any time be chosen governor, deputy governor, or director, or shall be or become a member of the said corporation, it shall be sufficient for such person or persons to make his or their solemn affirmation, to the purport and effect of the oaths prescribed by the said charter and by this Act to be taken by governors, deputy governors, directors, or members respectively of the said corporation.

Oaths to be taken by directors, &c., of the Bank of Ireland.

VIII. And be it enacted, That every banker claiming to be entitled to issue bank notes in *Ireland* shall, within one month next after the passing of this Act, give notice in writing to the Commissioners of Stamps and Taxes, at their head office in *London*, of such claim, and of the place and name and firm at and under which such banker has issued such notes in *Ireland* during the year next

Bankers claiming to be entitled to issue bank notes to give notice to Commission-

8 & 9 Vict. c. 37.

ers of Stamps and Taxes.

Commissioners to certify existing banks of issue and limitation of issue.

preceding the first day of *May* one thousand eight hundred and forty-five, and thereupon the said commissioners shall ascertain if such banker was on the sixth day of *May* one thousand eight hundred and forty-four, and from thence up to the first day of *May* one thousand eight hundred and forty-five, carrying on the business of a banker, and lawfully issuing his own bank notes in *Ireland*, and if it shall so appear, then the said commissioners shall proceed to ascertain the average amount of the bank notes of such banker which were in circulation during the said period of one year preceding the first day of *May* one thousand eight hundred and forty-five, according to the returns made by such banker in pursuance of the Act passed in the fourth and fifth years of the reign of Her present Majesty, intituled *An Act to make further Provisions relative to the Returns to be made by Banks of the Amount of their Notes in Circulation*, and the said commissioners, or any two of them, shall certify under their hands to such banker the average amount, when so ascertained as aforesaid, omitting the fractions of a pound, if any; and it shall be lawful for every such banker to continue to issue his own bank notes after the sixth day of *December* one thousand eight hundred and forty-five, to the extent of the amount so certified, and of the amount of the gold and silver coin held by such banker, in the proportion and manner hereinafter mentioned, but not to any further extent; and from and after the sixth day of *December* one thousand eight hundred and forty-five it shall not be lawful for any banker to make or issue bank notes in *Ireland*, save and except only such bankers as shall have obtained such certificate from the Commissioners of Stamps and Taxes.

4 & 5 Vict. c. 50.

Prohibiting issue by uncertified bankers.

Provision for united banks.

IX. Provided always, and be it enacted, That if it shall be made to appear to the Commissioners of Stamps and Taxes that any two or more banks have, by written contract or agreement (which contract or agreement shall be produced to the said commissioners), become united within the year next preceding such first day of *May* one thousands eight hundred and forty-five, it shall be lawful for the said commissioners to ascertain the average amount of the notes of each such bank in the manner hereinbefore directed, and to certify a sum equal to the average amount of the notes of the two or more banks so united as the amount which the united bank shall thereafter be authorized to issue, subject to the regulations of this Act.

Duplicate of certificate to be published in the 'Gazette.'

'Gazette' to be evidence.

X. And be it enacted, That the Commissioners of Stamps and Taxes shall, at the time of certifying to any banker such particulars as they are hereinbefore required to certify, also publish a duplicate of their certificate thereof in the next succeeding *Dublin Gazette* in which the same may be conveniently inserted; and the Gazette in which such publication shall be made shall be conclusive evidence in all courts whatsoever of the amount of bank notes which the banker named in such certificate or duplicate is by law authorized to issue and to have in circulation as aforesaid, exclusive of an amount equal to the monthly average amount of the gold and silver coin held by such banker as herein provided.

In case banks become united, commissioners to

XI. And be it enacted, That in case it shall be made to appear to the Commissioners of Stamps and Taxes at any time hereafter that any two or more banks have, by written contract or agreement (which contract or agreement shall be produced to the said commissioners), become united subsequently to the passing of this Act, it shall be lawful to the said commissioners, upon the application of such united bank, to certify, in manner hereinbefore mentioned, the aggregate of the amount of bank notes which such separate banks were previously authorized to issue under the separate certificates previously delivered to them, and so from time to time; and every such certificate shall be published in manner hereinbefore directed; and from and after such publication the amount therein stated shall be and be deemed to be the limit of the amount of bank notes which such united bank may have in circulation, exclusive of an amount equal to the monthly average amount of the gold and silver coin held by such banker as herein provided.

8 & 9 Vict. c. 37.

certify the amount of bank notes which each bank was authorized to issue.

XII. And be it enacted, That it shall be lawful for any banker in *Ireland* who under the provisions of this Act is entitled to issue bank notes to contract and agree with the Governor and Company of the Bank of *Ireland*, by an agreement in writing, for the relinquishment of the privilege of issuing such notes in favour of the said governor and company, and in each such case a copy of such agreement shall be transmitted to the Commissioners of Stamps and Taxes; and the said commissioners shall thereupon certify, in manner hereinbefore mentioned, the aggregate of the amount of bank notes which the Bank of *Ireland* and the banker with whom such agreement shall have been made were previously authorized to issue under the separate certificates previously delivered to them; and every such certificate shall be published in manner hereinbefore directed; and from and after such publication the amount therein stated shall be the limit of the amount of bank notes which the Governor and Company of the Bank of *Ireland* may have in circulation, exclusive of an amount equal to the amount of the gold and silver coin held by the Bank of *Ireland* as herein provided.

Banks entitled to the privilege of issuing notes may relinquish the same;

XIII. And be it enacted, That it shall not be lawful for any banker who shall have so agreed to relinquish the privilege of issuing bank notes at any time thereafter to issue any such notes.

but not resume the issue.

XIV. And be it enacted, That from and after the sixth day of *December* one thousand eight hundred and forty-five it shall not be lawful for any banker in *Ireland* to have in circulation, upon the average of a period of four weeks, to be ascertained as hereinafter mentioned, a greater amount of notes than an amount composed of the sums certified by the Commissioners of Stamps and Taxes as aforesaid, and the monthly average amount of gold and silver coin held by such banker during the same period of four weeks, to be ascertained in manner hereinafter mentioned.

Limitation of bank notes in circulation.

XV. And be it enacted, That all bank notes to be issued or reissued in *Ireland* after the sixth day of *December* one thousand eight hundred and forty-five shall be expressed to be for payment of a sum in pounds sterling, without any fractional parts of a pound; and if any banker in *Ireland* shall from and after that day make, sign, issue, or reissue any bank note for the fractional part of a pound sterling, or for any sum together with the frac-

Issue of notes for fractional parts of a pound prohibited.

8 & 9 Vict. c. 37.

tional part of a pound sterling, every such banker so making, signing, issuing, or reissuing any such note as aforesaid shall for each note so made, signed, issued, or reissued forfeit or pay the sum of twenty pounds.

Issuing banks to render accounts weekly.

XVI. And be it enacted, That every banker who after the sixth day of *December* one thousand eight hundred and forty-five shall issue bank notes in *Ireland* shall, on some one day in every week after the thirteenth day of *December* one thousand eight hundred and forty-five (such day to be fixed by the Commissioners of Stamps and Taxes), transmit to the said commissioners a just and true account of the amount of bank notes of such banker in circulation at the close of the business on the next preceding *Saturday*, distinguishing the notes of five pounds and upwards, and the notes below five pounds, and also an account of the total amount of gold and silver coin held by such banker at each of the head offices or principal places of issue in *Ireland* of such banker at the close of business on each day of the week ending on that *Saturday*, and also an account of the total amount of gold and silver coin in *Ireland* held by such banker at the close of business on that day; and on completing the first period of four weeks, and so on completing each successive period of four weeks, every such banker shall annex to such account the average amount of bank notes of such banker in circulation during the said four weeks, distinguishing the bank notes of five pounds and upwards, and the notes below five pounds, and the average amount of gold and silver coin respectively held by such banker at each of the head offices or principal places of issue in *Ireland* of such banker during the said four weeks, and also the amount of bank notes which such banker is, by the certificate published as aforesaid, authorized to issue under the provisions of this Act; and every such account shall be verified by the signature of such banker or his chief cashier, or in the case of a company or partnership by the signature of the chief cashier or other officer duly authorized by the directors of such company or partnership, and shall be made in the form to this Act annexed marked (A); and if any such banker shall neglect or refuse to render any such account in the form and at the time required by this Act, or shall at any time render a false account, such banker shall forfeit the sum of one hundred pounds for every such offence.

What shall be deemed to be bank notes in circulation.

XVII. And be it enacted, That all bank notes shall be deemed to be in circulation from the time the same shall have been issued by any banker, or any servant or agent of such banker, until the same shall have been actually returned to such banker, or some servant or agent of such banker.

Commissioners of Stamps to make a monthly return.

XVIII. And be it enacted, That from the returns so made by each banker to the Commissioners of Stamps and Taxes the said commissioners shall, at the end of the first period of four weeks after the said sixth day of *December* one thousand eight hundred and forty-five, and so at the end of each successive period of four weeks, make out a general return in the form to this Act annexed marked (B) of the monthly averge amount of bank notes in circulation of each banker in *Ireland* during the last preceding four weeks, and of the average amount of all the gold and silver coin held by such banker during the same period, and certifying, under the hand of any officer of the said commissioners duly authorized for that purpose in the case of each such banker, whether such banker has held the amount of coin required by law during the period to which the said return shall apply, and shall publish the same in the next succeeding *Dublin Gazette* in which the same can be conveniently inserted.

8 & 9 Vict. c. 37.

XIX. And be it enacted, That for the purpose of ascertaining the monthly average amount of bank notes of each banker in circulation, the aggregate of the amount of bank notes of each such banker in circulation at the close of the business on the *Saturday* in each week during the first complete period of four weeks next after the sixth day of *December* one thousand eight hundred and forty-five shall be divided by the number of weeks, and the average so ascertained shall be deemed to be the average of bank notes of each such banker in circulation during such period of four weeks, and so in each successive period of four weeks; and the monthly average amount of gold and silver coin respectively held as aforesaid by such banker shall be ascertained in like manner from the amount of gold and silver coin held by such banker at the head offices or principal places of issue of such banker in *Ireland*, as after mentioned, at the close of business on such day in each week; and the monthly average amount of bank notes of each such banker in circulation during any such period of four weeks is not to exceed a sum made up by adding the amount certified by the Commissioners of Stamps and Taxes as aforesaid and the monthly average amount of gold and silver coin held by such banker as aforesaid during the same period.

Mode of ascertaining the average amount of bank notes of each banker in circulation, and gold coin, during the first four weeks after the 6th day of December 1845.

XX. And be it enacted, That in taking account of the coin held by any banker in *Ireland* with respect to which bank notes to a further extent than the sum certified as aforesaid by the Commissioners of Stamps and Taxes may, under the provisions of this Act, be made and issued, there shall be included only the gold and silver coin held by such banker at the several head offices or principal places of issue in *Ireland* of such banker, such head offices or principal places of issue not exceeding four in number, of which not more than two shall be situated in the same province; and every banker shall give notice in writing to the said commissioners, on or before the sixth day of *December* next, of such head offices or principal places of issue at which the account of gold and silver coin held by him is to be taken as aforesaid; and no amount of silver coin exceeding one fourth part of the gold coin held by such banker as aforesaid shall be taken into account, nor shall any banker be authorized to make and issue bank notes in *Ireland* on any amount of silver coin held by such banker exceeding the proportion of one fourth part of the gold coin held by such banker as aforesaid.

What shall be taken in the account of coin held by any banker.

Silver coin not to exceed the proportion of one quarter of gold.

XXI. And whereas in order to ensure the rendering of true and faithful accounts of the amount of bank notes in circulation, and the amount of gold and silver coin held by each banker, as directed by this Act, it is necessary that the Commissioners of Stamps and Taxes should be empowered to cause the books of bankers issuing

Commissioners of Stamps and Taxes empowered to cause the books of bankers,

8 & 9 Vict. c. 37.

containing accounts of their bank notes in circulation, and of gold coin, to be inspected.

such notes, and the amount of gold and silver coin held by such bankers as aforesaid, to be inspected as hereinafter mentioned; be it therefore enacted, That all and every the book and books of any banker who shall issue bank notes under the provisions of this Act, in which shall be kept, contained, or entered any account, minute, or memorandum of or relating to the bank notes issued or to be issued by such bank, of or relating to the amount of such notes in circulation from time to time, or of or relating to the gold or silver coin held by such banker from time to time, or any account, minute, or memorandum the sight or inspection whereof may tend to secure the rendering of true accounts of the average amount of such notes in circulation and gold or silver coin held as directed by this Act, or to test the truth of any such account, shall be open for the inspection and examination at all seasonable times of any officer of stamp duties authorized in that behalf by writing signed by the Commissioners of Stamps and Taxes, or any two of them; and every such officer shall be at liberty to take copies of or extracts from any such book or account as aforesaid, and to inspect and ascertain the amount of any gold or silver coin held by such banker; and if any banker or other person keeping any such book, or having the custody or possession thereof or power to produce the same, shall, upon demand made by any such officer showing (if required) his authority in that behalf, refuse to produce any such book to such officer for his inspection and examination, or to permit him to inspect and examine the same, or to take copies thereof or extracts therefrom, or of or from any such account, minute, or memorandum as aforesaid, kept, contained, or entered therein, or if any banker or other person having the custody or possession of any coin belonging to such banker shall refuse to permit or prevent the inspection of such gold and silver coin as aforesaid, every such banker or other person so offending shall for every such offence forfeit the sum of one hundred pounds: Provided always, that the said commissioners shall not exercise the powers aforesaid without the consent of the Commissioners of Her Majesty's Treasury.

Penalty for refusing to allow such inspection.

All bankers to return their names once a year, to the Stamp Office.

XXII. And be it enacted, That every banker in *Ireland*, other than the Bank of *Ireland*, who is now carrying on or shall hereafter carry on business as such, shall, on the first day of *January* in each year, or within fifteen days thereafter, make a return to the Commissioners of Stamps and Taxes, at their office in *Dublin*, of his name, residence, and occupation, or in the case of a company or partnership, of the name, residence, and occupation of every person composing or being a member of such company or partnership, and also the name of the firm under which such banker, company, or partnership carry on the business of banking, and of every place where such business is carried on; and if any such banker shall omit or refuse to make such return within fifteen days after the said first day of *January*, or shall wilfully make other than a true return of the persons as herein required, every banker so offending shall forfeit or pay the sum of fifty pounds; and the said Commissioners of Stamps and Taxes shall on or before the first day of *March* in every year publish in the *Dublin Gazette* a copy of the return so made by every banker.

XXIII. And be it enacted, That if the monthly average circulation of bank notes of any banker, taken in the manner herein directed, shall at any time exceed the amount which such banker is authorized to issue and to have in circulation under the provisions of this Act, such banker shall in every such case forfeit a sum equal to the amount by which the average monthly circulation, taken as aforesaid, shall have exceeded the amount which such banker was authorized to issue and to have in circulation as aforesaid.

8 & 9 Vict. c. 37.

Penalty on banks issuing in excess.

XXIV. And be it enacted, That all promissory or other notes, bills of exchange, or drafts, or undertakings in writing, being negotiable or transferable, for the payment of any sum or sums of money, or any orders, notes, or undertakings in writing, being negotiable or transferable, for the delivery of any goods, specifying their value in money less than the sum of twenty shillings in the whole, heretofore made or issued, or which hereafter shall be made or issued in *Ireland*, shall, from and after the first day of *January* one thousand eight hundred and forty-six, be and the same are hereby declared to be absolutely void and of no effect, any law, statute, usage, or custom to the contrary thereof in anywise notwithstanding; and that if any person or persons shall, after the first day of *January* one thousand eight hundred and forty-six, by any art, device, or means whatsoever, publish or utter in *Ireland* any such notes, bills, drafts, or engagements as aforesaid, for a less sum than twenty shillings, or on which less than the sum of twenty shillings shall be due, and which shall be in anywise negotiable or transferable, or shall negotiate or transfer the same in *Ireland*, every such person shall forfeit and pay for every such offence any sum not exceeding twenty pounds nor less than five pounds, at the discretion of the justice of the peace who shall hear and determine such offence.

Notes for less than 20*s.* not negotiable in Ireland.

XXV. And be it enacted, That all promissory or other notes, bills of exchange, or drafts, or undertakings in writing, being negotiable or transferable, for the payment of twenty shillings, or any sum of money above that sum and less than five pounds, or on which twenty shillings, or above that sum and less than five pounds, shall remain undischarged, and which shall be issued within *Ireland* at any time after the first day of *January* one thousand eight hundred and forty-six, shall specify the names and places of abode of the persons respectively to whom or to whose order the same shall be made payable, and shall bear date before or at the time of drawing or issuing thereof, and not on any day subsequent thereto, and shall be made payable within the space of twenty-one days next after the date thereof, and shall not be transferable or negotiable after the time hereby limited for payment thereof, and that every indorsement to be made thereon shall be made before the expiration of that time, and to bear date at or not before the time of making thereof, and shall specify the name and place of abode of the person or persons to whom or to whose order the money contained in every such note, bill, draft, or undertaking is to be paid; and that the signing of every such note, bill, draft, or undertaking, and also of every such indorsement, shall be attested by one subscribing witness at the least; and which said notes, bills of exchange, or drafts, or undertakings in writing, may be made or drawn in words to the purport or effect as set out in the Schedules to this Act annexed

Notes for 20*s.* and above, and less than 5*l.*, to be drawn in certain form.

8 & 9 Vict. c. 37.

marked (D) and (E); and that all promissory or other notes, bills of exchange, or drafts, or undertakings in writing, being negotiable or transferable, for the payment of twenty shillings, or any sum of money above that sum and less than five pounds, or in which twenty shillings, or above that sum and less than five pounds, shall remain undischarged, and which shall be issued in *Ireland* at any time after the said first day of *January* one thousand eight hundred and forty-six, in any other manner than as aforesaid, and also every indorsement on any such note, bill, draft, or other undertaking to be negotiated under this Act, other than as aforesaid, shall and the same are hereby declared to be absolutely void, any law, statute, usage, or custom to the contrary thereof in anywise notwithstanding; provided that nothing in this clause contained shall be construed to extend to any such bank notes as shall be lawfully issued by any banker in *Ireland* authorized by this Act to continue the issue of bank notes.

Penalty for persons other than bankers hereby authorized issuing notes payable on demand for less than 5*l*.

XXVI. And be it enacted, That if any body politic or corporate or any person or persons shall, from and after the said first day of *January* one thousand eight hundred and forty-six, make, sign, issue, or reissue in *Ireland* any promissory note payable on demand to the bearer thereof for any sum of money less than the sum of five pounds, except the bank notes of such bankers as are hereby authorized to continue to issue bank notes as aforesaid, then and in either of such cases every such body politic or corporate or person or persons so making, signing, issuing, or reissuing any such promissory note as aforesaid, except as aforesaid, shall for every such note so made, signed, issued, or reissued forfeit the sum of twenty pounds.

Penalty for persons other than bankers hereby authorized uttering or negotiating notes, bills of exchange, &c., transferable, for payment of 20*s*. or less than five pounds.

XXVII. And be it enacted, That if any body politic or corporate or person or persons shall, from and after the passing of this Act, publish, utter, or negotiate in *Ireland* any promissory or other note (not being the bank note of a banker hereby authorized to continue to issue bank notes), or any bill of exchange, draft, or undertaking in writing, being negotiable or transferable, for the payment of twenty shillings, or above that sum and less than five pounds, or on which twenty shillings, or above that sum and less than five pounds, shall remain undischarged, made, drawn, or indorsed, in any other manner than as is hereinbefore directed, every such body politic or corporate or person or persons so publishing, uttering, or negotiating any such promissory or other note (not being such bank note as aforesaid), bill of exchange, draft, or undertaking, in writing as aforesaid, shall forfeit and pay the sum of twenty pounds.

Not to prohibit checks on bankers.

XXVIII. Provided always, and be it enacted, That nothing herein contained shall extend to prohibit any draft or order drawn by any person on his banker, or on any person acting as such banker, for the payment of money held by such banker or person to the use of the person by whom such draft or order shall be drawn.

Mode of enforcing penalties.

XXIX. And be it enacted, That all pecuniary penalties under this Act may be sued or prosecuted for and recovered for the use of Her

Majesty, in the name of Her Majesty's Attorney General or Solicitor General in *Ireland*, or of the Solicitor of Stamps in *Ireland*, or of any person authorized to sue or prosecute for the same, by writing under the hands of the Commissioners of Stamps and Taxes, or in the name of any officer of stamp duties, by action of debt, bill, plaint, or information in the Court of Exchequer in *Dublin*, or by civil bill in the court of the recorder, chairman, or assistant barrister within whose local jurisdiction any offence shall have been committed, in respect of any such penalty, or, in respect of any penalty not exceeding twenty pounds, by information or complaint before one or more justice or justices of the peace in *Ireland*, in such and the same manner as any other penalties imposed by any of the laws now in force relating to the duties under the management of the Commissioners of Stamps; and it shall be lawful in all cases for the Commissioners of Stamps and Taxes, either before or after any proceedings commenced for recovery of any such penalty, to mitigate or compound any such penalty, as the said commissioners shall think fit, and to stay any such proceedings after the same shall have been commenced, and whether judgment may have been obtained for such penalty or not, on payment of part only of any such penalty, with or without costs, or on payment only of the costs incurred in such proceedings, or of any part thereof, or on such other terms as such commissioners shall judge reasonable: Provided always, that in no such proceeding as aforesaid shall any essoign, protection, wager of law, nor more than one imparlance be allowed; and all pecuniary penalties imposed by or incurred under this Act, by whom or in whose name soever the same shall be sued or prosecuted for or recovered, shall go and be applied to the use of Her Majesty, and shall be deemed to be and shall be accounted for as part of Her Majesty's revenue arising from stamp duties, any thing in any Act contained, or any law or usage, to the contray in anywise notwithstanding: Provided always, that it shall be lawful for the Commissioners of Stamps and Taxes, at their discretion, to give all or any part of such penalties as rewards to any person or persons who shall have detected the offenders, or given information which may have led to their prosecution and conviction. 8 & 9 Vict. c. 37.

Companies to sue and be sued in the names of their officers.

XXX. And be it enacted, That after the passing of this Act every company or copartnership of more than six persons established before the passing of this Act, for the purpose of carrying on the trade or business of bankers within the distance of fifty miles from *Dublin*, shall have the same powers and privileges of suing and being sued, and of presenting petitions to found sequestrations or fiats in bankruptcy, in the name of any one of the public officers of such company or copartnership, as the nominal plaintiff, petitioner, or defendant, on behalf of such company or copartnership, as are provided with respect to companies carrying on the said trade or business at any place in *Ireland* exceeding the distance of fifty miles from *Dublin*, under the provisions of an Act passed in the sixth year of the reign of King *George* the Fourth, intituled *An Act for the better Regulation of Copartnerships of certain Bankers in* Ireland: 6 G. 4, c. 42
and all judgments, decrees, and orders made and obtained in any action, suit, or other proceeding brought, instituted, or carried on by or against any such company or copartnership carrying on business within the distance of fifty miles from *Dublin*, in the name of their

8 & 9 Vict. c. 37.

public officer, shall have the same effect and operation, and may be enforced in like manner in all respects, as is provided in and by the last-mentioned Act with respect to the judgments, decrees, and orders therein mentioned; provided that every such company or copartnership as last aforesaid shall make out and deliver from time to time to the Commissioners of Stamps and Taxes the several accounts or returns required by the last-mentioned Act; and all the provisions of the last-mentioned Act as to such accounts or returns shall be taken to apply to the accounts or returns so made out and delivered by the said last-mentioned companies, as if they had been originally included in the provisions of the last-mentioned Act.

Provision in case of determination of existing agreement between Bank of Ireland and Tipperary Joint Stock Bank.

XXXI. And whereas a certain joint stock banking company, called and known as "The *Tipperary* Joint Stock Bank," refrained from issuing its own bank notes, under a certain agreement with the Governor and Company of the Bank of *Ireland* for the issue of the bank notes of the said governor and company, which agreement is determinable by either party upon certain notice to the other party, and it is just that in case such agreement should at any time hereafter during the continuance of this Act be determined and put an end to by the Governor and Company of the Bank of *Ireland*, that the said *Tipperary* Joint Stock Bank should receive by way of compensation such composition as hereafter mentioned; be it therefore enacted, That if the said agreement shall be at any time hereafter during the continuance of this Act determined or put an end to by the Governor and Company of the Bank of *Ireland*, then and in such case the said governor and company shall from the termination of the said agreement pay and allow to the said *Tipperary* Joint Stock Bank, so long as the latter shall continue to carry on the business of a bank and to issue exclusively the notes of the Governor and Company of the Bank of *Ireland*, a composition at and after the rate of one *per centum per annum* on the average annual amount of the Bank of *Ireland* notes issued by the said *Tipperary* Joint Stock Bank, and kept in circulation, such average annual amount to be ascertained by the Bank of *Ireland* in the manner provided for regulating the compensation to be made to certain bankers by the Bank of *England* in and by the Act passed in the seventh and eighth years of the reign of Her present Majesty, intituled *An Act to regulate the Issue of Bank Notes, and for giving to the Governor and Company of the Bank of* England *certain Privileges for a limited Period:* Provided always, that the total sum payable to the *Tipperary* Joint Stock Bank by way of composition as aforesaid in any one year shall not exceed one *per cent.* on an amount that hath been agreed on by and between the Bank of *Ireland* and the *Tipperary* Joint Stock Bank, and certified by both banks to the Commissioners of Stamps and Taxes; and such composition shall cease to be payable from and after the first day of *January* one thousand eight hundred and fifty-six.

7 & 8 Vict. c. 32.

Interpretation of Act.

XXXII. And be it enacted, That the term "bank note" used in this Act shall extend and apply to all bills or notes for the payment of money to the bearer on demand; and that the term "banker" shall, when the Bank of *Ireland* be not specially excepted, extend and apply to the Governor and Company of the Bank of *Ireland*,

and to all other corporations, societies, partnerships, and persons, and every individual person carrying on the business of banking, whether by the issue of bank notes or otherwise; and that the word "coin" shall be construed to mean the coin of this realm; and that the word "person" used in this Act shall include corporations; and that the singular number used in this Act shall include the plural number, and the plural number the singular, except where there is any thing in the context repugnant to such construction; and that the masculine gender in this Act shall include the feminine, except where there is any thing in the context repugnant to such construction. 8 & 9 Vict. c. 37.

XXXIII. And be it enacted, That this Act may be amended or repealed by any Act to be passed in the present session of Parliament. Alteration of Act.

SCHEDULES referred to in the foregoing Act.

SCHEDULE (A).

Name and title set forth in licence . . ________ bank.
Name of the firm . . . . . . ________ firm.
Head offices or principal places of issue . ________ place.

Amount of Notes in circulation on Saturday the day of	£5 and upwards . .	£
	under £5 . .	£
	Total . .	£

Amount of Gold and Silver Coin held at the head office or principal place of issue at the close of business on—

	Head Office at		Head Office at		Head Office at		Head Office at	
	Gold.	Silver.	Gold.	Silver.	Gold.	Silver.	Gold.	Silver.
Monday the								
Tuesday the								
Wednesday the								
Thursday the								
Friday the								
Saturday the								

8 & 9 Vict. c. 37.

Total Amount of Coin held at the close of business on Saturday the day of 18 .

Gold	£
Silver	£
Total .	£

[*To be inserted in the Account at the End of each Period of Four Weeks.*]

Amount of notes authorized by certificate		£
Average amount of notes in circulation during the four weeks ending as above	£5 and upwards	£
	under £5 .	£
Average amount of coin held during the said four weeks	Gold .	£
	Silver .	£
	Total .	£

I, being the [banker, chief cashier, director, *or* partner, *as the case may be*], do hereby certify, that the above is a true account of the notes in circulation, and of the coin held by the said bank, as required under the Act 8 & 9 Vict. c. .

(Signed)________________

Dated this day of 18 .

8 & 9 Vict. c. 37.

SCHEDULE (B).

Name and Title, as set forth in the Licence.	Name of the Firm.	Head Office, or principal Place of Issue.	Circulation authorized by Certificate.	Average Circulation during Four Weeks ending the			Average Amount of Coin held during Four Weeks ending		
				£5 and upwards.	Under £5.	TOTAL.	Gold.	Silver.	TOTAL.

I hereby certify, that each of the bankers named in the above Return who have in circulation an amount of notes beyond that authorized in their certificate [with the exception of *A. B.* or *C. D.*, *as the case may be*], have held an amount of gold and silver coin not less than that which they are required to hold during the period to which this Return relates.

Dated this day of 18 . (Signed) ——————Officer of Stamp Duties.

8 & 9 Vict. c. 37.

SCHEDULE (D).

[*Place*] [*Day*] [*Month*] [*Year*]

Twenty-one days after date, I promise to pay to *A. B.* of [*Place*], or his order, the sum of for value received by *C. D.*

Witness, *E. F.*

And the Indorsement, toties quoties.

[*Day*] [*Month*] [*Year*]

Pay the contents to *G. H.* of [*Place*], or his order. *A. B.*

Witness, *J. K.*

SCHEDULE (E).

[*Place*] [*Day*] [*Month*] [*Year*]

Twenty-one days after date, pay to *A. B.* of [*Place*], or his order, the sum of value received, as advised by *C. D.*

to *E. F.* of [*Place*].

Witness, *G. H.*

And the Indorsement, toties quoties.

[*Day*] [*Month*] [*Year*]

Pay the contents to *J. K.* of [*Place*], or his order. *A. B.*

Witness, *L. M.*

[8 & 9 Vict. c. 38.]

8 & 9 Vict. c. 38.

An Act to regulate the Issue of Bank Notes in Scotland. [21*st July*, 1845.]

7 & 8 Vict. c. 32, s. 10.

WHEREAS by an Act made and passed in the eighth year of the reign of Her Majesty, intituled *An Act to regulate the Issue of Bank Notes, and for giving to the Governor and Company of the Bank of* England *certain Privileges for a limited Period*, it was enacted, that from and after the passing of that Act no person, other than a banker who on the sixth day of *May* one thousand eight hundred and forty-four was lawfully issuing his own bank notes, should make or issue bank notes in any part of the United Kingdom: And whereas it is expedient to regulate the issue of bank notes by such bankers as are now by law authorized to issue the same in *Scotland:* Be it therefore enacted by the Queen's most excellent Majesty, by and with the advice and consent of the Lords spiritual and temporal, and Commons, in this present Parliament assembled, and by the authority of the same, That every banker claiming to be entitled to issue bank notes in *Scotland* shall, within one month next after the passing of this Act, give notice in writing to the Commissioners of Stamps and Taxes, at their head office in *London*, of such claim, and of the place and name and firm at and under which such banker has

Bankers claiming to be entitled to issue bank notes to give notice to Commis-

issued such notes in *Scotland* during the year next preceding the first day of *May* one thousand eight hundred and forty-five, and thereupon the said commissioners shall ascertain if such banker was on the sixth day of *May* one thousand eight hundred and forty-four, and from thence up to the first day of *May* one thousand eight hundred and forty-five, carrying on the business of a banker and lawfully issuing his own bank notes in *Scotland*, and if it shall so appear then the said commissioners shall proceed to ascertain the average amount of the bank notes of such banker which were in circulation during the said period of one year preceding the first day of *May* one thousand eight hundred and forty-five, according to the returns made by such banker in pursuance of the Act passed in the fourth and fifth years of the reign of Her present Majesty, intituled *An Act to make further Provision relative to the Returns to be made by Banks of the Amount of their Notes in Circulation;* and the said commissioners, or any two of them, shall certify under their hands to such banker the average amount when so ascertained as aforesaid, omitting the fractions of a pound, if any; and it shall be lawful for every such banker to continue to issue his own bank notes after the sixth day of *December* one thousand eight hundred and forty-five, to the extent of the amount so certified, and of the amount of gold and silver coin held by such banker at the head office or principal place of issue of such banker, in the proportion and manner hereinafter mentioned, but not to any further extent; and from and after the sixth day of *December* one thousand eight hundred and forty-five it shall not be lawful for any banker to make or issue bank notes in *Scotland*, save and except only such bankers as shall have obtained such certificate from the Commissioners of Stamps and Taxes.

8 & 9 Vict. c. 38.

sioners of Stamps and Taxes.

4 & 5 Vict. c. 50.

Commissioners to certify existing banks of issue and limitation of issue.

II. Provided always, and be it enacted, That if it shall be made to appear to the Commissioners of Stamps and Taxes that any two or more banks have by written contract or agreement (which contract or agreement shall be produced to the said commissioners) become united within the year next preceding such first day of *May* one thousand eight hundred and forty-five, it shall be lawful for the said commissioners to ascertain the average amount of the notes of each such bank in the manner hereinbefore directed, and to certify a sum equal to the average amount of the notes of the two or more banks so united, as the amount which the united bank shall thereafter be authorized to issue, subject to the regulations of this Act.

Provision for united banks.

III. And be it enacted, That the Commissioners of Stamps and Taxes shall, at the time of certifying to any banker such particulars as they are hereinbefore required to certify, also publish a duplicate of their certificate thereof in the next succeeding *London Gazette* in which the same may be conveniently inserted; and the Gazette in which such publication shall be made shall be conclusive evidence in all courts whatsoever of the amount of bank notes which the banker named in such certificate or duplicate is by law authorized to issue and to have in circulation as aforesaid, exclusive of an amount equal to the monthly average amount of the gold and silver coin held by such banker as herein provided.

Duplicate of certificate to be published in the 'Gazette.'

'Gazette' to be evidence.

IV. And be it enacted, That in case it shall be made to appear to

In case banks be-

8 & 9 Vict c. 38.

Come united, Commissioners to certify the amount of bank notes which each bank was authorized to issue.

the Commissioners of Stamps and Taxes, at any time hereafter, that any two or more banks have by written contract or agreement (which contract or agreement shall be produced to the said commissioners) become united subsequently to the passing of this Act, it shall be lawful to the said commissioners, upon the application of such united bank, to certify in manner hereinbefore mentioned the aggregate of the amount of bank notes which such separate banks were previously authorized to issue under the separate certificates previously delivered to them, and so from time to time; and every such certificate shall be published in manner hereinbefore directed, and from and after such publication the amount therein stated shall be and be deemed to be the limit of the amount of bank notes which such united bank may have in circulation, exclusive of an amount equal to the monthly average amount of the gold and silver coin held by such bank, as herein provided.

Issue of notes for fractional parts of a pound prohibited.

V. And be it enacted, That all bank notes to be issued or reissued in *Scotland* shall be expressed to be for payment of a sum in pounds sterling, without any fractional parts of a pound; and if any banker in *Scotland* shall, from and after the sixth day of *December* one thousand eight hundred and forty-five, make, sign, issue, or reissue, any bank note for the fractional part of a pound sterling, or for any sum together with the fractional part of a pound sterling, every such banker so making, signing, issuing, or reissuing any such note as aforesaid shall for each note so made, signed, issued, or reissued forfeit or pay the sum of twenty pounds.

Limitation of bank notes in circulation

VI. And be it enacted, That from and after the sixth day of *December* one thousand eight hundred and forty-five it shall not be lawful for any banker in *Scotland* to have in circulation, upon the average of a period of four weeks, to be ascertained as hereinafter mentioned, a greater amount of notes than an amount composed of the sum certified by the Commissioners of Stamps and Taxes as aforesaid and the monthly average amount of gold and silver coin held by such banker at the head office or principal place of issue of such banker during the same period of four weeks, to be ascertained in manner hereinafter mentioned.

Issuing banks to render accounts weekly.

VII. And be it enacted, That every banker who after the sixth day of *December* one thousand eight hundred and forfty-five shall issue bank notes in *Scotland* shall, on some one day in every week after the thirteenth day of *December* one thousand eight hundred and forty-five (such day to be fixed by the Commissioners of Stamps and Taxes), transmit to the said commissioners a just and true account of the amount of bank notes of such banker in circulation at the close of the business on the next preceding *Saturday*, distinguishing the notes of five pounds and upwards, and the notes below five ponnds, and also an account of the total amount of gold and silver coin held by such banker at the head office or principal place of issue in *Scotland* of such banker at the close of business an each day of the week ending on the same *Saturday*, and also on account of the total amount of gold and silver coin in *Scotland* held by such banker at the close of business on that day; and on completing the first period of four weeks, and so on completing each successive period of four weeks, every such banker shall annex to such account the average amount of bank notes of such banker in circulation during the said four weeks, distinguishing the bank notes of five pounds and upwards and the notes below five pounds, and the average amount of gold and silver coin respectively held by such banker at the head office or principal place of issue in *Scotland* of such banker during the said four weeks, and also the amount of bank notes which such banker is, by the certificate published as aforesaid in the *London Gazette*, authorized to issue under the provisions of this Act; and every such account shall specify the head office or principal places of issue in *Scotland* of such banker, and shall be verified by the signature of such banker or his chief cashier, or in case of a company or partnership by the signature of the chief cashier or other officer duly authorized by the directors of such company or partnership, and shall be made in the form to this Act annexed marked (A); and if any such banker shall neglect or refuse to render any such account in the form and at the time required by this Act, or shall at any time render a false account, such banker shall forfeit the sum of one hundred pounds for every such offence.

8 & 9 Vict. c. 38.

VIII. And be it enacted, That all bank notes shall be deemed to be in circulation from the time the same shall have been issued by any banker, or any servant or agent of such banker, until the same shall have been actually returned to such banker, or some servant or agent of such banker.

What shall be deemed to be bank notes in circulation.

IX. And be it enacted, That from the returns so made by each banker to the Commissioners of Stamps and Taxes the said commissioners shall, at the end of the first period of four weeks after the said sixth day of *December* one thousand eight hundred and forty-five, and so at the end of each successive period of four weeks, make out a general return in the form to this Act annexed marked (B) of the monthly average amount of bank notes in circulation of each banker in *Scotland* during the last preceding four weeks, and of the average amount of all the gold and silver coin held by such banker, and certifying under the hand of any officer of the said commissioners duly authorized for that purpose, in the case of each such banker, whether such banker has held the amount of coin required by law during the period to which the said return shall apply, and shall publish the same in the next succeeding *London Gazette* in which the same can be conviently inserted.

Commissioners of Stamps and Taxes to make a monthly return.

X. And be it enacted, That for the purpose of ascertaining the monthly average amount of bank notes of each banker in circulation, the aggregate of the amount of bank notes of each such banker in circulation at the close of the business on *Saturday* of each week during the first complete period of four weeks next after the sixth day of *December* one thousand eight hundred and forty-five shall be divided by the number of weeks, and the average so ascertained shall be deemed to be the average of bank notes of each such bank in circulation during such period of four weeks, and so in each successive period of four weeks; and the monthly average amount of gold and silver coin respectively held as aforesaid by such banker shall be ascertained in like manner from the amount of gold and silver coin held by such banker at the head

Mode of ascertaining the average amount of bank notes of each banker in circulation, and gold coin, during the first four weeks after 31st December 1845.

8 & 9 Vict. c. 38.

office or principal place of issue in *Scotland* of such banker at the close of business on *Saturday* in each week during the same period; and the monthly average amount of bank notes of each such banker in circulation during any such period of four weeks is not to exceed a sum made up by adding the amount certified by the Commissioners of Stamps and Taxes as aforesaid and the monthly average amount of gold and silver coin held by such banker as aforesaid during the same period.

In taking the account of coin held by bankers, silver coin not to exceed the proportion of one fourth of of gold.

XI. And be it enacted, That in taking account of the coin held by any such banker as aforesaid, with respect to which bank notes to a further extent than the sum certified as aforesaid by the Commissioners of Stamps and Taxes may, under the provisions of this Act be made and issued, no amount of silver coin exceeding one fourth part of the gold coin held by such banker as aforesaid shall be taken into account, nor shall any banker be authorized to make and issue bank notes in *Scotland* on any amount of silver coin held by such banker exceeding the proportion of one fourth part of the gold coin held by such banker as aforesaid.

Commissioners of Stamps and Taxes empowered to cause the books of bankers containing accounts of their bank notes in circulation, and of gold coin, to be inspected.

XII. And whereas, in order to ensure the rendering of true and faithful accounts of the amount of bank notes in circulation, and the amount of gold and silver coin held by each banker as directed by this Act, it is necessary that the Commissioners of Stamps and Taxes should be empowered to cause the books of bankers issuing such notes, and the gold and silver coin held by such bankers as aforesaid, to be inspected as hereinafter mentioned; be it therefore enacted, That all and every the book and books of any banker who shall issue bank notes under the provisions of this Act, in which shall be kept, contained, or entered any account, minute, or memorandum of or relating to the bank notes issued or to be issued by such banker, or of or relating to the amount of such notes in circulation from time to time, or of or relating to the gold and silver coin held by such banker from time to time, or any account, minute, or memorandum the sight or inspection whereof may tend to secure the rendering of true accounts of the average amount of such notes in circulation and gold and silver coin held as directed by this Act, or to test the truth of any such account, shall be open for the inspection and examination at all seasonable times of any officer of stamp duties authorized in that behalf by writing signed by the Commissioners of Stamps and Taxes, or any two of them; and every such officer shall be at liberty to take copies of or extracts from any such book or account as aforesaid, and to inspect and ascertain the amount of any gold or silver coin held by such banker; and if any banker or other person keeping any such book, or having the custody or possession thereof or power to produce the same, shall, upon demand made by any such officer showing (if required) his authority in that behalf, refuse to produce any such book to such officer for his inspection and examination, or to permit him to inspect and examine the same, or to take copies thereof or extracts therefrom, or of or from any such account, minute, or memorandum as aforesaid, kept, contained, or entered therein, or if any banker or other person having the custody or possession of any coin belonging to such banker shall refuse to permit or prevent the inspection of such gold and silver coin as afore-

Penalty for refusing to allow such inspection.

said, every such banker or other person so offending shall for every such offence forfeit the sum of one hundred pounds: Provided always, that the said commissioners shall not exercise the powers aforesaid without the consent of the Commissioners of Her Majesty's Treasury.

8 & 9 Vict. c. 38.

All bankers to return their names once a year to the Stamp Office.

XIII. And be it enacted, That every banker in *Scotland* who is now carrying on or shall hereafter carry on business as such, other than the Bank of *Scotland*, the Royal Bank of *Scotland*, and the *British* Linen Company, shall, on the first day of *January* in each year, or within fifteen days thereafter, make a return to the Commissioners of Stamps and Taxes, at their head office in *London*, of his name, residence, and occupation, or, in the case of a company or partnership, of the name, residence, and occupation of every person composing or being a member of such company or partnership, and also the name of the firm under which such banker, company, or partnership carry on the business of banking, and of every place where such business is carried on; and if any such banker, company, or partnership shall omit or refuse to make such return within fifteen days after the said first day of *January*, or shall wilfully make other than a true return of the persons as herein required, every banker, company, or partnership so offending shall forfeit or pay the sum of fifty pounds; and the said Commissioners of Stamps and Taxes shall on or before the first day of *March* in every year publish in some newspaper circulating within each town or county respectively in which the head office or principal place of issue of any such banker be situated a copy of the return so made by every banker, company, or partnership carrying on the business of bankers within such town or county respectively, as the case may be.

Penalty on banks issuing in excess.

XIV. And be it enacted, That if the monthly average circulation of bank notes of any banker, taken in the manner herein directed shall at any time exceed the amount which such banker is authorized to issue and to have in circulation under the provisions of this Act, such banker shall in every such case forfeit a sum equal to the amount by which the average monthly circulation, taken as aforesaid, shall have exceeded the amount which such banker was authorized to issue and to have in circulation as aforesaid.

Bank of England notes not a legal tender in Scotland.

XV. And whereas by an Act passed in the third and fourth years of the reign of His late Majesty King *William* the Fourth, intituled *An Act for giving to the Corporation of the Governor and Company of the Bank of* England *certain Privileges for a limited Period, under certain Conditions*, it was enacted, that from and after the first day of *August* one thousand eight hundred and thirty-four, unless and until Parliament should otherwise direct, a tender of a note or notes of the Governor and Company of the Bank of *England*, expressed to be payable to bearer on demand, should be a legal tender to the amount expressed in such note or notes, and should be taken to be valid as a tender to such amount for all sums above five pounds on all occasions on which any tender of money may be legally made, so long as the Bank of *England* should continue to pay on demand their said notes in legal coin; provided always, that no such note or notes should be deemed a legal tender of payment

8 & 9 Vict. c. 38.

by the Governor and Company of the Bank of *England*, or any branch bank of the said governor and company: And whereas doubts have arisen as to the extent of the said enactment; for removal whereof be it enacted and declared, That nothing in the said last-recited Act contained shall extend or be construed to extend to make the tender of a note or notes of the Governor and Company of the Bank of *England* a legal tender in *Scotland*: Provided always, that nothing in this Act contained shall be construed to prohibit the circulation in *Scotland* of the notes of the Governor and Company of the Bank of *England*, as heretofore.

Proviso.

Notes for less than 20*s*. not negotiable in Scotland.

XVI. And be it enacted, That all promissory or other notes, bills of exchange, or drafts, or undertakings in writing, being negotiable or transferable, for the payment of any sum or sums of money, or any orders, notes, or undertakings in writing, being negotiable or transferable, for the delivery of any goods, specifying their value in money less than the sum of twenty shillings in the whole, heretofore made or issued, or which shall hereafter be made or issued in *Scotland*, shall, from and after the first day of *January* one thousand eight hundred and forty-six, be and the same are hereby declared to be absolutely void and of no effect, any law, statute, usage, or custom to the contrary thereof in anywise notwithstanding; and that if any person or persons shall, after the first day of *January* one thousand eight hundred and forty-six, by any art, device, or means whatsoever, publish or utter in *Scotland* any such notes, bills, drafts, or engagements as aforesaid for a less sum than twenty shillings, or on which less than the sum of twenty shillings shall be due, and which shall be in anywise negotiable or transferable, or shall negotiate or transfer the same in *Scotland*, every such person shall forfeit and pay for every such offence any sum not exceeding twenty pounds nor less than five pounds, at the discretion of the justice of the peace who shall hear and determine such offence.

Notes of 20*s*. or above, and less than 5*l*., to be drawn in certain form.

XVII. And be it enacted, That all promissory or other notes, bills of exchange, or drafts, or undertakings in writing, being negotiable or transferable, for the payment of twenty shillings, or any sum of money above that sum and less than five pounds, or on which twenty shillings, or above that sum and less than five pounds, shall remain undischarged, and which shall be issued within *Scotland* at any time after the first day of *January* one thousand eight hundred and forty-six, shall specify the names and places of abode of the persons respectively to whom or to whose order the same shall be made payable, and shall bear date before or at the time of drawing or issuing thereof, and not on any day subsequent thereto, and shall be made payable within the space of twenty-one days next after the day of the date thereof, and shall not be transferable or negotiable after the time hereby limited for payment thereof, and that every indorsement to be made thereon shall be made before the expiration of that time, and to bear date at or not before the time of making thereof, and shall specify the name and place of abode of the person or persons to whom or to whose order the money contained in every such note, bill, draft, or undertaking is to be paid; and that the signing of every such note, bill, draft, or undertaking, and also of every such indorsement, shall be attested by one subscribing witness at the least; and which said notes, bills of exchange, or drafts, or undertakings in writing, may be made or drawn in words to the purport or effect as set out in the Schedules to this Act annexed marked (C) and (D); and that all promissory or other notes, bills of exchange, or drafts, or undertakings in writing, being negotiable or transferable, for the payment of twenty shillings, or any sum of money above that sum and less than five pounds, or in which twenty shillings, or above that sum and less than five pounds, shall remain undischarged, and which shall be issued in *Scotland* at any time after the said first day of *January* one thousand eight hundred and forty-six, in any other manner than as aforesaid, and also every indorsement on any such note, bill, draft, or other undertaking to be negotiated under this Act, other than as aforesaid, shall and the same are hereby declared to be absolutely void, any law, statute, usage, or custom to the contrary thereof in anywise notwithstanding: Provided always, that nothing in this clause contained shall be construed to extend to any such bank notes as shall be lawfully issued by any banker in *Scotland* authorized by this Act to continue the issue of bank notes (*a*).

8 & 9 Vict. c. 38.

XVIII. And be it enacted, That if any body politic or corporate or any person or persons shall, from and after the said first day of *January* one thousand eight hundred and forty-six, make, sign, issue, or reissue in *Scotland* any promissory note payable on demand to the bearer thereof for any sum of money less than the sum of five pounds, except the bank notes of such bankers as are hereby authorized to continue to issue bank notes as aforesaid, then and in either of such cases every such body politic or corporate or person or persons so making, signing, issuing, or reissuing any such promissory note as aforesaid, except as aforesaid, shall for every such note so made, signed, issued, or reissued forfeit the sum of twenty pounds.

Penalty for persons, other than bankers hereby authorized, issuing notes payable on demand for less than 5*l*.

XIX. And be it enacted, That if any body politic or corporate or person or persons shall, from and after the passing of this Act, publish, utter, or negotiate in *Scotland* any promissory or other note (not being the bank note of a banker hereby authorized to continue to issue bank notes), or any bill of exchange, draft, or undertaking in writing, being negotiable or transferable, for the payment of twenty shillings, or above that sum and less than five pounds, or on which twenty shillings, or above that sum and less than five pounds, shall remain undischarged, made, drawn, or indorsed in any other manner than as is hereinbefore directed, every such body politic or corporate or person or persons so publishing, uttering, or negotiating any such promissory or other note (not being such bank note as aforesaid), bill of exchange, draft, or undertaking in writing as aforesaid, shall forfeit and pay the sum of twenty pounds.

Penalty for persons, other than bankers hereby authorized, uttering or negotiating notes, bills of exchange, &c., transferable, for payment of 20*s*. or less than 5*l*.

XX. Provided always, and be it enacted, That nothing herein contained shall extend to prohibit any draft or order drawn by any person on his banker, or on any person acting as such banker, for the payment of money held by such banker or person to the use of the person by whom such draft or order shall be drawn.

Not to prohibit checks on bankers.

(*a*) Repealed until December 31, 1877, by 26 & 27 Vict. c. 105, and 39 & 40 Vict. c. 69.

8 & 9 Vict. c. 38.

Mode of recovering penalties.

XXI. And be it enacted, That all pecuniary penalties under this Act may be sued or prosecuted for and recovered for the use of Her Majesty, in the name of Her Majesty's Advocate General or Solicitor General in *Scotland*, or of the Solicitor of Stamps and Taxes in *Scotland*, or of any person authorized to sue or prosecute for the same, by writing under the hands of the Commissioners of Stamps and Taxes, or in the name of any officer of stamp duties, by action of debt, bill, plaint, or information in the Court of Exchequer in *Scotland*, or, in respect of any penalty not exceeding twenty pounds, by information or complaint before one or more justice or justices of the peace in *Scotland*, in such and the same manner as any other penalties imposed by any of the laws now in force relating to the duties under the management of the Commissioners of Stamps; and it shall be lawful in all cases for the Commissioners of Stamps and Taxes, either before or after any proceedings commenced for recovery of any such penalty, to mitigate or compound any such penalty, as the said commissioners shall think fit, and to stay any such proceedings after the same shall have been commenced, and whether judgment may have been obtained for such penalty or not, on payment of part only of such penalty, with or without costs, or on payment only of the costs incurred in such proceedings, or of any part thereof, or on such other terms as such commissioners shall judge reasonable: Provided always, that in no such proceeding aforesaid shall any essoign, protection, wager of law, nor more than one imparlance be allowed; and all pecuniary penalties imposed by or incurred under this Act, by whom or in whose name soever the same shall be sued or prosecuted for or recovered, shall go and be applied to the use of Her Majesty, and shall be deemed to be and shall be accounted for as part of Her Majesty's revenue arising from stamp duties, anything in any Act contained, or any law or usuage, to the contrary in anywise notwithstanding: Provided always, that it shall be lawful for the Commissioners of Stamps and Taxes, at their discretion, to give all or any part of such penalties as rewards to any person or persons who shall have detected the offenders, or given information which may have led to their prosecution and conviction.

Interpretation of Act.

XXII. And be it enacted, That the term "bank notes" used in this Act shall extend and apply to all bills or notes for the payment of money to the bearer on demand, other than bills and notes of the Governor and Company of the Bank of *England;* and that the term "banker" shall extend and apply to all corporations, societies, partnerships, and persons, and every individual person carrying on the business of banking, whether by the issue of bank notes or otherwise; and that the word "person" used in this Act shall include corporations; and that the word "coin" shall mean the coin of this realm; and that the singular number in this Act shall include the plural, and the plural number the singular, except where there is anything in the context repugnant to such construction; and that the masculine gender in this Act shall include the feminine, except where there is anything in the context repugnant to such construction.

Alteration of Act.

XXIII. And be it enacted, That this Act may be amended or repealed by any Act to be passed in the present session of Parliament.

SCHEDULES to which this Act refers.—SCHEDULE (A).

Name and Title, as set forth in Licence.	Name of the Firm.	Head Office, or principal Place of Issue.	Amount of Circulation authorized by Certificate.	Notes in Circulation during the Week ending Day of .		*Average of Four Weeks of all Notes.		Account of Coin held by the Banker at the Head Office or principal Place of Issue, on the Day of .		*Average Total Amount of Coin held by the Bank during Four Weeks ending	
				£5 and upwards.	Under £5.	£5 and upwards.	Under £5.	Gold.	Silver.	Gold.	Silver.
								£	£		
								Held on each Day of the Week preceding that Day.			
								. Gold.	Silver.		
								Monday - -			
								Tuesday - -			
								Wednesday -			
								Thursday - -			
								Friday - - -			
								Saturday - -			

* To be inserted at the end of each period of four weeks.

I [being the banker, chief cashier, managing director, *or* partner of the bank, *or other officer duly authorized by the director, as the case may be*], do hereby certify, that the above is a true account of the notes in circulation and coin held by the said bank during the week above written.
Dated the day of 18 . (Signed)

SCHEDULE (B).

Name and Title as set forth in Licence.	Name of the Firm.	Head Office, or principal Place of Issue.	Amount of Circulation authorized by Certificate.	Average Amount of Notes in Circulation during the four Weeks ending the Day of .			Average Total Amount of Coin held during Four Weeks ending	
				£5 and upwards.	Under £5.	TOTAL.	Gold.	Silver.

X

I hereby certify, that each of the bankers named in the above Return who have issued an amount of notes beyond that authorized in their certificate [with the exception of *A. B. or C. D., as the case may be*], have held an amount of gold and silver coin not less than that which they are required to hold during the Period to which this Return refers.

Dated

Officer of the Stamps.

8 & 9 Vict. c. 38.

SCHEDULE (C).

[*Place*] [*Day*] [*Month*] [*Year*]

Twenty-one days after date I promise to pay to *A.B.* of [*Place*], or his order, the sum for value received by *C. D.*

Witness, *E. F.*

And the Indorsement, toties quoties.

[*Day*] [*Month*] [*Year*]

Pay the contents to *G. H.* of [*Place*], or his order. *A. B.*

Witness, *J. K.*

SCHEDULE (D).

[*Place*] [*Day*] [*Month*] [*Year*]

Twenty-one days after date pay to *A.B.* of [*Place*], or his order, the sum of value received, as advised by *E.D.*

To *E. F.* of [*Place*].

Witness, *G. H.*

And the Indorsement, toties quoties.

[*Day*] [*Month*] [*Year*]

Pay the contests to *J.K.* of [*Place*], or his order. *A. B.*

Witness, *L. M.*

[8 & 9 Vict. c. 76.]

8 & 9 Vict. c. 76.

An Act to increase the Stamp Duty on Licences to Appraisers; to reduce the Stamp Duties on Registry Searches in Ireland; to amend the Law relating to the Duties on Legacies; and also to amend an Act of the last Session of Parliament, for regulating the Issue of Bank Notes in England. [*4th August*, 1845.]

Provision for recovery and application of penalties under 7 & 8 Vict. c. 32

V. And whereas an Act was passed in the last session of Parliament, intituled *An Act to regulate the Issue of Bank Notes, and for giving to the Governor and Company of the Bank of* England *certain Privileges for a limited Period*, and certain penalties are thereby imposed for offences against the provisions of the same Act, and it is expedient to provide for the recovery and application of such penalties; be it therefore enacted, That from and after the passing of this Act all pecuniary penalties imposed by or incurred under the said last-recited Act may be sued or prosecuted for and recovered, for the use of Her Majesty, in the name of Her Majesty's Attorney-General or Solicitor-General, or of any person authorized to sue or prosecute for the same, by writing under the hands of the Commissioners of Stamps and Taxes, or in the name of any officer of stamp duties, by action of debt, bill, plaint, or information in the Court of Exchequer at *Westminster*, in such and the same manner as any penalties imposed by any of the laws now in force relating to the duties under the management of the said commissioners; and it shall be lawful in all cases for the said commissioners, either before or after any proceedings commenced for recovery of any such penalty, to mitigate or compound any such penalty as they shall think fit, and to stay any such proceedings after the same shall have been commenced, and whether judgment may have been obtained for such penalty or not, on payment of part only of any such penalty, with or without costs, or on payment only of the costs incurred in such proceedings, or of any part thereof, or on such other terms as such commissioners shall judge reasonable: Provided always, that in no such proceeding as aforesaid shall any essoign, protection, wager of law, or more than one imparlance, be allowed; and all pecuniary penalties imposed by or incurred under the said last-recited Act, by whom or in whose name soever the same shall be sued or prosecuted for or recovered, shall go and be applied to the use of Her Majesty, and shall be deemed to be and shall be accounted for as part of Her Majesty's revenue arising from stamp duties, any thing in any Act contained, or any law or usage, to the contrary in anywise notwithstanding: Provided always, that it shall be lawful for the said commissioners, at their discretion, to give all or any part of such penalties as rewards to any person or persons who shall have detected the offenders, or given information which may have led to their prosecution and conviction.

8 & 9 Vict. c. 76.

[16 & 17 Vict. c. 59.]

An Act to repeal certain Stamp Duties, and to grant others in lieu thereof, to amend the Laws relating to Stamp Duties, and to make perpetual certain Stamp Duties in Ireland. [*4th August*, 1853.]

16 & 17 Vict. c. 59.

XIX. Provided always, That any draft or order drawn upon a banker for a sum of money payable to order on demand which shall, when presented for payment, purport to be indorsed by the person to whom the same shall be drawn payable, shall be a sufficient authority to such banker to pay the amount of such draft or order to the bearer thereof; and it shall not be incumbent on such banker to prove that such indorsement, or any subsequent indorsement, was made by or under the direction or authority of the person to whom the said draft or order was or is made payable either by the drawer or any indorser thereof.

Drafts on bankers payable to order on demand sufficient authority for payment without proof of indorsement.

XX. And whereas by an Act passed in the session of Parliament held in the fifth and sixth years of Her Majesty's reign, chapter

X 2

17 & 18 Vict. c. 59.

eighty-two, certain rates and duties denominated stamp duties were granted and made payable in *Ireland* for a limited term; and by four several Acts passed respectively in the eighth, eleventh, fourteenth, and fifteenth years of Her Majesty's reign the same rates and duties were continued for four other several and successive terms, the last of which will expire on the tenth day of *October* one thousand eight hundred and fifty-three; and it is expedient to make the said rates and duties perpetual:

Stamp duties in Ireland granted by 5 & 6 Vict. c. 82, and continued by 8 & 9 Vict. c. 2. 11 & 12 Vict. c. 9, 14 & 15 Vict. c. 18, 15 & 16 Vict. c 21, made perpetual. Acts continued in force.

All the several sums of money and duties and composition for duties granted and made payable in *Ireland* by the said Act of the fifth and sixth years of Her Majesty, chapter eighty-two, and not repealed by any subsequent Act, and also all duties now payable in lieu or instead of any of the said duties which may have been so repealed, shall be and the same are hereby continued and made perpetual, and shall be charged, raised, levied, collected, and paid unto and for the use of Her Majesty, her heirs and successors for ever: The said Act of the fifth and sixth years of Her Majesty, and all and every other Act and Acts now in force in relation to the duties and composition for duties which are continued by this Act, shall severally be continued and remain in full force in all respects in relation to the said duties and composition for duties hereby continued and granted, and all and every the powers and authorities, rules, regulations, directions, penalties, forfeitures, clauses, matters, and things contained in the said Acts or any of them, and in force as aforesaid, shall severally and respectively be duly observed, practised, applied, and put in execution in relation to the said duties and composition for duties hereby continued and granted, for the charging, raising, levying, paying, accounting for, and securing of the said duties and composition for duties, and all arrears thereof, and for the preventing, detecting, and punishing of all frauds, forgeries, and other offences relating thereto, as fully and effectually to all intents and purposes as if the same powers, authorities, rules, regulations, directions, penalties, forfeitures, clauses, matters, and things were particularly repeated and re-enacted in the body of this Act with reference to the said duties and composition for duties hereby granted.

[16 & 17 Vict. c. 63.]

16 & 17 Vict. c. 63.

An Act to repeal certain Duties, and to grant others in lieu thereof, to give Relief with respect to the Stamp Duties on Newspapers and Supplements thereto, to repeal the Duty on Advertisements, and otherwise to amend the Laws relating to Stamp Duties.

[*4th August*, 1853.]

VII. And whereas under and by virtue of certain Acts of Parliament now in force the Governor and Company of the Bank of *Scotland*, and the Royal Bank of *Scotland*, and the *British* Linen Company in *Scotland* are respectively authorized and empowered to make and issue and reissue their promissory notes payable to bearer on demand on unstamped paper, giving security, and keeping and producing true accounts of all the notes so issued by them respectively, and accounting for and paying the stamp duties payable in respect of such notes: And whereas it is expedient to authorize and empower the Commissioners of Her Majesty's Treasury to compound with the said banks, as well as all bankers in *Scotland*, for the stamp duties on their promissory notes payable to bearer on demand, as well as for stamps payable on their bills of exchange: It shall be lawful for the Commissioners of Her Majesty's Treasury for the time being, or any three of them, and they are hereby authorized and empowered to compound and agree with the said Governor and Company of the Bank of *Scotland*, and the Royal Bank of *Scotland*, and the *British* Linen Company in *Scotland*, and all or any other bankers in *Scotland*, or elsewhere respectively, for a composition in lieu of the stamp duties payable on the promissory notes of the said banks and bankers respectively payable to the bearer on demand, as well as for stamps payable on their bills of exchange; and such composition shall be made on such terms and conditions, and with such security for the payment of the same, and for keeping, producing, and rendering of such accounts, as the said last-mentioned commissioners may deem to be proper in that behalf; and upon such composition being entered into by such banks and bankers respectively it shall be lawful for them to issue and reissue all notes and to draw all such bills for which such composition shall have been made on unstamped paper, anything in any Act contained to the contrary notwithstanding.

17 & 18 Vict. c. 63.

Power to Treasury to compound with bankers in Scotland for the stamp duties on their promissory notes.

[17 & 18 Vict. c. 73.]

An Act to amend the Acts for the Regulation of Joint Stock Banks in Scotland. [31*st July*, 1854.]

17 & 18 Vict. c. 73.

WHEREAS an Act passed in the eighth year of the reign of Her present Majesty, intituled *An Act to regulate Joint Stock Banks in* England: And whereas the said Act was extended to *Scotland* and *Ireland* by an Act passed in the ninth and tenth years of the reign of Her Majesty, intituled *An Act to regulate Joint Stock Banks in* Scotland *and* Ireland: And whereas it is expedient that the recited Acts should be amended in certain of the provisions thereof, in so far as the same apply to *Scotland:* Be it enacted by the Queen's most excellent Majesty, by and with the advice and consent of the Lords spiritual and temporal, and Commons, in this present Parliament assembled, and by the authority of the same, as follows:

7 & 8 Vict. c. 113.

9 & 10 Vict. c. 75.

I. No clause directed by the said Acts to be inserted in the deed of partnership of any joint stock banking company in *Scotland* to be executed previous to such company being incorporated under the recited Acts shall take away or impair the right of retention or lien which, in virtue of the common law of *Scotland*, such company has or may be entitled to exercise over the shares of its partners, for or

Right of retention or lien over shares of partners not to be affected.

17 & 18 Vict. c. 73.

in respect of any debt or liability incurred or obligation undertaken by them to the company.

The company to sell shares acquired in virtue of right of lien.

II. Provided, That as often as the company may, in virtue of their right of lien or retention acquire any shares in the company's stock, they shall be bound to sell the same within six months after the same shall have been so acquired, and in such manner as is by the said first-recited Act provided for the sale of forfeited shares; and the company shall be bound to account to the party or parties interested in such shares, or to their creditors, or heirs or executors, for the balance of the price or prices which may have been realized by such sale, after paying the debt due to the company, and the expenses incurred by them in securing their debt and selling the shares.

Provision to be made as to signing bills and notes.

III. In such deed of partnership there shall be inserted provisions regulating the manner in which bills of exchange or promissory notes of the company may be made, accepted, or indorsed, and it shall not be necessary that such bills of exchange or promissory notes be signed in the manner prescribed by the first-recited Act.

[17 & 18 Vict. c. 83.]

17 & 18 Vict. c. 83.

An Act to amend the Laws relating to the Stamp Duties. [*9th August*, 1854.]

What shall be deemed bank notes within the meanings of 7 & 8 Vict. c. 32, and 8 & 9 Vict. cc. 38 & 37.

XI. And whereas an Act was passed in the seventh and eighth years of Her Majesty's reign, chapter thirty-two, to regulate the issue of bank notes; and an Act was passed in the eighth and ninth years of Her Majesty's reign, chapter thirty-eight, to regulate the issue of bank notes in *Scotland;* and another Act was passed in the last-mentioned years, chapter thirty-seven, to regulate the issue of bank notes in *Ireland;* and in order to prevent evasions of the regulations and provisions of the said respective Acts it is expedient to define what shall be deemed to be bank notes within the meaning thereof respectively: Be it enacted, That all bills, drafts, or notes (other than notes of the Bank of *England*) which shall be issued by any banker or the agent of any banker for the payment of money to the bearer on demand, and all bills, drafts, or notes so issued which shall entitle or be intended to entitle the bearer or holder thereof, without indorsement, or without any further or other indorsement than may be thereon at the time of the issuing thereof, to the payment of any sum of money on demand, whether the same shall be so expressed or not, in whatever form and by whomsoever such bills, drafts, or notes shall be drawn or made, shall be deemed to be bank notes of the bankers by whom or by whose agent the same shall be issued within the meaning of the said three several Acts last mentioned, and within all the clauses, provisions, and regulations thereof respectively.

17 & 18 Vict. c. 83.

All bills, drafts, and notes deemed bank notes under the above-recited Acts liable to stamp duties, &c.

XII. All bills, drafts, and notes which by or under this Act, or the said three several Acts last mentioned, or any of them respectively, are declared or deemed to be bank notes, shall be subject and liable to the stamp duties, and composition for stamp duties, imposed by or payable under any Act or Acts in force upon or in respect of promissory notes for the payment of money to the bearer on demand; and all clauses, provisions, regulations, penalties, and forfeitures contained in any Act or Acts relating to the issuing of such promissory notes, or for securing the said stamp duties and composition respectively, or for preventing or punishing frauds or evasions in relation thereto, shall respectively be deemed to apply to all such bills, drafts, and notes as aforesaid, and to the stamp duties and composition payable upon or in respect thereof, anything in this Act, or any other Act or Acts, to the contrary notwithstanding.

[19 Vict. c. 3.]

19 Vict. c. 3.

An Act to extend the Period for which Her Majesty may grant Letters Patent of Incorporation to Joint Stock Banks in Scotland existing before the Act of One thousand eight hundred and forty-six.

[*7th March*, 1856.]

WHEREAS, under the provisions of the Act of the ninth and tenth years of Her present Majesty, chapter seventy-five (whereby the Act of the seventh and eighth years of Her Majesty, chapter one hundred and thirteen, was extended to joint stock banks in *Scotland*), Her Majesty, with the advice of her privy council, is empowered to grant letters patent of incorporation to any company of more than six persons who were carrying on the business of bankers in *Scotland* on or before the ninth day of *August* one thousand eight hundred and forty-five, upon the terms and in manner in the said Act mentioned or referred to, but only for a term of years not exceeding twenty years: And whereas it is expedient that Her Majesty should be empowered in certain cases to grant such letters patent of incorporation for a longer period: Now be it enacted by the Queen's most excellent Majesty, by and with the advice and consent of the Lords spiritual and temporal, and Commons, in this present Parliament assembled, and by the authority of the same, as follows:

Extending period for which Her Majesty may grant letters patent of incorporation to certain joint stock banks in Scotland.

I. That, notwithstanding anything in the said Acts contained, it shall be lawful for Her Majesty to grant letters patent of incorporation under the said Acts to any company of more than six persons in *Scotland* who were carrying on the business of bankers before the said ninth day of *August* one thousand eight hundred and forty-five, either for a term of years or in perpetuity, but so that the same shall be liable to be dealt with by or under the provisions of any future Acts of Parliament in every respect as if this Act had not been passed.

[19 Vict. c. 20.]

19 Vict. c. 20. *An Act to continue certain Compositions payable to Bankers who have ceased to issue Bank Notes.* [*5th June,* 1856.]

7 & 8 Vict. c. 32. Whereas under sections twenty-three and twenty-four of the Act of the session holden in the seventh and eighth years of Her Majesty, chapter thirty-two, certain compositions are made payable by the Governor and Company of the Bank of *England* to bankers who have discontinued the issue of their own bank notes; and by section twenty-five of the said Act it is provided that all such compositions shall, if not previously determined by the act of such banker as thereinbefore provided, cease and determine on the first day of *August* one thousand eight hundred and fifty-six, or on any earlier day on which Parliament may prohibit the issue of bank notes: And whereas it is expedient to provide for the further continuance of such compositions: Be it enacted by the Queen's most excellent Majesty, by and with the advice and consent of the Lords spiritual and temporal, and Commons, in this present Parliament assembled, and by the authority of the same, as follows:

Section 25 of the said Act repealed. I. Section twenty-five of the said Act shall be repealed.

Compositions continued. II. All the compositions payable under the said Act as amended by this Act to bankers who have discontinued, or who shall agree with the said governor and company to discontinue, the issue of their own bank notes, shall, if not previously determined by the act of such bankers as by the said Act provided, and unless Parliament shall otherwise provide, continue in force and be payable until Parliament shall prohibit the issue of bank notes as defined by section twenty-eight of the said recited Act, or until the exclusive privileges of the said governor and company mentioned in section twenty-seven of the said Act shall be determined in pursuance of such section, or otherwise be determined or altered by authority of Parliament.

[19 & 20 Vict. c. 100.]

19 & 20 Vict. c. 100. *An Act to amend the Law with respect to the Election of Directors of Joint Stock Banks in England.* [*29th July,* 1856.]

7 & 8 Vict. c. 113. Whereas by the Act of the seventh and eighth years of the Queen, chapter one hundred and thirteen, it is enacted, that the deed of

partnership of every banking company to be established under that Act shall contain a specific provision for the retirement of at least one fourth of the directors yearly, and for preventing the re-election of the retiring directors for at least twelve calendar months: And whereas it is expedient that so much of the said enactment as relates to the re-election of such retiring directors should be repealed: Be it therefore enacted by the Queen's most excellent Majesty, by and with the advice and consent of the Lords spiritual and temporal, and Commons, in this present Parliament assembled, and by the authority of the same, as follows; that is to say, 19 & 20 Vict. c. 100.

I. It shall not be necessary in the deed of partnership of any banking company established after the passing of this Act to insert any provision for preventing the re-election of retiring directors, either absolutely or for any limited period. Retiring directors in banking companies eligible for re-election.

II. In every banking company already established under the provisions of the said recited Act, and whose deed of partnership or settlement contains a provision in accordance with the enactment hereinbefore repealed, the directors retiring at any general meeting after the passing of this Act shall and may, if duly qualified in other respects, be immediately eligible for re-election, anything in the deed of partnership of such company contained to the contrary notwithstanding. Provision for existing banking companies established under recited Act.

[20 & 21 Vict. c. 49.]

An Act to amend the Law relating to Banking Companies. [17*th August*, 1857.]

20 & 21 Vict. c. 49.

Whereas it is expedient to amend the law relating to copartnerships and companies carrying on the business of banking, and hereinafter included under the term banking companies: Be it enacted by the Queen's most excellent Majesty, by and with the advice and consent of the Lords spiritual and temporal, and Commons, in this present Parliament assembled, and by the authority of the same, as follows:

Preliminary.

I. This Act may be cited for all purposes as "The Joint Stock Banking Companies Act, 1857." Short title.

II. The Joint Stock Companies Acts, 1856, 1857, shall be deemed to be incorporated with and to form part of this Act. Joint Stock Companies Acts to be incorporated with this Act.

Registration of existing Banking Companies.

III. The second section of the Joint Stock Companies Act, 1856, shall be repealed so far as relates to persons associated together for the purpose of banking, subject to this proviso, that no existing or future banking company shall be registered as a limited company. Sect. 2, of 19 & 20 Vict. c. 47, repealed.

20 & 21 Vict. c. 49.

Banking companies required to register under this Act.

IV. Every banking company consisting of seven or more persons, and formed under the Acts following, or either of them, that is to say,

(1.) An Act passed in the eighth year of the reign of Her present Majesty, chapter one hundred and thirteen, and intituled *An Act to regulate Joint Stock Banks in* England,

(2.) An Act passed in the tenth year of the reign of Her present Majesty, chapter seventy-five, and intituled *An Act to regulate Joint Stock Banks in* Scotland *and* Ireland,

shall, on or before the first day of *January* one thousand eight hundred and fifty-eight, register itself as a company under this Act.

Penalty on neglect to register.

V. If any banking company hereby required to register under this Act makes default in registering on or before the said first day of *January* one thousand eight hundred and fifty-eight, then, from and after such day, until the day on which such company is registered under this Act, the following consequences shall ensue; (that is to say),

(1.) The company shall be incapable of suing either at law or in equity, but shall not be incapable of being made a defendant to a suit either at law or in equity:

(2.) No dividend shall be payable to any shareholder in such company:

(3.) Each director or manager of the company shall for each day during which the company is in default incur a penalty of five pounds, and such penalty may be recovered by any person, whether a shareholder or not in the company, and be applied by him to his own use:

Nevertheless such default shall not render the company so being in default illegal, nor subject it to any penalty or disability, other than as specified in this section.

Banking companies permitted to register under this Act.

VI. Any banking company, consisting of seven or more persons, having a capital of fixed amount and divided into shares also of fixed amount, legally carrying on the business of banking previously to the passing of this Act, and not being a company hereby required to be registered, may at any time hereafter, with the assent of a majority of such of its shareholders as may have been present in person, or in cases where proxies are allowed by the regulations of the company, by proxy, at some general meeting summoned for the purpose, register itself as a company other than a limited company under this Act, and when so registered all such provisions contained in any Act of Parliament, letters patent, or deed of settlement constituting or regulating the company, as are inconsistent with the Joint Stock Companies Acts, 1856, 1857, or with this Act, shall no longer apply to the company so registered; but such registration shall not take away or affect any powers previously enjoyed by such company of banking, issuing notes payable on demand, or of doing any other thing.

Existing companies

VII. No fees shall be payable in respect of the registration under this Act of any banking company existing at the time of the passing of this Act. 20 & 21 Vict. c. 49.

VIII. The registration under this Act of any banking company existing at the time of the passing of this Act, and hereby required or authorized to be registered, shall not affect or prejudice the liability of such company to have enforced against it or its right to enforce any debt or obligation incurred, or any contract entered into by, to, with, or on account of such company, previously to such registration, and all such debts, obligations, and contracts shall be binding on the company when so registered, and the other parties thereto, to the same extent as if such registration had not taken place.

not to pay fees.

Registration under this Act not to affect obligations incurred previously to registration.

IX. Every person who at or previously to the date of the registration under this Act of any banking company hereby required or authorized to be registered may have held shares in such company shall, in the event of the same being wound up by the court or voluntarily, be liable to contribute to the assets of the company the same amount that he would if this Act had not been passed have been liable to pay to the company, or for or on account of any debt of the company in pursuance of any action, suit, judgment, or other legal proceeding that might, if this Act had not been passed, have been instituted or enforced against himself or the company.

Saving of liabilities of persons holding shares before registration under Act.

X. All such actions, suits, and other legal proceedings as may at the time of the registration under this Act of any company hereby required or authorized to be registered have been commenced by or against such company or the public officer thereof may be continued in the same manner as if such registration had not taken place; nevertheless execution shall not issue against the effects of any individual shareholder in or member of such company upon any judgment, decree, or order obtained against such company in any action, suit, or proceeding so commenced as aforesaid; but, in the event of the property and effects of the company being insufficient to satisfy such judgment, decree, or order, an order may be obtained for winding up the company in manner directed by the Joint Stock Companies Acts, 1856, 1857.

Continuation of existing actions and suits.

Winding up of the Banking Companies.

XI. The following Acts, that is to say,

(1.) The Act of the eleventh year of the reign of Her present Majesty, chapter forty-five,

(2.) The Act of the thirteenth year of the reign of Her present Majesty, chapter one hundred and eight,

(3.) The Act of the eighth year of the reign of Her present Majesty, chapter one hundred and eleven,

(4.) The Act of the ninth year of the reign of Her present Majesty, chapter ninety-eight,

shall not apply to companies registered under this Act or under the Acts incorporated herewith or either of them; and all companies so registered shall be wound up in manner directed by the said incorporated Acts.

Certain Acts not to apply to companies registered under this Act or Acts incorporated herewith.

20 & 21 Vict. c. 49.

Repeal.

7 & 8 Vict. c. 113, and 9 & 10 Vict. c. 75, repealed.

XII. The above-mentioned Acts, that is to say,

The said Act passed in the eighth year of the reign of Her present Majesty, chapter one hundred and thirteen, and

The said Act passed in the tenth year of the reign of Her present Majesty, chapter seventy-five,

shall forthwith be repealed as respects any banking company to be formed hereafter, and shall, from and after such time as any company formed in pursuance of such Acts or either of them may have registered as a company under this Act, but not before, be repealed as respects the company so registered; and the Articles of Table B in the Schedule annexed to the Joint Stock Companies Act, 1856, relating to "shares," to "transmission of shares," and to "forfeiture of shares," and numbered from one to nineteen, both inclusive, shall, from and after such time as last aforesaid, but subject to the power of alteration conferred by the Joint Stock Companies Acts, 1858, 1857, be deemed to be regulations of any company formed in pursuance of the said Acts passed in the eighth and tenth years of Her present Majesty; nevertheless such repeal shall not affect any penalty, forfeiture, or other punishment incurred or to be incurred in respect of any offence against any Acts hereby repealed committed before such repeal comes into operation; and notwithstanding anything contained in the said Act of the eighth year of the reign of Her present Majesty, chapter one hundred and thirteen, or in any other Act, it shall be lawful for any number of persons, not exceeding ten, to carry on in partnership the business of banking in the same manner and upon the same conditions in all respects as any company, if not more than six persons, could before the passing of this Act have carried on such business.

Formation of new Banking Companies.

New banking companies.

XIII. Seven or more persons associated for the purpose of banking may register themselves under this Act as a company other than a limited company, subject to this condition, that the shares into which the capital of the company is divided shall not be of less amount than one hundred pounds each; but not more than ten persons shall after the passing of this Act, unless registered as a company under this Act, form themselves into a partnership for the purpose of banking, or if so formed carry on the business of banking.

Examination of Affairs in Company.

One third in number and value of shareholders to apply for inspectors.

XIV. No appointment of inspectors to examine into the affairs of any banking company shall be made by the Board of Trade, in pursuance of the Joint Stock Companies Act, 1856, except upon the application of one third at the least in number and value of the shareholders in such company.

Nineteenth Section of Joint Stock Companies Act not to apply.

Sect. 19, of 19 & 20 Vict.

XV. The nineteenth section of the Joint Stock Companies Act,

1856, shall not apply to any banking company in *Scotland* registered under this Act. 20 & 21 Vict. c. 49.

Transfer of Trust Property.

c. 47, not applicable to companies in Scotland.

Transfer of trust property to company.

XVI. All such estate or interest in real and personal property in *England* and *Ireland*, and in property, heritable and movable, in *Scotland*, and all such deeds, bonds, obligations, and rights as may belong to or be vested in any person or persons in trust for any banking company at the date of its registration under this Act, or in trust for any other company at the date of its registration under the Joint Stock Companies Acts, 1856, 1857, shall immediately on registration vest in such banking or other company; but no merger shall take place of any estates by reason of their uniting in the company under this section, without the express consent of the company, certified by some instrument under their common seal.

Banking Companies not registered as such.

Liability of banking company that is not registered as such.

XVII. If, through inadvertence or otherwise, a company that is in fact a banking company has, previously to the passing of this Act, been registered as a limited company under the Joint Stock Companies Act, 1856, or if, through inadvertence or otherwise, a company that is in fact a banking company is hereafter registered under the said Joint Stock Companies Acts, 1856, 1857, as a limited company, any company so registered shall not be illegal, nor shall the registration thereof be invalid, but it shall be subject to the following liabilities; that is to say,

(1.) Any creditor or member of the company may petition the court to have it wound up, and the fact of its being registered as a limited company shall of itself be a sufficient circumstance on which an order shall be made for winding up the same:

(2.) In the event of such company being wound up the contributories shall, whether the company is or not registered as a limited company, be liable to contribute to the assets of the company to an amount sufficient to pay its debts, and the costs, charges, and expenses of winding up the same.

Saving Clauses.

Exemption of certain existing banking companies from joint stock companies Acts.

XVIII. The Joint Stock Companies Acts, 1856, 1857, shall not apply to any banking company legally carrying on the business of banking previously to the passing of this Act, and not hereby required to be registered, until such time as such company registers itself under this Act, in pursuance of the power hereby given in that behalf.

Not to affect provisions of 7 & 8 Vict. c. 32, and 8 & 9 Vict. c. 38.

XIX. Nothing herein contained shall affect an Act passed in the eighth year of the reign of Her present Majesty, and intituled *An Act to regulate the Issue of Bank Notes, and for giving to the Governor and Company of the Bank of* England *certain Privileges for a limited Period*, or an Act passed in the ninth year of the reign of Her present Majesty, chapter thirty-eight, intituled *An Act to regulate the Issue of Bank Notes in* Scotland, or any other Act relating to the issue or circulation of bank notes.

[21 & 22 Vict. c. 91.]

21 & 22 Vict. C. 91.

An Act to enable Joint Stock Banking Companies to be formed on the Principle of Limited Liability. [*2nd August*, 1858.]

WHEREAS it is expedient to enable banking companies to be formed on the principle of limited liability: Be it enacted by the Queen's most excellent Majesty, by and with the advice and consent of the Lords spiritual and temporal, and Commons, in this present Parliament assembled, and by the authority of the same, as follows:

So much of 20 & 21 Vict. c. 49, as prohibits banking companies from being registered with limited liability repealed.

Proviso as to bankers issuing notes.

I. So much of the Joint Stock Banking Companies Act, 1857, as prohibits a banking company from being formed under that Act with limited liability, or prohibits an existing banking company from being registered under that Act with limited liability, shall be repealed, subject to the following proviso, that no banking company claiming to issue notes in the United Kingdom shall be entitled to limited liability in respect of such issue, but shall continue subject to unlimited liability in respect thereof, and that, if necessary, the assets shall be marshalled for the benefit of the general creditors, and the shareholders shall be liable for the whole amount of the issue, in addition to the sum for which they would be liable as shareholders of a limited company.

Registration of banking companies not to prejudice re-registration as limited.

II. The registration of a banking company under the Joint Stock Banking Companies Act, 1857, or under any other Act, shall not prejudice the right of such company to register itself again as a limited company under the said Joint Stock Banking Companies Act, 1857, and the Acts incorporated therewith.

On reregistration with limited liability notice to be given to customers.

III. Provided, That every company so registering itself again as a limited company, and every existing banking company which shall register itself as a limited banking company, shall, at least thirty day previous to obtaining a certificate of registration with limited liability, give notice that it is intended so to register the same to every person and partnership firm who shall have a banking account with the company, and such notice shall be given either by delivering the same to such person or firm, or leaving the same or putting the same into the post addressed to him or them at such address as shall have been last communicated or otherwise become known as his or their address to or by the company; and in case the company shall omit to give any such notice as is hereinbefore required to be given, then as between the company and the person or persons only who are for the time being interested in the account in respect of which such notice ought to have been given, and so far as respects such account and all variations thereof down to the time at which such notice shall be given, but not further or otherwise, the certificate of registration with limited liability shall have no operation.

In default of notice unlimited liability to continue as to such customers.

IV. Every limited joint stock banking company shall, before it commences business, or, if a banking company at the time carrying on business with unlimited liability, before it avails itself of the provisions of this Act, and also on the first day of *February* and first day of *August* in every year during which it carries on business, make a statement in the form contained in the Schedule hereto, or as near thereto as circumstances will admit, and a copy of such statement shall be put up in a conspicuous place in the registered office of the company, and in every branch office or place where the banking business of the company is carried on; and if default is made in due compliance with the provisions of this section, each director shall be liable to a penalty not exceeding five pounds for every day during which such default continues, and such penalties shall be recovered in a summary manner.

21 & 22 Vict. c. 91.

Banking company to annex a statement to their memorandum of association.

V. Limited joint stock banking companies shall be wound up in the same manner and under the same jurisdiction as that in and under which joint stock banking companies other than limited are required to be wound up by the Joint Stock Banking Companies Act, 1857.

How limited banking companies are to be wound up.

SCHEDULE referred to in the foregoing Act.

Form of Statement to be published by a Limited Joint Stock Banking Company.

The liability of the shareholders is limited.

The capital of the company is one million, divided into ten thousand shares of one hundred pounds each.

The number of shares issued is ten thousand.

Calls to the amount of twenty pounds per share have been made, under which the sum of one hundred and eighty thousand pounds has been received.

The liabilities of the company on the first day of January (*or* July) were,	£ . *d.*
Notes issued	
Deposits not bearing interest . . .	
Deposits bearing interest . . .	
Seven day and other bills . . .	
Total	

The assets of the company on that day were,	
Government securities.	
Bills of exchange	
Loans on mortgage	
Other loans	
Bank premises	
Other securities, exclusive of unpaid calls on shares	
Total	

Dated the first day of February *or* August one thousand eight hundred and fifty-nine.

[23 & 24 Vict. c. 111.]

23 & 24 Vict. c. 111.

An Act for granting to Her Majesty certain Duties of Stamps, and to amend the Laws relating to the Stamp Duties. [28*th August*, 1860.]

Sect. 18 of 55 Geo. 3, c. 184, prohibiting the issuing of bankers' notes with printed dates, repealed.

Drafts on bankers for less than 20*s.* to be lawful.

XIX. Whereas by the eighteenth section of the Act passed in the fifty-fifth year of the reign of King *George* the Third, chapter one hundred and eighty-four, the issuing of promissory notes payable to bearer on demand with printed dates therein is prohibited, and such prohibition is an unnecessary restriction: Be it enacted, That the said section of the said last-mentioned Act shall be and is hereby repealed: Provided always, that, notwithstanding anything in any Act of Parliament contained to the contrary, it shall be lawful for any person to draw upon his banker, who shall *bonâ fide* hold money to or for his use, any draft or order for the payment, to the bearer or to order on demand, of any sum of money less than twenty shillings.

[24 & 25 Vict. c. 91.]

24 & 25 Vict. c. 91.

An Act to amend the Laws relating to the Inland Revenue. [6*th August*, 1861.]

Licences to joint stock banks not required to specify the names of more than six persons.

XXXV. Whereas the licences and certificates granted to bankers and persons acting as bankers in *Great Britain* and *Ireland* respectively, by or under the authority of the Commissioners of Inland Revenue, are required by law to specify, amongst other things, the names and places of abode of all the persons composing the respective companies or partnerships to whom they are granted: Be it enacted, That in any case where a company or copartnership of bankers consists of more than six persons it shall be sufficient to specify in any such licence or certificate the names and places of abode of any six or more of such persons who may be presented to the commissioners or their officer, or whom they or he may select for the purpose, and to grant the licence or certificate to them as and for the whole of the company or copartnership, or otherwise to specify only the name or style of the company or copartnership, and to grant the licence or certificate to such company or copartnership in and by the said name or style, as the commissioners or their officer shall think fit; and every such licence and certificate respectively shall be as good, valid, and available as if the names and places of abode of all the members of the company or copartnership had been specified therein, and the licence had been granted to them, anything in any Act of Parliament to the contrary notwithstanding; but this shall not in any way alter or affect the provisions of any Act of Parliament whereby any banking company or copartnership is required to make any account or return of the name and places of abode of all the members or partners of such company or copartnership, and any other particulars relating thereto.

24 & 25 Vict c. 91.

[25 & 26 Vict. c. 89.]

An Act for the Incorporation, Regulation, and Winding-up of Trading Companies and other Associations. [*7th August*, 1862.]

25 & 26 Vict. c. 89.

II. This Act, with the exception of such temporary enactment as is hereinafter declared to come into operation immediately, shall not come into operation until the second day of *November* one thousand eight hundred and sixty-two, and the time at which it so comes into operation is hereinafter referred to as the commencement of this Act.

Commencement of Act.

IV. No company, association, or partnership consisting of more than ten persons shall be formed, after the commencement of this Act, for the purpose of carrying on the business of banking, unless it is registered as a company under this Act, or is formed in pursuance of some other Act of Parliament, or of letters patent; and no company, association, or partnership consisting of more than twenty persons shall be formed, after the commencement of this Act, for the purpose of carrying on any other business that has for its object the acquisition of gain by the company, association, or partnership, or by the individual members, thereof unless it is registered as a company under this Act, or is formed in pursuance of some other Act of Parliament, or of letters patent, or is a company engaged in working mines within and subject to the jurisdiction of the Stannaries.

Prohibition of partnerships exceeding certain number.

XLIV. Every limited banking company and every insurance company, and deposit, provident or benefit society under this Act shall, before it commences business, and also on the first *Monday* in *February* and the first *Monday* in *August* in every year during which it carries on business, make a statement in the form marked D in the First Schedule hereto, or as near thereto as circumstances will admit, and a copy of such statement shall be put up in a conspicuous place in the registered office of the company, and in every branch office or place where the business of the company is carried on, and if default is made in compliance with the provisions of this section the company shall be liable to a penalty not exceeding five pounds for every day during which such default continues, and every director and manager of the company who shall knowingly and wilfully authorize to permit such default shall incur the like penalty.

Certain companies to publish statement entered in Schedule.

Every member and every creditor of any company mentioned in this section shall be entitled to a copy of the above-mentioned statement on payment of a sum not exceeding sixpence.

Part IX.

Repeal of Acts and temporary Provisions.

CCV. After the commencement of this Act there shall be repealed the several Acts specified in the First Part of the Third Schedule hereto, with this qualification, that so much of the said Acts as is set forth in the Second Part of the said Third Schedule shall be hereby re-enacted and continue in force as if unrepealed.

Repeal of Acts.

25 & 26 Vict. c. 89.

THIRD SCHEDULE.

First Part.

Date and Chapter of Act.	Title of Act.
21 & 22 Geo. 3, c.46 (Parlmt. of Ireland).	An Act to promote Trade and Manufactures by regulating and encouraging Partnerships.
7 & 8 Vict. c. 110 -	An Act for the Registration, Incorporation, and Regulation of Joint Stock Companies.
7 & 8 Vict. c. 111 -	An Act for facilitating the winding up the Affairs of Joint Stock Companies unable to meet their pecuniary Engagements.
7 & 8 Vict. c. 113 -	An Act to regulate Joint Stock Banks in England.
8 & 9 Vict. c. 98 -	An Act for facilitating the winding up the Affairs of Joint Stock Companies in Ireland unable to meet their pecuniary Engagements.
9 & 10 Vict. c. 28 -	An Act to facilitate the Dissolution of certain Railway Companies.
9 & 10 Vict. c. 75 -	An Act to regulate Joint Stock Banks in Scotland and Ireland.
10 & 11 Vict. c. 78	An Act to amend an Act for the Registration, Incorporation, and Regulation of Joint Stock Companies.
11 & 12 Vict. c. 45	An Act to amend the Acts for facilitating the winding up the Affairs of Joint Stock Companies unable to meet their pecuniary Engagements, and also to facilitate the Dissolution and winding up of Joint Stock Companies and other Partnerships.
12 & 13 Vict. c. 108	An Act to amend the Joint Stock Companies Winding-up Act, 1848.
19 & 20 Vict. c. 47	An Act for the Incorporation and Regulation of Joint Stock Companies and other Associations.
20 & 21 Vict. c. 14	An Act to amend the Joint Stock Companies Act, 1856.
20 & 21 Vict. c. 49	An Act to amend the Law relating to Banking Companies.
20 & 21 Vict. c. 78	An Act to amend the Act Seven and Eight Victoria, Chapter One hundred and eleven, for facilitating the winding up the affairs of Joint Stock Companies unable to meet their pecuniary Engagements, and also the Joint Stock Companies Winding-up Acts, 1848 and 1849.
20 & 21 Vict. c. 80	An Act to amend the Joint Stock Companies Act, 1856.
21 & 22 Vict. c. 60	An Act to amend the Joint Stock Companies Acts, 1856 and 1857, and the Joint Stock Banking Companies Act, 1857.
21 & 22 Vict. c. 91	An Act to enable Joint Stock Banking Companies to be formed on the Principle of Limited Liability.

SECOND PART.

25 & 26 Vict. c. 89.

7 & 8 Vict. c. 113, s. 47.

Existing companies to have the powers of suing and being sued.

Every company of more than six persons established on the sixth day of May one thousand eight hundred and forty-four, for the purpose of carrying on the trade or business of bankers within the distance of sixty-five miles from London, and not within the provisions of the Act passed in the session holden in the seventh and eighth years of the reign of Her present Majesty, chapter one hundred and thirteen, shall have the same powers and privileges of suing and being sued in the name of any one of the public officers of such copartnership as the nominal plaintiff, petitioner, or defendant on behalf of such copartnership; and all judgments, decrees, and orders, made and obtained in any such suit may be enforced in like manner as is provided with respect to such companies carrying on the said trade or business at any place in England exceeding the distance of sixty-five miles from London, under the provisions of an Act passed in the seventh year of the reign of King George the Fourth, chapter forty-six, intituled "An Act for the better regulating Copartnerships of certain Bankers in England, and for amending so much of an Act of the Thirty-ninth and Fortieth Years of the Reign of His late Majesty King George the Third, intituled 'An Act for establishing an Agreement with the Governor and Company of the Bank of England for advancing the Sum of Three millions towards the Supply for the Service of the Year One thousand eight hundred,' as relates to the same," provided that such first-mentioned company shall make out and deliver from time to time to the Commissioners of Stamps and Taxes the several accounts or returns required by the last-mentioned Act, and all the provisions of the last-recited Act as to such accounts or returns shall be taken to apply to the accounts or returns so made out and delivered by such first-mentioned companies as if they had been originally included in the provisions of the last-recited Act.

20 & 21 Vict. c. 49, Part of Section XII.

Power to form banking partnerships of ten persons.

Notwithstanding anything contained in any Act passed in the session holden in the seventh and eighth years of the reign of Her present Majesty, chapter one hundred and thirteen, and intituled "An Act to regulate Joint Stock Banks in England," or in any other Act, it shall be lawful for any number of persons, not exceeding ten, to carry on in partnership the business of banking, in the same manner and upon the same conditions in all respects as any company of not more than six persons could before the passing of this Act have carried on such business.

[27 & 28 Vict. c. 32.]

27 & 28 Vict. c. 32. *An Act to enable certain Banking Copartnerships which shall discontinue the Issue of their own Bank Notes to sue and be sued by their public Officer.*

[30*th June*, 1864.]

WHEREAS by an Act passed in the session holden in the seventh year of the reign of His late Majesty King *George* the Fourth,
7 G. 4, c. 46 chapter forty-six, intituled *An Act for the better regulating Copartnerships of certain Bankers in* England, *and for amending so much of an Act of the Thirty-ninth and Fourtieth Years of the Reign of His late Majesty King* George *the Third, intituled 'An Act for establishing an Agreement with the Governor and Company of the Bank of* England *for advancing the Sum of Three Millions towards the Supply for the Service of the Year One thousand eight hundred,' as relates to the same*, banking copartnerships registered and carrying on business under the Act now in recital, and entitled to issue their own bank notes, under an Act passed in the session holden in the seventh and eighth years of the reign of Her Majesty Queen *Victoria*, chapter
7 & 8 Vict. c. 32. thirty-two, intituled *An Act to regulate the Issue of Bank Notes, and for giving to the Governor and Company of the Bank of* England *certain Privileges for a limited Period*, have certain powers and privileges of suing and being sued in the name of any one of their public officers, so long as such copartnerships carry on business under the provisions of the first recited Act: And whereas by the secondly recited Act such copartnerships are empowered to agree with the Governor and Company of the Bank of *England* to discontinue the issue of bank notes, and it is thereby enacted, that if
Sect. 24. any such banking copartnership shall discontinue the issue of bank notes, either by agreement with the Governor and Company of the
Sect. 12. Bank of *England*, or otherwise, it shall not be lawful for such copartnerships at any time thereafter to issue such notes: And whereas doubts are entertained whether the powers and privileges so given by the first recited Act will extend to such of the said banking copartnerships as shall discontinue the issue of bank notes, and shall afterwards commence and carry on the trade or business of bankers in *London*, or within sixty-five miles from *London*, in such manner as they will then by law be authorized to do; and it is expedient that such doubts be removed: Be it therefore declared and enacted by the Queen's most excellent Majesty, by and with the advice and consent of the Lords spiritual and temporal, and Commons, in this present Parliament assembled, and by the authority of the same, as follows:

Banks discontinuing the issue of bank notes empowered

I. From and after the passing of this Act, every banking copartnership registered and carrying on business under the first recited Act, and entitled to issue their own bank notes under the secondly recited Act, which shall discontinue the issue of such bank notes, and shall afterwards commence and carry on the trade or business of bankers in *London*, or within sixty-five miles from *London*, in such manner as they will then by law be authorized to do, shall have the same powers and privileges of suing and being sued in the name of any one of the public officers of such copartnership, as the nominal plaintiff, petitioner, or defendant, on behalf of such copartnership; and all judgments, decrees, and orders made and obtained in any such suits may be enforced in like manner as is provided by the first recited Act with respect to copartnerships carrying on business under the provisions of that Act; provided that nothing in this Act contained shall empower any copartnership to carry on the trade or business of bankers in *London*, or within sixty-five miles therefrom, in any case where by the existing law they are not authorized so to do.

27 & 28 Vict. c. 32.

to sue and be sued by their Public officer.

Act not to empower any bank carry on business in London.

[27 & 28 Vict. c. 86.]

An Act to permit for a limited Period Compositions for Stamp Duty on Bank Post Bills of Five Pounds and upwards in Ireland. [29*th July*, 1864.]

27 & 28 Vict. c 86.

WHEREAS by an Act passed in the sixteenth and seventeenth years of Her Majesty's reign, chapter sixty-three, the Commissioners of Her Majesty's Treasury are authorized and empowered to compound and agree with all or any bankers in *Scotland* or elsewhere for a composition in lieu of the stamp duties payable on the bills of exchange of such bankers: And whereas it is expedient to permit bankers in *Ireland* for a limited period to compound for the stamp duties payable on their bank post bills as well as on their bills of exchange: Be it enacted by the Queen's most excellent Majesty, by and with the advice and consent of the Lords spiritual and temporal, and Commons, in this present Parliament assembled, and by the authority of the same, as follows:

16 & 17 Vict. c. 63.

I. It shall be lawful for the Commissioners of Her Majesty's Treasury and they are hereby authorized and empowered to compound and agree with any banker in *Ireland* for a composition in lieu of the stamp duties payable on the bank post bills to be made or drawn by such banker at any time during the period of three years from the passing of this Act, for any sum of money amounting to five pounds or upwards, and such composition shall be made on the like terms and conditions and with such security as the said commissioners are by the said Act empowered to require in the case of compounding for the stamp duties on bills of exchange; and upon such composition being entered into by such banker it shall be lawful for him, during the period aforesaid, to make, draw, and issue all such bank post bills, for which composition shall have been made, on unstamped paper, anything in any Act contained to the contrary notwithstanding.

Power to Treasury to compound with bankers in Ireland for the stamp duty on bank Post bills for a period of three years.

[30 Vict. c. 29.]

30 Vict. c. 29.

An Act to amend the Law in respect of the Sale and Purchase of Shares in Joint Stock Banking Companies. [17*th June*, 1867.]

WHEREAS it is expedient to make provision for the prevention of contracts for the sale and purchase of shares and stock in joint stock banking companies of which the sellers are not possessed or over which they have no control:

May it therefore please Your Majesty that it may be enacted; and be it enacted by the Queen's most excellent Majesty, by and with the advice and consent of the Lords spiritual and temporal, and Commons, in this present Parliament assembled, and by the authority of the same:

Contracts for sale, &c., of shares to be void unless the numbers by which such shares are distinguished are set forth in contract.

I. That all contracts, agreements, and tokens of sale and purchase which shall, from and after the first day of *July* one thousand eight hundred and sixty-seven, be made or entered into for the sale or transfer, or purporting to be for the sale or transfer, of any share or shares, or of any stock or other interest, in any joint stock banking company in the United Kingdom of *Great Britain* and *Ireland* constituted under or regulated by the provisions of any Act of Parliament, royal charter, or letters patent, issuing shares or stock transferable by any deed or written instrument, shall be null and void to all intents and purposes whatsoever, unless such contract, agreement, or other token shall set forth and designate in writing such shares, stock, or interest by the respective numbers by which the same are distinguished at the making of such contract, agreement, or token on the register or books of such banking company as aforesaid, or where there is no such register of shares or stock by distinguishing number, then unless such contract, agreement, or other token shall set forth the person or persons in whose name or names such shares, stock, or interest shall at the time of making such contract stand as the registered proprietor thereof in the books of such banking company; and every person, whether principal, broker, or agent, who shall wilfully insert in any such contract, agreement, or other token any false entry of such numbers, or any name or names other than that of the person or persons in whose name such shares, stock, or interest shall stand as aforesaid, shall be guilty of a misdemeanor, and be punished accordingly, and, if in *Scotland*, shall be guilty of an offence punishable by fine or imprisonment.

Registered shareholders may see lists.

II. Joint stock banking companies shall be bound to show their list of shareholders to any registered shareholder during business hours, from ten of the clock to four of the clock.

Extent of Act limited.

III. This Act shall not extend to shares or stock in the Bank of *England* or the Bank of *Ireland*.

[30 & 31 Vict. c. 89.]

An Act to render perpetual an Act passed in the Session holden in the Twenty-seventh and Twenty-eighth Years of Her present Majesty, intituled An Act to permit for a limited Period Compositions for Stamp Duty on Bank Post Bills of Five Pounds and upwards in Ireland. [12*th August*, 1867.] 30 & 31 Vict. c. 89.

WHEREAS by an Act passed in the session holden in the twenty-seventh and twenty-eighth years of the reign of Her present Majesty, chapter eighty-six, intituled *An Act to permit for a limited Period Compositions for Stamp Duty on Bank Post Bills of Five Pounds and upwards in* Ireland, the Commissioners of Her Majesty's Treasury are empowered to compound and agree, in manner therein mentioned, with any banker in *Ireland* for a composition in lieu of the stamp duties payable on the bank post bills to be made or drawn by such banker at any time during the period of three years from the passing of the said Act for any sum of money amounting to five pounds and upwards: 27 & 28 Vict. c. 86.

And whereas it is expedient to make perpetual the powers conferred by the said Act:

Be it enacted by the Queen's most excellent Majesty, by and with the advice and consent of the Lords spiritual and temporal, and Commons, in this present Parliament assembled, and by the authority of the same, as follows:

I. The powers conferred by the said Act of the session of the twenty-seventh and twenty-eighth years of the reign of Her present Majesty shall be perpetual, and the said Act shall be construed as if the words "during the period of three years from the passing of this Act" had been omitted therefrom. Powers of 27 & 28 Vict. c. 86, made perpetual.

II. This Act may be cited for all purposes as "The Stamp Duty Composition (*Ireland*) Act, 1867." Short title.

[33 & 34 Vict. c. 97.]

An Act for granting certain Stamp Duties in lieu of Duties of the same kind now payable under various Acts, and consolidating and amending Provisions relating thereto. [10*th August*, 1870.] 33 & 34 Vict. c. 97.

I. This Act may be cited as "The Stamp Act, 1870" and shall come into operation on the first day of January one thousand eight Short title, and com-

33 & 34 Vict. c 97.

hundred and seventy-one, which date is hereinafter referred to as the commencement of this Act.

mencement of Act.

All duties to be paid according to the regulations of this Act, and the Schedule to be read as part of this Act.

VI. (1.) All stamp duties which may from time to time be chargeable by law upon any instruments are to be paid and denoted according to the general and special regulations in this Act contained.

(2.) The said Schedule, and everything therein contained, is to be read and construed as part of this Act.

Terms upon which instruments may be stamped after execution.

XV. (1.) Except where express provision to the contrary is made by this or any other Act, any unstamped or insufficiently stamped instrument may be stamped after the execution thereof, on payment of the unpaid duty and a penalty of ten pounds, and also by way of further penalty, where the unpaid duty exceeds ten pounds, of interest on such duty, at the rate of five pounds *per centum per annum*, from the day upon which the instrument was first executed up to the time when such interest is equal in amount to the unpaid duty.

And the payment of any penalty or penalties is to be denoted on the instrument by a particular stamp.

Proviso.

(2.) Provided as follows:

As to instruments executed abroad.

(*a.*) Any unstamped or insufficiently stamped instrument, which has been first executed at any place out of the United Kingdom, may be stamped, at any time within two months after it has been first received in the United Kingdom, on payment of the unpaid duty only:

As to the remission of penalties.

(*b.*) The commissioners may, if they think fit, at any time within twelve months after the first execution of any instrument, remit the penalty or penalties, or any part thereof.

Terms upon which unstamped or insufficiently stamped instruments may be received in evidence in any court.

XVI. (1.) Upon the production of an instrument chargeable with any duty as evidence in any court of civil judicature in any part of the United Kingdom, the officer whose duty it is to read the instrument shall call the attention of the judge to any omission or insufficiency of the stamp thereon, and if the instrument is one which may legally be stamped after the execution thereof, it may, on payment to the officer of the amount of the unpaid duty, and the penalty payable by law on stamping the same as aforesaid, and of a further sum of one pound, be received in evidence, saving all just exceptions on other grounds.

The officer of the court to account for duties and penalties.

(2.) The officer receiving the said duty and penalty shall give a receipt for the same, and make an entry in a book kept for that purpose of the payment and of the amount thereof, and shall communicate to the commissioners the name or title of the cause or proceeding in which, and of the party from whom, he received the said duty and penalty, and the date and description of the instrument, and shall pay over to the Receiver General of Inland Revenue or to such other person as the commissioners may appoint, the money received by him for the said duty and penalty.

(3.) Upon production to the commissioners of any instrument in respect of which any duty or penalty has been paid as aforesaid, together with the receipt of the said officer, the payment of such duty and penalty shall be denoted on such instrument accordingly.

XVII. Save and except as aforesaid, no instrument executed in any part of the United Kingdom, or relating, wheresoever executed to any property situate, or to any matter or thing done or to be done, in any part of the United Kingdom, shall, except in criminal proceedings, be pleaded or given in evidence, or admitted to be good, useful, or available in law or equity, unless it is duly stamped in accordance with the law in force at the time when it was first executed.

33 & 34 Vict. c. 97.

Instrument not duly stamped inadmissible.

XXIII. Except where express provision is made to the contrary, all duties are to be denoted by impressed stamps only.

How duties to be denoted.

XXIV. (1.) An instrument, the duty upon which is required, or permitted by law, to be denoted by an adhesive stamp, is not to be deemed duly stamped with an adhesive stamp unless the person required by law to cancel such adhesive stamp cancels the same by writing on or across the stamp his name or initials, or the name or initials of his firm, together with the true date of his so writing, so that the stamp may be effectually cancelled, and rendered incapable of being used for any other instrument, or unless it is otherwise proved that the stamp appearing on the instrument was affixed thereto at the proper time.

General direction as to the cancellation of adhesive stamps.

(2.) Every person who, being required by law to cancel an adhesive stamp, wilfully neglects or refuses duly and effectually to do so in manner aforesaid, shall forfeit the sum of ten pounds.

Penalty for neglect or refusal, 10*l*.

XXV. Any person who—

(1.) Fraudulently removes or causes to be removed from any instrument any adhesive stamp, or affixes any adhesive stamp which has been so removed to any other instrument with intent that such stamp may be used again:

Penalty for frauds in relation to adhesive stamps,

(2.) Sells or offers for sale, or utters, any adhesive stamps which has been so removed, or utters any instrument having thereon any adhesive stamp which has to his knowledge been so removed as aforesaid:

(3.) Practises or is concerned in any fraudulent act, contrivance, or device not specially provided for, with intent to defraud Her Majesty, her heirs or successors, of any duty,

shall forfeit, over and above any other penalty to which he may be liable, the sum of fifty pounds.

or to any duty, 50*l*.

As to Bank Notes, Bills of Exchange, and Promissory Notes.

XLV. The term "banker" means and includes any corporation, society, partnership, and persons, and every individual person carrying on the business of banking in the United Kingdom.

Interpretation of terms.

The term "bank notes" means and includes—

(1.) Any bill of exchange or promissory note issued by any banker, other than the Governor and Company of the Bank of England, for the payment of money not exceeding one hundred pounds to the bearer on demand:

(2.) Any bill of exchange or promissory note so issued which

33 & 34 Vict. c. 97.

entitles or is intended to entitle the bearer or holder thereof, without indorsement, or without any further or other indorsement than may be thereon at the time of the issuing thereof, to the payment of money not exceeding one hundred pounds on demand, whether the same be so expressed or not, and in whatever form, and by whomsoever such bill or note is drawn or made.

Bank notes may be re-issued.

XLVI. A bank note issued duly stamped, or issued unstamped by a banker duly licensed or otherwise authorized to issue unstamped bank notes, may be from time to time reissued without being liable to any stamp duty by reason of such reissuing.

Penalty for issuing an unstamped bank note, 50*l.*;

XLVII. (1.) If any banker, not being duly licensed or otherwise authorized to issue unstamped bank notes, issues, or causes or permits to be issued, any bank note not being duly stamped, he shall forfeit the sum of fifty pounds.

for receiving, 20*l.*

(2.) If any person receives or takes any such bank note in payment or as a security, knowing the same to have been issued unstamped contrary to law, he shall forfeit the sum of twenty pounds.

Interpretation of term "bill of exchange."

XLVIII. (1.) The term "bill of exchange" for the purposes of this Act includes also draft, order, cheque, and letter of credit, and any document or writing (except a bank note) entitling or purporting to entitle any person, whether named therein or not, to payment by any other person of, or to draw upon any other person for, any sum of money therein mentioned.

(2.) An order for the payment of any sum of money by a bill of exchange or promissory note, or for the delivery of any bill of exchange or promissory note in satisfaction of any sum of money, or for the payment of any sum of money out of any particular fund which may or may not be available, or upon any condition or contingency which may or may not be performed or happen, is to be deemed for the purposes of this Act a bill of exchange for the payment of money on demand.

(3.) An order for the payment of any sum of money weekly, monthly, or at any other stated periods, and also any order for the payment by any person at any time after the date thereof of any sum of money, and sent or delivered by the person making the same to the person by whom the payment is to be made, and not to the person to whom the payment is to be made, or to any person on his behalf, is to be deemed for the purposes of this Act a bill of exchange for the payment of money on demand.

Interpretation of term "promissory note."

XLIX. (1.) The term "promissory note" means and includes any document or writing (except a bank note) containing a promise to pay any sum of money.

(2.) A note promising the payment of any sum of money out of any particular fund which may or may not be available, or upon any condition or contingency which may or may not be performed or happen, is to be deemed for the purposes of this Act a promissory note for the said sum of money.

L. The fixed duty of one penny on a bill of exchange for the payment of money on demand may be denoted by an adhesive stamp, which is to be cancelled by the person by whom the bill is signed before he delivers it out of his hands, custody, or power.

33 & 34 Vict. c. 97.

The fixed duty may be denoted by adhesive stamp.

LI. (1.) The ad valorem duties upon bills of exchange and promissory notes drawn or made out of the United Kingdom are to be denoted by adhesive stamps.

Ad valorem duties to be denoted in certain cases by adhesive stamps.

(2.) Every person into whose hands any such bill or note comes in the United Kingdom before it is stamped shall, before he presents for payment, or indorses, transfers, or in any manner negotiates, or pays such bill or note, affix thereto a proper adhesive stamp or proper adhesive stamps of sufficient amount, and cancel every stamp so affixed thereto.

(3.) Provided as follows:

Provisoes for the protection of bona fide holders;

(a.) If at the time when any such bill or note comes into the hands of any bonâ fide holder thereof there is affixed thereto an adhesive stamp effectually obliterated, and purporting and appearing to be duly cancelled, such stamp shall, so far as relates to such holder, be deemed to be duly cancelled, although it may not appear to have been so affixed or cancelled by the proper person.

(b.) If at the time when any such bill or note comes into the hands of any bonâ fide holder thereof there is affixed thereto an adhesive stamp not duly cancelled, it shall be competent for such holder to cancel such stamp as if he were the person by whom it was affixed, and upon his so doing such bill or note shall be deemed duly stamped, and as valid and available as if the stamp had been duly cancelled by the person by whom it was affixed.

(4.) But neither of the foregoing provisoes is to relieve any person from any penalty incurred by him for not cancelling any adhesive stamp.

not to relieve any other person.

LII. A bill of exchange or promissory note purporting to be drawn or made out of the United Kingdom is, for the purposes of this Act, to be deemed to have been so drawn or made, although it may in fact have been drawn or made within the United Kingdom.

Bills and notes purporting to be drawn, &c., abroad to be deemed to have been so drawn, &c.

LIII. (1.) Where a bill of exchange or promissory note has been written on material bearing an impressed stamp of sufficient amount but of improper denomination, it may be stamped with the proper stamp on payment of the duty, and a penalty of forty shillings if the bill or note be not then payable according to its tenor, and of ten pounds if the same be so payable.

Terms upon which bills and notes may be stamped after execution.

(2.) Except as aforesaid, no bill of exchange or promissory note shall be stamped with an impressed stamp after the execution thereof.

LIV. (1.) Every person who issues, indorses, transfers, negotiates, presents for payment, or pays any bill of exchange or promissory note liable to duty and not being duly stamped shall forfeit the sum

Penalty for issuing, &c., any unstamped

33 & 34 Vict. c. 97.

bill or note 10*l.*; and bill or note to be unavailable.

of ten pounds, and the person who takes or receives from any other person any such bill or note not being duly stamped either in payment or as a security, or by purchase or otherwise, shall not be entitled to recover thereon, or to make the same available for any purpose whatever.

Proviso as to the fixed duty,

(2.) Provided that if any bill of exchange for the payment of money on demand, liable only to the duty of one penny, is presented for payment unstamped, the person to whom it is so presented may affix thereto a proper adhesive stamp, and cancel the same, as if he had been the drawer of the bill, and may, upon so doing, pay the sum in the said bill mentioned, and charge the duty in account against the person by whom the bill was drawn, or deduct such duty from the said sum, and such bill is, so far as respects the duty, to be deemed good and valid.

not to relieve from penalty.

(3.) But the foregoing proviso is not to relieve any person from any penalty he may have incurred in relation to such bill.

One bill only out of a set need be stamped.

LV. When a bill of exchange is drawn in a set according to the custom of merchants, and one of the set is duly stamped, the other or others of the set shall, unless issued or in some manner negotiated apart from such duly stamped bill, be exempt from duty; and upon proof of the loss or destruction of a duly stamped bill forming one of a set, any other bill of the set which has not been issued or in any manner negotiated apart from such lost or destroyed bill may, although unstamped, be admitted in evidence to prove the contents of such lost or destroyed bill.

As to Notarial Acts.

Duty may be denoted by adhesive stamp.

CXVI. The duty upon a notarial act, and upon the protest by a notary public of a bill of exchange or promissory note, may be denoted by an adhesive stamp, which is to be cancelled by the notary.

As to Receipts.

Interpretation of term.

CXX. The term "receipt" means and includes any note, memorandum, or writing whatsoever whereby any money amounting to two pounds or upwards, or any bill of exchange or promissory note for money amounting to two pounds or upwards, is acknowledged or expressed to have been received or deposited or paid, or whereby any debt or demand, or any part of a debt or demand, of the amount of two pounds or upwards, is acknowledged to have been settled, satisfied, or discharged, or which signifies or imports any such acknowledgment, and whether the same is or is not signed with the name of any person.

Duty may be denoted by adhesive stamp.

CXXI. The duty upon a receipt may be denoted by an adhesive stamp, which is to be cancelled by the person by whom the receipt is given before he delivers it out of his hands.

Penalty for offences.

CXXIII. If any person—

(1.) Gives any receipt liable to duty and not duly stamped;

(2.) In any case where a receipt would be liable to duty refuses to give a receipt duly stamped; 33 & 34 Vict. c. 97.

(3.) Upon a payment to the amount of two pounds or upwards gives a receipt for a sum not amounting to two pounds, or separates or divides the amount paid with intent to evade the duty;

he shall forfeit the sum of ten pounds.

SCHEDULE.

	£	s.	d.
BILL OF EXCHANGE—			
Payable on damand	0	0	1
BILL OF EXCHANGE of any other kind whatsoever (*except a bank note*) and PROMISSORY NOTE of any kind whatsoever (*except a bank note*)—drawn, or expressed to be payable, or actually paid, or indorsed, or in any manner negotiated in the United Kingdom.			
Where the amount or value of the money for which the bill or note is drawn or made does not exceed 5*l*.	0	0	1
Exceeds 5*l*. and does not exceed 10*l*.	0	0	2
" 10*l*. " 25*l*.	0	0	3
25*l*. 50*l*.	0	0	6
50*l*. " 75*l*.	0	0	9
" 75*l*. " 100*l*.	0	1	0
" 100*l*. for every 100*l*., and also for any fractional part of 100*l*., of such amount or value .	0	1	0

Exemptions.

(1.) Bill or note issued by the Governor and Company of the Bank of England or Bank of Ireland.

(2.) Draft or order drawn by any banker in the United Kingdom upon any other banker in the United Kingdom, not payable to bearer or to order, and used solely for the purpose of settling or clearing any account between such bankers.

(3.) Letter written by a banker in the United Kingdom to any other banker in the United Kingdom, directing the payment of any sum of money, the same not being payable to bearer or to order, and such letter not being sent or delivered to the person to whom payment is to be made, or to any person on his behalf.

(4.) Letter of credit granted in the United Kingdom authorizing drafts to be drawn out of the United Kingdom payable in the United Kingdom.

(5.) Draft or order drawn by the Accountant General of the Court of Chancery in England or Ireland.

(6.) Warrant or order for the payment of any annuity granted by the Commissioners for the Reduction

33 & 34 Vict. c. 97.

£ s. d.

of the National Debt, or for the payment of any dividend or interest on any share in the Government or Parliamentary stocks or funds.

(7.) Bill drawn by the Lords Commissioners of the Admiralty, or by any person under their authority, under the authority of any Act of Parliament upon and payable by the Accountant General of the Navy.

(8.) Bill drawn (according to a form prescribed by Her Majesty's orders by any person duly authorized to draw the same) upon and payable out of any public account for any pay or allowance of the army or other expenditure connected therewith.

(9.) Coupon or warrant for interest attached to and issued with any security.

And *see* sections 48, 49, 50, 51, 52, 53, 54, and 55.

PROTEST of any bill of exchange or promissory note :

Where the duty on the bill or note does not exceed 1*s.* { The same duty as the bill or note.

In any other case 0 1 0

And *see* section 116.

RECEIPT given for, or upon the payment of, money amounting to 2*l.* or upwards 0 0 1

Exemptions.

(1.) Receipt given for money deposited in any bank, or with any banker, to be accounted for and expressed to be received of the person to whom the same is to be accounted for.

(2.) Acknowledgment by any banker of the receipt of any bill of exchange or promissory note for the purpose of being presented for acceptance or payment.

(3.) Receipt given for or upon the payment of any parliamentary taxes or duties, or of money to or for the use of Her Majesty.

(4.) Receipt given by the Accountant-General of the Navy for any money received by him for the service of the navy.

(5.) Receipt given by any agent for money imprested to him on account of the pay of the army.

(6). Receipt given by any officer, seaman, marine or soldier, or his representatives, for or on account of any wages, pay or pension, due from the Admiralty or Army Pay Office.

(7.) Receipt given for the consideration money for the purchase of any share in any of the Government or Parliamentary stocks or funds, or in stock of the East India Company, or in the stocks and funds of the Secretary of State in Council of

£ s. d. 33 & 34 Vict. c. 97.

India, or of the Governor and Company of the Bank of England, or of the Bank of Ireland, or for any dividend paid on any share of the said stocks or funds respectively.

(8.) Receipt given for any principal money or interest due on an exchequer bill.

(9.) Receipt written upon a bill of exchange or promissory note duly stamped.

(10.) Receipt given upon any bill or note of the Governor and Company of the Bank of England or the Bank of Ireland.

(11.) Receipt indorsed or otherwise written upon or contained in any instrument liable to stamp duty, and duly stamped, acknowledging the receipt of the consideration money therein expressed, or the receipt of any principal money, interest, or annuity thereby secured or therein mentioned.

(12.) Receipt given for drawback or bounty upon the exportation of any goods or merchandise from the United Kingdom.

(13.) Receipt given for the return of any duties of customs upon certificates of over entry.

(14.) Receipt indorsed upon any bill drawn by the Lords Commissioners of the Admiralty, or by any person under their authority or under the authority of any Act of Parliament upon and payable by the Accountant General of the Navy.

And *see* sections 120, 121, 122, and 123.

[34 Vict. c. 17.]

An Act to make Provision for Bank Holidays, and respecting Obligations to make Payments and do other Acts on such Bank Holidays. 34 Vict. c. 17.

[25*th May*, 1871.]

WHEREAS it is expedient to make provision for rendering the day after Christmas Day, and also certain other days, bank holidays, and for enabling bank holidays to be appointed by royal proclamation:

Be it enacted by the Queen's most excellent Majesty, by and with the advice and consent of the Lords spiritual and temporal, and Commons, in this present Parliament assembled, and by the authority of the same, as follows:

I. After the passing of this Act, the several days in the Schedule to this Act mentioned (and which days are in this Act hereinafter referred to as bank holidays) shall be kept as close holidays in all banks in England and Ireland and Scotland respectively, and

Bills due on bank holidays to be payable on the following day.

34 Vict. c. 17.

all bills of exchange and promissory notes which are due and payable on any such bank holiday shall be payable, and in case of non-payment may be noted and protested, on the next following day, and not on such bank holiday; and any such noting or protest shall be as valid as if made on the day on which the bill or note was made due and payable; and for all the purposes of this Act the day next following a bank holiday shall mean the next following day on which a bill of exchange may be lawfully noted or protested.

Provision as to notice of dishonour and presentation for honour.

II. When the day on which any notice of dishonour of an unpaid bill of exchange or promissory note should be given, or when the day on which a bill of exchange or promissory note should be presented or received for acceptance, or accepted or forwarded to any referee or referees, is a bank holiday, such notice of dishonour shall be given and such bill of exchange or promissory note shall be presented or forwarded on the day next following such bank holiday.

As to any payments on bank holidays.

III. No person shall be compelled to make any payment or to do any act upon such bank holidays which he would not be compelled to do or make on Christmas Day or Good Friday; and the obligation to make such payment and do such act shall apply to the day following such bank holiday; and the making of such payment and doing such act on such following day shall be equivalent to payment of the money or performance of the act on the holiday.

Appointment of special bank holidays by royal proclamation.

IV. It shall be lawful for Her Majesty, from time to time, as to Her Majesty may seem fit, by proclamation, in the manner in which solemn fasts or days of public thanksgiving may be appointed, to appoint a special day to be observed as a bank holiday, either throughout the United Kingdom or in any part thereof, or in any county, city, borough, or district therein, and any day so appointed shall be kept as a close holiday in all banks within the locality mentioned in such proclamation, and shall, as regards bills of exchange and promissory notes payable in such locality, be deemed to be a bank holiday for all the purposes of this Act.

Day appointed for bank holiday may be altered by order in council.

V. It shall be lawful for Her Majesty in like manner, from time to time, when it is made to appear to Her Majesty in council in any special case that in any year it is inexpedient that a day by this Act appointed for a bank holiday should be a bank holiday, to declare that such day shall not in such year be a bank holiday, and to appoint such other day as to Her Majesty in council may seem fit to be a bank holiday instead of such day, and thereupon the day so appointed shall in such year be substituted for the day so appointed by this Act.

Exercise of powers conferred by sections 4 and 5 in Ireland by Lord Lieutenant.

VI. The powers conferred by sections 3 and 4 of this Act on Her Majesty may be exercised in Ireland, so far as relates to that part of the United Kingdom, by the Lord Lieutenant of Ireland in council.

Short title.

VII. This Act may be cited for all purposes as "The Bank Holidays Act, 1871."

SCHEDULE.

34 Vict. c. 17.

Bank Holidays in England and Ireland.

Easter Monday.
The Monday in Whitsun week.
The first Monday in August.
The twenty-sixth day of December, if a week day.

Bank Holidays in Scotland.

New Year's Day.
Christmas Day.
If either of the above days falls on a Sunday, the next following Monday shall be a bank holiday.
Good Friday.
The first Monday of May.
The first Monday of August.

[34 & 35 Vict. c. 74.]

An Act to abolish Days of Grace in the Case of Bills of Exchange and Promissory Notes payable at Sight or on Presentation. [14*th August*, 1871.]

34 & 35 Vict. c. 74.

WHEREAS doubts have arisen whether by the custom of merchants a bill of exchange or promissory note purporting to be payable at sight or on presentation is payable until the expiration of a certain number of "days of grace":

And whereas it is expedient that such bills of exchange and promissory notes should bear the same stamp, and should be payable in the same manner as bills of exchange and promissory notes purporting to be payable on demand:

Be it enacted by the Queen's most excellent Majesty, by and with the advice and consent of the Lords spiritual and temporal, and Commons, in this present Parliament assembled, and by the authority of the same, as follows:

I. This Act may be cited as "The Bills of Exchange Act, 1871." Short title.

II. Every bill of exchange or promissory note, drawn after this Act comes into operation and purporting to be payable at sight or on presentation, shall bear the same stamp and shall, for all purposes whatsoever, be deemed to be a bill of exchange or promissory note payable on demand, any law or custom to the contrary notwithstanding. Bills payable at sight or on presentation to be payable on demand.

III. For the purposes of this Act, the terms "bill of exchange" Definition of terms

34 & 35 Vict. c. 74. and "promissory note" shall have the same meanings as are given to them in the Stamp Act, 1870.

Admissibility in evidence of past bills. IV. A bill of exchange purporting to be payable at sight and drawn at any time between the first day of *January* one thousand eight hundred and seventy-one and the day of the passing of this Act, both inclusive, and stamped as a bill of exchange payable on demand, shall be admissible as evidence on payment of the difference between the amount of stamp duty paid on such bill and the amount which would have been payable if this Act had not passed.

[39 & 40 Vict. c. 48.]

39 & 40 Vict. c. 48. *An Act to amend the Law with reference to Bankers' Books Evidence.* [11*th August*, 1876.]

WHEREAS serious inconvenience has been occasioned to bankers and also to the public by reason of the ledgers and other account books having been removed from the banks for the purpose of being produced in legal proceedings:

And whereas it is expedient to facilitate the proof of the transactions recorded in such ledgers and account books:

Be it therefore enacted by the Queen's most excellent Majesty, by and with the advice and consent of the Lords spiritual and temporal, and Commons, in this present Parliament assembled, and by the authority of the same, as follows:

Short title. I. This Act may be cited for all purposes as the Bankers' Books Evidence Act, 1876.

Interpretation clause. II. The word "bank" in this Act shall mean any person or persons, partnership or company, carrying on the business of bankers, and who at the commencement of each year shall have made their return to the Commissioners of Inland Revenue, and any savings bank certified under the Act of 1863.

The words "legal proceedings" in this Act shall include all proceedings, whether preliminary or final, in courts of justice, both criminal and civil, legal and equitable, and shall include all proceedings, whether preliminary or final, by way of arbitration, examination of witnesses, assessment of damages, compensation or otherwise, in which there is power to administer an oath.

The words "the court" in this Act shall mean the court, judge, magistrate, sheriff, arbitrator, or other person authorized to preside over the said legal proceedings for the time being, and shall include all persons, judges, or officers having jurisdiction and authorized to preside over or to exercise judicial control over the said legal proceedings or the procedure or any steps therein.

The words "a judge of one of the superior courts" shall mean respectively a judge of Her Majesty's High Court of Justice in so far as this Act applies to *England* and *Wales*, a lord ordinary of the outer house of the Court of Session in *Scotland* in so far as it applies to *Scotland*, and a judge of one of the superior courts at *Dublin* in so far as it applies to *Ireland*.

39 & 40 Vict. c. 48.

Entries in books by affidavit admissible in evidence.

III. From and after the commencement of this Act the entries in ledgers, day books, cash books, and other account books of any bank shall be admissible in all legal proceedings as primâ facie evidence of the matters, transactions, and accounts recorded therein on proof being given by the affidavit in writing of one of the partners, managers, or officers of such bank, or by other evidence that such ledgers, day books, cash books, or other account books are or have been the ordinary books of such bank, and that the said entries have been made in usual and ordinary course of business, and that such books are in or come immediately from the custody or control of such bank. Nothing in this clause contained shall apply to any legal proceeding to which any bank whose ledgers, day books, cash books, and other account books may be required to be produced in evidence shall be a party.

Originals need not be produced.

IV. Copies of all entries in any ledgers, day books, cash books, or other account books used by any such bank may be proved in all legal proceedings as evidence of such entries without production of the originals, by means of the affidavit of a person who has examined the same, stating the fact of said examination, and that the copies sought to be put in evidence are correct.

Proviso as to notice to parties in a suit

V. Provided always, That no ledger, day book, cash book, or other account book of any such bank, and no copies of entries therein contained, shall be adduced or received in evidence under this Act, unless five days' notice in writing, or such other notice as may be ordered by the court, containing a copy of the entries proposed to be adduced and of the intention to adduce the same in evidence, shall have been given by the party proposing to adduce the same in evidence to the other party or parties to the said legal proceeding, and that such other party or parties is or are at liberty to inspect the original entries and the accounts of which such entries form a part.

Power under order of court to inspect books and take copies.

VI. On the application of any party to any legal proceedings who has received such notice, a judge of one of the superior courts may order that such party be at liberty to inspect and to take copies of any entry or entries in the ledger, day books, cash books, or other account books of any such bank relating to the matters in question in such legal proceedings, and such orders may be made by such judge at his discretion either with or without summoning before him such banker or the other party or parties to such legal proceedings, and shall be intimated to such bank at least three days before such copies are required.

Judge may order that copies are not admissible.

VII. On the application of any party to any legal proceedings who has received notice, a judge of one of the superior courts may order that such entries and copies mentioned in the said notice shall not be admissible as evidence of the matters, transactions, and accounts recorded in such ledgers, day books, cash books, and other account books.

Bank not compellable

VIII. No bank shall be compellable to produce the ledgers, day

39 & 40 Vict. c. 48.

to produce books except in certain cases.

books, cash books, or other account books of such bank in any legal proceedings, unless a judge of one of the superior courts specially orders that such ledgers, day books, cash books, or other account books should be produced at such legal proceedings.

Proof as to status of bank.

IX. The fact of any such bank having duly made their return to the Commissioners of Inland Revenue may be proved in any legal proceedings by production of a copy of such return, verified as having been duly made by the affidavit in writing of one of the partners, or of the manager, or of one of the officers of such bank, or by the production of a copy of a newspaper purporting to contain a copy of such return, published in such newspaper by the said Commissioners of Inland Revenue.

[39 & 40 Vict. c. 81.]

39 & 40 Vict. c. 81.

An Act for amending the Law relating to Crossed Cheques. [*15th August*, 1876.]

Be it enacted by the Queen's most excellent Majesty, by and with the advice and consent of the Lords spiritual and temporal, and Commons, in this present Parliament assembled, and by the authority of the same, as follows:

Short title.

I. This Act may be cited as "The Crossed Cheques Act, 1876."

Repeal of Acts in Schedule.

II. The Acts described in the Schedule to this Act are hereby repealed, but this repeal shall not affect any right, interest, or liability acquired or accrued before the passing of this Act.

Interpretation.

III. In this Act—

"Cheque" means a draft or order on a banker payable to bearer or to order on demand, and includes a warrant for payment of dividend on stock sent by post by the Governor and Company of the Bank of England or of Ireland, under the authority of any Act of Parliament for the time being in force:

"Banker" includes persons or a corporation or company acting as bankers.

General and special crossings.

IV. Where a cheque bears across its face an addition of the words "and company," or any abbreviation thereof, between two parallel transverse lines, or of two parallel transverse lines simply, and either with or without the words "not negotiable," that addition shall be deemed a crossing, and the cheque shall be deemed to be crossed generally.

Where a cheque bears across its face an addition of the name of a banker, either with or without the words "not negotiable," that addition shall be deemed a crossing, and the cheque shall be deemed to be crossed specially, and to be crossed to that banker.

V. Where a cheque is uncrossed, a lawful holder may cross it generally or specially. 39 & 40 Vict. c. 81.

Crossing after issue.

Where a cheque is crossed generally, a lawful holder may cross it specially.

Where a cheque is crossed generally or specially, a lawful holder may add the words "not negotiable."

Where a cheque is crossed specially, the banker to whom it is crossed may again cross it specially to another banker, his agent for collection.

Crossing material part of cheque.

VI. A crossing authorized by this Act shall be deemed a material part of the cheque, and it shall not be lawful for any person to obliterate or, except as authorized by this Act, to add to or alter the crossing.

Payment to banker only.

VII. Where a cheque is crossed generally, the banker on whom it is drawn shall not pay it otherwise than to a banker

Where a cheque is crossed specially, the banker on whom it is drawn shall not pay it otherwise than to the banker to whom it is crossed, or to his agent for collection.

Cheque crossed specially more than once not to be paid.

VIII. Where a cheque is crossed specially to more than one banker, except when crossed to an agent for the purpose of collection, the banker on whom it is drawn shall refuse payment thereof.

Protection of banker and drawer where cheque crossed specially.

IX. Where the banker on whom a crossed cheque is drawn has in good faith and without negligence paid such cheque, if crossed generally to a banker, and if crossed specially to the banker to whom it is crossed, or his agent for collection being a banker, the banker paying the cheque and (in case such cheque has come to the hands of the payee) the drawer thereof shall respectively be entitled to the same rights, and be placed in the same position in all respects, as they would respectively have been entitled to and have been placed in if the amount of the cheque had been paid to and received by the true owner thereof.

Banker paying cheque contrary to provisions of Act to be liable to lawful owner.

X. Any banker paying a cheque crossed generally otherwise than to a banker, or a cheque crossed specially otherwise than to the banker to whom the same shall be crossed, or his agent for collection, being a banker, shall be liable to the true owner of the cheque for any loss he may sustain owing to the cheque having been so paid.

Relief of banker from responsibility in some cases.

XI. Where a cheque is presented for payment, which does not at the time of presentation appear to be crossed, or to have had a crossing which has been obliterated, or to have been added to or altered otherwise than as authorized by this Act, a banker paying the cheque, in good faith and without negligence, shall not be responsible or incur any liability, nor shall the payment be questioned, by reason of the cheque having been crossed, or of the crossing having been obliterated, or having been added to or altered otherwise than as authorized by this Act, and of payment being made otherwise than to a banker or the banker to whom the cheque is or was crossed, or to his agent for collection being a banker (as the case may be).

39 & 40 Vict. c. 81.

Title of holder of cheque crossed specially.

XII. A person taking a cheque crossed generally or specially, bearing in either case the words "not negotiable," shall not have and shall not be capable of giving a better title to the cheque than that which the person from whom he took it had.

But a banker who has in good faith and without negligence received payment for a customer of a cheque crossed generally or specially to himself shall not, in case the title to the cheque proves defective, incur any liability to the true owner of the cheque by reason only of having received such payment.

SCHEDULE.

Acts Repealed.

19 & 20 Vict. c. 25.	-	An Act to amend the Law relating to Drafts on Bankers.
21 & 22 Vict. c. 79.	-	An Act to amend the Law relating to Cheques or Drafts on Bankers.

INDEX.

A.

C.

F.

H.

I.

J.

L.

M.

P.

S.

W.

THE END.

LONDON: STEVENS & RICHARDSON, PRINTERS, 5, GREAT QUEEN STREET, W.C.

June, 1877.

A CATALOGUE OF LAW WORKS,

PUBLISHED BY

STEVENS AND SONS,

(LATE STEVENS AND NORTON),

119, CHANCERY LANE, LONDON, W.C.,

(*Formerly of Bell Yard, Lincoln's Inn*).

Law Books Purchased or Valued.

Now ready, 8vo. cloth lettered, price 6d., post free.

A Catalogue of Modern Law Works; *together with a complete Chronological List of all the English, Irish, and Scotch Reports, Abbreviations used in reference to Law Reports and Text Books, and an Index of Subjects.*

ACTS OF PARLIAMENT.—Public and Local Acts are sold singly, and may be had of the Publishers of this Catalogue, who have also on sale the largest collection of Private Acts, relating to Estates, Enclosures, Railways, Roads, &c., &c.

ACTION AT LAW.—Smith's (John W.) Action at Law. —Twelfth Edition, adapted to the practice of the Supreme Court. By W. D. I. FOULKES, Esq., Barrister-at-Law, Joint Editor of the "Licensing Acts," and "Judicature Acts." 12mo. 1876. 10*s.* 6*d.*

"The author, indeed, must look to students in both branches of the profession for patrons, and we can heartily advise students to avail themselves of his assistance. His style is simple and perspicuous; his method orderly."—*Law Journal*, August 19, 1876.

"The student will find in 'Smith's Action' a manual, by the study of which he may easily acquire a general knowledge of the mode of procedure in the various stages of an action in the several divisions of the High Court of Justice. It is a book, the pages of which neither lawyers nor laymen need hesitate to consult, inasmuch as the information, as far as it goes, is perfectly accurate."—*Law Times*, September 2, 1876.

ADMIRALTY.—Boyd.—*Vide* "Shipping."

Lowndes.—*Vide* "Collisions."

Pritchard's Admiralty Digest.—A Digest of the Law and Practice of the High Court of Admiralty of England, with Notes from Text Writers, and the Scotch, Irish, and American Reports. Second Edition. By ROBERT A. PRITCHARD, D.C.L., of the Inner Temple, Barrister-at-Law, and WILLIAM TARN PRITCHARD. With Notes of Cases from French Maritime Law. By ALGERNON JONES, Avocat à la Cour Impériale de Paris. 2 vols. Royal 8vo. 1865. 3*l.*

Stuart's Cases heard and determined in the Vice-Admiralty Court at Quebec, 1836-75. Edited by GEORGE OKILL STUART, Esq., Q.C. 2 vols. Royal 8vo. 1858-75. *Net*, 5*l.*

*** *All standard Law Works are kept in Stock, in law calf and other bindings.*

AGENCY.—**Petgrave's Principal and Agent.**—A Manual of the Law of Principal and Agent. By E. C. PETGRAVE, Solicitor. 12mo. 1857. 7*s.* 6*d.*

Petgrave's Code of the Law of Principal and Agent, with a Preface. By E. C. PETGRAVE, Solicitor Demy 12mo. 1876. *Net,* 2*s.*

Rogers.—*Vide* "Elections."

Russell's Treatise on Mercantile Agency.—Second Edition. 8vo. 1873. 14*s.*

AGRICULTURAL LAW.—**Addison's Practical Guide to the Agricultural Holdings (England) Act, 1875** (38 & 39 Vic. c. 92), and Treatise thereon, shewing the Alterations in the Law, and containing many useful Hints and Suggestions as to the carrying out of the Provisions of the Act; with Handy Forms and a Carefully Prepared Index. Designed chiefly for the use of Agricultural Landlords and Tenants. By ALBERT ADDISON, Solicitor of the Supreme Court of Judicature. 12mo. 1876. *Net,* 2*s.* 6*d.*

Cooke on Agricultural Law.—The Law and Practice of Agricultural Tenancies, with Numerous Precedents of Tenancy Agreements and Farming Leases, &c., &c. By G. WINGROVE COOKE, Esq., Barrister-at-Law. 8vo. 1851. 18*s.*

Dixon's Farm.—*Vide* "Farm."

ARBITRATION.—**Russell's Treatise on the Duty and Power of an Arbitrator, and the Law of Submissions and Awards;** with an Appendix of Forms, and of the Statutes relating to Arbitration. By FRANCIS RUSSELL, Esq., Recorder of Tenterden. Fourth Edition. Royal 8vo. 1870. *Net,* 1*l.* 16*s.*

ARTICLED CLERKS.—**Butlin's New and Complete Examination Guide and Introduction to the Law;** for the use of Articled Clerks and those who contemplate entering the legal profession, comprising Courses of Reading for the Preliminary and Intermediate Examinations and for Honours, or a Pass at the Final, with Statute, Case, and Judicature (Time) Tables, Sets of Examination Papers, &c., &c. By JOHN FRANCIS BUTLIN, Solicitor, &c. 8vo. 1877. 18*s.*

"A sensible and useful guide for the legal tyro."—*Solicitors' Journal,* April 21, 1877.

"In supplying law students with materials for preparing themselves for examination, Mr. Butlin, we think, has distanced all competitors. The volume before us contains hints on reading, a very neat summary of law, which the best read practitioner need not despise. There are time tables under the Judicature Act, and an excellent tabular arrangement of leading cases, which will be found of great service . . . . Tuition of this kind will do much to remove obstacles which present themselves to commencing students, and when examinations are over the book is one which may be usefully kept close at hand, and will well repay 'noting up.'"—*Law Times,* February 24, 1877.

Rubinstein and Ward's Articled Clerks' Handbook.—Being a Concise and Practical Guide to all the Steps Necessary for Entering into Articles of Clerkship, passing the Preliminary, Intermediate and Final Examinations, obtaining Admission and Certificate to Practise, with Notes of Cases affecting Articled Clerks, and Suggestions as to Mode of Reading and Books to be read during Articles. By J. S. RUBINSTEIN and S. WARD, Solicitors. Demy 12mo. 1877. 3*s.*

"No articled clerk should be without it."—*Law Times,* February 17, 1877.

"Will serve as a simple and practical guide to all the steps necessary for entering into articles of clerkship to solicitors, for passing the several examinations, and for procuring admission on the Roll."—*Law Times,* February 24, 1877.

*** *All standard Law Works are kept in Stock, in law calf and other bindings.*

ARTICLED CLERKS.—*Continued.*

Wharton's Articled Clerk's Manual.—A Manual for Articled Clerks: being a comprehensive Guide to their successful Examination, Admission, and Practice as Attorneys and Solicitors of the Superior Courts. Ninth Edition. Greatly enlarged. By CHARLES HENRY ANDERSON, Senior Prizeman of the Incorporated Law Society, &c. Royal 12mo. 1864. 18*s.*

ASSURANCE.—*Vide* "Insurance."

ATTORNEYS.—**Pulling's Law of Attorneys,** General and Special, Attorneys-at-Law, Solicitors, Notaries, Proctors, Conveyancers, Scriveners, Land Agents, House Agents, &c., and the Offices and Appointments usually held by them. Their several Qualifications and legitimate Province, Rights, Duties, Privileges, Exemptions, Disabilities, and Liabilities in the General Practice of the Law, in Legal Proceedings, in Legal Negotiations, and Legal Formalities. And the Law of Costs as between Party and Party and Attorney and Client. By ALEXANDER PULLING, Serjeant-at-Law. Third Edition. 8vo. 1862. 18*s.*

"It is a laborious work, a careful work, the work of a lawyer, and, beyond comparison, the best that has ever been produced upon this subject."—*Law Times.*

Smith.—The Lawyer and his Profession.—A Series of Letters to a Solicitor commencing Business. By J. ORTON SMITH. 12mo. 1860. 4*s.*

AVERAGE.—**Hopkins' Hand-Book on Average.**—Third Edition. 8vo. 1868. 18*s.*

Lowndes' Law of General Average.—English and Foreign. Third Edition. By RICHARD LOWNDES, Author of "The Admiralty Law of Collisions at Sea." (*In preparation.*)

BAILMENTS.—**Jones on the Law of Bailments.**—Fourth Edition. By W. THEOBALD. 8vo. 1834. *Net,* 5*s.*

BALLOT.—**FitzGerald's Ballot Act.**—With an INTRODUCTION. Forming a Guide to the Procedure at Parliamentary and Municipal Elections. Second Edition. Enlarged, and containing the Municipal Elections Act, 1875, and the Parliamentary Elections (Returning Officers) Act, 1875. By GERALD A. R. FITZGERALD, M.A., of Lincoln's Inn, Esq., Barrister-at-Law. Fcap. 8vo. 1876. 5*s.* 6*d.*

"A useful guide to all concerned in Parliamentary and Municipal Elections."—*Law Magazine,* February, 1877.

"We should strongly advise any person connected with elections, whether acting as candidate, agent, or in any other capacity, to become possessed of this manual."—Nov. 26, 1876.

BANKING.—**Walker's Treatise on Banking Law.** Including the Crossed Checks Act, 1876, with dissertations thereon, also references to some American Cases, and full Index. By J. DOUGLAS WALKER, of Lincoln's Inn, Esq., Barrister-at-Law. Demy 8vo. 1877. 14*s.*

BANKRUPTCY.—**Bedford's Final Examination Guide to Bankruptcy.**—Third Edition. (*In preparation.*)

Lynch's Tabular Analysis of Proceedings in Bankruptcy, for the use of Students for the Incorporated Law Society's Examinations. Second Edition. 8vo. 1874. *Net,* 1*s.*

Parker's Analysis of the Principal Steps in a Bankruptcy Proceeding, taken from the Bankruptcy Act and Rules; with an Index. By FRANK R. PARKER, one, &c. Folio. 1870. 5*s.*

Scott's Costs in Bankruptcy.—*Vide* "Costs."

*** *All standard Law Works are kept in Stock, in law calf and other bindings.*

BANKRUPTCY.—*Continued.*

Smith's Manual on Bankruptcy.—A Manual relating to Bankruptcy, Insolvency, and Imprisonment for Debt; comprising the New Statute Law verbatim, in a consolidated and readable form. With the Rules, a Copious Index, and a Supplement of Decisions. By JOSIAH W. SMITH, Esq., B.C.L., Q.C., Judge of County Courts. 12mo. 1873. 10*s.*

*** The Supplement may be had separately, *net,* 2*s.* 6*d.*

Williams' Law and Practice in Bankruptcy, comprising the Bankruptcy Act, the Debtors Act, and the Bankruptcy Repeal and Insolvent Court Act of 1869, and the Rules and Forms made under those Acts. Second Edition. By ROLAND VAUGHAN WILLIAMS, of Lincoln's Inn, Esq., and WALTER VAUGHAN WILLIAMS, of the Inner Temple, Esq, assisted by FRANCIS HALLETT HARDCASTLE, of the Inner Temple, Esq., Barristers-at-Law. 8vo. 1876. 1*l.* 8*s.*

"'Williams on Bankruptcy' is quite satisfactory, the more so, perhaps, as the authors have wisely 'not attempted to give all the old authorities, even where the law seems unchanged, but rather the result of those authorities.'"—*Law Magazine,* Nov. 1876.

"The present edition is a great improvement"—*Solicitors' Journal,* August 26, 1876.

"It would be difficult to speak in terms of undue praise of the present work. . . . The present edition brings down the law to May, 1876, and the profession has now not only the most recent, but certainly one of the best, if not the best, treatise on the Law of Bankruptcy."—*Public Opinion,* July 1, 1876.

BILLS OF EXCHANGE.—**Chitty on Bills of Exchange and Promissory Notes.**—Eleventh Edition. By JOHN A. RUSSELL, one of Her Majesty's Counsel, and Judge of County Courts. (*In preparation.*)

Eddis' Rule of Ex parte Waring. By A. C. EDDIS, B.A., of Lincoln's Inn, Barrister-at-Law. Post 8vo. 1876. *Net,* 2*s.* 6*d.*

BILLS OF SALE.—**Millar and Collier's Bills of Sale.**—A Treatise on Bills of Sale, with an Appendix containing the Acts for the Registration of Bills of Sale, Precedents, &c. Third Edition. By F. C. J. MILLAR Barrister-at-Law. 12mo. 1871. *Net,* 10*s.* 6*d.*

BOOK-KEEPING.—**Bedford's Intermediate Examination Guide to Book-keeping.**—Second Edition. 12mo. 1875. *Net,* 2*s.* 6*d.*

BUILDING ACTS.—**Woolrych.**—*Vide* "Metropolis Building Acts."

CANAL TRAFFIC ACT.—**Lely's Railway and Canal Traffic Act, 1873.**—And other Railway and Canal Statutes; with the General Orders, Forms, and Table of Fees. Post 8vo. 1873. 8*s*

CARRIERS.—**Browne on Carriers.**—A Treatise on the Law of Carriers of Goods and Passengers by Land and Water. With References to the most recent American Decisions. By J. H. BALFOUR BROWNE, of the Middle Temple, Esq., Barrister-at-Law, Registrar to the Railway Commission. 8vo. 1873. 18*s.*

CHANCERY *and Vide* "**EQUITY.**"

Daniell's Chancery Practice.—The Practice of the High Court of Chancery, with some observations on the Pleadings in that Court. By the late EDMUND ROBERT DANIELL, Barrister-at-Law. Fifth Edition, by LEONARD FIELD and EDWARD CLENNELL DUNN, Barristers-at-Law; with the assistance of JOHN BIDDLE, of the Master of the Rolls' Chambers. 2 vols. 8vo. 1871. 4*l.* 4*s.*

CHANCERY—*Continued.*

The Practice of the High Court of Chancery and the Court of Chancery (Funds) Act, 1872, together with Appendices containing the Act, and the Rules and Orders thereunder, and a Collection of Forms. By LEONARD FIELD and EDWARD CLENNELL DUNN, Barristers-at-Law. 8vo. 1873. 8*s.* 6*d.*

"It is the merit of Mr. Daniell's 'Practice' that it takes nothing as known. The reader is minutely instructed *what* he is to do and *how* he is to do it, and if he closely follows his guide he cannot go wrong."—*Law Times.*

Daniell's Chancery Forms.—Forms and Precedents of Pleadings and Proceedings in the High Court of Chancery, with Practical Notes and Observations, and References to the Fourth Edition of Daniell's Chancery Practice; and incorporating the Forms in Braithwaite's Record and Writ Practice. By LEONARD FIELD and EDWARD CLENNELL DUNN, Barristers-at-Law, and JOHN BIDDLE, of the Master of the Rolls' Chambers. Second Edition. By JOHN BIDDLE. 8vo. 1871. 1*l.* 12*s.*

Morgan's Acts and Orders, Fifth Edition. 1876.—The Statutes, General Orders, and Rules of Court relating to the Practice, Pleading, and Jurisdiction of the Supreme Court of Judicature, particularly with reference to the Chancery Division, and the Actions assigned thereto. With copious Notes. Fifth Edition. Carefully revised and adapted to the new Practice by GEORGE OSBORNE MORGAN, M.P., one of Her Majesty's Counsel, and CHALONER W. CHUTE, of Lincoln's Inn, Barrister-at-Law, and late Fellow of Magdalen College, Oxford. In 1 vol. Demy 8vo. 1876. 1*l.* 10*s.*

"A most valuable feature is the annotation of the Rules of Court, which give all the recent cases, and is as useful as a new edition of any of the works on Judicature Acts only. This edition of Mr. Morgan's treatise must, we believe, be the most popular with the profession."—*Law Times*, December 9, 1876.

"In the shape in which it now appears we have no doubt this edition will meet with a very favourable reception by the professions, and will exceed in demand any of its predecessors."—*Law Journal*, Dec. 30, 1876.

"The practitioner will find in the present edition, a lucid and compendious statement of the substance of the Consolidated and other Orders of the Court of Chancery, which, though not expressly incorporated in the new enactments, are, by implication, left untouched by them, placed side by side with the Judicature Acts and Rules of Court. . . . . This new edition will maintain and enhance the high reputation deservedly gained by the original work"—*Law Magazine and Review*, February, 1877.

Morgan and Davey's Chancery Costs.—*Vide* "Costs."

Orders and Rules of the High Court of Justice, Chancery Division.—Published by authority, as issued.

CHURCH AND CLERGY.—Phillimore.—*Vide* "Ecclesiastical Law."

Stephen's Laws relating to the Clergy.—2 vols. Royal 8vo. 1848. 2*l.* 18*s.*

CIVIL LAW.—Bowyer's Commentaries on the Modern Civil Law.—By Sir GEORGE BOWYER, D.C.L., Royal 8vo. 1848. 18*s.*

Bowyer's Introduction to the Study and Use of the Civil Law.—By Sir GEORGE BOWYER, D.C.L. Royal 8vo. 1874. 5*s.*

Cumin's Manual of Civil Law.—A Manual of Civil Law, containing a Translation of, and Commentary on, the Fragments of the XII. Tables, and the Institutes of Justinian; the Text of the Institutes of Gaius and Justinian arranged in parallel columns; and the Text of the Fragments of Ulpian, and of Selections from Paul's Receptæ Sententiæ. By P. CUMIN, M.A., Barrister-at-Law. Second Edition. Medium 8vo. 1865. 18*s.*

CIVIL LAW.—*Continued.*

Greene.—*Vide* "Roman Law."

Mears.—*Vide* "Roman Law."

Voet Commentarius ad Pandectas, Translated into English.—Part I. The Contract of Sale. (Book xviii.) By SIR ROLAND KNYVET WILSON, Bart., of Lincoln's Inn, Barrister-at-Law. Royal 8vo. 1876. *Net* 1*l.* 1*s.*

COLLISIONS.—Lowndes' Admiralty Law of Collisions at Sea.—8vo. 1867. 7*s.* 6*d.*

COLONIAL LAW.—Clark's Colonial Law.—A Summary of Colonial Law and Practice of Appeals from the Plantations. 8vo. 1834. 1*l.* 4*s.*

Vanderlinden.—*Vide* "Dutch Law."

COMMENTARIES ON THE LAWS OF ENGLAND.—Bowyer.—*Vide* "Constitutional Law."

Broom and Hadley's Commentaries on the Laws of England.—By HERBERT BROOM, LL.D., of the Inner Temple, Barrister-at-Law; Reader in Common Law to the Inns of Court; Author of "A Selection of Legal Maxims," &c.; and EDWARD A. HADLEY, M.A., of Lincoln's Inn, Barrister-at-Law; late Fellow of Trinity Coll., Cambridge. 4 vols. 8vo. 1869. 3*l.* 3*s.*

"Messrs. Broom and Hadley have been unsparing in their editorial labours. There are abundant reference notes, so that the diligent student can consult the authorities if he is so disposed. Besides the table of contents, there are an appendix and a copious index to each volume. Nothing that could be done to make the work useful and handy has been left undone."—*Law Journal*, Nov. 19, 1869.

COMMERCIAL LAW.—Levi's International Commercial Law.—Being the Principles of Mercantile Law of the following and other Countries—viz.: England, Scotland, Ireland, British India, British Colonies, Austria, Belgium, Brazil, Buenos Ayres, Denmark, France, Germany, Greece, Hans Towns, Italy, Netherlands, Norway, Portugal, Prussia, Russia, Spain, Sweden, Switzerland, United States, and Würtemburg. By LEONE LEVI, Esq., F.S.A., F.S.S., of Lincoln's Inn, Barrister-at-Law, Professor of the Principles and Practice of Commerce at King's College, London, &c. Second Edition. 2 vols. Royal 8vo. 1863. 1*l.* 15*s.*

Smith.—*Vide* "Mercantile Law."

COMMON LAW.—Braithwaite.—*Vide* "Oaths."

Fisher.—*Vide* "Digests."

Orders and Rules of the High Court of Justice, Common Law Divisions.—Published by Authority, as issued.

Smith's Manual of Common Law.—A Manual of Common Law, comprising the fundamental principles and the points most usually occurring in daily life and practice; for the Practitioner, Student, and General Reader. By JOSIAH W. SMITH, B.C.L., Q.C., Judge of County Courts. Seventh Edition, with Notices of the Judicature Acts. 12mo. 1876. 14*s.*

"Admirably conceived and executed. . . . . Eminently lucid and concise . . . . . A pocket-book of pith and essence of common law."—*Legulcian.*

"Mr. Josiah Smith possesses, in an eminent degree, that kind of logical skill which exhibits itself in the simple arrangement, but exhaustive division, of wide and complicated subjects, and is, moreover, gifted with the rare power of accurate condensation."—*Solicitors' Journal.*

"To more advanced students, and to the practitioner, whether barrister or attorney, we think the 'Manual of Common Law' a most useful and convenient companion. . . . . It is compiled with the scrupulous care and the ability which distinguish Mr. Smith's previous works."—*Jurist.*

"Smith's Manuals of Common Law and Equity must be resorted to as the open sesames to the learning requisite in the Final Examination of the Incorporated Law Society."—*From* Dr. ROLLIT's *Lecture*, p. 11.

COMMONS AND INCLOSURES.—Chambers' Digest of the Law relating to Commons and Open Spaces. —Including Public Parks and Recreation Grounds; with Official Documents, Bye-Laws, Statutes and Cases. By GEORGE F. CHAMBERS, of the Inner Temple, Esq., Barrister-at-Law. Imperial 8vo. 1877. (*Nearly ready.*) 6*s.* 6*d.*

Cooke on Inclosures.—The Acts for facilitating the Inclosure of Commons in England and Wales; with a Treatise on the Law of Rights of Commons, in reference to these Acts, &c., &c. With Forms as settled by the Inclosure Commissioners. By G. WINGROVE COOKE, Esq., Barrister-at-Law. Fourth Edition. 12mo. 1864. 16*s.*

COMPANY LAW.—*Vide* "Joint Stocks."

COMPANY PRECEDENTS.—Palmer.—*Vide* "Conveyancing."

CONSTITUTIONAL LAW.—Bowyer's Commentaries on the Constitutional Law of England.—By Sir GEORGE BOWYER, D.C.L. Second Edition. Royal 8vo. 1846. 1*l.* 2*s.*

CONTRACTS.—Addison on Contracts.—Being a Treatise on the Law of Contracts. By C. G. ADDISON, Esq., Author of the "Law of Torts." Seventh Edition. By L. W. CAVE, Esq., one of Her Majesty's Counsel, Recorder of Lincoln. Royal 8vo. 1875. 1*l.* 18*s.*

"At present this is by far the best book upon the Law of Contract possessed by the Profession, and it is a thoroughly practical book."—*Law Times.*

"We cannot speak too highly of the great amount of well-arranged information which is to be found in this second book. It is a magazine of learning which the legal practitioner will find of very great value."—*Solicitors' Journal*, March 20, 1875.

"Mr. Cave's edition of Addison must prove a great acquisition to every lawyer's library." —*Law Times*, April 3, 1875.

Leake on Contracts.—The Elements of the Law of Contracts. Second Edition. By STEPHEN MARTIN LEAKE, of the Middle Temple, Barrister-at-Law. (*Preparing for publication*).

Pollock's Principles of Contract at Law and in Equity; being a Treatise on the General Principles relating to the Validity of Agreements, with a special view to the comparison of Law and Equity, and with references to the Indian Contract Act, and occasionally to American and Foreign Law. By FREDERICK POLLOCK, of Lincoln's Inn, Esq., Barrister-at-Law. 8vo. 1876. 1*l.* 4*s.*

The Lord Chief Justice in his judgment in *Metropolitan Railway Company* v. *Brogden and others*, said, "The Law is well put by Mr. Frederick Pollock in his very able and learned work on Contracts."—*The Times*, February 19, 1877.

"He has succeeded in writing a book on Contracts which the working lawyer will find as useful for reference as any of its predecessors, and which at the same time will give the student what he will seek for in vain elsewhere, a complete *rationale* of the law."—*Law Magazine and Review*, August, 1876.

"Mr. Pollock's work ought, in our opinion, to take a high place among treatises of its class. The 'fusion of law and equity' so far as that fusion is possible, is in his pages an accomplished fact."—*Pall Mall Gazette*, March 3, 1876.

"This is a work of undoubted merit. . . . . We can only regret that there is not more of such teaching about, bearing fruit similar to the book now before us. A prominent characteristic especially valuable at the present time is that the principles of equity are read in with what used to be common law principles, and we have, therefore, in this one volume, the law relating to Contracts as administered by the Supreme Court of Judicature under the Judicature Acts."—*Law Times*, Feb. 12, 1876.

"A work which, in our opinion, shows great ability, a discerning intellect, a comprehensive mind, and painstaking industry. The book ought to be a success.'—*Law Journal*, March 18, 1876.

"There is no part of the work that does not please us by the freshness of the style and the ingenuity of the treatment. The author may be congratulated on having achieved a marked success in a field where others before him have written well."—*Solicitors' Journal*, April 8, 1876.

*** *All standard Law Works are kept in Stock in law calf and other bindings.*

CONTRACTS,—*Continued.*

Smith's Law of Contracts.—By the late J. W. SMITH, Esq., Author of "Leading Cases," &c. Sixth Edition. By VINCENT T. THOMPSON, Esq., Barrister-at-Law. 8vo. 1874. 16*s.*

CONVEYANCING.—**Greenwood's Manual of Conveyancing.**—A Manual of the Practice of Conveyancing, showing the present Practice relating to the daily routine of Conveyancing in Solicitors' Offices. To which are added Concise Common Forms and Precedents in Conveyancing; Conditions of Sale, Conveyances, and all other Assurances in constant use. Fifth Edition. By H. N. CAPEL, B.A., LL.B., Solicitor. Demy 8vo. 1877. 15*s.*

"The information under these heads is just of that ordinary practical kind which is learned from experience and is not to be gathered from treatises. . . . A careful study of these pages would probably arm a diligent clerk with as much useful knowledge as he might otherwise take years of desultory questioning and observing to acquire."—*Solicitors' Journal.*

"We believe that the present edition will be found by articled clerks and young solicitors a trustworthy guide to the present practice relating to the daily routine of conveyancing in solicitors' offices."—*Law Magazine and Review*, August, 1876.

"The young solicitor will find this work almost invaluable, while the members of the higher branch of the profession may refer to it with advantage. We have not met with any book that furnishes so simple a guide to the management of business entrusted to articled clerks."—*Sheffield Post.*

Martin's Student's Conveyancer.—A Manual on the Principles of Modern Conveyancing, illustrated and enforced by a Collection of Precedents, accompanied by detailed Remarks. Part I. Purchase Deeds. By THOMAS FREDERIC MARTIN, Solicitor. Demy 8vo. 1877. 5*s.* 6*d.*

Palmer's Company Precedents.—Conveyancing and other Forms and Precedents relating to Companies' incorporated under the Companies' Acts, 1862 and 1867. Arranged as follows:—Agreements, Memoranda of Association, Articles of Association, Resolutions, Notices, Certificates, Provisional Orders of Board of Trade, Debentures, Reconstruction, Amalgamation, Petitions, Orders. With Copious Notes. By FRANCIS BEAUFORT PALMER, of the Inner Temple, Esq., Barrister-at-Law. Demy 8vo. 1877. 1*l.* 5*s.*

"The compilation and arrangement of the subjects treated, appear to have been dealt with most exhaustively . . . a most copious index accompanies the work."—May 5, 1877.

Prideaux's Precedents in Conveyancing.—With Dissertations on its Law and Practice. Eighth Edition. By FREDERICK PRIDEAUX, late Professor of Real and Personal Property to the Inns of Court, and JOHN WHITCOMBE, Esqrs., Barristers-at-Law. 2 vols. Royal 8vo. 1876. 3*l.* 10*s.*

"Prideaux has become an indispensable part of the Conveyancer's library. . . . The new edition has been edited with a care and accuracy of which we can hardly speak too highly. . . . . The care and completeness with which the dissertation has been revised leaves us hardly any room for criticisms."—*Solicitors' Journal*, Oct 14, 1876.

"We really can hardly imagine a conveyancer being required to prepare any instrument which he will not find sketched out in the work under notice. . . . . We may also be allowed to add our tribute of praise to these Precedents for their conciseness perspicuity, precision, and perfection of drafting."—*Law Journal*. Sept. 23, 1876.

"The effect of the recent cases is in every instance that we have examined them remarkably well stated, and Prideaux's Precedents retains its reputation as a valuable repertory of law on the subject of conveyancing."—*Law Times*, October 28, 1876.

CONVICTIONS.—**Paley on Summary Convictions.**—Fifth Edition. By H. T. J. MACNAMARA, Esq., Barrister-at-Law. 8vo. 1866. 1*l.* 1*s.*

"A good, practical, and valuable treatise, which we can safely recommend to the profession."—*The Law Journal.*

"'Paley on Convictions' has enjoyed a high reputation and extensive popularity. No better man could have been found for such a work than Mr. Macnamara."—*Law Times.*

Stone.—*Vide* "Petty Sessions."

*** *All standard Law Works are kept in Stock, in law calf and other bindings.*

COPYRIGHT.—**Phillips' Law of Copyright.**—The Law of Copyright in Works of Literature and Art, and in the Application of Designs. With the Statutes relating thereto. By CHARLES PALMER PHILLIPS, of Lincoln's Inn, Esq., Barrister-at-Law. 8vo. 1863. 12*s*

"Mr. Phillips' work is at once an able law-book and a lucid treatise, in a popular form, on the rights of authors and artists."—*Jurist.*

CORONERS.—**Jervis on the Office and Duties of Coroners.**—With Forms and Precedents. Third Edition. By C. W. LOVESY, of the Middle Temple, Esq. 12mo. 1866. 12*s.*

COSTS.—**Carew's Precedents of Bills of Costs,** for obtaining Grants of Probate and Letters of Administration in the Principal Registry of the Court of Probate. 1869. 5*s.*

Morgan and Davey's Treatise on Costs in Chancery.—By GEORGE OSBORNE MORGAN, M.A., Barrister-at-Law, late Stowell Fellow of University College, Oxford, and Eldon Scholar; and HORACE DAVEY, M.A., Barrister-at-Law, late Fellow of University College, Oxford, and Eldon Scholar. With an Appendix, containing Forms and Precedents of Bills of Costs. 8vo. 1865. 1*l.* 1*s.*

Morris' Solicitors' Fees and Court Fees, under the Judicature Acts.—With Copious Index. By WILLIAM MORRIS, Solicitor. 12mo. 1876. 4*s.*

Scott's Costs in the Superior Courts of Common Law, and Probate and Divorce, and in Conveyancing; also in Bankruptcy (Act of 1869). Proceedings in the Crown Office, on Circuit and at Sessions, and in the County Court, &c. With an Appendix, containing Costs under Parliamentary Elections Act, 1868. By JOHN SCOTT, of the Inner Temple, Esq., Barrister-at-Law. Third Edition. Royal 12mo. 1868-73. 1*l.* 4*s.*

*** The Supplement, containing "Bankruptcy Costs (Act of 1869)," may be had separately. *Net,* 3*s.*

"Mr Scott's work is well known to the profession. It is an extensive collection of taxed bills of costs in all branches of practice, supplied to him probably by the taxing masters. Such a work speaks for itself. Its obvious utility is its best recommendation."—*Law Times.*

Scott's Costs under the Judicature Acts, 1873 and 1875; containing the "Additional Rules" and Scale of Costs; together with PRECEDENTS OF TAXED BILLS. By JOHN SCOTT, Esq., Barrister-at-Law. Royal 12mo. 1876. 5*s.* 6*d.*

Summerhays and Toogood's Precedents of Bills of Costs in the Chancery, Queen's Bench, Common Pleas, Exchequer, Probate and Divorce Divisions of the High Court of Justice, in Conveyancing, Bankruptcy, &c., with Scales of Allowances and Court Fees, &c., &c. Royal 8vo. 1877. 8*s.* 6*d.*

Webster's Parliamentary Costs.—Private Bills, Election Petitions, Appeals, House of Lords. By EDWARD WEBSTER, Esq., of the Taxing Office, House of Commons, and of the Examiners' Office, House of Lords and House of Commons. Third Edition. Post 8vo. 1867. 20*s.*

"The object of this work is to give the scale of costs allowed to Solicitors in relation to private bills before Parliament, the conduct of Election Petitions and Appeal Causes, and the allowance to Witnesses. The connection of the author with the Taxing Office of the House of Commons gives authority to the work."—*Solicitors' Journal.*

**** All standard Law Works are kept in Stock, in law calf and other bindings.*

COUNTY COURTS.—**The Consolidated County Court Orders and Rules, 1875, with Forms and Scales of Costs and Fees,** as issued by the Lord Chancellor and Committee of County Court Judges. Authorized Edition. Super-royal 8vo. 1875. *Net*, 3*s*.

County Court Rules, 1876. Authorised Edition. *Net*, 6*d*.

Pitt-Lewis' County Court Practice.—A Complete Manual of the Practice of the County Courts, including Admiralty and Bankruptcy, embodying the Act, Rules, Forms and Costs, with Table of Cases and Full Index. By G. PITT-LEWIS, of the Middle Temple and Western Circuit, Esq., Barrister-at-Law, sometime Holder of the Studentships of the Four Inns of Court. (*In preparation.*)

CRIMINAL LAW.—**Archbold's Pleading and Evidence in Criminal Cases.**—With the Statutes, Precedents of Indictments, &c., and the Evidence necessary to support them. By JOHN JERVIS, Esq. (late Lord Chief Justice of Her Majesty's Court of Common Pleas). Eighteenth Edition, including the Practice in Criminal Proceedings by Indictment. By WILLIAM BRUCE, of the Middle Temple, Esq., Barrister-at-Law, and Stipendiary Magistrate for the Borough of Leeds. Royal 12mo. 1875. 1*l*. 11*s*. 6*d*.

Cole on Criminal Informations and Quo Warranto.—By W. R. COLE, Esq., Barrister-at-Law. 12mo. 1843. 12*s*.

Greaves' Criminal Law Consolidation and Amendment Acts of the 24 & 25 Vict.—With Notes, Observations, and Forms for Summary Proceedings. By CHARLES SPRENGEL GREAVES, Esq., one of Her Majesty's Counsel, who prepared the Bills and attended the Select Committees of both Houses of Parliament to which the Bills were referred. Second Edition. Post 8vo. 1862. 16*s*.

Roscoe's Digest of the Law of Evidence in Criminal Cases.—Eighth Edition. By HORACE SMITH, Esq., Barrister-at-Law. Royal 12mo. 1874. 1*l*. 11*s*. 6*d*.

Russell's Treatise on Crimes and Misdemeanors.—Fifth Edition. By SAMUEL PRENTICE, Esq., one of Her Majesty's Counsel. 3 vols. Royal 8vo. 1877. 5*l*. 15*s*. 6*d*.

'We may safely assert that the fifth edition of 'Russell on Crimes' has, under the careful hand of Mr. Prentice, fully reached the standard attained to by the preceding editions." —*Law Journal*, January 27, 1877.

"No more trustworthy authority, or more exhaustive expositor than 'Russell' can be consulted."—*Law Magazine and Review*, February, 1877.

"Alterations have been made in the arrangement of the work which without interfering with the general plan are sufficient to show that great care and thought have been bestowed. . . . . We are amazed at the patience, industry and skill which are exhibited in the collection and arrangement of all this mass of learning."—*The Times*, Dec. 26, 1876.

This treatise is so much more copious than any other upon all the subjects contained in it, that it affords by far the best means of acquiring a knowledge of the Criminal Law in general, or of any offence in particular; so that it will be found peculiarly useful as well to those who wish to obtain a complete knowledge of that law, as to those who desire to be informed on any portion of it as occasion may require.

This work also contains a very complete treatise on the Law of Evidence in Criminal Cases, and in it the manner of taking the depositions of witnesses, and the examinations of prisoners before magistrates, is fully explained.

"What better Digest of Criminal Law could we possibly hope for than 'Russell on Crimes?' "—*Sir James Fitzjames Stephen's Speech on Codification.*

*** *All standard Law Works are kept in Stock, in law calf and other bindings.*

DECREES.—Seton.—*Vide* "Equity."

DIARY.—Lawyer's Companion (The), Diary, and Law Directory.—For the use of the Legal Profession, Public Companies, Justices, Merchants, Estate Agents, Auctioneers, &c., &c. PUBLISHED ANNUALLY. Thirty-first Issue for 1877.

The Work is 8vo. size, strongly bound in cloth, and published at the following Prices :—

		s.	d.
1.	Two days on a page, plain	5	0
2.	The above, INTERLEAVED for ATTENDANCES	7	0
3.	Two days on a page, ruled, with or without money columns	5	6
4.	The above, INTERLEAVED for ATTENDANCES	8	0
5.	Whole page for each day, plain	7	6
6.	The above, INTERLEAVED for ATTENDANCES	9	6
7.	Whole page for each day, ruled, with or without money columns	8	6
8.	The above, INTERLEAVED for ATTENDANCES	10	6
9.	Three days on a page, ruled blue lines, without money columns	5	0

The Diary is printed on JOYNSON'S paper of superior quality, and contains memoranda of Legal Business throughout the Year.

The Lawyer's Companion for 1877.—Is edited by JOHN THOMPSON, of the Inner Temple, Esq., Barrister-at-Law; and contains a Digest of Recent Cases on Costs; Monthly Diary of County, Local Government, and Parish Business; Forms of Jurat; Summary of Legislation of 1876; Alphabetical Index to the Practical Statutes; a Copious Table of Stamp Duties; Legal Time, Interest, Discount, Income, Wages and other Tables; Probate, Legacy and Succession Duties; a London and Provincial Law Directory, and a variety of matters of practical utility.

"A publication which has long ago secured to itself the favour of the profession, and which, as heretofore, justifies by its contents the title assumed by it. The new volume presents all the attractive features of its predecessors, combined with much matter compiled specially for the coming year."—*Law Journal*, Nov. 4, 1876.

"The present issue contains all the information which could be looked for in such a work, and gives it in a most convenient form and very completely. We may unhesitatingly recommend the work to our readers."—*Solicitors' Journal*, Nov. 25, 1876.

"The 'Lawyer's Companion and Diary' is a book that ought to be in the possession of every lawyer, and of every man of business."

"The 'Lawyer's Companion' is, indeed, what it is called, for it combines everything required for reference in the lawyer's office."—*Law Times*.

DICTIONARY.—Wharton's Law Lexicon.—A Dictionary of Jurisprudence, explaining the Technical Words and Phrases employed in the several Departments of English Law; including the various Legal Terms used in Commercial Transactions. Together with an Explanatory as well as Literal Translation of the Latin Maxims contained in the Writings of the Ancient and Modern Commentators. Sixth Edition. Enlarged and revised in accordance with the Judicature Acts, by J. SHIRESS WILL, of the Middle Temple, Esq., Barrister-at-Law. Super royal 8vo. 1876. 2*l*. 2*s*.

"As a work of reference for the library, the handsome and elaborate edition of 'Wharton's Law Lexicon' which Mr. Shiress Will has produced, must supersede all former issues of that well-known work."—*Law Magazine and Review*, August, 1876.

"No law library is complete without a law dictionary or law lexicon. To the practitioner it is always useful to have at hand a book where, in a small compass, he can find an explanation of terms of infrequent occurrence, or obtain a reference to statutes on most subjects, or to books wherein particular subjects are treated of at full length. To the student it is almost indispensable." [*Continued*.

*** *All standard Law Works are kept in Stock, in law calf and other bindings.*

DICTIONARY.—Wharton's Law Lexicon.—*Continued.*

"We have simply to notice that the same ability and accuracy mark the present edition which were conspicuous in its predecessor. Mr. Will has done all that was rendered necessary by the Judicature Acts, in the shape of incorporation and elimination, and has brought the Statute Law down to the date of publication."—*Law Times*, March 4, 1876.

"We have been at the pains of perusing many words or titles in the Lexicon which seemed likely to contain the results of recent legislation, and we have been led by that perusal to the conclusion that Mr. Will has performed this part of his task with skill and care."—*Law Journal*, March 18, 1876.

"Wharton's perennial Law Lexicon has just been adapted to the new condition of the Law, brought about by the Judicature Act. The task of revision has been ably performed by Mr. Shiress Will."—*Saturday Review*, April 15, 1876.

DIGESTS.—Bedford.—*Vide* "Examination Guides."

Chamber's—*Vide* "Public Health."

Chitty's Equity Index.—Chitty's Index to all the Reported Cases, and Statutes, in or relating to the Principles, Pleading, and Practice of Equity and Bankruptcy, in the several Courts of Equity in England and Ireland, the Privy Council, and the House of Lords, from the earliest period. Third Edition. By J. MACAULAY, Esq., Barrister-at-Law. 4 vols. Royal 8vo. 1853. *7l. 7s.*

Fisher's Digest of the Reported Cases determined in the House of Lords and Privy Council, and in the Courts of Common Law, Divorce, Probate, Admiralty and Bankruptcy, from Michaelmas Term, 1756, to Hilary Term, 1870; with References to the Statutes and Rules of Court. Founded on the Analytical Digest by Harrison, and adapted to the present practice of the Law. By R. A. FISHER, Esq., Judge of the County Courts of Bristol and of Wells. Five large volumes, royal 8vo. 1870. *12l. 12s.*

(*Continued Annually.*)

"Mr. Fisher's Digest is a wonderful work. It is a miracle of human industry."—*Mr. Justice Willes.*

"The fact is, that we have already the best of all possible digests. I do not refer merely to the works which pass under that title—though, I confess, I think it would be very difficult to improve upon Mr. Fisher's 'Common Law Digest'—I refer to the innumerable text books of every branch of the law. What better digest of criminal law could we possibly hope for than 'Russell on Crimes,' and the current Roscoe and Archbold, to say nothing of the title, 'Criminal Law,' in 'Fisher's Digest.'"—*Sir James Fitzjames Stephen, Q. C., in his Address to the Law Amendment Society on Codification in India and England, Session* 1872-3.

Leake.—*Vide* "Real Property."

Notanda Digest in Law, Equity, Bankruptcy, Admiralty, Divorce, and Probate Cases.—By H. TUDOR BODDAM, of the Inner Temple, and HARRY GREENWOOD, of Lincoln's Inn, Esqrs., Barristers-at-Law. The NOTANDA DIGEST, from the commencement, December, 1862, to October, 1876. In 1 volume, half-bound. *Net*, *3l. 3s.*

Ditto, in 2 volumes, half-bound. *Net*, *3l. 10s.*

Ditto, Third Series, 1873 to 1876 inclusive, half-bound. *Net*, *1l. 11s. 6d.*

Ditto, for 1876, with Indexes, sewed. *Net*, *12s. 6d.*

Ditto, Fourth Series, Plain Copy and Two Indexes, or Adhesive Copy for insertion in Text-Books.

Annual Subscription, payable in advance. *Net*, *21s.*

*** The Cases under the Judicature Acts and Rules of Court commence in No. 4 of 1876. The numbers are now issued regularly every alternate month. Each number will contain a concise analysis of every case reported in the *Law Reports*, *Law Journal*, *Weekly*

DIGESTS.—*Continued.*

Reporter, *Law Times*, and the *Irish Law Reports*, up to and including the cases contained in the parts for the current month, with references to Text-books, Statutes, and the Law Reports Consolidated Digest. An ALPHABETICAL INDEX of the subjects contained IN EACH NUMBER will form a new feature in this series.

Pollock.—*Vide* "Partnership."

Roscoe's.—*Vide* "Criminal Law" and "Nisi Prius."

DISCOVERY.—Seton.—*Vide* "Equity."

DIVORCE.—Browne's Treatise on the Principles and Practice of the Court for Divorce and Matrimonial Causes:—With the Statutes, Rules, Fees, and Forms relating thereto. Third Edition. By GEORGE BROWNE, Esq., B.A., of the Inner Temple, Barrister-at-Law. 8vo. 1876. 1*l.* 4*s.*

"We think this Edition of Mr. Browne's Treatise has been edited with commendable care. The book, as it now stands, is a clear, practical, and, so far as we have been able to test it, accurate exposition of divorce law and procedure."—*Solicitors' Journal*, April 22, 1876

Macqueen on Divorce and Matrimonial Causes.—Including Scotch Marriages and Scotch Law of Divorce, &c. With numerous Precedents. Second Edition, greatly enlarged. By JOHN FRASER MACQUEEN, Esq., Barrister-at-Law. 8vo. 1860. 18*s.*

DOMICIL.—Phillimore's (Dr. R.) Law of Domicil.—8vo. 1847. 9*s.*

DUTCH LAW.—Vanderlinden's Institutes of the Laws of Holland.—8vo. 1828. 1*l.* 18*s.*

EASEMENTS.—Goddard's Treatise on the Law of Easements.—By JOHN LEYBOURN GODDARD, of the Middle Temple, Esq., Barrister-at-Law. Second Edition. Demy 8vo. 1877. 16*s.*

*** The Author was appointed by Her Majesty's Digest of Law Commissioners to prepare a specimen Digest of the Law of Easements.

"Nowhere has the subject been treated so exhaustively, and, we may add, so scientifically, as by Mr. Goddard. We recommend it to the most careful study of the law student, as well as to the library of the practitioner."—*Law Times*

Woolrych.—*Vide* "Lights."

ECCLESIASTICAL.—Phillimore's (Sir R.) Ecclesiastical Law.—The Ecclesiastical Law of the Church of England. With Supplement, containing the Statutes and Decisions to end of 1875. By SIR ROBERT PHILLIMORE, D.C.L., Official Principal of the Arches Court of Canterbury; Member of Her Majesty's Most Honourable Privy Council. 2 vols. 8vo. 1873-76. 3*l.* 7*s.* 6*d.*

*** The Supplement may be had separately, price 4*s.* 6*d.*, sewed.

Rogers' Ecclesiastical Law.—Second Edition. 8vo. 1849. 1*l.* 16*s.*

Stephens.—*Vide* "Church and Clergy."

ELECTIONS.—FitzGerald.—*Vide* "Ballot."

Rogers on Elections, Registration, and Election Agency.—With an Appendix of Statutes and Forms. Twelfth Edition. By F. S. P. WOLFERSTAN, of the Inner Temple, Esq., Barrister-at-Law. 12mo. 1876. 1*l.* 10*s.*

"The book maintains its reputation as a well arranged magazine of all the authorities on the subject."—*Law Journal*, August 19, 1876.

"Mr. Wolferstan has added a new chapter on election agency, which contains a careful and valuable digest of the decisions and dicta on this thorny subject."—*Solicitors' Journal*, October 28, 1876.

*** *All standard Law Works are kept in Stock, in law calf and other bindings.*

ENGLAND, LAWS OF.—Bowyer.—*Vide* "Constitutional Law."

Broom and Hadley.—*Vide* "Commentaries."

Syms' Code of English Law (Principles and Practice) for handy reference in a Solicitor's office. By F. R. SYMS, Solicitor. 12mo. 1870. 16*s.*

EQUITY, *and Vide* **CHANCERY.**

Seton's Forms of Decrees, Judgments, and Orders in the High Court of Justice and Courts of Appeal, having especial reference to the Chancery Division, with Practical Notes. Fourth Edition. By R. H. LEACH, Esq., Senior Registrar of the Court of Chancery; F. G. A. WILLIAMS, of the Inner Temple, Esq.; and H. W. MAY, of Lincoln's Inn, Esq., Barristers-at-Law. In 2 vols. Vol. I. Royal 8vo. 1877. 1*l.* 10*s.*

"This Volume contains Judgment by Default and at Trial; Motion for Judgment; Transfer and Payment of Funds into and out of Court; Proceedings in Chambers; Discovery and Production; Injunctions; Stop Orders and Charging Orders; *Ne Exeat* Attachment of Debts; Transfer and Consolidation of Actions; Prohibition Patents; Interpleader; Issues; Referees and Arbitration Receivers; Trustees (including Trustees Act); Charities; Orders affecting Solicitors; and Taxation of Bills of Costs, &c., &c.

"Cannot fail to commend itself to practitioners. Nothing need be said as to the value of the work, which is one of settled authority, and we have only to congratulate the profession upon the fact that this edition comes out under circumstances peculiarly calculated to enhance its value."—*Law Times,* February 24, 1877.

"The impression derived from our perusal of the book is that it represents the result of conscientious and intelligent labour on the part of the editors, and we think it deserves, and will obtain, the confidence of the profession."—*Solicitors' Journal,* April 7, 1877.

(*Vol. II. in the press.*)

Smith's Manual of Equity Jurisprudence.—A Manual of Equity Jurisprudence founded on the Works of Story, Spence, and other writers, and on the subsequent cases, comprising the Fundamental Principles and the points of Equity usually occurring in General Practice. By JOSIAH W. SMITH, B.C.L., Q.C., Judge of County Courts. Eleventh Edition. 12mo. 1873. 12*s.* 6*d.*

"To sum up all in a word, for the student and the jurisconsult, the Manual is the nearest approach to an equity code that the present literature of the law is able to furnish."—*Law Times.*

"It will be found as useful to the practitioner as to the student."—*Solicitors' Journal.*

"Mr. Smith's Manual has fairly won for itself the position of a standard work."—*Jurist.*

"It retains and that deservedly, the reverence of both examiners and students."—*From a Lecture on a Course of Reading by* A. K. ROLLIT, *LL.D., Gold Medallist of the University of London, and Prizeman of the Incorporated Law Society.*

"There is no disguising the truth; the proper mode to use this book is to learn its pages by heart."—*Law Magazine and Review.*

Smith's (Sidney) Principles of Equity.—8vo. 1856. 1*l.* 5*s.*

EVIDENCE.—Archbold.—*Vide* "Criminal."

Roscoe.—*Vide* "Criminal."

Roscoe.—*Vide* "Nisi Prius."

EXAMINATION GUIDES.—Bedford's Guide to the Preliminary Examination for Solicitors.—Fourth Edition. 12mo. 1874. *Net,* 3*s.*

Bedford's Digest of the Preliminary Examination Questions on English and Latin, Grammar, Geography, History, French Grammar, and Arithmetic, with the Answers. 8vo. 1875. 18*s.*

Bedford's Preliminary Guide to Latin Grammar.—12mo. 1872. *Net,* 3*s.*

Bedford's Intermediate Examination Guide to Bookkeeping.—Second Edition. 12mo. 1875. *Net,* 2*s.* 6*d.*

Bedford's Final Examination Guide to Bankruptcy.—Second Edition. 12mo. 1873. 4*s.*

*** *All standard Law Works are kept in Stock, in law calf and other bindings.*

EXAMINATION GUIDES.—*Continued.*

The following are published the day after each Examination :—

Bedford's Preliminary.—Containing the Questions of the Preliminary Examinations. Edited by E. H. BEDFORD, Solicitor. Sewed. *Net,* 1s.

Bedford's Intermediate and Final.—Containing the Questions and Answers at the Intermediate and Final Examinations. Edited by E. H. BEDFORD, Solicitor. Sewed. *Each, net,* 6*d.*

Butlin.—*Vide* "Articled Clerks."

Lynch.—*Vide* "Bankruptcy," "Judicature Acts," and "Statutes."

Lynch and Smith.—*Vide* "Judicature Acts."

Rubinstein and Ward.—*Vide* "Articled Clerks."

EXECUTORS.—**Williams' Law of Executors and Administrators.**—A Treatise on the Law of Executors and Administrators. Seventh Edition. By the Rt. Hon. Sir EDWARD VAUGHAN WILLIAMS, late one of the Judges of Her Majesty's Court of Common Pleas, and WALTER VAUGHAN WILLIAMS, Esq., Barrister-at-Law. 2 vols. Royal 8vo. 1873. 3*l.* 16*s.*

FACTORY ACTS.—**Notcutt's Factory and Workshop Acts.**—Comprising all the Laws now in force (including the Act of 1874) for the regulation of Labour in Factories and Workshops, with Introduction, Explanatory Notes, and Notes of decided cases, by GEORGE JARVIS NOTCUTT, of the Middle Temple, Esq., Barrister-at-Law. 12mo. 1874. 9*s.*

FARM, LAW OF.—**Addison; Cooke.**—*Vide* "Agricultural Law."

Dixon's Law of the Farm.—A Treatise on the Law of the Farm. Fourth Edition. By HENRY PERKINS, of the Inner Temple, Esq., Barrister-at-Law. (*In the Press.*)

FIXTURES.—**Amos and Ferard on Fixtures.**—Second Edition. Royal 8vo. 1847. 16*s.*

Woodfall.—*See* "Landlord and Tenant."

FORMS.—**Chitty's Forms.** Eleventh Edition. By THOMAS CHITTY, Esq. (*In preparation.*)

Corner's Forms of Writs and other Proceedings on the Crown side of the Court of Queen's Bench.—8vo. 1844. 7*s.* 6*d.*

Daniell's Chancery Forms.—Forms and Precedents of Pleadings and Proceedings in the High Court of Chancery, with Practical Notes and Observations, and References to the Fourth Edition of Daniell's Chancery Practice; and incorporating the Forms in Braithwaite's Record and Writ Practice. By LEONARD FIELD and EDWARD CLENNELL DUNN, Barristers-at-Law, and JOHN BIDDLE, of the Master of the Rolls' Chambers. Second Edition. By JOHN BIDDLE. 8vo. 1871. 1*l.* 12*s.*

Moore's Solicitor's Book of Practical Forms.—12mo. 1852. 7*s.* 6*d.*

Palmer.—*Vide* "Conveyancing."

Seton.—*Vide* "Equity."

HEALTH.—*Vide* "Public Health."

HIGHWAYS.—**Bateman's General Highway Acts.**—Second Edition. By W. N. WELSBY, Esq. With a Supplement containing the Highway Act of 1864, &c. With Notes and a Revised Index by C. MANLEY SMITH, of the Inner Temple, Esq., Barrister-at-Law. 12mo. 1865. 10*s.* 6*d.*

HIGHWAYS.—*Continued.*

Shelford's Law of Highways.—The Law of Highways; including the General Highway Acts for England and Wales, and other Statutes, with copious Notes of the Decisions thereon; with Forms. The Third Edition. With Supplement by C. MANLEY SMITH, Esq., Barrister-at-Law. 12mo. 1865. 15*s.*

*** The Supplement may be had separately, price 3*s.* sewed.

INCLOSURES.—*Vide* "Commons."

INDIAN LAW.—**Montriou; the Hindu Will of Bengal.** With an Introductory Essay, &c. Royal 8vo. 1870. *Net,* 1*l.* 10*s.*

Norton's Law of Evidence applicable to India. By JOHN BRUCE NORTON, late Advocate-General of Madras. Ninth Edition. (*In the press.*)

Norton's Leading Cases on the Hindu Law of Inheritance.—2 vols. Royal 8vo. 1870-71. *Net,* 2*l.* 10*s.*

INFANTS.—**Ebsworth's Law of Infants.**—A Handy Book of the Law of Infants. By JOHN EBSWORTH, Esq., Solicitor. 12mo. 1861. 3*s.*

Forsyth's Law relating to the Custody of Infants in Cases of difference between Parents or Guardians.—8vo. 1850. 8*s.*

INJUNCTIONS.—**Seton.**—*Vide* "Equity."

INSURANCE.—**Arnould on the Law of Marine Insurance.**—Fourth Edition. By DAVID MACLACHLAN, Esq., Barrister-at-Law. 2 vols. Royal 8vo. 1872. 2*l.* 12*s.* 6*d.*

Hopkins' Manual of Marine Insurance.—8vo. 1867. 18*s.*

Lowndes.—*Vide* "Average."

INTERNATIONAL LAW.—**Amos' Lectures on International Law.**—Delivered in the Middle Temple Hall to the Students of the Inns of Court, by SHELDON AMOS, M.A., of the Inner Temple, Barrister-at-Law; Professor of Jurisprudence (including International Law) to the Inns of Court; Professor of Jurisprudence in University College, London. Royal 8vo. 1874. 10*s.* 6*d.*

Kent's International Law.—Kent's Commentary on International Law, Revised, with Notes and Cases brought down to the present time. Edited by J. T. ABDY, LL.D., Judge of County Courts. Second Edition. (*In the press.*)

"Dr. Abdy has done all Law Students a great service in presenting that portion of Kent's Commentaries which relates to public international Law in a single volume, neither large, diffuse, nor expensive."

"Altogether Dr. Abdy has performed his task in a manner worthy of his reputation His book will be useful not only to Lawyers and Law Students, for whom it was primarily intended, but also for laymen. It is well worth the study of every member of an enlightened and civilized community."—*Solicitors' Journal,* March 15, 1867.

Levi's International Commercial Law.—Being the Principles of Mercantile Law of the following and other Countries—viz.: England, Ireland, Scotland, British India, British Colonies, Austria, Belgium, Brazil, Buenos Ayres, Denmark, France, Germany, Greece, Hans Towns, Italy, Netherlands, Norway, Portugal, Prussia, Russia, Spain, Sweden, Switzerland, United States, and Würtemberg. By LEONE LEVI, Esq., F.S.A., F.S.S., of Lincoln's Inn, Barrister-at-Law, Professor of the Principles and Practice of Commerce at King's College, London, &c. Second Edition. 2 vols. Royal 8vo. 1863. 1*l.* 15*s.*

INTERNATIONAL LAW.—*Continued.*

Prize Essays on International Law—By A. P. SPRAGUE, Esq., Counsellor of Law in the United States, and M. PAUL LACOMBE, Advocate in France. With an Introduction by His Excellency DON ARTURO DE MARCOARTU, Ex-Deputy to the Cortes. Royal 8vo. 1876. 7*s.* 6*d.*

Vattel's Law of Nations.—A New Edition. By JOSEPH CHITTY, Esq. Royal 8vo. 1834. 1*l.* 1*s.*

Wildman's International Law.—Institutes of International Law, in Time of Peace and Time of War. By RICHARD WILDMAN, Barrister-at-Law. 2 vols. 8vo. 1849-50. 1*l.* 2*s.* 6*d.*

INTESTATE SUCCESSIONS—Colin's Essay on Intestate Successions.—According to the French Code. By BARTHELEMY HARDY COLIN, of the Middle Temple. 12mo. 1876. 6*s.*

"A very intelligent essay."—*Law Times,* February 24, 1877.

JOINT STOCKS.—Jordan's Joint Stock Companies.—A Handy Book of Practical Instructions for the Formation and Management of Joint Stock Companies. Fifth Edition. 12mo. 1875. *Net,* 2*s.* 6*d.*

Palmer—*Vide* "Conveyancing."

Thring's (Sir H.) Joint Stock Companies' Law.—The Law and Practice of Joint Stock and other Public Companies, including the Statutes, with Notes, and the Forms required in Making, Administering, and Winding-up a Company, with a Supplement containing the Companies' Act, 1867, and Notes of Recent Decisions. By SIR HENRY THRING, K.C.B., The Parliamentary Counsel. Third Edition. By GERALD A. R. FITZGERALD, of Lincoln's Inn, Esq., Barrister-at-Law, and Fellow of St. John's College, Oxford. 12mo. 1875. 1*l.*

"This, as the work of the original draughtsman of the Companies Act of 1862, and well-known Parliamentary Counsel, Sir Henry Thring, is naturally the highest authority on the subject."—*The Times,* April 21, 1876.

JUDGMENTS.—Pask's Judgments, Executions, and Crown Debts.—The Judgments Law Amendment Acts relating to Real Property, 22 & 23 Vict., c. 35, and 23 & 24 Vict., c. 38, 23 & 24 Vict. c. 115, and 27 & 28 Vict. c. 112. With Notes, References to Cases, and Index: forming an Appendix to "The Practice of Registering," &c. By JAMES PASK, Chief Clerk to the Registrar to the Court of Common Pleas, Westminster. Third Edition. 12mo. 1866. Sewed. *Net,* 2*s.*

Seton.—*Vide* "Equity."

JUDICATURE ACTS.—Braithwaite.—*Vide* "Oaths."

Clowes' Compendious Index to the Supreme Court of Judicature Acts, and to the Orders and Rules issued thereunder. By W. CLOWES, Esq., one of the Registrars of the Court of Chancery. Second Edition, revised and enlarged. (*Uniform in size with the Queen's Printer's Edition of the Acts and Rules.*) 1875. *Half bound.* 10*s.* 6*d.*

*** THE ABOVE, with the Acts and Rules (Authorized Edition), Orders in Council, and additional rules, court fees, &c., COMPLETE IN ONE VOLUME, *bound in limp leather.* 1*l.* 5*s.*

*** *All standard Law Works are kept in Stock in law calf and other bindings.*

JUDICATURE ACTS.—*Continued.*

Leys' Complete Time-Table to the Rules under the Supreme Court of Judicature Act, 1875. Showing all the periods fixed by the Rules within or after which any proceedings may be taken. By JOHN KIRKWOOD LEYS, M.A., of the Middle Temple, Esq., Barrister-at-Law. Royal 8vo. 1875. *Net*, 1*s*. 6*d*.

Lynch and Smith's Introduction to the Final Examination.—Being a collection of the questions set by the Incorporated Law Society, with the answers adapted to meet the recent extensive alterations made by the JUDICATURE ACT, 1873. By H. FOULKS LYNCH, Solicitor, and ERNEST AUGUSTUS SMITH, Solicitor, Clifford's Inn, Prizeman; Senior Prizeman of the Incorporated Law Society, and Brodrip Gold Medalist, 1872. Vol. I. The Principles of the Law. Post 8vo. 1874. 12*s*.

Lynch's Epitome of Practice in the Supreme Court of Judicature in England. With References to Acts, Rules, and Orders. For the Use of Students. Royal 8vo. Third Edition. Incorporating the Appellate Jurisdiction Act, 1876, and the Rules of the Supreme Court, December, 1875, and June, 1876. 1876. *Net*, 1*s*.

Morgan.—*Vide* "Chancery."

Morris.—*Vide* "Costs."

Scott.—*Vide* "Costs."

Stephen's Judicature Acts 1873, 1874, and 1875, consolidated. With Notes and an Index. By Sir JAMES STEPHEN, one of Her Majesty's Counsel. 12mo. 1875. 4*s*. 6*d*.

Summerhays and Toogood.—*Vide* "Costs."

Wilson's Judicature Acts, Rules and Forms. With Notes and a copious Index, and additional Rules, forming a COMPLETE GUIDE TO THE NEW PRACTICE. By ARTHUR WILSON, of the Inner Temple, Esq., Barrister-at-Law. Royal 12mo. 1875. 18*s*.

(*Bound in limp leather for the pocket*, 22*s*. 6*d*., *or the same*, *Interleaved*, 25*s*.)

*** A LARGE PAPER EDITION OF THE ABOVE (for marginal notes), with Additional Rules. Royal 8vo. 1875. 1*l*. 5*s*. (*Bound in limp leather*, 1*l*. 10*s*.).

"The references are ample, and the description of the matter referred to is clear. The result of a very careful examination of Mr. Wilson's book is that it is executed with great care and thoroughness, and that it will be of the utmost value to all those on whom the task falls, whether as practitioners or as administrators of the law, of applying and adapting the new practice and procedure."—*Solicitors' Journal*, Oct. 23, 1875.

"We have nothing but praise to bestow upon the annotating of the rules. We have no doubt it will maintain a position in the front rank of the works upon the all-engrossing subject with which it deals."—*Law Times*, Oct. 16, 1875.

"Mr. Wilson has appended to the Acts and Rules, especially the latter, a valuable body of notes, which we are sure will be found useful."—*Law Journal*, Oct. 30, 1875.

"Mr. Arthur Wilson, as might have been expected, is particularly successful in dealing with the Rules of Court, to which, indeed, his notes are an almost indispensable accompaniment."—*Law Magazine*, Nov. 1875.

JURISPRUDENCE.—**Amos, Law as a Science and as an Art.**—An Introductory Lecture delivered at University College at the commencement of the session 1874-5. By SHELDON AMOS, Esq., M.A., Barrister-at-Law. 8vo. 1874. *Net*, 1*s*. 6*d*.

Phillimore's (J. G.) Jurisprudence.—An Inaugural Lecture on Jurisprudence, and a Lecture on Canon Law, delivered at the Hall of the Inner Temple, Hilary Term, 1851. By J. G. PHILLIMORE, Esq., Q.C. 8vo. 1851. Sewed. 3*s*. 6*d*.

JUSTICE OF THE PEACE.—Arnold's Summary of the Duties of a Justice of the Peace out of Sessions.—Summary Convictions. By Sir THOMAS JAMES ARNOLD, Chief Metropolitan Police Magistrate. 8vo. 1860. 1*l.* 6*s.*

Burn's Justice of the Peace and Parish Officer.—Edited by the following Barristers, under the General Superintendence of JOHN BLOSSETT MAULE, Esq., Q.C., Recorder of Leeds. The Thirtieth Edition. Vol. I. containing titles "Abatement" to "Dwellings for Artizans;" by THOS. SIRRELL PRITCHARD, of the Inner Temple, Esq. Vol. II. containing titles "Easter Offering" to "Hundred;" by SAML. BOTELER BRISTOWE, of the Inner Temple, Esq. Vol. III. containing titles "Indictment' to "Promissory Notes;" by LEWIS W. CAVE, of the Inner Temple, Esq. Vol. IV. containing the whole title "Poor;" by JAMES EDWD. DAVIS, Esq., Stipendiary Magistrate for Stoke-upon-Trent. (*Sold separately, price* 1*l.* 11*s.* 6*d.*) Vol. V. containing titles "Quo Warranto" to "Wreck;" by JOHN BLOSSETT MAULE, Esq., Q.C., Recorder of Leeds. Five vols. 8vo. 1869. 7*l.* 7*s.*

Since the publication in 1845 of the former Edition of *Burn's Justice of the Peace and Parish Officer* the whole range of the Law which Magistrates had to administer has undergone more or less alteration, and, indeed, the time which has elapsed since that publication appeared has doubtless worked as great a change in the Magistrates themselves: so that to very many of the Gentlemen now composing the body of Justices the Encyclopedic Work of Burn must be, if not entirely unknown, at least unfamiliar as a book of reference.

Paley.—*Vide* "Convictions."

Stone.—*Vide* "Petty Sessions."

JUSTINIAN, INSTITUTES OF.—Cumin.—*Vide* "Civil Law."
Greene.—*Vide* "Roman Law."
Mears.—*Vide* "Roman Law."
Voet.—*Vide* "Civil Law."

LAND DRAINAGE.—Thring's Land Drainage Act.—With an Introduction, Practical Notes, an Appendix of Statutes relating to Drainage, and Forms. By THEODORE THRING, Esq., Barrister-at-Law. 12mo. 1861. 7*s.*

LAND TAX.—Bourdin's Land Tax.—An Exposition of the Land Tax; its Assessment and Collection, with a statement of the rights conferred by the Redemption Acts. By MARK A. BOURDIN, of the Inland Revenue Office, Somerset House (late Registrar of Land Tax). Second Edition. Crown 8vo. 1870. 4*s.*

LANDLORD AND TENANT.—Woodfall's Law of Landlord and Tenant.—A Practical Treatise on the Law of Landlord and Tenant, with a full Collection of Precedents and Forms of Procedure. Tenth Edition. By W. R. COLE, Esq., Barrister-at-Law. Royal 8vo. 1871. *Net,* 1*l.* 18*s.*

LAW, GUIDE TO.—A Guide to the Law for General Use. By a Barrister. Twenty-first Edition. Crown 8vo. 1877. *Net,* 3*s.* 6*d.*

"There may be many students of both branches of the profession who will find the following pages an assistance to them in the course of their reading, not in substitution of but together with, or preliminary to, the voluminous and highly technical works which they have necessarily to examine."

*** *All standard Law Works are kept in Stock, in law calf and other bindings.*

LAW LIST.—Law List (The).—Comprising the Judges and Officers of the different Courts of Justice, Counsel, Special Pleaders, Draftsmen, Conveyancers, Attorneys, Notaries, &c., in England and Wales; to which are added the Circuits, Judges, Treasurers, Registrars, and High Bailiffs of the County Courts, District Registries and Registrars under the Probate Act, Lords Lieutenant of Counties, Recorders, Clerks of the Peace, Town Clerks, Coroners, Colonial Judges, and Colonial Lawyers having English Agents, Metropolitan Police Magistrates, Law Agents, Law and Public Officers, Circuits of the Judges and Counsel attending Circuit and Sessions, List of Sheriffs and Agents, London Commissioners to Administer Oaths in the Supreme Court of Judicature in England, Conveyancers Practising in England under Certificates obtained in Scotland, &c., &c., and a variety of other useful matters so far as relates to Special Pleaders, Draftsmen, Conveyancers, Attorneys, Solicitors, Proctors and Notaries. Compiled by WILLIAM HENRY COUSINS, of the Inland Revenue Office, Somerset House, Registrar of Stamped Certificates, and of Joint Stock Companies. Published annually. By authority. 1877. (*Now ready.*) 10*s.* 6*d.*

LAW REPORTS.—*Vide* pages 29-30.

LAWYER'S COMPANION.—*Vide* "Diary."

LEGACIES.—Roper's Treatise on the Law of Legacies.—Fourth Edition. By H. H. WHITE. 2 vols. Royal 8vo. 1847. 3*l.* 3*s.*

LEXICON.—*Vide* "Dictionary."

LICENSING.—Lely and Foulkes' Licensing Acts, 1828, 1869, 1872, and 1874; Containing the Law of the Sale of Liquors by Retail and the Management of Licensed Houses; with Notes to the Acts, a Summary of the Law, and an Appendix of Forms. Second Edition. By J. M. LELY and W. D. I. FOULKES, Esqrs., Barristers-at-Law. Royal 12mo. 1874. 8*s.*

"Messrs. Lely and Foulkes's plan is to print in full the principal Acts, and to interpolate between the sections of each of these statutes all subsidiary enactments, distinguishing them by brackets and marginal notes . . . . to most of the sections of the Act of last Session notes are added. These notes are usually sensible and to the point and give evidence both of care and knowledge of the subject."—*Solicitors' Journal.*

LIEN.—Cross' Treatise on the Law of Lien and Stoppage in Transitu.—8vo. 1840. 15*s.*

LIGHTS—Woolrych's Practical Treatise on the Law of Window Lights.—Second Edition. 12mo. 1864. 6*s.*

LOCAL GOVERNMENT.—*Vide* "Public Health."

LUNACY.—Elmer's Lunacy Practice.—Sixth Edition. By JOSEPH ELMER, of the Office of the Masters in Lunacy. (*In preparation.*)

MAGISTERIAL LAW.—Burn.—*Vide* "Justice of Peace."

Leeming and Cross.—*Vide* "Quarter Sessions."

Paley.—*Vide* "Convictions."

Pritchard.—*Vide* "Quarter Sessions."

Stone.—*Vide* "Petty Sessions."

*** *All standard Law Works are kept in Stock, in law calf and other bindings.*

MAINTENANCE AND CHAMPERTY.—Tapp on Maintenance and Champerty.—An Inquiry into the present state of the Law of Maintenance and Champerty, principally as affecting Contracts. By WM. JOHN TAPP, of Lincoln's Inn, Esq., Barrister-at-Law. 12mo. 1861. *4s. 6d.*

MANDAMUS.—Tapping on Mandamus.—The Law and Practice of the High Prerogative Writ of Mandamus as it obtains both in England and Ireland. Royal 8vo. 1848. 1*l.* 1*s.*

MARINE INSURANCE.—*Vide* "Insurance."

MARTIAL LAW.—Finlason's Treatise on Martial Law, as allowed by the Law of England in time of Rebellion; with Practical Illustrations drawn from the Official Documents in the Jamaica Case, and the Evidence taken by the Royal Commission of Enquiry, with Comments Constitutional and Legal. By W. F. FINLASON, Esq., Barrister-at-Law. 8vo. 1866. 12*s.*

MERCANTILE LAW.—Boyd.—*Vide* "Shipping."

Brooke.—*Vide* "Notary."

Russell.—*Vide* "Agency."

Smith's Mercantile Law.—A Compendium of Mercantile Law. By the late JOHN WILLIAM SMITH, Esq. Ninth Edition. By G. M. DOWDESWELL, of the Inner Temple, Esq. one of Her Majesty's Counsel. (*Nearly ready.*)

Tudor's Selection of Leading Cases on Mercantile and Maritime Law.—With Notes. By O. D. TUDOR, Esq., Barrister-at-Law. Second Edition. Royal 8vo. 1868. 1*l.* 18*s.*

MERCHANDISE MARKS ACT.—*Vide* "Trade Marks."

METROPOLIS BUILDING ACTS.—Woolrych's Metropolis Building Acts, together with such Clauses of the Metropolis Management Acts, 1855 and 1862, and other Acts, as more particularly relate to the Buildings Acts, with Notes, Explanatory of the Sections and of the Architectural Terms contained therein. Second Edition. By NOEL H. PATERSON, M.A., of the Middle Temple, Esq., Barrister-at-Law. 12mo. 1877. 8*s.* 6*d.*

MINES.—Rogers' Law relating to Mines, Minerals, and Quarries in Great Britain and Ireland; with a Summary of the Laws of Foreign States and Practical Directions for obtaining Government Grants to work Foreign Mines. Second Edition Enlarged. By ARUNDEL ROGERS, Esq., Barrister-at-Law. 8vo. 1876. 1*l.* 11*s.* 6*d.*

"Mr. Arundel Rogers' Second Edition, which is increased by about 200 pages, will afford a really useful work of reference alike for the Government Inspector and for the practising Barrister who is engaged in cases involving the Law of Mines."—*Law Magazine*, May, 1877.

"Most comprehensive and complete."—*Law Times*, June 17, 1876.

"Although issued as a Second Edition, the work appears to have been almost entirely re-written and very much improved. . . . The volume will prove invaluable as a work of legal reference."—*The Mining Journal*, May 13, 1876.

MORTGAGE.—Coote's Treatise on the Law of Mortgage.—Third Edition. Royal 8vo. 1850. *Net*, 1*l.*

MUNICIPAL ELECTIONS.—*Vide* "Ballot."

*** *All standard Law Works are kept in Stock, in law calf and other bindings.*

NISI PRIUS.—Roscoe's Digest of the Law of Evidence on the Trial of Actions at Nisi Prius.—Thirteenth Edition. By JOHN DAY, one of Her Majesty's Counsel, and MAURICE POWELL, Barrister-at-Law. Royal 12mo. 1875. 2*l.*
(*Bound in one thick volume calf or circuit, 5s. 6d., or in two convenient vols. calf or circuit, 10s. net, extra.*)

"The work itself has long ago won a position altogether unique, and in the hands of its present editors there is no fear that the position will be lost."—*Law Journal*, July 10, 1875

Selwyn's Abridgment of the Law of Nisi Prius.—Thirteenth Edition. By DAVID KEANE, Q.C., Recorder of Bedford, and CHARLES T. SMITH, M.A., one of the Judges of the Supreme Court of the Cape of Good Hope. 2 vols. Royal 8vo. 1869. (*Published at 2l. 16s.*) *Net*, 1*l.*

NOTANDA.—*Vide* "Digests."

NOTARY.—Brooke's Treatise on the Office and Practice of a Notary of England.—With a full collection of Precedents. Fourth Edition. By LEONE LEVI, Esq., F.S.A., of Lincoln's Inn, Barrister-at-Law. 8vo. 1876. 1*l.* 4*s.*

Tennant's Notary's Manual; containing Instructions for the Notaries at the Cape of Good Hope, with Practical Directions for making Wills; the Law of Executors and Tutors, a Summary of the Law of Testaments and of Inheritance *ab intesto* in force within the colony of the Cape of Good Hope, and a collection of Precedents, &c., &c. Fourth Edition. By HERCULES TENNANT, of the Inner Temple, Esq., Barrister-at-Law. Demy 8vo. 1877. *Net*, 1*l.* 1*s.*

NUISANCES.—FitzGerald.—*Vide* "Public Health."

OATHS.—Braithwaite's Oaths in the Supreme Court of Judicature.—A Manual for the use of Commissioners to Administer Oaths in the Supreme Court of Judicature in England. Part I. containing practical information respecting their Appointment, Designation, Jurisdiction, and Powers; Part II. comprising a collection of officially recognised Forms of Jurats and Oaths, with Explanatory Observations. By T. W. BRAITHWAITE, of the Record and Writ Clerks' Office. Fcap. 8vo. 1876. 4*s.* 6*d.*

"Specially useful to Commissioners."—*Law Magazine*, February, 1877.

"The work will, we doubt not, become the recognized guide of commissioners to administer oaths."—*Solicitors' Journal*, May 6, 1876.

PARTNERSHIP.—Pollock's Digest of the Law of Partnership. By FREDERICK POLLOCK, of Lincoln's Inn, Esq., Barrister-at-Law. Author of "Principles of Contract at Law and in Equity." Demy 8vo. 1877. 8*s.* 6*d.*

*** The object of this work is to give the substance of the Law of Partnership (excluding Companies) in a concise and definite form.

"Mr. Pollock's work appears eminently satisfactory . . . the book is praiseworthy in design, scholarly and complete in execution."—*Saturday Review*, May 5, 1877.

"Mr. Pollock is most accurate in his law, which is a matter of much importance, in a book whose contents may almost be got by heart by a hard-working student."—*The Spectator*, May 12, 1877.

"A few more books written as carefully as the 'Digest of the Law of Partnership,' will, perhaps, remove some drawbacks, and render English law a pleasanter and easier subject to study than it is at present."—*The Examiner*, March 31, 1877.

PATENTS.—Hindmarch's Treatise on the Law relating to Patents.—8vo. 1846. 1*l.* 1*s.*

Seton.—*Vide* "Equity."

PAWNBROKERS.—Turner's Pawnbrokers' Act, 1872.—With Explanatory Notes. By FRANCIS TURNER, Esq., Barrister-at-Law, Author of the "Contract of Pawn." 12mo. 1872. *Net*, 2*s.*

*** *All standard Law Works are kept in Stock, in law calf and other bindings.*

PERSONAL PROPERTY.—Smith's Real and Personal Property.—A Compendium of the Law of Real and Personal Property Primarily Connected with Conveyancing; Designed as a Second Book for Students, and as a Digest of the most useful Learning for Practitioners. By JOSIAH W. SMITH, B.C.L., Q.C., Judge of County Courts. Fourth Edition. 2 vols. 8vo. 1870. 1*l.* 18*s.*

PETTY SESSIONS.—Stone's Petty Sessions Practice.—With the Statutes, and an Appendix of Forms. Eighth Edition. By THOMAS SIRRELL PRITCHARD, of the Inner Temple, Esq., Barrister-at-Law. Recorder of Wenlock. (*In the press.*)

PLEADING.—Archbold.—*Vide* "Criminal."

Stephen on Pleading.—A Treatise on the Principles of Pleading in Civil Actions; comprising a Summary Account of the whole proceedings in a Suit at Law. Seventh Edition. By FRANCIS F. PINDER, Barrister-at-Law. 8vo. 1866. 16*s.*

POOR LAW.—Davis' Treatise on the Poor Laws.—Being Vol. IV. of Burn's Justice of the Peace. 8vo. 1869. 1*l.* 11*s.* 6*d.*

POWERS.—Farwell on Powers.—A Concise Treatise on Powers. By GEORGE FARWELL, B.A., of Lincoln's Inn, Barrister-at-Law. 8vo. 1874. 1*l.* 1*s.*

"We recommend Mr. Farwell's book as containing within a small compass what would otherwise have to be sought out in the pages of hundreds of confusing reports."—*The Law*, November, 1874.

PRECEDENTS.—*Vide* "Conveyancing."

PRINCIPAL AND AGENT.—Petgrave's Principal and Agent.—A Manual of the Law of Principal and Agent. By E. C. PETGRAVE, Solicitor. 12mo. 1857. 7*s.* 6*d.*

Petgrave's Code of the Law of Principal and Agent, with a Preface. By E. C. PETGRAVE, Solicitor. Demy 12mo. 1876. *Net, sewed,* 2*s.*

PRIVY COUNCIL.—Lattey's Handy Book on the Practice and Procedure before the Privy Council.—By ROBERT THOMAS LATTEY, Attorney of the Court of Queen's Bench, and of the High Court of Bengal; and Advocate of the Courts of British Burmah. 12mo. 1869. 6*s.*

PROBATE.—Browne's Probate Practice: a Treatise on the Principles and Practice of the Court of Probate, in Contentious and Non-Contentious Business, with the Statutes, Rules, Fees, and Forms relating thereto. By GEORGE BROWNE, Esq., Barrister-at-Law. (Author of "Practice for Divorce and Matrimonial Causes.") 8vo. 1873. 1*l.* 1*s.*

"A cursory glance through Mr. Browne's work shows that it has been compiled with more than ordinary care and intelligence. We should consult it with every confidence, and consequently recommend it to those who require an instructor in Probate Court practice."—*Law Times*, June 21, 1873.

PUBLIC HEALTH.—Chambers' Digest of the Law relating to Public Health and Local Government.—With notes of 1073 leading Cases. Various official documents; precedents of By-laws and Regulations. The Statutes in full. A Table of Offences and Punishments, and a Copious Index. Seventh Edition, enlarged and revised. Imperial 8vo. 1875. 18*s.*

Chambers' Popular Summary of Public Health and Local Government Law. Imperial 8vo. 1875. *Net,* 1*s.* 6*d.*

*** *All standard Law Works are kept in Stock, in law calf and other bindings.*

PUBLIC HEALTH.—*Continued.*

Chambers' Exhaustive Index to the Public Health Act, 1875; with the full Text of the Act, and of most of the Incorporated Acts. By GEO. F. CHAMBERS, of the Inner Temple, Esq., Barrister-at-Law. Imperial 8vo. 1877. 4*s.* 6*d.*

FitzGerald's Public Health and Rivers Pollution Prevention Acts.—The Law relating to Public Health and Local Government, as contained in the Public Health Act, 1875, with Introduction and Notes, showing all the alterations in the Existing Law, with reference to the Cases, &c.; together with a Supplement containing "The Rivers Pollution Prevention Act, 1876." With Explanatory Introduction, Notes, Cases, and Index. By GERALD A. R. FITZGERALD, of Lincoln's Inn, Esq., Barrister-at-Law, Editor of "Thring's Joint Stocks." Royal 8vo. 1876. 1*l.* 1*s.*

*** The Supplement containing "THE RIVERS POLLUTION PREVENTION ACT, 1876," may be had separately. 3*s.* 6*d.*

"A copious and well-executed analytical index completes the work which we can confidently recommend to the officers and members of sanitary authorities, and all interested in the subject matter of the new Act."—*Law Magazine and Review*, February, 1877.

"Mr. FitzGerald's treatise is well adapted for the professional advisers of sanitary boards."—*Public Health*, December 1, 1876.

"Mr. FitzGerald comes forward with a special qualification for the task, for he was employed by the Government in the preparation of the Act of 1875; and, as he himself says, has necessarily, for some time past, devoted attention to the Law relating to public health and local government."—*Law Journal*, April 22, 1876.

PUBLIC LAW.—**Bowyer's Commentaries on Universal Public Law.**—By Sir GEORGE BOWYER, D.C.L. Royal 8vo. 1854. 1*l.* 1*s.*

QUARTER SESSIONS.—**Leeming & Cross's General and Quarter Sessions of the Peace.**—Their Jurisdiction and Practice in other than Criminal matters. Second Edition. By HORATIO LLOYD, Esq., Recorder of Chester, Judge of County Courts, and Deputy-Chairman of Quarter Sessions, and H. F. THURLOW, of the Inner Temple, Esq., Barrister-at-Law. 8vo. 1876. 1*l.* 1*s.*

"The present editors appear to have taken the utmost pains to make the volume complete, and, from our examination of it, we can thoroughly recommend it to all interested in the practice of quarter sessions."—*Law Times*, March 18, 1876.

Pritchard's Quarter Sessions.—The Jurisdiction, Practice and Procedure of the Quarter Sessions in Criminal, Civil, and Appellate Matters. By THOS. SIRRELL PRITCHARD, of the Inner Temple, Esq., Barrister-at-Law, Recorder of Wenlock. 8vo. 1875. 2*l.* 2*s.*

"We congratulate Mr. Pritchard on the state of order he has produced out of the chaotic mass he has dealt with, and we think much credit is due to him for his evident painstaking."—*Law Journal*, April 24, 1875.

"We can confidentally say that it is written throughout with clearness and intelligence, and that both in legislation and in case law it is carefully brought down to the most recent date."—*Solicitors' Journal*, May 1, 1875.

RAILWAYS.—**Browne.**—*Vide* "Carriers."

Lely's Railway and Canal Traffic Act, 1873.—And other Railway and Canal Statutes; with the General Orders, Forms, and Table of Fees. By J. M. LELY, Esq., Barrister-at-Law. Post 8vo. 1873. 8*s.*

"This book contains all that such a book should contain. The arrangement is clear and convenient, and from it at a glance can be seen the subject matter of complaint, the decision of the Court, and the ground of each decision."—*Law Magazine*, April, 1874.

*** *All standard Law Works are kept in Stock, in law calf and other bindings.*

RAILWAYS.—*Continued.*

Simon's Law relating to Railway Accidents, including an Outline of the Liabilities of Railway Companies as Carriers generally, concisely Discussed and Explained. 12mo. 1862. 3s.

REAL PROPERTY.—Dart.—*Vide* "Vendors and Purchasers."

Leake's Elementary Digest of the Law of Property in Land.—Containing: Introduction. Part I. The Sources of the Law.—Part II. Estates in Land. By STEPHEN MARTIN LEAKE, Barrister-at-Law. 8vo. 1874. 1*l.* 2*s.*

*** The above forms a Complete Introduction to the Study of the Law of Real Property

Shelford's Real Property Statutes.—Eighth Edition. By T. H. CARSON, of Lincoln's Inn, Esq. 8vo. 1874. 1*l.* 10*s.*

Smith's Real and Personal Property.—A Compendium of the Law of Real and Personal Property, primarily connected with Conveyancing. Designed as a second book for Students, and as a digest of the most useful learning for Practitioners. By JOSIAH W. SMITH, B.C.L., Q.C., Judge of County Courts. Fourth Edition. In two convenient volumes, 8vo. 1870. 1*l.* 18*s.*

"As a refresher to the memory, and a repository of information that is wanted in daily practice, it will be found of great value."—*Jurist.*

. . . "He has given to the student a book which he may read over and over again with profit and pleasure."—*Law Times.*

"The work before us will, we think, be found of very great service to the practitioner."—*Solicitors' Journal.*

. . . "I know of no volume which so entirely fulfils the requirements of a student's text book."—*From* DR. ROLLIT'S *Lecture.*

RECEIVERS.—Seton.—*Vide* "Equity."

RECORD AND WRIT.—Braithwaite's Record and Writ Practice.—With Practical Directions. By T. W. BRAITHWAITE, of the Record and Writ Clerks' Office. 8vo. 1858. 18*s.*

REGISTRATION.—Rogers.—*Vide* "Elections."

REGISTRATION CASES.—Hopwood and Coltman's Registration Cases.—Vol. I. (1868-1872). Calf. *Net*, 2*l.* 18*s.*; Vol. II. Part I. (1873). Sewed. *Net*, 10*s.*; Vol. II. Part II. (1874). Sewed. *Net*, 10*s.* 6*d.*; Vol. II. Part III. (1875). Sewed. *Net*, 4*s.* 6*d.*; Vol. II. Part. IV. (1876). Sewed. *Net*, 4*s.*

REPORTS.—*Vide* pages 29-30.

RIVERS POLLUTION PREVENTION.—FitzGerald's Rivers Pollution Prevention Act, 1876.—With Explanatory Introduction, Notes, Cases, and Index. Royal 8vo. 1876. 3*s.* 6*d.*

"A well-timed addition to the author's previous work on Sanitary Law."—*Law Magazine*, February, 1877.

ROMAN LAW.—Cumin.—*Vide* "Civil."

Greene's Outlines of Roman Law.—Consisting chiefly of an Analysis and Summary of the Institutes. For the use of Students. By T. WHITCOMBE GREENE, B.C.L., of Lincoln's Inn, Barrister-at-Law. Third Edition. Foolscap 8vo. 1875. 7*s.* 6*d.*

Mears' Student's Ortolan.—An Analysis of M. Ortolan's Institutes of Justinian, including the History and Generalization of ROMAN LAW. By T. LAMBERT MEARS,

ROMAN LAW.—*Continued.*

M.A., LL.D. Lond., of the Inner Temple, Barrister-at-Law. *Published by permission of the late M. Ortolan.* Post 8vo. 1876. 12*s.* 6*d.*

"By far the most valuable part of the work, however, was that contained in the two later volumes, which, while merely purporting to be a commentary on the Institutes of Justinian, are in reality an exhaustive treatise on the whole Roman Law, and practically contain all the learning on the subject. Dr. Mears presents the public with an admirable analysis of the first volume, and what we have pointed out above is, as a matter o fact, a translation of the other two."—*Law Times*, October 7, 1876.

"We have no doubt that this book is intended to meet a real demand. Nor have we any reason to doubt that the work has been well and faithfully executed . . . However, both students and their teachers are at the mercy of examiners, and this book will very probably be found useful by all parties."—*Athenæum*, October 28, 1876.

"Dr. Mears has made his edition *the* edition *par excellence* of that great French writer."—*Irish Law Times*, December 30, 1876.

SALE.—The Contract of Sale with a View to its Codification.—By ARTHUR COHEN, one of Her Majesty's Counsel, FREDERIC THOMPSON, of Lincoln's Inn, and H. D. WARR, of the Middle Temple, Barristers-at-Law. (*In preparation.*)

SAUNDERS' REPORTS.—Williams' (Sir E. V.) Notes to Saunders' Reports.—By the late Serjeant WILLIAMS. Continued to the present time by the Right Hon. Sir EDWARD VAUGHAN WILLIAMS. 2 vols. Royal 8vo. 1871. 2*l.* 10*s.*

SETTLED ESTATES.—Brickdale's Leases and Sales of Settled Estates Act.—19 & 20 Vict., c. 120, and the General Orders and Regulations relating thereto. With an Introduction and Notes. 12mo. 1861. 5*s.*

SHIPPING, and *vide* "Admiralty."

Boyd's Merchant Shipping Laws; being a Consolidation of all the Merchant Shipping and Passenger Acts from 1854 to 1876, inclusive; with Notes of all the leading English and American Cases on the subjects affected by Legislation, and an Appendix containing the New Rules issued in October, 1876; forming a complete Treatise on Maritime Law. By A. C. BOYD, LL.B., of the Inner Temple, Esq., Barrister-at-Law, and Midland Circuit. 8vo. 1876. 1*l.* 5*s.*

"As compared with other text-books on the subject, this has, at any rate the not inconsiderable merit of conciseness . . . . Mr. Boyd confines himself to short, and as far as we can judge correct, statements of the effect of actual decisions."—*Solicitor's Journal*, Jan. 20, 1877.

"The great desideratum is obviously a good index, and this Mr. Boyd has taken particular care to supply. We can recommend the work as a very useful compendium of shipping law."—*Law Times*, Dec. 30, 1876.

"For practical purposes the work now produced by Mr. Boyd has accomplished almost all that could be desired in a legislative code. . . . The value of such a work can hardly be over estimated."—*Irish Law Times*, December 9, 1876.

STAMP LAWS.—Tilsley's Stamp Laws.—A Treatise on the Stamp Laws, being an Analytical Digest of all the Statutes and Cases relating to Stamp Duties, with practical remarks thereon. Third Edition. With Tables of all the Stamp Duties payable in the United Kingdom after the 1st January, 1871, and of Former Duties, &c., &c. By EDWARD HUGH TILSLEY, of the Inland Revenue Office. 8vo. 1871. 18*s.*

STATUTES, and *vide* "Acts of Parliament."

Biddle's Table of Statutes.—A Table of References to unrepealed Public General Acts, arranged in the Alphabetical Order of their Short or Popular Titles. Second Edition, including References to all the Acts in Chitty's Collection of Statutes. Royal 8vo. 1870. (*Published at* 9*s.* 6*d.*) *Net*, 2*s.* 6*d.*

*** *All standard Law Works are kept in Stock, in law calf and other bindings.*

STATUTES.—*Continued.*

Chitty's Collection of Statutes, with Supplements, to 1875.—A Collection of Statutes of Practical Utility; with notes thereon. The Third Edition, containing all the Statutes of Practical Utility in the Civil and Criminal Administration of Justice to the Present Time. By W. N. WELSBY and EDWARD BEAVAN, Esqrs., Barristers-at-Law. In 4 very thick vols. Royal 8vo. 1865. 12*l.* 12*s.*

Supplemental Volume to the above, comprising the Statutes 1865—72. By HORATIO LLOYD, Esq., Judge of County Courts, and Deputy-Chairman of Quarter Sessions for Cheshire. Vol. I. Royal 8vo. 1872. 3*l.* 4*s.*

Vol. II., Part I., 1873, 7*s.* 6*d.* Part II., 1874, 6*s.* Part III., 1875, 16*s.* Part IV., 1876, 6*s.* 6*d.*, sewed.

*** Continued Annually.

"When he (Lord Campbell) was upon the Bench he always had this work by him, and no statutes were ever referred to by the Bar, which he could not find in it."

Lynch's Statute Law of 1870, for the use of Students for the Incorporated Law Society's Examinations. 8vo. Sewed. *Net*, 1*s.*

" " 1872, *Net*, 1*s.*; 1873, 1*s.* 6*d.*; 1874, 1*s.*; 1875, 1*s.*; 1876, 1*s.* *sewed.*

***Public General Statutes**, issued in parts and in complete volumes, royal 8vo, during and after each session, and supplied by the Publishers of this Catalogue immediately on publication.

***The Revised Edition of the Statutes**, prepared under the direction of the Statute Law Committee, and published by the authority of Her Majesty's Government. Imperial 8vo.

Vol.	Contents	Years	*l.*	*s.*	*d.*
Vol. 1.	Henry III. to James II.,	1235–1685	1*l.*	1*s.*	0*d.*
,, 2.	Will. & Mary to 10 Geo. III.,	1688–1770	1	0	0
,, 3.	11 Geo. III. to 41 Geo. III.,	1770–1800	0	17	0
,, 4.	41 Geo. III. to 51 Geo. III.,	1801–1811	0	18	0
,, 5.	52 Geo. III. to 4 Geo. IV.,	1812–1823	1	5	0
,, 6.	5 Geo. IV. to 1 & 2 Will. IV.,	1824–1831	1	6	0
,, 7.	2 & 3 Will. IV. to 6 & 7 Will. IV.,	1831–1836	1	10	0
,, 8.	7 Will. IV. & 1 Vict. to 5 & 6 Vict.,	1837–1842	1	12	6
,, 9.	6 & 7 Vict. to 9 & 10 Vict.,	1843–1846	1	11	6
,, 10.	10 & 11 Vict. to 13 & 14 Vict.,	1847–1850	1	7	6
,, 11.	14 & 15 Vict. to 16 & 17 Vict.,	1851–1853	1	4	0
,, 12.	17 & 18 Vict. to 19 & 20 Vict.,	1854–1856	1	6	0

*** Volume XIII. in preparation.

***Chronological Table of and Index to the Statutes** to the end of the Session of 1874. Third Edition, imperial 8vo. 1*l.* 5*s.*

* Published by Her Majesty's Printers, and Sold by STEVENS & SONS.

TORTS.—Addison on Wrongs and their Remedies.—Being a Treatise on the Law of Torts. By C. G. ADDISON, Esq., Author of "The Law of Contracts." Fourth Edition. By F. S. P. WOLFERSTAN, Esq., Barrister-at-Law. Royal 8vo. 1873. 1*l.* 18*s.*

TRADE MARKS.—Rules under the Trade Marks' Registration Act, 1875 (by Authority). Sewed. *Net*, 1*s.*

Trade Marks' Journal.—4to. Sewed. (*Issued twice a week.*) *Nos. 1 to 90 are now ready.* *Net, each* 1*s.*

Wood's Law of Trade Marks.—Containing the Merchandise Marks' Act, 1862, and the Trade Marks' Registration Act, 1875; with the Rules thereunder, and Practical Directions for obtaining Registration; with Notes, full Table of Cases and Index. By J. BIGLAND WOOD, of the Inner Temple, Esq, Barrister-at-Law. 12mo. 1876. 5*s.*

"Mr. Wood's 'Table of Cases' is novel and ingenious, each case being distinguished by a concise description in a parallel column."—*The Athenæum*, June 24, 1876.

*** *All standard Law Works are kept in Stock, in law calf and other bindings.*

TRAMWAYS.—Sutton's Tramway Acts.—The Tramway Acts of the United Kingdom, with Notes on the Law and Practice, and an Appendix containing the Standing Orders of Parliament, Rules of the Board of Trade relating to Tramways, and Decisions of the Referees with respect to Locus Standi. By HENRY SUTTON, B.A., of Lincoln's Inn, Barrister-at-Law. Post 8vo. 1874. 12*s.*

USES.—Jones (W. Hanbury) on Uses.—8vo. 1862. 7*s.*

VENDORS AND PURCHASERS.—Dart's Vendors and Purchasers.—A Treatise on the Law and Practice relating to Vendors and Purchasers of Real Estate. By J. HENRY DART, of Lincoln's Inn, Esq., Barrister-at-Law, one of the Six Conveyancing Counsel of the High Court of Justice, Chancery Division. Fifth Edition. By the AUTHOR and WILLIAM BARBER, of Lincoln's Inn, Esq., Barrister-at-Law. 2 vols. Royal 8vo. 1876. 3*l.* 13*s.* 6*d.*

"A standard work like Mr. Dart's is beyond all praise."—*The Law Journal*, February 12, 1876.

VICE.—Amos (Professor Sheldon) on the Laws for the Regulation of Vice.—A comparative Survey of Laws in Force, for the Prohibition, Regulation, and Licensing of Vice in England and other Countries. With an Appendix giving the text of Laws and Police Regulations as they now exist in England, in British Dependencies, in the chief towns of Continental Europe, and in other parts of the world; a precise narrative of the passing of the English Statutes; and an Historical Account of English Laws and Legislation on the subject from the earliest times to the present day. By SHELDON AMOS, M.A., Barrister-at-Law and Professor of Jurisprudence in University College, London. 8vo. 1877. 18*s.*

WATERS.—Woolrych on the Law of Waters.—Including Rights in the Sea, Rivers, Canals, &c. Second Edition. 8vo. 1851. *Net*, 10*s.*

Goddard.—*Vide* "Easements."

WILLS.—Montriou.—*Vide* "Indian Law."

Rawlinson's Guide to Solicitors on taking Instructions for Wills.—8vo. 1874. 4*s.*

Theobald's Concise Treatise on the Construction of Wills.—With Table of Cases and Full Index. By H. S. THEOBALD, of the Inner Temple, Esq., Barrister-at-Law, and Fellow of Wadham College, Oxford. 8vo. 1876. 1*l.*

"Mr. Theobald has certainly given evidence of extensive investigation, conscientious labour, and clear exposition."—*Law Magazine*, May, 1877.

"This book has a wider scope than its title might imply; it deals with rules of administration as well as rules of construction, and also with the several general rules of law which, from their constant application in reference to the terms of testamentary dispositions, are conveniently treated of in a text book on wills. In this respect the extended plan of Mr. Theobald's work gives it, for practical purposes, an advantage over that of Mr. Hawkins. . . . The substance of the law is summarized by Mr. Theobald with considerable skill, and generally with accuracy. . . . We desire to record our decided impression, after a somewhat careful examination, that this is a book of great ability and value. It bears on every page traces of care and sound judgment. It is certain to prove of great practical usefulness, for it supplies a want which was beginning to be distinctly felt."—*Solicitors' Journal*, February 24, 1877.

"His arrangement being good, and his statement of the effect of the decisions being clear, his work cannot fail to be of practical utility, and as such we can commend it to the attention of the profession."—*Law Times*, Dec. 23, 1876.

"We have not space to make quotations from Mr. Theobald's book; but we may say that it is remarkably well arranged, and its contents embrace all the principal heads on the subject."—*Law Journal*, February 3, 1877.

Williams.—*Vide* "Executors."

WINDOW LIGHTS.—Woolrych.—*Vide* "Lights.

WRONGS.—*Vide* "Torts."

REPORTS.

STEVENS AND SONS HOLD THE QUIRE STOCK OF THE FOLLOWING, AND HAVE A LARGE STOCK OF SECOND-HAND REPORTS.—PRICES ON APPLICATION

Adolphus and Ellis, Queen's Bench, 12 vols., 1834-40.
„ „ N. S. 15 vols., 1841-50.
Barnewall and Adolphus, King's Bench, 5 vols., 1830-34.
„ „ Alderson, „ 5 vols., 1817-22.
„ „ Cresswell, „ 10 vols., 1822-30.
Barron and Austin, Election Cases, 1 vol., 1842.
Barron and Arnold, „ „ 1 vol., 1843-46.
Beavan, Rolls Court, 36 vols., 1838-66.
Bell, Crown Cases, 1 vol., 1858-60.
Calthrop, King's Bench, 1 vol., 1609-18.
Cary, Chancery, 1 vol., 1557-1604.
Central Criminal Court Sessions Papers (*published after every Session*).
Clark and Finnelly, House of Lords, 12 vols., 1831-46.
Craig and Phillips, Chancery, 1 vol., 1841.
Common Bench Reports, vols. 1 to 8, 1845-9.
Cooper temp. Cottenham, Chancery, 2 vols., 1834-48.
„ temp. Eldon, Chancery, 1 vol., 1815.
Dearsley, Crown Cases, 1 vol., 1852-56.
„ and Bell, Crown Cases, 1 vol., 1856-58.
De Gex, Macnaghten and Gordon.
Chancery, 8 vols., 1851-57.
„ and Jones, „ 4 vols., 1857-60.
„ Fisher and Jones, „ 4 vols., 1860-62.
„ Jones and Smith, „ 4 vols., 1862-66.
De Gex, Bankruptcy Appeals, 1 vol., 1845-48.
„ Fisher and Jones, „ 1 part, 1860.
„ Jones and Smith, „ 1 vol., 1862-65.
Denison, Crown Cases. 2 vols., 1844—52.
Dow and Clark, House of Lords, 2 vols., 1827-32.
Drewry, 4 vols. 1852—59.
Drewry and Smale, Chancery, 2 vols., 1860-65.
Exchequer Reports, (Welsby, Hurlstone and Gordon,) 11 vols., 1847-56.
Foster and Finlason, Nisi Prius, 4 vols., 1858-67.
Haggard, Consistory, 2 vols., 1789-1821.
„ Ecclesiastical, 3 vols. and vol. 4, parts 1 and 2, 1827-33.
Harrison and Rutherford, Common Pleas, 1 vol., 1866—68.

Hopwood and Coltman, Registration Cases, vols. 1 and 2, parts 1, 2, 3 and 4, 1868-76.
Hurlstone and Coltman, Exchequer, 4 vols., 1862-65.
Jacob, Chancery, 1 vol., 1821-22.
Jurist, The Reports in all the Courts, 1837—66.
Keen, Chancery (Rolls Court), 2 vols., 1836-38.
Knapp and Ombler, Election Cases, 1 vol., 1834.
Leigh and Cave, Crown Cases, 1 vol., 1861-5.
Lloyd and Goold, Temp. Sugden, Irish Chancery, 1 vol., 1835.
Lutwyche, Registration Cases, 2 vols., 1843-53.
Macnaghten and Gordon, Chancery, 3 vols., 1849-51.
Macrory, Patent Cases, 2 parts, 1836-54.
McCleland, Exchequer, 1 vol., 1824.
" **and Younge**, Exchequer, 1 vol., 1825.
Moody and Malkin, Nisi Prius, 1 vol., 1827-30.
Moore, Privy Council Cases, 15 vols., 1836-62.
" Ditto N.S., 9 vols., 1862-73.
" Indian Appeals, 14 vols., 1836-73.
" Gorham Case.
Mylne and Craig, Chancery, 5 vols., 1836-46.
" " **Keen**, Chancery, 3 vols., 1833-35.
Nelson, Chancery, 1 vol., 1625-93.
Peake, Nisi Prius, 2 vols., 1790-1812.
Phillips, Chancery, 2 vols., 1841-9.
Ridgway, Irish Appeals, 3 vols., 1784-96.
Rose, Bankruptcy, 2 vols., 1810-16.
Russell and Mylne, Chancery, 2 vols., 1829-31.
" **and Ryan**, Crown Cases, 1 vol., 1799-1823.
Sessions Cases, King's Bench, 1 vol., 1710-48.
Simons, Vice-Chancellors', 17 vols., 1826-49.
" New Series, " 2 vols., 1850-2.
" **and Stuart** " 2 vols., 1822-6.
Stuart Cases selected from those heard and determined in the Vice-Admiralty Court at Quebec, 2 vols. 1836-75.
Tothill, Chancery, 1 vol., 1559-1646.
Webster, Patent Cases, vols. 1 and 2, part 1, 1844-55.
Wolferstan and Dew, Election, 1 vol., 1856-8.
" **and Bristow**, 2 vols., 1859-65.
Younge, Exchequer Equity, 1830-2.
" **and Collyer**, Chancery, 2 vols., 1841-43.
" **and Jervis**, Exchequer, 3 vols., 1826-30.

*** ESTIMATES ON APPLICATION.

*** *All standard Law Works are kept in Stock, in law calf and other bindings.*

Addison on Contracts.—Being a Treatise on the Law of Contracts. By C. G. ADDISON, Esq., Author of the "Law of Torts." *Seventh Edition.* By L. W. CAVE, of the Inner Temple, Esq., Barrister-at-Law, Recorder of Lincoln. *Royal 8vo.* 1875. *Price 1l. 18s. cloth.*

"At present this is by far the best book upon the Law of Contract possessed by the profession; and it is a thoroughly practical book."—*Law Times.*

Addison on Wrongs and their Remedies; being a Treatise on the Law of Torts. *Fourth Edition.* By F. S. P. WOLFERSTAN, Esq., Barrister-at-Law. *Royal 8vo.* 1873. *Price 1l. 18s. cloth.*

Wharton's Law Lexicon, or Dictionary of Jurisprudence, Explaining the Technical Words and Phrases employed in the several Departments of English Law; including the various Legal Terms used in Commercial Business; with an Explanatory as well as Literal translation of the Latin Maxims contained in the Writings of the Ancient and Modern Commentators. *Sixth Edition.* Revised in accordance with the Judicature Acts, by J. SHIRESS WILL, of the Middle Temple, Esq., Barrister-at-Law. *Super-royal 8vo.* 1876. *Price 2l. 2s.* cloth.

"As a work of reference for the library the handsome and elaborate edition of 'Wharton's Law Lexicon' which Mr. Shiress Will has produced, must supersede all former issues of that well-known work."—*Law Magazine and Review*, August, 1876.

"Mr. Will has done all that was rendered necessary by the Judicature Acts, in the shape of incorporation and elimination, and has brought the Statute Law down to the date of publication."—*Law Times*, March 4, 1876.

Smith's (John W.) Action at Law.—An Elementary View of the Proceeding in an Action at Law. *Twelfth Edition.* Adapted to the practice of the Supreme Court. By W. D. I. FOULKES, Esq., Barrister-at-Law, Joint Editor of the "Licensing Acts," and the "Judicature Acts." *12mo.* 1876. *Price 10s. 6d. cloth.*

"The student will find in 'Smith's Action' a manual by the study of which he may easily acquire a general knowledge of the mode of procedure in the various stages of an action in the several divisions of the High Court of Justice. It is a book the pages of which neither lawyers nor laymen need hesitate to consult, inasmuch as the information, as far as it goes, is perfectly accurate."—*Law Times*, September 2, 1876.

FitzGerald's Public Health and Rivers Pollution Prevention Acts.—The Law relating to Public Health and Local Government, as contained in the Public Health Act, 1875. With Introduction and Notes showing all the Alterations in the Existing Law; with References to all the Cases Decided on Sections of Former Acts, which are re-enacted in this Act, together with a Supplement containing "THE RIVERS POLLUTION PREVENTION ACT, 1876." With Explanatory Introduction, Notes, Cases, and Index. By GERALD A. R. FITZGERALD, of Lincoln's Inn, Esq., Barrister-at-Law. *Royal 8vo.* 1876. *Price 1l. 1s. cloth.*

*** The Supplement, containing "THE RIVERS POLLUTION PREVENTION ACT, 1876," may be had separately. *Price 3s. 6d. cloth.*

"Mr. G. A. R. FitzGerald was employed by the Government in the preparation of the Act of 1875, and is therefore specially well fitted to comment upon its provisions and discuss the judicial decisions which have been engrafted on the older statutes incorporated in it."—*Pall Mall Gazette*, April 3, 1876.

Brooke's Treatise on the Office and Practice of a Notary of England.—With a full collection of Precedents. *Fourth Edition.* Including "THE CROSSED CHEQUES ACT, 1876." By LEONE LEVI, Esq., F.S.A., of Lincoln's Inn, Barrister-at-Law. *Demy 8vo.* 1876. *Price 1l. 4s. cloth.*

Farwell on Powers.—A Concise Treatise on Powers. By GEORGE FARWELL, B.A., of Lincoln's Inn, Barrister-at-Law. *Demy 8vo.* 1874. *Price 1l. 1s. cloth.*

"We recommend Mr. Farwell's book as containing within a small compass what would otherwise have to be sought out in the pages of hundreds of confusing reports."—*The Law*, Nov. 1874.

Pritchard's Quarter Sessions.—The Jurisdiction, Practice, and Procedure of the Quarter Sessions in Criminal, Civil, and Appellate Matters. By THOMAS SIRRELL PRITCHARD, of the Inner Temple, Barrister-at-Law, Recorder of Wenlock. *Thick 8vo.* 1875. *Price 2l. 2s. cloth.*

"We congratulate Mr. Pritchard on the state of order he has produced out of the chaotic mass he has dealt with, and we think much credit is due to him for his evident painstaking."—*Law Journal*, April 24, 1875.

Browne's (G.) Principles and Practice of the Court for Divorce, and Matrimonial Causes, with the Statutes, Rules, Fees and Forms relating thereto. *Third Edition.* By GEORGE BROWNE, Esq., Barrister-at-Law. *8vo.* 1876. *Price 1l. 4s. cloth.*

"Mr. G. Browne fully deserves all the credit which from time to time has been bestowed on him, not only by reviewers, but also by practitioners of both branches of the profession, for his 'Treatise on the Law and Practice of Divorce;' and we welcome heartily this third edition of his careful and exhaustive work."—*The Law Journal*, April 15, 1876.

*** *See also Catalogue at end of this Volume.*

Prideaux's Precedents in Conveyancing.—With Dissertations on its Law and Practice. *Eighth Edition.* By FREDERICK PRIDEAUX, late Professor of Real and Personal Property to the Inns of Court, and JOHN WHITCOMBE, Esqrs., Barristers-at-Law. 2 *vols.* *Royal* 8*vo.* 1876. *Price* 3*l.* 10*s.* *cloth.*

"'Prideaux' has become an indispensable part of the conveyancer's library. . . . . The new edition has been edited with a care and accuracy of which we can hardly speak too highly."—*Solicitors' Journal*, October 14, 1876.

"We may also be allowed to add our tribute of praise to these precedents for their conciseness, perspicuity, precision, and perfection of drafting."—*The Law Journal*, September 23, 1876.

Rogers' Elections, Registration, and Election Agency, with an Append
WOLFERSTAN,
"Mr. Wolferstan
valuable digest of th
1876.
"The book main
subject."—*Law Jour*

Rogers' Law r
in Great Britain
wall, and Local
States, and Prac
Mines. *Second*
Barrister-at-La
"Most comprehe

Scott's Costs
containing the '
of Taxed Bi
Price 5*s.* 6*d.* *cl*

Braithwaite's
A Manual for t
of Judicature i
Appointment,
tion of officiall
tions. By T.
8*vo.* 1876.
"The work wi
oaths."—*Solicito*

Dart's Vend
and Practice
DART, of L
Counsel of t
WILLIAM
1876. *Price*
"A standard

Thring's (Si
and Practic
with Notes,
and all th
Companies.
Third Edit
time. By
and Fellow
"This, as
Parliamenta
Times, April

Wilson's
Notes and a copious ...
TO THE NEW PRACTICE. B
Barrister-at-Law. *Royal* 12*mo.* 1875.
(*Bound in limp leather for the pocket.* *Price* 1*l.* 2*s.* 6*d.*)

*** A LARGE PAPER EDITION of the above with Additional Rules (for marginal notes). *Royal* 8*vo.* 1875. *Price* 1*l.* 5*s.* *cloth.* (*Bound in limp leather.* *Price* 1*l.* 10*s.*)

"The result of a very careful examination of Mr. Wilson's book is that it is executed with great care and thoroughness, and that it will be of the utmost value to all those on whom the task falls, whether as practitioners or as administrators of the law."—*Solicitors' Journal*, Oct. 23, 1875.

Lightning Source UK Ltd.
Milton Keynes UK
UKHW012000181218
334232UK00010B/549/P

9 781331 218777